Amelia Earhart's SHOES

Updated Edition

Amelia Earhart's SHOES

Is the Mystery Solved?
Updated Edition

Thomas F. King
Randall S. Jacobson
Karen R. Burns
Kenton Spading

On behalf of The International Group for
Historic Aircraft Recovery

ALTAMIRA
PRESS

A Division of
ROWMAN & LITTLEFIELD PUBLISHERS, INC.
Lanham • New York • Toronto • Plymouth, UK

ALTAMIRA PRESS
A division of Rowman & Littlefield Publishers, Inc.
A wholly owned subsidary of The Rowman & Littlefield Publishing Group, Inc.
4501 Forbes Boulevard, Suite 200
Lanham, MD 20706
www.altamirapress.com

Estover Road
Plymouth PL6 7PY
United Kingdom

British Library Cataloguing in Publication Information Available

The Library of Congress catalogued the hardcover edition as follows:

Amelia Earhart's shoes : is the mystery solved? / Thomas F. King . . . [et al.].
    p. cm.
Includes bibliographical references and index.
    1. Earhart, Amelia, 1897–1937—Death and burial. 2. Women air pilots—United
States—Biography. 3. Air pilots—United States—Biography. 4. Aircraft accidents—
Investigation—Kiribati—Phoenix Islands. I. King, Thomas F., 1942–

TL540.E3 A74 2001
629.13'092—dc21   2001022771
ISBN 0-7591-0130-2 (cloth : alk. paper)
ISBN 0-7591-0131-0 (pbk : alk. paper)

Printed in the United States of America

To the memories of Teng Koata of Onotoa and Gerald B. Gallagher, pioneers of the Phoenix Islands who may well have found Amelia Earhart, this book is respectfully dedicated.

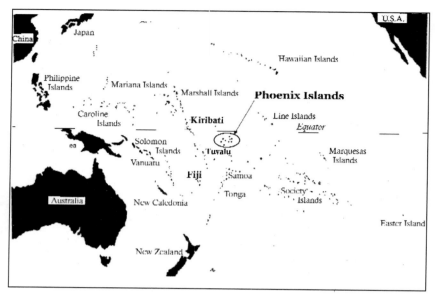

The Phoenix Islands in the Pacific Ocean.

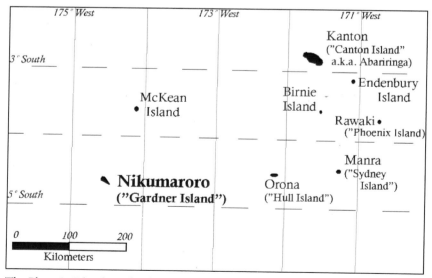

The Phoenix Islands and Nikumaroro.

Contents

CONTENTS

CHAPTER I

Where in the World Is Amelia Earhart?

Happy landings to you, Amelia Earhart.
Farewell, First Lady of the Air.
—RED RIVER DAVE McENERY, "Amelia Earhart's Last Flight"

So ENDED A BRIEFLY POPULAR SONG OF 1937, THE YEAR aviation pioneer Amelia Earhart and her navigator, Fred Noonan, disappeared over the Pacific Ocean. Record-setting pilot, writer, lecturer, role model for ambitious women, and major celebrity, Earhart was coming to the end of a globe-circling "World Flight" when she and Noonan vanished.

Vanished without a trace, just as they were approaching Howland Island, a tiny outcrop of coral in the mid-Pacific where they were scheduled to refuel before hopping on to Honolulu and California, to the welcome accorded heroes by their adoring fans. Vanished without a trace, despite tantalizing radio messages suggesting that they were so close they should have seen the island or the Coast Guard cutter waiting there to guide them in. Vanished, never to be found, despite a tremendous effort to find them.

Never to be found until, perhaps, now.

"You're writing about Amelia Earhart?"

Tom King looked up from his laptop at the attractive young woman in the seat next to him in the jam-packed airliner. Some people find King rather forbidding—gray-bearded, bald, rather weather-beaten. She quickly apologized.

"I'm sorry; I couldn't help noticing—didn't mean to read over your shoulder, but . . ."

"No problem. Yes, I'm working on a book, with a few colleagues. Are you interested in Earhart?"

"Oh, she's one of my heroines; I've always admired her. I heard they found her shoe on some island."

"Well, that's us, and we're not really all that sure it's her shoe, but we've found quite a bit of other stuff, too. That's what the book's about—what we've found, how we've found it, what we think happened."

"You mean you found the shoe?"

"No, I wasn't on that expedition, but I'm the project archaeologist—it's kind of my recreation. My wife says it's cheaper than a shrink."

"So you think she crashed on—what's the island?"

"Nikumaroro, in the Phoenix group. Really beautiful, uninhabited island about as far from anyplace as you can get. But actually we don't think she crashed; we think she landed, but then died."

"Why did she die? Why wasn't she found."

King saved his file. The battery was running low anyway, and it was still three hours to San Francisco and his grandchildren.

"Well, would you like to hear the whole story?"[1]

It's hard for us, in the early twenty-first century, to imagine the way someone like Earhart captured the public's imagination in the 1930s. A time before television, before instant celebrity. A time between world wars, with the nation struggling through a crushing depression. A time when air travel was still a new thing, still an adventure. Following hard on the heels of the wildly popular Charles Lindbergh, but very much her own person, Earhart was a dashing, heroic figure. Her disappearance into thin air was a headline-grabbing shock felt across the nation.

The Roosevelt administration responded accordingly, sending the U.S. Navy to join the Coast Guard on what was, at the time, the most massive air-sea rescue mission ever undertaken. The battleship *Colorado*, the aircraft carrier *Lexington*, their support ships and aircraft, the Coast Guard cutter *Itasca*, the minesweeper *Swan* were all involved. The British colonial government in the Gilbert Islands lent a hand; the Japanese authorities in the Marshall Islands conducted their own search. Nothing was found; not a life raft, not a piece of wreckage, not an oil slick. No living aviators, safe on an island or reef. No floating bodies.

Eventually the search had to end, and it did, with the conclusion that Earhart and Noonan, for some reason unable to find Howland Island, had run out of gas, crashed into the trackless Pacific, and sunk. A logical, efficient conclusion, but one that has never entirely satisfied the many people who have been, and remain, intrigued by the flyers' fate.

Why does the "crashed and sank" explanation not satisfy? Partly, no doubt, because we don't easily give up our heroes. We still have Elvis sightings, after all. Partly because it's rather boring, relative to other possibilities. But partly, too, because it's based entirely on "negative data"— in other words, on the *absence* of information. They didn't land on Howland, they haven't turned up anyplace else, therefore they must have crashed and sunk.

And partly because there are things about it that don't quite add up— notably the fact that the plane had taken on enough fuel for about twenty-four hours of flying at the speed Earhart was primed to fly, and when it disappeared it had been in the air only a bit more than twenty hours. Are there ways to account for this? Sure. Fuel may have been lost somehow, or miscalculated, or Earhart could have flown in an inefficient way, wasting fuel, or there could have been some kind of catastrophic system failure. But here again we're thrown back on negative data. There's no actual evidence that anything like that happened, other than the fact that the flyers didn't show up on Howland.

In the absence of certainty, scores of writers have suggested—indeed insisted on, and defended tooth and claw—a number of alternative explanations. Captured by the Japanese. Engaged in a secret spy mission and captured by the Japanese. Engaged in a spy mission and *not* captured by the Japanese, still alive in one place or another—even New Jersey!—under false identities. Taken by space aliens.[2] Some of these notions are more plausible than others, but they all share one important feature: there is nothing but anecdotal evidence—things people have said—to support any of them. All are based on what someone says they saw or heard, or what someone says someone told them they'd seen or heard, often years or decades after they ostensibly saw or heard it. Maybe one or more of these anecdotes is true, accurately remembered, and accurately reported, and maybe one or more of them reflects what happened to the famous flyers, but without some sort of hard—at least semihard—data to back them up, they all amount to hearsay.

There *is* a body of evidence that's not just hearsay, though.

3

- The last radio message known to have come from Earhart said they were flying along "the line 157-337," looking for Howland. That means a line bearing 337 degrees (north-northwest) and 157 degrees (south-southeast) that Noonan had plotted as running through Howland Island. In navigator language it's known as the "line of position," or "LOP."
- North of Howland Island along the LOP there's nothing but open water for thousands of miles. About 400 miles south along the LOP is Nikumaroro—in 1937 known as Gardner Island. A beautiful coral island in the Phoenix Group, part of the modern island nation of Kiribati. Uninhabited in 1937, uninhabited today.
- In 1940, pioneers for a new colony on Nikumaroro found a partial human skeleton. With it were the remains of shoes—apparently a woman's shoe and a man's shoe—together with a sextant box. The box had numbers on it that closely resemble those on a similar box known to have belonged to Fred Noonan.
- A medical doctor measured the bones in 1941. When modern forensic anthropologists analyzed his measurements, the results suggested that the skeleton most resembled that of a woman of northern European origin, about 5 feet 7 inches tall—a dead ringer for Earhart.
- In 1991, the remains of two more shoes were found on Nikumaroro— a blucher-style oxford, probably a woman's, probably from the 1930s, and the heel from what appears to be a man's shoe. Photographs of Earhart taken during the World Flight show her wearing blucher oxfords.
- People who lived on the island during its colonial period—1938 to 1963—say (okay, it's anecdotal) that there was airplane wreckage on the fringing reef and—in one case—on the lagoon shore. One such report is from 1940, another from the 1950s, and both identify wreckage as being at about the same location on the reef. They say that the colonists warned their children not to play with the wreckage because it was haunted by the ghosts of the airplane's crew. There is no record of any airplane crashes on Nikumaroro.
- During archaeological work on Nikumaroro in 1989, '91, '96, '97, and '99, dozens of airplane parts have been found in and around the site of the colonial village. Most of them can't be traced to any particular airplane, and some are definitely from World War II military

planes, probably brought in from crash sites and airfields on other islands. A few, however, more closely resemble Earhart's plane than they do any other aircraft known to have operated in the area.

Aha! So obviously, Earhart and Noonan, when they couldn't find Howland, flew southeast along the LOP, crashed on Nikumaroro, and died there. Mystery solved.

Well, not so fast. Certainly the evidence we've just summarized points that way, toward what we call the "Nikumaroro Hypothesis." But does it prove it? Absolutely not. The Nikumaroro Hypothesis is just what its name indicates—a hypothesis, an idea about what happened, that can be tested against more information, through research.

That's what TIGHAR is trying to do: test the hypothesis.

TIGHAR? That's The International Group for Historic Aircraft Recovery. Pronounced "tiger," of course, as in "go get 'em . . . ," except by some of our British compatriots who insist on pronouncing it "tigger." Which is appropriate in some respects; it's a pretty bouncy organization.

In 1984, aviation insurance investigator Ric Gillespie got sick of flying around the country looking at crash sites and ferreting out insurance scams, so he quit. Like other people sliding into midlife, Gillespie wanted something meaningful to do. A lifelong love affair with airplanes, and a fascination with history, combined to bring him into the esoteric field of aviation historic preservation. Time after time he had seen historic aircraft "restored" to a point where there was nothing original left. Time after time he had seen such airplanes flown and crashed, destroying unique relics of aviation's history. And time after time he had seen and read of vintage airplanes being "recovered" from old airfields, crash sites, swamps, lagoons, the ocean floor, using such sloppy techniques that the "recovery" amounted to destruction. Encouraged and joined in the enterprise by his wife, Pat Thrasher, Gillespie decided to form an organization to grapple with such problems—to recover historic aircraft right, to help establish standards for deciding what should be flown and what should be put in museums, to work out ways to interpret them for the public without destroying them. Thus was TIGHAR born.

Today, TIGHAR has some 750 members worldwide, a Web site (www.tighar.org), an Internet discussion and research group called the Earhart Forum, a newsletter called *TIGHAR Tracks,* and modest offices—TIGHAR Central—in Wilmington, Delaware. The Web site contains accessible copies

Ric Gillespie, Chief TIGHAR, on Nikumaroro, 1991. TIGHAR photo by
Russ Matthews.

of most of the unpublished material we'll refer to in this book, or directions
for where it can be found. Thrasher is TIGHAR's president, Gillespie is its
executive director, and with a little clerical help they make up the organization's staff. They're assisted, supported, argued with, and troubled by a large
number of volunteer researchers, including King and his co-conspirators in
this book, Randall S. Jacobson, Karen R. Burns, and Kenton Spading.

Gillespie is a controversial fellow in historic airplane circles. He can be
brash, he can be abrasive. He's a true polymath, as is Thrasher—they have
amazing encyclopedic knowledge of the most dizzying assortment of things,
and both can be impatient, even haughty, with lesser mortals—and almost
everyone winds up in the "lesser mortal" category from time to time.
Gillespie is—well, dashing might be the word, with his beat-up pilot's
leather jacket and sometime Clark Gable moustache. He's articulate and
clever, and can be maddeningly pigheaded. And he promotes ideas that

make others uncomfortable. Like the notion that fixing up and flying old airplanes isn't necessarily a laudable historical endeavor. And like the idea that you can't solve a mystery like Earhart's disappearance by stringing together selected anecdotes and announcing a solution. And, of course, like the idea that what really happened to Earhart is perhaps that—subject to confirmation through scientific research—she and Noonan landed and died on Nikumaroro.

There's some tendency among aviation historians, airplane buffs, and Earhart fans to dismiss TIGHAR's investigation of the Earhart disappearance as merely Ric's schtick—Gillespie's personal crusade, with no more scientific or historical legitimacy than the Alien Capture Hypothesis. We're here to tell you that—unless Gillespie is a far better con man than we think he is—it's a lot more than that.

And who are "we"? We are four of TIGHAR's volunteer researchers. In our day jobs King is an archaeologist who consults, writes, and teaches about historic preservation and environmental impact assessment. Jacobson is a civilian scientist who manages programs in oceanography and mine countermeasures for the U.S. Navy; Burns is a forensic anthropologist with a penchant for the study of genocide; and Spading is a civilian engineer with the U.S. Army. Over the years each of us has stumbled into TIGHAR's investigation and been unable to get out. And we're having such a good time with it that we thought it unconscionable not to share the fun with the reading public. Besides, the story is getting too long to tell verbally, even to nice young college students on transcontinental flights.

Why tell the story, though—a mystery story, after all—when we don't yet have a definitive, thoroughly proven solution? Well, because we may very well never solve the mystery to the satisfaction of everyone we might want to satisfy—including ourselves—but in trying to solve it we've come up with what we think are some intriguing facts, and had some exciting times doing it. Because in some ways a mystery's more interesting before it's solved than it is afterward. And besides, each reader can decide for herself or himself, having read what we have to say, just how close TIGHAR actually is to a real solution. We think we may be close.

Our story is told largely from King's point of view, in King's voice. This is mostly because King has spent the most time working on it, and because, unlike Jacobson, Spading, and Burns, he's been with the project almost from the beginning. But his coauthors have contributed their own stories, their own perspectives, and kept King alert by questioning his interpretations, recollections, and portrayals of the facts.

This book is only one of TIGHAR's many reports on the Earhart search, and it certainly is not the last. It does not portray the search as it's perceived by TIGHAR's executive leadership, Ric Gillespie and Pat Thrasher, though Ric and Pat have cooperated with us in writing it, commented on drafts, and generously shared photographs, documents, and other material. When and if TIGHAR's research yields a firm conclusion, Gillespie plans to write the definitive book on the subject, and we wish him well in doing so. But in the meantime, we have a story to tell.

CHAPTER **2**

The Lady in Question

Amelia grinned: "Hi! I've come from America!"
"Have you now," Farmer Gallagher exclaimed.
　　　—JEAN BACKUS, *Letters from Amelia*[1]

Where She Came From

This book is not about Amelia Earhart; it's about one investigation into the mystery of her disappearance. But we wouldn't be investigating her disappearance if she hadn't been a remarkable person whose exploits stirred the public imagination and whose loss seemed like everyone's loss. Though her life and career have been thoroughly documented,[2] we need to say a little about them to place her disappearance, and our search, in context.

She was born in Atchison, Kansas, in 1897, and was in Toronto, Ontario, in 1918 serving as a nurse's aid tending wounded soldiers home from World War I when she visited a local flying field and developed what was apparently at first a rather mild interest in airplanes. Moving on to study medicine at Columbia University, she went to California in 1920 to visit her parents. At an air show in west Los Angeles her father bought her a $10 airplane ride, and she was hooked. By the latter part of 1921 she had completed flying lessons, bought her first plane, and entered her first air show—where she set a new altitude record for women, topping 14,000 feet.

The elder Earharts, Amy and Edwin, had a troubled marriage that ended in 1924. Amy moved to Boston, where her younger daughter Muriel was living. Amelia went with her, selling her plane and buying a car. She returned to Columbia, but quit in early 1925 and went to work to support herself and help her mother. Supporting herself and her family seems to have been a powerful and continuing concern in her life. In letters to her mother throughout her career, Earhart routinely included "little checkies" for various amounts, and expressed concern about whether Amy and Muriel were adequately provided for.[3]

Earhart's main employment in Boston was as a university extension teacher, instructing foreign students; she held a second job as a social worker. However, she also arranged with aircraft manufacturer Bert Kinner to demonstrate one of his planes to potential buyers, in return for the opportunity to use the plane herself, so many weekends were spent flying.

Across the Atlantic

In May 1927, Charles Lindbergh succeeded in flying across the Atlantic, and returned to the United States a celebrity. Earhart at this time was still only a weekend pilot, and took a full-time job as a social worker shortly after Lindbergh's flight. In April 1928, however, she was recruited by publicist George Palmer Putnam to become the first woman to cross the ocean by air. Flying more or less as a passenger on *Friendship*, piloted by Wilmer L. Stultz and Louis E. Gordon, she landed in Wales on June 18, 1928. The flight was unsatisfying to her—she said she felt like "baggage"—but it transformed her life. Suddenly she, like Lindbergh, was a celebrity, with contracts for a book, magazine articles, and lectures, as well as arrangements for endorsements on lines of stationery, luggage, and clothing. All arranged by . . .

Putnam

George Palmer Putnam, grandson of the founder of Putnam's Sons publishing house, was generally referred to as "G. P." G. P. was running the publishing house in 1928, and had just published a best-seller by Lindbergh. An adept entrepreneur who reached out well beyond book publishing into the lecture circuit, magazines, and movies, Putnam seems to have had a good idea of what the public wanted during the difficult days of the Great Depression: heroes, heroines, inspirations. Articulate, adventurous, hardworking, with good solid American roots, Earhart could give the public

Amelia Earhart. TIGHAR
Collection from Purdue
University Special
Collections.

something of what it wanted, and Putnam knew how to help her do it. He
promoted her enthusiastically, and Earhart was no slouch herself. She seems
to have been a talented public speaker and a natural writer, and she vigorously put these skills to use.

But she didn't spend all her time writing and speaking. In late 1928 she
became the first woman to fly solo across the United States, and by 1929
she was active in air shows, races, and other aerial events. With Putnam's
support and salesmanship, she wrote and lectured extensively about everything she did. She wrote well, giving people the feeling that they were partic-
ipating in her adventures, and she was charismatic as a speaker and especially
appealing to young women. A thoroughly modern woman, embodying much
of what women in the '30s wanted to be, were struggling to become.

Putnam, forty-three at the time to Earhart's thirty-one, and married to
boot, became increasingly involved not only in Earhart's writing contracts,
speaking tours, endorsements, and flying events, but also in her personal
life. In 1930 he obtained a Nevada divorce and began seriously wooing his

George Putnam was Earhart's partner in all her adventures, including the last. TIGHAR Collection from Purdue University Special Collections.

protégé. Earhart was busy setting new women's speed records and helping organize a new airline company; she clearly valued her freedom and was not very receptive to Putnam's attentions. Eventually, though, she softened, and married Putnam in February 1931.

Putnam is often casually thought of as a rich man, but in fact he and Earhart were never personally wealthy. He came from a wealthy family, ran an important company, and traveled in high social circles, but money was always an issue, especially as the Great Depression spread gloom over the nation and the world. Each adventure that Earhart embarked on required that both Earhart and Putnam work at scraping together money, banking on the rewards to be gleaned from publicity and endorsements once it was done.

Putnam is also sometimes criticized as an adventurer who took advantage of Earhart's celebrity, or alternatively as a showman who manufactured her celebrity out of whole cloth. Both portraits are probably wrong, or at least far too one-dimensional. Earhart and Putnam seem to have had complementary strengths that they put to good, concerted use. Earhart had plenty of star quality all by herself, but Putnam helped her burnish it, while certainly benefiting from his association with her. They made a very good team.

Solo to Ireland

By 1932, they had gathered together the support to make a solo flight across the Atlantic possible. On May 21 of that year Earhart landed her bright red Lockheed Vega—now in the Smithsonian Institution's National Air and Space Museum—in a pasture near Londonderry, Northern Ireland. The farm field where she landed was the property of a family named Gallagher—as we'll see, an odd coincidence.

If she had been a celebrity before, she was really a celebrity now. She was received by the pope, traveled in royal style across the Continent, and returned to the United States aboard the *Ile de France* to a tumultuous welcome in New York City. She plunged back into her life of writing, lecturing, and setting flying records, while G. P. left the book publishing game to become affiliated with Paramount Studios. Earhart became a partner in another new airline company, Boston-Maine Airways—one of the ancestors of today's Delta Airlines.

The Road to the World Flight

In 1934 Earhart began planning another audacious solo flight: from Hawaii to the U.S. mainland. She hired Paul Mantz, a skilled stunt pilot, aircraft technician, and charter operator, as her technical assistant, and learned a good deal—though in the end, it seems, not enough—about the radio operations that were becoming increasingly important for over-ocean pilots. In January 1935 she took off from Wheeler Field in Honolulu and landed about eighteen hours later in Oakland, California. A few months later she flew from California to Mexico City to a huge welcome, and from there to New York.

Earhart was viewed by many women as a role model, and she played the part with vigor. She took part in organizing Zonta International, an organization of professional women, and the Ninety-Nines, a women's aviation society. And she became a part-time career counselor for women at Purdue University in Indiana, an institution that was to play an important role in her final flight.

Looking to the future, Earhart began to work with Mantz to set up a flight school. But there was at least one more record she wanted to set. She wanted to be the first to circle the globe by air at the equator. With Putnam, Mantz, and Harry Manning, a sea captain she had met after the *Friendship* flight, she began to plan.

Heroics or Hype?

Today, as public consciousness of Earhart fades, many who do remember her idolize her as an "American heroine," while others scoff at her accomplishments as mere publicity stunts. Some see her as a daring pilot with great skill, while others write her off as only marginally competent.

Both portraits probably contain a little truth, but both are certainly too simplistic. Earhart was obviously daring, and she went where few women were going at the time. She became a celebrity, certainly, but she used that celebrity for good causes—notably the rights of women to walk through every door that is open to men. As a pilot she made her share of mistakes, some of which quite likely contributed to her demise. But it was, and is, a rare pilot—or human being—who doesn't make mistakes. As far as we can tell, Earhart was a thoroughly competent professional who completed a lot of tricky long-distance flights at a time when such flights were serious business. Earhart was no more perfect than anyone else—indeed there were gaps in her knowledge, and flaws in her planning, that probably turned out to be fatal. Maybe not the person you'd want at the controls of a 747 carrying hundreds of passengers across the ocean. But if Earhart were alive today that's not likely what she would be doing. She'd probably be working on becoming the first woman on Mars.

This may be a good point at which to say something to those who insist that the very act of seeking a solution to the Earhart mystery somehow denigrates her memory. "Why can't you leave her in peace?" we are sometimes asked. "Why can't you celebrate her life instead of probing into her death?"

We don't think the two activities—celebrating life and investigating death—are incompatible. In fact, we don't think they even have much to do with one another. We have great respect for Earhart's professionalism, her skill, her charisma, her dedication to her family, to the advancement of women, and to those less fortunate than herself. But why should this respect cause us not to wonder what really happened to her, to invest some effort in trying to find out? The respect the people of the United States feel for President Kennedy is not diminished by curiosity about his death, or by attempts to resolve the mysteries that surround it. Likewise, we don't think that curiosity about Earhart's fate, or attempts to find out what it was, in any way diminish appreciation for her life.

At the time of her disappearance, Amelia Earhart was one of the most famous women of her generation. Even today she is probably the best-known female aviator of all time. As the first woman pilot to fly solo across the Atlantic, she established herself as a major figure in an era when aviation was making daily headlines. The World Flight would make her a legend, even as it ended her life.

CHAPTER 3

The Navigator
and the Airplane

Noonan, look for Noonan;
He's the navigator no one knows.
When you search for Noonan,
You can go to places no one goes.*
    —TIGHAR TUNES[1]

Who Was Fred Noonan?

If Amelia Earhart's life before the World Flight is well known, Fred
Noonan's is shrouded in mystery. This does not seem to reflect a deliberate effort on Noonan's part to be mysterious; it is just the way things
turned out. In the last few years several TIGHAR researchers have put
together the "Noonan Project"[2] to dig into his history. Their research
has provided a good deal of basic information on this often-forgotten
navigator.

Frederick Joseph Noonan was born April 4, 1893, in Chicago. He later
said that he left school in the summer of 1905 and headed for Seattle,
Washington. According to his maritime records, he soon shipped as an ordi-

---

*Sung to the tune of the "Flintstones" theme, by Bill Hanna and Joe Barbara; music by
Hoyt Curtin.

nary seaman on the bark *Hecla,* probably bound for South America. By 1910, rated as able-bodied seaman, he was aboard the British bark *Crompton.* Three years and six ships later, the records show him rated quartermaster and boatswain's mate aboard the *Corinthian.*

This was the time when sailing vessels were giving way to steamships, and Noonan served on both, in a wide range of jobs. But he seems never to have stuck in a single billet; he must have displayed a range of skills. He also seems never to have been at a loss for work, however much he bounced around. The records show him shipping as an able seaman, ✦ boatswain's mate, and quartermaster on a variety of ships through World War I, sailing widely over the Atlantic and Pacific. In 1918, having luckily missed being aboard SS *Cairnhill* when she was torpedoed (he had missed the ship's sailing but all his belongings were lost), he was rated second mate aboard the bark *Launberga.* After many more voyages at various ratings, by the end of 1923 he had received his officer's papers and was first mate on SS *Eastern Victor.*

Three years later, Noonan received his master's license, but there's no evidence that he ever served as captain of a ship. We don't know why he didn't, but suspect that in these postwar years there may have been a glut of senior officers, so he may not have been able to find a berth. Five years later he was relicensed as a master for "any ocean," but at about the same time he left his seagoing career behind and took to the air.

From Sea to Sky

By the end of 1929, Noonan was living in New Orleans with his wife of three years, the former Josie Sullivan of Savannah, Georgia. The Mississippi Shipping Company employed him in various ships' crew capacities, several times as a chief mate. His next-door neighbor, Edward F. Stumpf, later said that Noonan had "quit the sea because he wanted to take up aviation, not necessarily as a pilot, but in a navigating capacity."[3] This he did, joining the New York, Rio & Buenos Aires Line in mid-1930. The NYRBA was a fledgling airline that had mail contracts with Argentina, Chile, Brazil, and Uruguay. When Noonan signed on it was losing money, however, and was soon acquired by Pan American Airways. It was as a navigator for Pan Am that Noonan would achieve his greatest fame—next to his notoriety as Earhart's colleague on the lost World Flight.

Fred Noonan at a dinner in
honor of AE at a French
aero club in Dakar, French
Senegal, probably the
evening of June 9, 1937.
TIGHAR Collection
from Purdue University
Special Collection.

Aboard the Clippers

In the 1930s, aircraft manufacturers were building huge "flying boats" that
could provide mail, cargo, and passenger service across even the vast
expanses of the Pacific. Of course, at the time it was impossible to make the
trip in a single hop, but this was the great advantage of the flying boat. It
could land and take off on the water, making any calm lagoon or harbor a
potential airport.

The United States and the British Empire competed for flying boat routes
across the Pacific, and Pan Am was the U.S. contestant. While the nations
negotiated and connived—and at one point almost stumbled into a shooting
war—over ownership of islands where flying boat bases might be established,
Pan Am pioneered the actual transpacific routes with its giant Clippers.

An important key to getting across a vast ocean, of course—and particularly to finding a little island where one could land and take on fuel—was
navigation. The art and science of radio navigation—homing in on radio

beacons, finding their bearing, and flying to them—was steadily being refined, but for the great distances between islands, celestial navigation was the way one found one's way around. Sextants and octants, sun shots and star sightings, dead reckoning and calculations of wind direction and velocity by observing the sea below, these were the stuff of the navigator's trade.

Presumably (though we have no direct evidence), Noonan had learned navigation in his many shipboard jobs, and as the 1930s progressed he adapted what he knew to navigating aircraft. After serving Pan Am in several capacities in Port-au-Prince and Miami, by March 1935 he was the navigator for Pan Am's lead flight crew, under Captain Edward Musick, training for transpacific operations. At the end of that month Noonan navigated a Pan Am Clipper over the Gulf of Mexico, across South America, and up the California coast to Alameda, Pan Am's brand new Pacific Division base on San Francisco Bay. During the next two years, as lead navigator, he helped pioneer the Clipper's routes to Asia, flying repeatedly to Honolulu, Midway, Wake Island, Guam, and Manila. At the same time, he provided navigation instruction for the airline's junior officers.

Late in 1936 or early in 1937, however, he left Pan Am and at about the same time sought a divorce from Josie. During this presumably turbulent period, too, he became involved in Earhart's preparations for the World Flight. His divorce became final in early March 1937, and on March 27 he married again, this time to Mary Beatrice Martinelli, who owned an Oakland beauty salon. Fred and Bea had little time to enjoy married life before Fred was off again, with Earhart, into history.

Was He a Drunk?

It's commonly accepted among many Earhart researchers that Fred Noonan was an alcoholic. Therefore, it is often asserted, he was dead drunk on the flight that ended in the disappearance, and of course the loss of the flight resulted from this debility. TIGHAR's research, including the detailed studies of his life carried out by the Noonan Project, doesn't support any of these assumptions.

The first published reference to Noonan's alleged alcoholism is in a 1966 best-seller by journalist Fred Goerner, *The Search for Amelia Earhart*.[4] Though Goerner's book confidently asserted Noonan's condition in some detail, the only actual evidence cited was thin—an April 4, 1937, auto accident that Fred and his second wife, Bea, experienced near Fresno, California. According to Goerner, the police accident report included the notation "Driver had been drinking." Efforts to find this accident report, in police files and in Goerner's own files (now at the Nimitz Museum in Texas) have thus far been unsuccessful.

Since publication of Goerner's book, several of Noonan's former colleagues have been quoted as reminiscing about Noonan's drinking and its results.[5] One account says that during his Pan American days, he slipped in a hotel bathroom, breaking some teeth and forcing Pan American to find a replacement navigator for the Manila Clipper. Another anecdote has him slipping off the dock while approaching the seaplane. Another story recalls that he sat on his glasses in an automobile, and had to buy several replacements. All of these episodes may or may not have been the results of drinking, of course, and all have come to light since 1966, raising the question of whether they were influenced by Goerner's allegations.

We know that Noonan drank. In a letter dated June 9, 1937, to his friend Eugene Pallette, he said he was looking forward to "a highball together" when he returned from the World Flight.[6] But social drinking is different from alcoholism, and alcoholism doesn't necessarily result in being blind drunk during a trip in which one's performance is a life-and-death matter.

Noonan's alleged alcohol problem has been cited—speculatively—as a reason for his leaving Pan Am; the idea is that he was fired for being routinely impaired. A 1939 book by William Grooch, a Pan Am pilot, gives a different story. According to Grooch, Noonan became fed up with continuing promises on the part of management to improve the grueling conditions under which Pan Am flight crews worked—including flying many more hours per month than the limits established by the U.S. Department of Commerce. When management was unresponsive to entreaties on the flight crews' behalf, Grooch says, Noonan quit.[7] So far, no letter of resignation or notification of termination has turned up in surviving Pan American files. Grooch's account, published two years after Noonan's disappearance, is the only near-contemporaneous written account that has come to light to explain the senior navigator's departure. Barring the discovery of a better source, it has to be regarded as the most credible.

In Lae, New Guinea, during preparations for the flight to Howland, Earhart sent a telegram to Putnam saying that a delay was necessary due to "personnel unfitness."[8] This has sometimes been interpreted as code for

Noonan's having been too drunk, or hung over, to navigate. That's one way to interpret it, but there are innumerable others. They had, after all, pushed themselves most of the way around the world in a rather cranky, loud, vibrating airplane, probably often hot, often cold. They had fought through all kinds of weather conditions, landed and taken off over and over. They had eaten all kinds of food, drunk water from all kinds of sources. It would hardly be surprising if one or both of the Electra's personnel had been dangerously fatigued, or just plain sick.

In a 1976 interview, James Collopy, who was superintendent of Civil Aviation in New Guinea in 1937, reportedly told of a drinking session with Noonan at Lae on the evening of June 29, the day the airplane arrived from Port Darwin, Australia.[9] In marked contrast to Collopy's story was the recollection of Francis "Fuzz" Furman, who spent several days and evenings with Noonan a few days earlier in Bandoeng, Java. In a 1989 interview with Ric Gillespie, Furman, who had helped oversee maintenance on the World Flight's Lockheed Electra during the stop in Java, was adamant that Noonan never had a drink even in social situations where Furman himself was drinking.[10] Either story, or neither, or both, may be true. A recently discovered letter from a reporter who covered the disappearance, and who says he knew Noonan, speculates that Noonan had to be "poured into the plane" before takeoff, but this isn't even offered as a truthful story; it is a guess by the reporter. How educated a guess it was, we have no way of knowing.

What we have in the way of documentary evidence pertinent to Noonan's condition when the flight left Lae is film of the Electra's takeoff.[11] This film, attributed to Sid Marshall of Guinea Airways, shows Earhart and Noonan boarding the plane, and both look quite chipper. Fred mounts the airplane's wing to go in through the hatch, turns, and gives Amelia a hand. Nobody staggers, nobody sways. If Noonan was drunk, or hung over, he was covering it up well.[12]

All in all, we haven't found any evidence that Noonan was an alcoholic, though of course we can't prove that he wasn't. If he did suffer from this disease, we can find no credible evidence that it affected his behavior at takeoff from Lae. Of course, one can speculate that he drank himself silly once the plane was in the air, or that he bravely held himself together until the Electra left the ground, and then passed out. One could also speculate that he had a nervous breakdown, went blind, or was possessed by the devil.

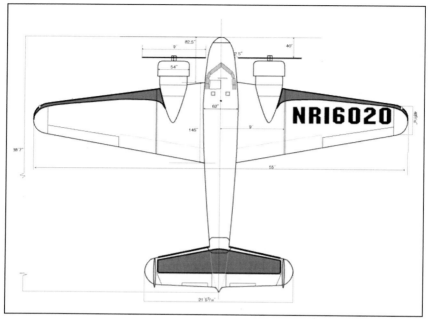

The Electra was an all-aluminum airplane with a 55-foot wingspan and two 550 hp Pratt & Whitney "Wasp" engines. TIGHAR Collection, based on drawing by William Harney.

There is—as yet, anyway—no evidence that alcohol abuse had anything to do with the flight's failure.

The Airplane

The aircraft in which Earhart and Noonan attempted their world flight, a Lockheed Model 10E Special, was a modification of the Burbank-based manufacturer's popular "Electra" 10-passenger airliner. Debuting in 1934, the Electra was Lockheed's first all-metal, twin-engined design. Together with the Boeing Model 247 and the Douglas DC-2, it represented a revolution in commercial air travel. The Model 10E, introduced in February 1936, featured 550 hp Pratt & Whitney "Wasp" engines, which provided a bit more speed and payload than the standard Electra's 450 hp "Wasp Juniors."

The Electra before departure from Miami, June 1, 1937. TIGHAR Collection from Purdue University Special Collections.

Lockheed eventually built fifteen of the big-engined version, most of which were purchased by airlines serving mountainous regions. Two Model 10Es were modified for long-distance flying and carried fuel tanks in the cabin instead of passenger seats. These special purpose aircraft were dubbed "10E Specials." One was built for newspaper magnate Harold Vanderbilt and christened *Daily Express*. In May 1937, piloted by legendary airline captain Dick Merrill, it made the first commercial transatlantic flight, carrying film of the Hindenburg disaster to England and bringing home film of King George VI's coronation.

The other 10E Special, Lockheed constructor's number 1055 (the fifty-fifth Model 10 built), was made for Amelia Earhart. The aircraft was purchased with $80,000 contributed to Purdue University's Amelia Earhart Fund for Aeronautical Research by David Ross, J. K. Lilly, and Vincent Bendix. Radios and other equipment were donated by aviation suppliers such as Western Electric, Goodrich, and Goodyear. The idea was that Earhart, who had worked for Purdue as a career adviser to female students, would use the aircraft to "develop scientific and engineering data of vital importance to the aviation industry."[13]

Delivered on Earhart's thirty-ninth birthday, July 24, 1936, it bore Bureau of Air Commerce registration number NR16020. Putnam dubbed it "the flying laboratory," but it was not used significantly in scientific research. Some of its equipment, such as its Sperry "Gyro-Pilot" automatic pilot, was state-of-the-art, but for the most part its equipment was unremarkable. On paper, the airplane had a top speed of 215 mph, but for long-distance flying it cruised at a far more economical 150 mph. In its final configuration it could carry 1,151 gallons of gasoline and some 80 gallons of oil, giving it a theoretical endurance of more than twenty-four hours aloft. The World Flight—circumnavigating the globe at its widest point, crisscrossing the Equator—was planned as a series of "legs," each requiring less than twenty hours in the air so as to allow a reasonable fuel reserve.

CHAPTER 4

Disappearance

Mr. Noonan told me that he was not a bit anxious about the flight to Howland Island and was quite confident that he would have little difficulty in locating it.

—JAMES COLLOPY, 1937

Prelude

The initial plan for the World Flight had Earhart and her Electra flying west from Oakland to Hawaii and on around the world. Earhart and Putnam recognized that the biggest problem would be crossing the Pacific. Even with extra fuel tanks, it was beyond the Electra's capacity to fly from Honolulu to anyplace near the Equator on the west side of the ocean in a single leg. Building on her notoriety and Putnam's contacts, Earhart discreetly contacted President Roosevelt and the Navy, seeking help for midair refueling between Hawaii and either Japan or the Philippines. While the Navy was capable of midair refueling, the logistics were cumbersome and the prospect of training Earhart in the techniques a bit daunting. Fortunately, an alternative emerged. As part of its competition with the British for islands that could serve as bases for transpacific airline and airmail routes (see chapter 3), the United States had launched a small-scale program of island colonization. Starting in 1935, William Miller of the U.S. Bureau of Air Commerce was charged with "populating" the islands of Howland, Baker, and Jarvis with Hawaiian schoolboys to underscore U.S. rights to the tiny but potentially strategic bits of coral. Miller's boss at Commerce was Gene Vidal (father of author Gore Vidal), a good friend of Earhart's. At Vidal's request, Miller met with Earhart in November 1936, explained what and where the islands were, and suggested that for the World Flight, Howland would make a good stepping stone between Hawaii and New Guinea or Australia. If Earhart used Howland Island as an intermediate stop, she would not need to fuel in midair.

The difficulty, though, was that Howland had no landing field. By June 1936, England had tacitly acquiesced in U.S. control of Howland, Baker, and Jarvis, and control of the islands was transferred to the Department of the Interior. Richard Black took over Miller's job of populating and supplying the islands, and a bit later a Works Projects Administration project was approved to build runways on Howland. In January 1937, construction gear was shipped to the island and grading began. The U.S. government also agreed to assist Earhart's flight by providing a Coast Guard cutter that routinely serviced the Howland operation, to provide radio communication and direction finding to help guide the Electra to its landing.

When the first attempt at the World Flight got under way, Noonan was aboard to assist but was not identified as its navigator. Captain Harry Manning—a navigator Earhart had met years before—filled this position, and Manning said only that "Noonan's going along with us as far as Howland"— that is, the first stop beyond Honolulu. The Electra departed Oakland on March 17 with Earhart, Manning, Paul Mantz, and Noonan aboard, and reached Honolulu without major incident (the starboard propeller froze in fixed pitch, and the transmitter became inoperative due to a blown fuse). On March 20, repairs complete, Earhart started her takeoff roll at Luke Field near Honolulu for the hop to Howland. Here disaster struck. For reasons that have never been quite clear, and that are the subjects of endless speculation among Earhart aficionados, the plane "groundlooped" (spun around on the ground), collapsing the landing gear and skidding down the runway on its belly. The Electra was sufficiently damaged that it had to be shipped back to California for repairs.

Noonan had apparently impressed Earhart considerably during the flight to Honolulu, and when the Electra was repaired and Earhart was ready to try again, she and Noonan were the World Flight's crew.

This time they would go east. Having flown a number of shakedown runs, Earhart and Noonan took off from Oakland and made their way to Miami. On June 1 they left North America behind.

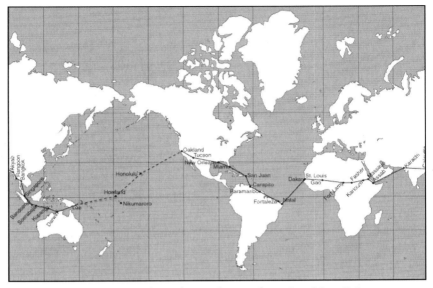

The World Flight as planned—and carried out as far as Lae, New Guinea.

To Lae

Earhart and Noonan flew the Electra across the Caribbean to South America, down along the coast to the great cape at Natal, then across the South Atlantic to Dakar in west Africa. Actually, they missed Dakar, crossing the African coast a little less than seventy miles north of their intended route. Fortunately they were able to land at Saint-Louis in Senegal and backtrack to Dakar to prepare for the next series of hops across Africa: Gao, Fort Lamy, El Fasher, Khartoum, Massawa, Assab on the Horn of Africa, and then a long jump along the Arabian coast and across the Persian Gulf to Karachi by the middle of June. As the flight progressed, Earhart regularly telegraphed reports to the *New York Herald* for publication, discussing the events of the day. These missives were published almost verbatim as the heart of *Last Flight,* her posthumously published book.[1]

The flight proceeded without major problems across the Indian subcontinent and down though Southeast Asia to Singapore, then through Bandoeng, Java, and on to Surabaya on the same island, where engine trouble sent them back to Bandoeng for repairs. In Bandoeng a photograph was taken of Earhart with her foot on the wing of the plane, her shoe neatly positioned on highly visible lines of rivets. Nothing special at the time, but about fifty-five years later TIGHAR would find that photo very interesting.

It was June 27 when the Electra finally left Java, landing the same day at Koepang on Timor. Leaving the next morning, by noon they landed in Darwin, on the north coast of Australia. On June 29 they climbed out of Darwin and flew east-northeast across the Arafura Sea to the rough little port town of Lae, on the northeastern shore of New Guinea.

The Lae-Howland Leg

At Lae, Earhart and Noonan faced the longest and most difficult leg of the entire journey: the 2,500-mile jump to Howland Island. Howland is a miniscule coral island in the mid-Pacific, but it now had runways, and the USCGC *Itasca* would be waiting there to help guide them in and to refuel the Lockheed for the flight to Hawaii. From there they would make their triumphal return to Oakland. The U.S. Navy seagoing tug *Ontario*, operating about midway between New Guinea and Howland, would also stand by for messages from the flight, and serve as a midflight radio navigation beacon.

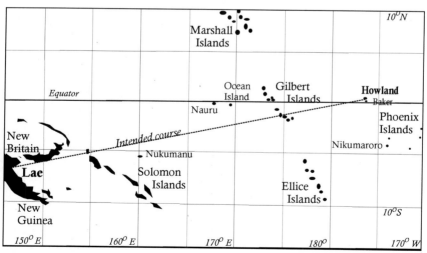

The Lae-Howland leg.

The Lae-Howland segment would be the longest Earhart and Noonan had flown. It would require Noonan to find an island only about 1.5 by 0.7 miles across, averaging about ten feet above sea level with no prominent landmarks. All Earhart's previous flights across broad expanses of water had been either to continents, which are hard to miss, or to the Hawaiian Islands—large, mountainous islands with ample radio facilities for direction finding. Noonan's Pan American experience, however, had given him extensive experience navigating over open water and finding small island targets—though none as small as Howland. Pan Am's navigational procedures, which Noonan had helped to develop, used celestial navigation to keep the plane close to its intended line of flight until it was within radio range of its destination. Once in range, both the plane and the station could use radio direction finding to locate one another; the plane could simply home in on the station's signals, or the station could instruct the pilot what course to fly, to bring the flight in safely.

July 2, 1937

Earhart and Noonan left Lae on July 2 at 10 A.M. local time—0000 Greenwich Civil Time.[2] The takeoff took almost the entire length of the grass runway, which fell off a few dozen feet into the Gulf of Huon. At the end of the runway the plane dipped slightly toward the sea, and continued outward just a few feet above the ocean. Across the International Date Line, the local time was 12:30 P.M. July 1 aboard *Itasca*, waiting at Howland Island. Midway along the route, USS *Ontario* stood by for radio contact. After some difficulty making contact with stations broadcasting accurate Greenwich Civil Time, Noonan had been able to calibrate his chronometers, so all seemed in readiness for takeoff and a smooth, if long, flight.

But the small crowd that gathered at Lae's airfield was the last group of people known to have seen Earhart and Noonan, or at least to have seen them alive.

Lae's radio operator received a few signals from Earhart as she traveled east, and sent weather reports but got no acknowledgement that they had been received. USS *Ontario* received no messages from her. *Itasca* began receiving messages some fourteen hours after the flight left Lae. As recorded in the ship's radio log and repeated by dozens of Earhart books and articles, they went like this:

2:45 a.m.: Earhart voice heard, but cannot make out information.

3:45 a.m.: Earhart states that she will listen on hour and half hour on 3105 kHz.

Itasca tried to call Earhart and establish two-way communication, but there was no evidence that Earhart received the ship's signals.

4:53 a.m.: Earhart states "Partly Cloudy."

6:14 a.m.: Earhart wants a bearing on 3105 kHz on the hour, will whistle in microphone, about 200 miles out approximately, now whistling.

Itasca tried to take bearings on Earhart's transmission, but wasn't able to do so.

6:41 a.m.: Earhart requests: "Please take bearing on us and report in half hour. I will make noise in mic—about 100 miles out."

Another attempt to take a bearing failed, and *Itasca* still had no two-way communication with Earhart.

7:42 a.m.: "KHAQQ [the call letters of Earhart's plane] calling Itasca we must be on you but cannot see you but gas is running low been unable to reach you by radio we are flying at 1000 feet."

A separate log kept by the operator of another radio aboard *Itasca* reports: "Earhart on now says running out of gas only half hour left can't hear us at all."

Itasca's skipper, Commander Warner K. Thompson, was getting worried by this time. His radio room kept trying to establish contact, but to no avail.

7:58 a.m.: "KHAQQ calling Itasca we are circling[3] but cannot hear you go ahead on 7500 with a long count either now or on the schedule time on half hour."

As requested, *Itasca* broadcast on 7500 kilohertz (kHz), and this time . . .

```
8:00 a.m.: "KHAQQ calling Itasca we received your signals but
      unable to get a minimum. Please take bearing on us and
      answer 3105 with voice."
```

 The other radio log reports: "Amelia on again at 0800 says hears us on 7.5 megs go ahead on 7500 again."

Itasca tried to take a bearing on Earhart's transmission, but again failed. With all the talk of the plane being low on fuel and "on" the island but unable to see it, it must have seemed likely to Thompson that Earhart was about to go into the water, if she weren't there already. But then . . .

```
8:43 a.m.: Earhart on the air: "KHAQQ to Itasca we are on the
      line 157 337 wl rept msg we will rept this on 6210 KCS
      wait, [(3105/A3 S5 (?/KHAQQ xmission we are running on
      N ES S line)]."4
```

The "157 337" message is the last message officially accepted as coming from the World Flight; twenty hours and thirteen minutes after leaving Lae, Earhart and Noonan vanished into legend.

To the Rescue

Since *Itasca* hadn't been able to get a bearing on any of Earhart's signals, Thompson had no way of knowing where the plane might be. After listening in vain for a couple more hours, however, Thompson had to conclude that it was down *someplace,* and the only thing to do was start looking. But where? The sky was clear in all directions except to the northeast, where a cloudbank hung about thirty to fifty miles out. Presumably reasoning that only if they had been in such clouds could Earhart and Noonan have failed to see the island, Thompson ordered *Itasca* underway at 10:40 local time and steamed northwest—where he found nothing but open sea.

After studying the facts as they knew them, the commandant of the Fourteenth Naval District in Pearl Harbor concluded that "the most probable reason for missing Howland Island would be that of stronger winds than normally expected in the region, and that the plane had been carried

U.S.S. *Colorado*'s float planes searched the Phoenix Islands. TIGHAR Collection from U.S. National Archives.

southeast of Howland."[5] The battleship USS *Colorado* was dispatched to search the area, while *Itasca* continued to sweep the seas, aided by USS *Swan*, which had been standing by between Howland and Hawaii.

The Cruise of the *Colorado*

Over the next few days, the *Colorado* steamed the 2,000 miles southward to begin the search. Meanwhile new radio signals thought to be from the lost plane were heard on the frequencies Earhart had been using. Lockheed experts said this meant that the plane had to be on land, so that it could turn an engine and recharge its batteries. Some of the signals were received by stations with radio direction finding equipment. Most of the bearings they were able to take, the U.S. Navy found, described lines that crossed in the vicinity of the mostly uninhabited Phoenix Islands, some 350 miles southeast of Howland.[6]

This information caused the Navy to alter its approach somewhat. Rather than searching for a plane or a raft floating in the vastness of the

Pacific, *Colorado* would use her three catapult-launched floatplanes to search the Phoenix Islands.

Colorado's pilots flew over each of the Phoenix Islands and landed in the lagoon at Hull, the only island of the group with inhabitants. They reported seeing no evidence of the Lockheed or its crew.

Giving Up—Officially

When the aircraft carrier USS *Lexington* and her destroyers took over on July 12, the search shifted away from the Phoenix Group to the open ocean areas north and west of Howland. *Itasca* and *Swan* were sent into the densely populated Gilbert Islands (now Kiribati) far to the west on the chance that Earhart had reversed her course,[7] but neither the *Lexington*'s intensive aerial search of the ocean nor the inquiries in the Gilberts turned up any hint of the missing flight. The United States also asked the Japanese to search the areas around the Marshall Islands, and official correspondence at the time indicated that the Japanese authorities asked the oceanographic survey ship *Koshu* to do so. The *Koshu* arrived in the Marshall Island area on or about July 9 and continued searching for about ten days. A 1949 U.S. Army Intelligence report states that although no documentation could be found in the records of the Japanese Navy, interviews of Japanese officials on Jaliut and elsewhere indicated that both the *Koshu* and the *Kamoi* searched the Marshall Islands, with the assistance of a large-type flying boat. Bridge logs of the *Kamoi* clearly state it was nowhere near the Marshalls during this time, however, and we have no documentary evidence that a flying boat was ever used to search for wreckage. The Army Intelligence report also says that no traces of the Electra were found.[8] The Japanese also offered to search the Gilberts, but—understandably—this offer apparently was not accepted.[9]

On July 18 the search was officially called off. The official verdict was that the plane had probably gone down at sea and sunk without a trace. The post-loss radio signals were declared to be either misunderstandings or outright hoaxes.[10]

Putnam Perseveres

Despite the official verdict that Earhart and Noonan were lost, Putnam apparently still had hope. TIGHAR's research has uncovered a good deal of information on his efforts, and those of the British colonial authorities, to continue the search.[11]

On July 17, just before the U.S. government withdrew its ships, Putnam contacted the U.S. Chief of Naval Operations (CNO):

```
Deeply grateful if steps be taken to search area
slightly north of intersection of longitude 170
East and equator contemporaneously with search of
Gilbert Island [sic]. Because peculiar intimate
nature alleged information this is a confidential
personal request to you. Most compelling unusual
circumstances dictate although sole obvious rea-
sonableness lies in westward prevailing drift
which might well carried floating plane through
Gilberts to indicated area. Anyway cannot pass up
this bet forlorn as it may be.[12]
```

In a follow-up telegram, Putnam said he "can't rationalize or make public why. This is written by practical person." We speculate that the proposed search location was provided by a friend of Putnam's, Jackie Cochran, a practicing clairvoyant. The CNO took the proposal up with his advisers and concluded that it wasn't worth pursuing.

Putnam then turned to his good friend Eugene Vidal, head of the Bureau of Air Commerce. Vidal brokered a meeting with President Roosevelt, which took place on July 30. No notes on this meeting have yet been found, but apparently Putnam asked that a search be made for an uncharted reef at 2°36'N, 174°10'E, bearing 106° from Makin Island.

The day after the meeting, Putnam wrote to Sumner Wells, the State Department's primary point of contact on Earhart matters, to clarify his request for a search for the uncharted reef. He said that a former copra vessel commander, his credibility confirmed by a reliable American, reported that such a reef was visited by Gilbertese seeking turtle eggs. He named Captain Isaac Handley of Tarawa as a knowledgeable person on the matter, though it is not clear whether Handley was the copra skipper who reported the reef.[13] We do not know how Putnam knew about Handley.

Wells asked the U.S. ambassador in London to contact the British Colonial Office and request a search, with Putnam reimbursing expenses and paying $2,000 for information leading to a definitive conclusion. Shortly, the Secretary of State for Colonies telegraphed the High Commissioner of the Western Pacific in Fiji:[14]

```
United States Ambassador states that evidence,
which to many sources seems positive, indicates
that Miss Earhart was on land two nights follow-
ing disappearance. Note proceeds to ask if fur-
ther search of Gilbert Islands could be made at
expense, if necessary, of husband, Putnam, who
urges immediate search of position 174 degrees
10 minutes east, 2 degrees 36 minutes north,
where he has reason to believe that uncharted
reef exists of which Captain Handley of Tarawa
said to know. Reward of 2,000 dollars offered for
any evidence leading to solution of disappearance.
Please telegraph what action can be taken.[15]
```

Search for a Spirit Isle

Official British resources in the area were stretched thin, but the Gilbert and Ellice Islands Colony officials had already alerted government personnel and trading vessels in the area to be on the lookout for evidence of the lost plane, and apparently called out residents of several islands to search the reefs for wreckage. With the cooperation of the Burns Philp Company, a major copra trading house, and Captain Isaac Handley himself, they now responded promptly to London's request—though little was reported back to Putnam, generating a good deal of frustration on his part. By August 12 Captain Handley, despite being in poor health and sixty-nine years old, was off with a Gilbertese crew of five in a borrowed sailing vessel.

On August 20 Handley returned to Tarawa, and reported to the District Officer in charge:

Sir,

At the mutual desire of yourself and the Manager of Messrs. Burns Philp S.S. Co. I undertook to go in search of Mrs. Putman [sic] alleged to be on an uncharted reef. Position given.

35

Nothing known locally of such a reef. There is a native tradition say, there is an isle of Spirits all right in this alleged position but the human eye is not permitted to see it.

However, after a search of three days within a radius of some twenty miles of given position. And no sign of Bird Life. I conclude that it is none existent there.

The natives of Marakei give the name Katagateman to the supposed isle. Half man half devil that discovered it.

Sorry the eventure [*sic*] was unsuccessful. But fate.

Yours faithfully,

(Signed) Isaac R. Handley[16]

It took a while for the results of Handley's search for Katagateman to reach Putnam, who was not immediately satisfied. Eventually, however, even he apparently accepted that Earhart was irrevocably lost. As for Captain Handley—who took the initiative to search for Katagateman even though he disbelieved in it—his fate was a sad one:

The Reverend Alfred Sadd . . . was brutally slaughtered in Tarawa on the 15 October 1942, together with twenty-one other British subjects, including two greatly respected veteran traders, McArthur and Handley, and several young New Zealanders. The Japanese tried in vain to make Sadd trample on the Union Jack, instead of which . . . he gathered it in his arms and kissed it.[17]

CHAPTER 5

After the Search: Assumptions, Assertions, and Conspiracy Theories

We'll blame Japan;
She's on Saipan;
Or maybe that's her now at the front door!
　　　　　　　　　—TIGHAR TUNES*

It Was Earhart's Fault

The U.S. Coast Guard and Navy had little trouble figuring out what had gone wrong: Earhart and Noonan had been unable to find Howland, and therefore had run out of fuel and crashed somewhere in the trackless ocean north of the island. First Lieutenant Daniel A. Cooper of the Army Air Corps, military observer aboard *Itasca*, summed up:

> It is my opinion that the Earhart plane missed Howland Island within 50 and probably within 30 miles to the North and that the airplane went down most probably within 180 miles of Howland to the Northwest and that wreckage or boat if still floating will drift to the Gilbert Islands, due to wind and current, arriving in that locality around August.

*Sung to the last bars of "The (U.S.) Air Force Song," by Robert Crawford.

He went on to recommend:

1. That no more flights of this nature be permitted.
2. That only flights backed by U.S. Army, Navy, or airlines similar to Pan American Airlines with competent personnel and adequate equipment be made to Howland Island.[1]

Cleaned up to reduce the potential for public distaste at criticism of Earhart, this became the U.S. government's official position. Predictably, it wasn't long before it was challenged.

Spies, Cover-Ups, and the Japanese Connection

The first allegation that there was more to the story of Earhart's disappearance than the U.S. government would admit came from *Smith's Weekly*, an Australian tabloid newspaper. The paper's October 16, 1937, issue charged that the U.S. Navy had used Earhart's disappearance as an excuse to send aircraft over the Marshall Islands, where it was suspected the Japanese were building military installations.[2] The Japanese controlled the Marshalls under a League of Nations mandate conferred when Germany's colonial holdings were divided up after World War I.[3] According to the logs of the *Colorado* and other ships that took part in the search, neither they nor their planes went into or over the Marshalls, and the Japanese hadn't yet developed fortifications there that anyone flying over them could have observed.[4] Nevertheless, *Smith's Weekly* had planted an idea that would grow into one of the twentieth century's most popular conspiracy theories.

The theory quickly evolved after war broke out in the Pacific. Not long after the attack on Pearl Harbor, a screenplay—of since-disputed authorship—appeared, titled "Stand By to Die," which took the *Smith's Weekly* idea and added the notion that Earhart was in on the plot. Purchased by RKO Pictures, the story was filmed and released under the title *Flight for Freedom* in April of 1943. Rosalind Russell and Fred MacMurray starred as "Toni Carter" and "Randy Britton"—Earhart and Noonan clones so thinly disguised that RKO reportedly paid George Putnam a fee to forestall a lawsuit.

Life began to imitate art as soon as the film was released. Within a week after opening night, a Georgia Tech University administrator, M. L. Brittain, who had been a guest aboard the *Colorado* during the Earhart search, announced that he had felt at the time that Earhart's flight was somehow involved with the government.[5] No doubt aided by the idea that it was not entirely fictional, *Flight for Freedom* was a commercial success and was widely talked about. By the time U.S. forces invaded the Marshall Islands and Saipan in 1944, the notion that Earhart may have been "captured by the Japanese" was well-established scuttlebutt.[6]

In 1949, Earhart's mother was quoted in the press as saying that she felt Amelia had been secretly involved with the government.[7] U.S. Army Intelligence and the United Press undertook independent investigations at this point, including interviews in the Marshalls, and reported no supporting evidence or corroborating witnesses.[8] At this point, "Earhart as spy" and "captured by Japanese" rumors seem to have died down. They remained quiescent for ten years.

As the 1960s began, however, the Japanese capture hypothesis grew new legs. Two U.S. Air Force officers stationed on Guam, Joseph Gervais and Robert Dinger, produced a long list of witnesses on Saipan who they said had reported seeing Earhart and Noonan in Japanese custody. Thomas E. Devine, who had been a U.S. Army sergeant on Saipan in 1945, reported that he had been told the location of Earhart's grave. An Office of Naval Intelligence investigation of Devine's claims showed that the alleged grave site wasn't what it was made out to be, but at the same time it speculated, based on secondhand hearsay evidence, that Earhart might have crashed in the Marshalls.[9]

Woven through all these stories was that of a California woman, Josephine Blanco Akiyama, who reported that as a girl on Saipan before the war, she had seen Earhart held prisoner. Mrs. Akiyama's story captured the imagination of San Francisco radio reporter Fred Goerner, who launched a serious on-site investigation of the Saipan Hypothesis. Goerner's work culminated in his 1966 book, *The Search for Amelia Earhart.*

The Japanese Capture/Conspiracy Hypothesis

In a nutshell, Goerner portrayed Earhart and Noonan as U.S. government agents whose secret mission it was to spy on Japanese forces in Truk (now Chuuk) Lagoon in the Caroline Islands. Having flown over Chuuk, he said, they had encountered bad weather, been unable to find Howland, and wound up landing on Mili Atoll in what is now the Republic of the Marshall Islands. After about ten days, he said, they were collected by the Japanese and taken to Saipan in the Mariana Islands. "The kind of questioning and hardships they endured can be imagined," he says, and recounts a number of stories told by people on Saipan about their death in Japanese hands. This, he says, "may have been a release they both desired."[10] He claims that the U.S. government did nothing to rescue them, and indeed covered up evidence of their real mission.

Goerner's book was a best-seller. Its success unleashed a flood of other conspiracy books by authors who proposed variations on the theme.[11] Like Goerner's book, all were based on anecdotal accounts of alleged eyewitnesses to the imprisonment and/or execution of people who allegedly looked like Earhart, or to the destruction of aircraft that looked like the Electra. All were largely based on hearsay, or on private sources to which no one else had access, so their interpretations couldn't easily be checked. All ascribed dark motives to various elements of the U.S. government that were thought to have kept Earhart's fate a secret from the public.

The Perils of Anecdote

If we seem a little snippy about how pervasive anecdotes are in the Earhart research game, it's true, we are. What people say they saw, heard, or did in the past are the lifeblood of oral history, but every oral historian knows that recollections have to be collected and interpreted with great care.

For one thing, people misremember. One person may say that the car that sped away from the crime scene was a green Toyota; another may say a blue Mazda. Neither is lying; each just remembers the incident differently, interpreted what he or she saw differently. This is why detectives talk to as many eyewitnesses as possible.

Time and events also blur, confuse, and mix up recollections. Was it last Christmas that Aunt Alice's mince pie was so awful, or the Christmas before? Was it the mince pie that made Cousin Jim sick, or the turkey liver stuffing?

Over time, recollections may evolve to serve psychological or social purposes. The oral historian Jan Vansina says, "The historian must always be on the lookout for unconscious distortions, as well as for the obvious alterations which might have been introduced for fun, profit, or esteem."[12]

People sometimes think things happened, or embroider on things that perhaps did happen, to add color to their lives, to impress others, to gain status, and over time they may come quite firmly to believe the stories they have told. This is why when we refer to a "war story" or a "fish story," we're not necessarily referring to a factual account of a battle or a fishing trip.

And it's easy for an interviewer to "lead" a witness, particularly if the witness feels somehow inferior to the interviewer, or wants to please the interviewer by giving him or her what's desired. This problem is compounded when the interviewer pays the witness for information.

All these factors have to be taken into account when you assess the stories about Earhart in the Marshalls, or Earhart on Saipan—or Earhart in the Phoenix Islands.

Although it doesn't always succeed, TIGHAR tries to be careful about how it collects and uses people's recollections. Ric Gillespie has been known to insist that anecdotal evidence really isn't evidence at all; others of us are a bit more liberal, but we all know that we have to be careful with it.

When we interview someone, we try to be careful not to "lead the witness." The question of payment for information has never arisen. If it did—and there are perfectly good and honorable reasons that it might—we'd want to make it as clear as we could that we were paying for whatever information the interviewee wanted to give us, not just for what he or she thought we wanted to hear. And even then we'd take what we were told with a larger grain of salt than we would information given for free.

Most importantly, we don't think of anecdotal evidence as fact, but as basis for testable hypotheses. When Emily Sikuli (see chapter 23) tells us that she saw airplane wreckage on Nikumaroro in 1940, we respect this as an accurate reflection of Mrs. Sikuli's recollection, but we don't assume that therefore there *was* airplane wreckage on Nikumaroro in 1940. We ask ourselves, "Is this consistent with other evidence?" If it is, that makes it more likely that it reflects some sort of objective truth, but it's still not definite. We then ask ourselves: "*If* in 1940 there was airplane wreckage at the spot indicated by Mrs. Sikuli, then where is that wreckage likely to be now?" And having come up with plausible ideas, we go out and look for the hard evidence that will either verify them or show that they're wrong.

Fred Goerner was a distinguished journalist and a dedicated, thoughtful Earhart scholar, but his conclusions were based almost entirely on anecdotal evidence, collected in a place where, and at a time when, any such evidence

A few of the many books that purport to solve the mystery of Earhart's disappearance. TIGHAR photo.

needs to be judged cautiously. At best, Goerner came up with a hypothesis about what happened to Earhart—a hypothesis that unfortunately is difficult to test, and that is contradicted by a good deal of evidence.[13]

Back to the Official Version: Crashed and Sank

It was inevitable that speculative propositions about captures, executions, and conspiracies—usually presented as truth discovered despite official lies and obfuscation—would spark a backlash. In 1972, public relations executive and Earhart student Richard G. Strippel wrote *Amelia Earhart: The Myth and the Reality*.[14] Strippel rebutted some of the allegations offered by Goerner and other conspiracy theorists, ignored others, and endorsed the original conclusion that Earhart ran out of gas and crashed at sea. Besides Strippel, some of today's leading proponents of this intuitively attractive premise are retired airline pilot Elgen Long and his wife, Marie, and the senior aviation curator at the National Air and Space Museum, Dr. Tom Crouch.

The "crashed and sank theory" has most recently been presented in detail in the Longs' 1999 book—rather adventurously titled *Amelia Earhart: The Mystery Solved.*[15] Beyond the title—not the authors' idea, we are told—the book doesn't actually purport to solve the mystery; it simply presents the Longs' excruciatingly detailed take on the "crashed and sank" hypothesis. The Longs think that Earhart and Noonan started off with less than a full load of fuel, wasted fuel on course jogs and fighting a stronger than expected (or recorded) headwind, and hence went down at a rather precisely identified location northwest of Howland. Maybe all those things happened, or maybe not. The Longs' book, touted in a jacket blurb by adventure novelist Clive Cussler as a "conclusive" validation of the crashed and sank hypothesis, is a frustrating tangle of demonstrable fact with anecdotes recounted long after the fact, logical deduction, more or less plausible assumption, and plain speculation.

Earhart "Research" As of the Late 1980s

As of the late 1980s, the major "theories" about the disappearance of Earhart and Noonan being pursued by various researchers around the world were (1) the "crashed and sank" hypothesis and (2) the cluster of proposals involving spying on the Japanese. Of course, there were other notions of what had happened. In 1982 a good deal of press coverage was given to the proposal that Earhart had in fact survived and was living in New Jersey[16]—an allegation vigorously denied by the woman whose identity she was alleged to have assumed. Alien abductions have been proposed, as has disappearance into another dimension through the Pacific equivalent of the Bermuda Triangle. A number of side allegations concern human factors that were supposed to have contributed to the flight's loss. It's been alleged that Earhart was pregnant and hence emotionally and hormonally off her stride, and that she wasn't really a very good pilot anyway. And then there's the premise that Noonan was an alcoholic whose bibulous habits led him to misnavigate the flight to its doom. Typically, such "theories," hypotheses, and assertions were—and continue to be—offered as statements of fact with little if any supporting data other than anecdote—and often unattributed anecdote at that. Proponents of opposing notions usually ignore those whose ideas they reject, or brush them off without data-based rebuttal, offering equally unsubstantiated counterclaims in their place. "What happened to Amelia Earhart" has become a question with a host of more or less mythic answers, each asserted and defended furiously by a coterie of advocates. It's a jungle out there.

A Way through the Woods: Evidence, Hypothesis, Test

Can the jungle be penetrated? Gillespie and his fellow TIGHARs think so; we think so. We think it can be done by applying as rigorous a scientific method as can be applied to historical research. That means recognizing the difference between a hypothesis and a proven fact, and applying rules to the interpretation of evidence.

What do we mean by evidence? Evidence comes in two flavors: direct evidence and indirect, or circumstantial, evidence. The boundaries between these two types of evidence are not always clear, and each includes subcategories.

A datable photograph of Earhart in the Electra, wearing a particular article of clothing, would be direct evidence that she wore it while in the plane. Assuming the photo was taken on the ground, it would be indirect evidence that she wore it while flying. A contemporaneous eyewitness account, written down at or soon after the time the event—like wearing a particular item—was observed would also generally be accepted as direct evidence. However, the longer the time that elapses between observation and documentation, the more indirect the evidence becomes. Where several contemporaneous accounts produce conflicting information or interpretations, the earliest account is usually given greater weight, as are multiple accounts that agree with one another, as opposed to the "odd man out." Anecdotal accounts, offered long after the fact, have the least weight of all.

Indirect evidence is not necessarily bad evidence, or wrong; it's just not directly associated with the event. The preponderance of indirect evidence is often what persuades an archaeologist, historian, crime scene investigator, or jury that a hypothesis is correct. DNA at a crime scene can show that an individual with such DNA was at the scene, but it doesn't demonstrate that a particular person committed the crime. Add other evidence—fingerprints on a gun, ownership of the weapon—and you may begin to build a case.

The major problem in assessing evidence for historical investigations is the passage of time. Direct evidence in the form of eyewitness accounts and photographs can, of course, be produced only at or near the time of the event in question. It's also limited in quantity—it can be produced only by those present and able to observe or photograph the event. Indirect evidence, too, is best collected at or near the time of the event. As the years pass, other events can occur—indeed, almost certainly do occur—that have nothing to do with the event in question but can contaminate the record. Somebody else wanders through wearing the same article of clothing as Earhart wore, and inadvertently drops it. The definitive Electra part is dug up and made into a belt buckle.

Our approach is to use the best available direct evidence—contemporaneous accounts and contemporaneous or near-contemporaneous documents—to generate hypotheses, and then to look for the body of indirect evidence (like Electra parts) that can provide a basis for judging whether the hypothesis is correct. Anecdotal accounts are used in hypothesis generation, too, as are expert—or not so expert—opinions ("They would have landed somewhere flat"), but these are not evidence in and of themselves.

Historical research isn't an exact science, though, and the boundaries among types of evidence are subject to interpretation. We argue a lot among ourselves about how much weight should be given a particular account, story, or logical deduction in generating and testing hypotheses.

So what's a hypothesis? According to Webster, it's "a system or theory imagined or assumed to account for what is not understood."[17] The authoritative (if a bit tongue-in-cheek) archaeological guidebook *Bluff Your Way in Archaeology* defines it as "a guess."[18] We hypothesize—that is, make an educated guess about something. Then we test the hypothesis by applying evidence—that is, pertinent information, or data. Our analysis of the evidence should allow us to determine whether our guess is—or at least probably is—true. But the evidence that we apply needs to be made up of demonstrably real data, or at least as real as we can get.

For example, suppose we hypothesize, as physicists do, that if we bring matter and antimatter together they will annihilate one another, producing a burst of energy, and suppose we then seek evidence to test our hypothesis. The extensively reported use of an antimatter drive to power the Starship *Enterprise* is not good evidence that our hypothesis is correct, because however plausible it may be, it's not "hard data"—that is, real, documented data about the real world. It's something Gene Roddenberry and his colleagues thought up. It wouldn't be hard data even if Roddenbury had insisted that he got his information from Spock or Scotty when they beamed him up and gave him a tour of the ship; he'd have to be able to show the rest of us here on Earth that the drive actually worked.

On the other hand, if we actually bring matter and antimatter together in a controlled setting like a laboratory and observe an explosion—a release of energy—that's strong evidence in support of our hypothesis. We can document how we do this—thus capturing our direct evidence—and then others can perform the same experiment over and over, demonstrating with a high degree of confidence that the hypothesis is correct.

In historical research, of course, we can't conduct experiments like those a physicist or chemist can carry out. We can't put Earhart and Noonan into an Electra and see where they go. But we can still develop hypotheses and test them. If our hypothesis is that Earhart and Noonan were captured by the Japanese, for example, we can ask ourselves what evidence we'd expect to find that would prove that this did or did not happen. The only way we can show conclusively that the flyers were *not* captured by the Japanese, of course, is to find strong evidence that something else happened to them,[19] but what evidence would prove that they *were*? A truly authoritative contemporaneous document—say, an unquestionably official Japanese prison record—would be good direct evidence. A well-documented piece of the Electra on Saipan, or bones whose DNA matched Earhart's or Noonan's, would be good indirect evidence. What about a diary composed by Earhart while in prison? Well, maybe, but we would have to find out whether the diary was genuine—which we might be able to do, but consider how hard it's been to decide about the Shroud of Turin. As for somebody's recollection of a captured woman pilot on Saipan, without something a lot more reliable to support it, it's only somebody's recollection. Interesting, maybe, perhaps correct, perhaps not. Perhaps a lead we can follow to something harder. But the further we get from the hard data—the piece of the airplane, the DNA, what Gillespie likes to call the "smoking gun" or the "any idiot artifact"[20]—the more caution we have to exercise in accepting the evidence as real. Earhart research to date has amounted to the mustering of anecdotal evidence and the announcement of solutions. With the Nikumaroro hypothesis, we're trying to do better than that.

But where did the hypothesis come from? And how did a bunch of seemingly sensible people start gallivanting around the Pacific testing such a hypothesis? Enter the Toms.

CHAPTER 6

Getting Hooked on Earhart

Off we go, seeking Amelia Earhart.
Come along, it'll be fun! *
                              —TIGHAR TUNES

F OR ABOUT THREE YEARS AFTER ITS FOUNDING IN 1985,
    TIGHAR resisted being drawn into the Earhart mystery.
    Like most people, Gillespie and Thrasher accepted the
"crashed and sank" hypothesis without serious consideration, and were reluctant to become involved in a question that (a) probably couldn't be answered, and (b) stirred so much passion among adherents to different hypotheses.

The Toms and the LOP

In 1988, however, two new members of the organization, Tom Willi and Tom Gannon—ever after known as "the Toms"—approached Gillespie and Thrasher with a "new" hypothesis about Earhart's disappearance—one that could be tested using accepted scientific research methods.

The Toms were both retired aviators and navigators, whose careers went back to the time when celestial navigation was still the rule of the day. As a result they had informed ideas about what Noonan did when he and Earhart found themselves in the position where they should have been in sight of Howland but couldn't see it. They found that last officially accepted radio message—about flying on "the line 157-337"—very meaningful.

*Sung to the first bars of "The (U.S.) Air Force Song," by Robert Crawford.

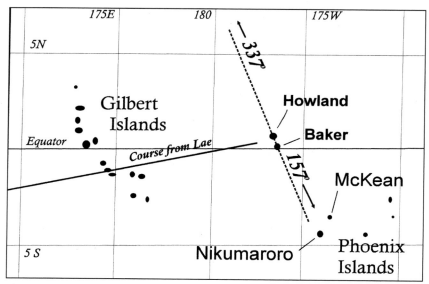

The Line of Position 157–337 degrees

When the sun rose on the morning of July 2, they said, Noonan would have measured its angular altitude using his bubble octant—a version of the traditional nautical sextant adapted for use in the air. The sun would rise at a bearing of 67 degrees—in the northeast—for an observer anywhere along Noonan's planned route to Howland (and for anyone within a couple of hundred miles on either side). Knowing the precise time from his well-calibrated chronometers, Noonan could use the sun's apparent altitude to calculate where he was along his track. At any given moment, the sun appears to be directly over a particular point on the earth's surface, called the subsolar point, or SSP. The exact position of the SSP, and its true bearing from any given latitude and longitude, is tabulated for any time of the day throughout the year and published in standard navigational publications. So, having measured the sun's apparent altitude at a precisely known time, and using an estimate of his position, Noonan could plot a line through his position and perpendicular to the sun's true bearing, and calculate how far west of the SSP that line ran. As it happened in this case, this "Line of Position," or LOP, was also nearly perpendicular to Noonan's track to Howland.

The perpendicular of 67 degrees off north on the compass is, of course, a line running from 157 to 337 degrees—from south-southeast to north-northwest. This was Noonan's LOP, and as of sunrise he could tell how far from the

SSP, and hence how far from Howland, he was. North or south was a different matter. Earhart had of course been following a compass heading designed to take them to Howland, but depending on wind direction and speed they could in fact be some distance off course in either direction. Latitude—north-south location—is most easily determined based on observations taken at high noon; it's difficult to work out based on early morning sightings. So what Noonan knew about their location north or south of their intended course depended on the accuracy of his calculations of wind direction and speed, and the celestial observations he'd been able to make during the night. These would not have been easy to make in an aircraft with limited window space, and would have been entirely dependent on the extent of cloud cover and turbulence. Unless his observations, instruments, or calculations were very wrong he shouldn't be very far off course, but he couldn't be certain that he was close enough to it to be able to spot Howland when it came up over the horizon.

He knew the Electra's airspeed, however, and he had forecasts of wind speed and direction, received before their departure from Lae. By observing the wave crests below he could judge wind direction, together giving him a fair measure of speed over the water. Standard navigational practice, the Toms said, would be to "advance" the LOP from the point at which Noonan found himself at sunrise, based on the plane's calculated ground speed. In other words, knowing how far west of Howland he was at daybreak, and knowing his ground speed, Noonan would calculate the time at which the Electra would arrive at a 157–337 degree LOP passing through the island. He would in effect imagine a line oriented 157–337 degrees, attached to and moving with the Electra. At the time when the line should have advanced far enough to cut through Howland, the Electra would necessarily be somewhere along that line, hopefully within sight and certainly within radio range of the island. But if the island wasn't visible or contactable by radio, then Noonan still knew that it had to be *somewhere* along the LOP, to the south-southeast (157 degrees) or north-northwest (337 degrees)[1] of Howland.

Of course, Noonan expected to be able to home in on radio signals from Howland long before Earhart could spot it, or to have *Itasca* be able to take bearings on Earhart's radio messages and guide them in. For whatever reason, these expectations turned out to be false. So Noonan's fallback, if they reached the vicinity of Howland but couldn't see it, would be to fly along the LOP until they *did* see it. In other words, to get "on the line 157–337" and fly along it to the north and/or south.

157 or 337?

But which way should they fly? Remember those messages about fuel being low, and having only a half-hour left. The latter message couldn't have been accurate, since it reportedly came in at 7:42 A.M. local time and the plane was still in the air and broadcasting the "157–337" message an hour later, but clearly the Electra was not fuel-rich. Earhart and Noonan couldn't afford to turn the wrong way.

If you head out from Howland Island at 337 degrees—toward the north—you'll eventually hit a nice big land mass—the Kamchatka Peninsula, a bit more than 4,000 miles away. You can't do that in an Electra 10E, especially after burning fuel for twenty hours; you're going into the ocean. If you fly at 157 degrees, however, it's a different story. If you're north of Howland when you start, then you come to Howland—assuming, of course, that your estimate of speed over the water has been accurate enough to have allowed you to advance the LOP accurately. If you're south, but not too far south, then you come to Baker Island, just a short way down the LOP. If you start out farther south, or miss Howland and Baker, then about 300 miles farther on, you come into the Phoenix group. No airfields to land on, but probably lots of beaches and exposed reef flats, and a whole lot better than the open ocean. The sensible thing for a navigator to do is turn south along the LOP.

So the most plausible fate of the Electra, the Toms suggested, was that it wound up on an island south of Howland. It didn't land on Baker, which was very small, devoid of vegetation in which an airplane could have disappeared, and inhabited at the time by the Department of the Interior's colonists. This left only a few possibilities, all in the Phoenix Island group. The two islands closest to the LOP south of Howland and Baker were McKean and Gardner, the latter now called Nikumaroro.

The Islands

Like most people, Gillespie and Thrasher had never heard of McKean or Gardner Island, but it didn't take long to acquire some basic information. The Phoenix Islands are a loose group of coral atolls, islands, and reefs about halfway between Hawaii and New Zealand, just south of the Equator. They're part of today's Republic of Kiribati (pronounced Kiribas with the "s" slightly slurred, or Kiribash with the "sh" very soft; in the Kiribati language "ti" is pronounced like it is in the English word "attention"). In colonial times—before the 1970s, in this case—western Kiribati was known as the Gilbert Islands, and was administered as part of the British Gilbert and Ellice Islands Colony. Americans who remember or have read about World War II will know Tarawa, now the capital of Kiribati, as the place where the Allies began to take the Pacific back from the Japanese. The Gilbert Islands proper lie west of the Phoenix Islands, and the Ellises, now Tuvalu, are southwest. Both are now members of the British Commonwealth. Formerly and sometimes still known as "Gilbertese," the people of Kiribati call themselves "I Kiribati," the "I" pronounced "E."

For the most part, the Phoenix Islands are uninhabited, except by millions of sea birds. McKean Island, in fact, is a world-renowned bird sanctuary. McKean was mined for bird guano in the nineteenth century and has been uninhabited since then. Nikumaroro (then called Gardner Island) was uninhabited in 1937 and was equally so in 1988 when TIGHAR began thinking about going there, but it had been occupied from the late 1930s into the 1960s. TIGHAR would learn a lot more about that occupation as time went by.

A Plausible Proposition?

Though their interest was piqued by the Toms' proposition, Gillespie and Thrasher weren't going to get TIGHAR involved in such a Quixotic quest as the Earhart game without asking a lot of questions and independently seeking answers. The first question was whether Earhart could possibly have had enough fuel to have made it to the Phoenix Islands. The Toms thought so. At the time, no one knew precisely how much fuel had been on board the Electra when it departed Lae, but the plane was equipped to carry about 1,100 U.S. gallons. This should have been sufficient for twenty-two to twenty-four hours in the air, and only a bit more than twenty hours elapsed between the departure from Lae and the "Should be on you" message. It's only about two and a half hours flying time at the Electra's standard cruising speed from Howland to either McKean or Nikumaroro.

And then there were those post-loss radio signals. It didn't take long to find the report of Wilhelm L. Friedell, captain of the *Colorado,* in the National Archives. In explaining the reason the battleship sailed south, Friedell said:

[R]eport received on 3 July that on 3105 Kcs a woman's voice had made four distress signal calls followed by KHAQQ, followed by "225 garble, off Howland, battery very weak, can't last long, garble indicated sandbank."

This report, he said, was given "considerable credence" by the Fourteenth Naval District, and he observed that "[t]he only [sand]banks charted are south and east of Howland Island." He went on to say that:

A report was received from Mr. Putnam stressing the Phoenix Island Group and stating that head winds aloft had been much stronger than expected. Again it was stated that the Lockheed Aircraft Engineers stated that the radio could not operate unless the plane was on land.

And there was more:

The Commander Coast Guard sent word that he had communicated with persons familiar with the methods of navigation of Mr. Noonan, and that Mr. Noonan would take a fix shortly before dawn, correct course for destination, and determine line of position when near the end of estimated run. . . . If short on gas, he probably would follow the line of position to the nearest land. . . .[2]

So the Toms' hypothesis was not exactly a new one; it was in fact quite an old one. It had been espoused by Putnam and navy experts, and had in fact been the reason for the cruise of the *Colorado* through the Phoenix Group. The Toms' idea was looking more and more plausible, more worthy of investigation.

"Signs of Recent Habitation"

But that cruise of the *Colorado* had tested the hypothesis, hadn't it? And found it wanting? According to Friedell's report as well as the media at the time, the battlewagon's float planes had flown over every one of the islands and had seen nothing that might be associated with Earhart. McKean Island, Friedell said, had shown "unmistakable signs of having at one time been inhabited," but these signs consisted of "buildings of the adobe type," hardly what Earhart and Noonan would have built. "No one was seen on either Gardner Island or McKean Island," and "(n)o dwellings appeared on Gardner or any other signs of inhabitation."

But some research in the library of the National Air and Space Museum in Washington, D.C., turned up the Navy Bureau of Aeronautics weekly newsletter for July 16, 1937, with an article by Lt. John O. Lambrecht, the battleship's Senior Aviator. Lambrecht had led the overflights. Lambrecht said:

> Gardner is a typical example of your south sea atoll . . . a narrow, circular strip of land . . . surrounding a large lagoon. Most of this island is covered with tropical vegetation with, here and there, a grove of coconut palms. Here signs of recent habitation were clearly visible but repeated circling and zooming failed to elicit any answering wave from possible inhabitants and it was finally taken for granted that none were there.[3]

Signs of recent habitation?

A quick scurry, then, to try to find Lambrecht, but alas, he was dead. Had anyone talked to him about his observations? As it turned out—though we didn't find this out until some years later, Fred Goerner had. Goerner, though he didn't believe that Earhart had wound up in the Phoenix Islands, was willing to share his data. He said that before he died, Lambrecht had told him in a telephone call that the "signs of recent habitation" had appeared to be "markers of some kind."[4]

Whatever Lambrecht had meant, his observation suggested that the Toms' hypothesis couldn't be discounted simply because the *Colorado*'s search had officially reported negative results. And of course, negative results in an aerial search operation have to be taken with large grains of salt. Finding an airplane on the ground from an airplane in the air can be very difficult, even if the airplane being sought is relatively intact and its surroundings aren't too confusing to the eye. A partially or entirely wrecked airplane in the visually complicated environment of a tropical island—wooded, surrounded by convoluted reefs and reflective surf lines—would make the job much more difficult.

The Colony on Gardner

There was another argument against the Phoenix hypothesis, though. Four of the Phoenix islands—Canton (now Kanton), Hull (now Orona), Sydney

53

(now Manra), and Gardner (now Nikumaroro)—had been colonized by people from the Gilbert Islands (now Kiribati) in 1938, and occupied until the early 1960s. If an airplane and its crew, dead or alive, had been on the islands, why hadn't they been found? Answering that question required some investigation into the nature and history of the colony.

Surprisingly enough, there were some readily available published sources on the colonization of the Phoenix Islands. Harry Maude, its instigator, had written a chapter about its inception for a book he edited called *Of Islands and Men*.[5] One of the Gilbert and Ellice colony's administrators, Paul Laxton, had written an article in a 1951 issue of the *Journal of the Polynesian Society* that picked up where Maude left off and carried the history of the Gardner/Nikumaroro colony up through the 1940s.[6] These papers indicated that the Gardner colony in particular had been a pretty small-scale affair during the years leading up to World War II, and that it had had a resident European administrator—a young British civil servant named Gallagher—only for a year or so during that time. It certainly didn't seem impossible that a wrecked airplane, far from the island's colonial village, could have gone undiscovered or unreported, at least until after World War II. And after the war, an airplane wreck might not have seemed particularly remarkable. Or, of course, the plane could have been on McKean, which was not part of the colonizing program.

There had also been a U.S. Coast Guard Loran station on Nikumaroro during World War II, which raised another question: why hadn't the "Coasties" found or reported anything? About the time Gillespie started wondering about that, he came across a 1960 article in the San Diego, California, *Tribune*, an interview with Floyd Kilts.

Bones on Nikumaroro?

Kilts, who unfortunately had died by the time Gillespie and Thrasher saw the article, had served in the Coast Guard during the war, and at its end, he said, he'd been assigned to a team dismantling Loran stations on various Pacific islands—including, apparently, Gardner/Nikumaroro. In the 1960 article by *Tribune* reporter Lew Scarr, titled "San Diegan Bares Clues to Earhart Disappearance,"[7] he speculated that Earhart and Noonan had landed and died there—partly because the reef flat around the island would have been a good place to land, and partly because of what "a native" had told him. According to Scarr's apparently verbatim quote from Kilts:

> It seems that in the latter part of 1938 there were 23 island people, all men, and an Irish magistrate planting coconut trees on Gardner for the government of New Zealand. They were about through and the native was walking along one end of the island. There in the bush about five feet from the shoreline he saw a skeleton. What attracted him was the shoes. Woman's shoes, American kind. No native wears shoes. Couldn't if they wanted to—feet too spread out and flat. The shoes were size nine narrow. Beside the body was a cognac bottle with fresh water in it for drinking.

Shoes? Women's shoes? True enough, Gillespie thought, that Gilbertese in those days didn't wear shoes—most probably don't even now. But if that were the case, how would they know what an "American kind" of "woman's shoe" looked like? How would they know they were size nine narrow?

Kilts went on to say that the "island doctor" had determined that the skeleton was that of a woman, and that the magistrate, a "young Irishman . . . got excited when he saw the bones," and "thought of Amelia Earhart right away." As quoted by Scarr:

> He put the bones in a gunnysack and with the native doctor, and three other natives in a 33-foot, four-oared boat started for Suva, Fiji, 887 nautical miles away. The magistrate was anxious to get the news to the world. But on the way the Irishman came down with pneumonia. When only 24 hours out of Suva he died. The Natives are superstitious as the devil and the next night after the young fellow died they threw the gunnysack full of bones overboard, scared of the spirits. And that was that.

At the time Gillespie didn't know enough about Nikumaroro's history to judge whether there might be any truth at all behind Kilts's account, but— well, Gallagher is an Irish name, and both Maude and Laxton referred to a time when there had been only a small male working party on the island. But Maude and Laxton also said that while Gallagher had died, it hadn't been in a boat en route to Fiji; it had been shortly after getting off a ship *returning* from Fiji. But still . . . Kilts at least was someone who had been there, who thought the place would be suitable for landing, and who must have been told *something* about a discovery there that *somebody* had associated with Earhart. Just as the Homeric epic of Troy has a kernel of truth at the heart of its mythic narrative, there might be something true behind what Kilts said he had been told.

All in all, it appeared that the Toms had an idea worth exploring—a proposition about Earhart's fate that could be subjected to objective investigation—something TIGHAR could sink its teeth into.

Non Sunt Multiplicanda Entia Praeter Necessitatem

What made the Phoenix Islands Hypothesis more attractive to TIGHAR than the other Earhart theories—and still does—comes down to the application of a basic principle of scientific research referred to as "Ockham's Razor." As articulated by the medieval Franciscan philosopher William of Ockham (1285–1347 or 1349), the "Razor" insists that "entities are not to be multiplied beyond necessity."[8] The basic idea is that as a matter of efficient research, one should first investigate the simplest set of factors that might answer the question. This doesn't mean that the simplest explanation is necessarily likely to be correct; it does mean that it ought to be easier to *disprove* a simple explanation than a complex one. So you examine the simple proposition first, and only once it's disproved do you move on to those that are more complicated.

None of the premises advanced by the various Earhart researchers was impossible, and certainly none had been definitively disproved. But those featuring secret spying missions, capture by the Japanese, and U.S. government cover-ups were very complicated, requiring that a lot of things not be as they seemed, that a lot of people be lying. Based on Ockham's Razor, time shouldn't be invested in pursuing these types of theories until it was ascertained that a less complicated explanation didn't account for all the facts.

Of course, the "crashed and sank" premise was superficially the simplest proposition, but it was among the hardest to disprove—or prove. An awful lot of ocean was out there for an Electra to fall into, along with an almost inexhaustible list of variables—including, as chaos theorists would assure us, the flapping of butterfly wings in Beijing—that might cause it to fall into any given square mile of water. In fact, to make "crashed and sank" work reasonably at all, one had to invent variables to deprive the Electra of at least a couple of hours' worth of fuel that it should have had aboard. Furthermore, it didn't really account for all the variables—notably the post-loss signals. To make "crashed and sank" work, one had to reject all the post-loss signals as bogus. They might be, of course, but proving that they either were or weren't would be tricky, too.

The Phoenix Islands Hypothesis, on the other hand, seemed to account for all the known facts without invoking a lot of complicated explanations like Japanese capture and U.S. cover-ups. It was, Gillespie and Thrasher decided, at least a sufficient justification for giving Nikumaroro and McKean the sort of hard look they had never received in the past.

Off to the Phoenix Islands

But you don't just hop in your plane and fly out to the Phoenix Islands for a look-around. The only airfield—the largely abandoned remains of a major World War II British-U.S. facility—is on Kanton (Canton), some 200 miles northeast of Nikumaroro and McKean, and there aren't any ships at Kanton to take you the rest of the way. In fact, the closest place to which one *could* fly and find reliable transport with enough space to carry a reasonable number of TIGHARs was Fiji, about 1,000 miles to the southwest. TIGHAR had run a number of expeditions, most of them to Maine in search of *l'Oiseau Blanc,* the biplane in which the French aviators Charles Nungesser and Francois Coli had tried to fly the Atlantic twelve days before Lindbergh.[9] These had been expensive, complicated enterprises; the *l'Oiseau Blanc* (White Bird) project had involved long, difficult treks through the cold, fly-infested woods, with substantial crews and plenty of logistical problems. A search of the Phoenix Islands for Earhart, however, put such enterprises entirely in the shade.

The first problem was money, of course. Something like a search for Amelia Earhart is not the kind of project that gets support from the big, "legitimate" granting agencies. No National Science Foundation, no Smithsonian, no National Geographic. Nor are there a lot of private foundations that put money into this sort of thing. The news media might eventually contribute something in return for exclusives, but not until they were convinced that there would be something worth covering. The only realistic sources of funding were private—individuals and corporations. And

TIGHAR limits its options further by declining to seek or accept support from alcohol or tobacco-related corporations.

But Gillespie and Thrasher can be persuasive, and TIGHAR's board of directors and members are pretty open-handed, and it turned out that Earhart captured some imaginations, so little by little, the funding started to come together. The projected bare-bones budget of $250,000 began to look attainable.

Meanwhile, there were arrangements to be made with the government of Kiribati, the island nation that owns the Phoenix Islands. Kiribati is made up of about 270 square miles of land scattered over 3 million square miles of ocean. Its capital, Tarawa, is itself about 800 miles from Nikumaroro and a whole lot farther from almost everything else. Just getting in touch with the government was a challenge, let alone reaching agreements about handling the expedition.

And of course, somebody had to do the work—a team was needed. It couldn't be a paid team—the money wasn't there for that. Quite a few

Tom King at Nikumaroro, 1989. TIGHAR photo by Mary DeWitt.

skilled, experienced volunteers were on hand from the *l'Oiseau Blanc* expeditions, but not too many could take the time off from their real work to sail away into the Pacific for a month or so. Luckily several veterans of the northwoods expeditions did find the time—John Clauss of Lake Tahoe, Veryl Fenlason from Minnesota, Leroy Knoll from Kansas, and Bill Decker from North Carolina, bringing talents that ranged from historical research to small boat operations.

Some specific kinds of expertise were needed. For one thing, an archaeologist would be good to have, this being an archaeological project. As luck—good or bad—would have it, an archaeologist was at hand.

Some years before, Gillespie and Thrasher had consulted with the Advisory Council on Historic Preservation, a tiny federal agency in Washington, D.C., about how to set standards for preserving historic aircraft. Here they had met Tom King, then the council's senior archaeologist. King had field experience in Micronesia, where he had worked with World War II sites.[10] Gillespie and King had remained in contact over the years, and King had become a member of TIGHAR. In 1988, weary of the bureaucracy, King was about to quit the government in a huff. Gillespie didn't know that, however, when he telephoned King with an ethical question.

From Tom King's journal of the 1989 Nikumaroro expedition:

"It seems," Ric said, "that Earhart was carrying some five thousand issues of a stamp commemorating the flight, which were supposed to be sold to help finance it. Some of our backers want to sell the stamps if we find them, and I wanted to check with you about how the archaeological community would view the ethics of that sort of thing."

Ric wasn't necessarily asking the best person. One of the several ways I've outraged a significant percentage of my professional peers in recent years has been by advocating détente with private collectors, taking the position that sale and private possession of artifacts shouldn't necessarily be treated as a hanging offense.

"Well," I said, "I can easily think of ways to regard it as perfectly ethical, but there are purists out there who'd certainly disagree. Strongly. But it seems like a pretty hypothetical problem, though. The likelihood of finding paper products on an airplane that crashed on a tropical island fifty-one years ago strikes me as only just this side of nil."

And then I made my mistake:

"Sounds like a neat project, though, and you know I've worked with World War II archaeology in Micronesia. If you need an archaeologist, let me know."

Gillespie did, and King agreed, and wound up a dozen years later as the lead author of this book.

A photographer was needed, and Mary DeWitt of Texas filled that bill. Medical support was a must; this was supplied by nurse Julie Williams and Dr. Tommy Love, an Air Force colonel who did double duty as a diver. A full team of divers was needed, since wreckage could well be on the reefs surrounding the island. In addition to Love, Joe Latvis and Dutch Kluge from Florida, and Mike Bowman from California were able to find the time. A good video record was essential, and Russ Matthews, a *l'Oiseau Blanc* veteran, was just beginning a career as a producer. Laboratory expertise might be needed, and microbiologist Jessica Krakow had that. Bart Whitehouse, a thoroughly experienced amateur radio operator from Colorado, would handle communications. The team came together.

As did a plan of action. Any decent piece of research is guided by a research design that lays out hypotheses and ways to test them, and then establishes what actual work will need to be done to run the tests. The overall hypothesis, of course, was that the World Flight had ended on Nikumaroro or McKean Island, but by itself that hypothesis didn't provide much guidance about what to do. Subhypotheses were needed. If they landed safely enough to be able to get off the post-loss signals, they must have landed someplace reasonably clear of vegetation, but if they had stayed there they probably would have been seen by the *Colorado* pilots, so the wooded fringes of clearings would be places to look. If the plane had been anyplace where the colonists or the U.S. Coast Guard cleared the native vegetation, it should have been found, so such areas were unlikely to contain anything of interest. If the landing had been on the beach and the plane had then come apart, pieces could be buried in the sand and coral, so metal detectors would be useful. If wreckage was back in the bush, it might be found by cutting swaths through the veggies, so lots of sharp machetes would be needed. If it had gone over the reef edge, it was going to be found only through systematic underwater survey. It was important not to develop a research design that was *too* detailed, though. Without a lot more knowledge of the islands it would be counterproductive to focus the search too narrowly. But this didn't seem like a problem; after all, Nikumaroro and McKean weren't very big islands.

The project design evolved into one featuring three elements. First would come archival research in Fiji, where there might be records of the colonial period that would help the team understand the historical context of whatever they found on the islands. It might even shed light on Floyd Kilts's story; maybe there was some record of bones being found, or a shoe, or both. The archival work would occupy a few team members for the week or so it would take for Gillespie, Thrasher, and others to pull together the last needed gear and complete the expedition's administrative details.

Once on Nikumaroro, and later on McKean, the team would simultaneously carry out the other two elements—archaeological survey on land and underwater. The common stereotype of archaeologists has them digging all the time, at least when they're not falling into tombs full of snakes and being chased around by bad guys. Actually, what archaeologists do most of the time when in the field is survey—looking for sites that might be worth digging, or worth studying some other way. Survey often involves such technology as aerial photography, ground-penetrating radar, and the like, but mostly it involves the use of what Pat Thrasher calls the "Mark-One Eyeball"—careful inspection of the ground, taking notes, making maps, finding things—it is hoped—and recording precisely where they are, how they relate to one another. On Nikumaroro such inspection would certainly require clearing a bit of vegetation, though neither King's experience in the populated islands of Micronesia nor Gillespie's rambles through the Maine woods gave them a full appreciation for how *big* that bit would be. Underwater survey would involve similar visual scanning, covering the face of the reef down to 100 feet or so—as deep as the divers could safely penetrate. Everyone would be tied together by hand-held radio, linked to the transceiver that Bart Whitehouse would man aboard whatever ship Gillespie was able to charter. Bart's radio, and a network of hams in the United States, would also be their tenuous link with the outside world—both families and media.

By summer's end, 1989, the necessary money had (barely) been raised, the basic research plan was in place, and the team was assembled—actually volunteers had to be turned away. Arrangements were complete with the Kiribati government, which would send a customs agent as its representative. Equipment was assembled. *Pacific Nomad* was chartered—an old

Japanese fishing boat converted to service dive tours, based in Fiji. The first TIGHAR Earhart expedition was launched.

There were seventeen Americans on that first expedition, roughly divided into three groups. One consisted of the Toms, who would staff a base in Fiji. Another team was made up of the divers under the direction of Joe Latvis; they would search the reefs of the two islands. The third and largest team would conduct archaeological survey on land, under King's supervision, with Gillespie and Thrasher in overall command of the whole shebang. Tommy Love and Julie Williams would keep the group healthy—and just in case, Love brought a body bag.

The team flew from Los Angeles via Tahiti to Nadi, the airport town on the west end of Fiji's largest island, Viti Levu. Motoring in to the capital, Suva—a fine old colonial city at the other end of the island, full of life and conflict between Fiji's two major ethnic groups, Native Fijians and Indo-Fijians—they plunged into archival research and preparations for putting to sea. As it turned out, the files of the Western Pacific High Commission, which had overseen the colony, had been distributed to archives in Kiribati, Tuvalu (the former Ellice Islands), England, and elsewhere. But published and unpublished works were available in Fiji that no one on the team had seen in the United States. Krakow, DeWitt, and Decker settled in at the University of the South Pacific, over the ridge from Suva, where the soft trade winds blow in through the open library windows. They found and reread books that were already old friends—for example, Harry Maude's *Of Islands and Men*—and some that were new discoveries, such as Sir Harry Luke's *From a South Seas Diary*.[11] Through their readings and nightly team briefings the TIGHARs began—just began—to form an image of the islands they were setting out to explore.

CHAPTER 7

McKean, Gardner, and the PISS

Stand up, O people of the Gilberts,
Grasp your working tools . . .
We shall stand up and clear the undergrowth,
And plant coconut trees
   —SONG OF THE PHOENIX ISLANDS SETTLERS[1]

Birds and Bukas

If you lay out the LOP through Howland Island and extend it southwest, it runs only about thirty nautical miles west of McKean Island.[2] McKean is a roughly circular coral island, surrounded by a reef flat and centered on a long-filled lagoon—long filled with bird droppings, for McKean is home to millions of sea birds. Now an officially designated and protected Kiribati bird refuge, it hasn't been inhabited by humans—other than by occasional ornithologists and shipwrecked fishermen—since the 1860s. Back then, bird guano was mined there to fuel the world trade in phosphates for fertilizer and explosives. There's not a tree growing on McKean—just low bushes and shrubs—but what the island lacks in flora it more than makes up in fauna; the birds stand almost shoulder-to-shoulder. Frigate birds, gannets, boobies, terns, gulls, flying and fluttering and perching and sitting on eggs. On the ground, in the air, on the coral stone walls left by the guano workers, swooping and screaming and pooping.[3]

Nikumaroro lies about sixty nautical miles southwest of McKean, and only a mile or so from the LOP plotted through Howland. It's a much larger, more complicated island. About 3.5 miles long and 1.5 miles wide, it's shaped more or less like a first-trimester fetus, with its bulbous head to the northwest and its tail to the southeast. At its center is a beautiful, aquamarine lagoon; around its margins are reefs teeming with fish. Two small passages connect the lagoon with the sea. Some parts of the island are as barren as McKean—sun-blasted coral rubble that the TIGHARs came to call "moonscape"—but most of the island is heavily wooded. The most impressive native tree is the buka—*Pisonia grandis* to botanists—a huge tree that from a distance rather resembles an oak. Up to eighty feet high and about as broad, with a great thick gray trunk, the buka is the kind of tree you imagine Tolkien had in mind when he dreamed up the Ent.

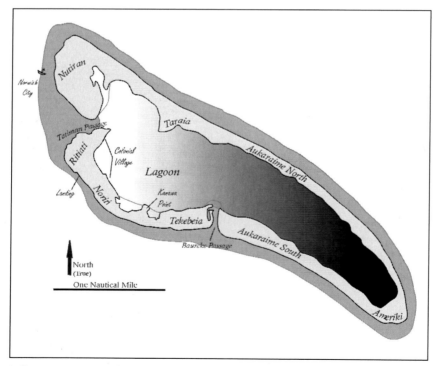

Nikumaroro's major land divisions and landmarks.

Like any good tropical paradise, Nikumaroro has palm trees, planted by the colonists and their predecessors and gone to riot. And then there's what the I Kiribati call *te mao*—scientific name *Scaevola frutescens*. The TIGHARs had read about scaevola before they left the States and Fiji, but hadn't thought much of it. This was a mistake.

Like McKean, Nikumaroro has plenty of birds, too, but they're not the dominating presence they are on the barren guano island. The other major critter on the island is the coconut or robber crab—*Birgus latro*—a big brown guy with a formidable set of pinchers, allegedly able to rip the husks off coconuts.[4] Nikumaroro has so many of these monsters that Polynesians from the Niue Islands used to call it *Motu Aonga*—the land of the coconut crabs.[5] The TIGHARs were to find out a whole lot about coconut crabs, too.

Unlike McKean, of course, Nikumaroro has been inhabited in recent times, though it was not occupied in 1937 and it is deserted today. During the week in Fiji the team learned some basic facts about the "Phoenix Islands Settlement Scheme," fondly known to its founder as the PISS.

The PISS

The Phoenix Island Settlement Scheme was the brainchild of a thoroughly remarkable man: Harry Maude, who at this writing is still alive in Australia, pushing a century old. Maude and his wife, Honor, are among the most respected members of the Pacific historical community, but they have influenced history as well as written about it. In 1937, Maude was a colonial administrator on the staff of the Western Pacific High Commission (WPHC), which oversaw the Crown Colony of the Gilbert and Ellice Islands among other British interests in the area.[6] The WPHC was based in Suva, Fiji, where the high commissioner also served as governor. Maude was assigned to the Gilberts and Ellices and here he and Honor became acutely aware of the plight of the southern Gilbertese.

On an island, the balance of population and resources is always a matter of great concern; an island can support only so many people. In precolonial times in the southern Gilberts, population size was kept in check in three major ways—disease, abortion, and warfare leading to emigration. The coming of European missionaries and colonizers, of course, put a stop to warfare and abortion (more or less), and exacerbated the situation by lengthening lives through modern medicine. By the time Harry and Honor Maude arrived in the southern Gilberts, the imbalance between people and land—which translates into food—was getting critical.

So Maude proposed the PISS, a program to colonize several of the uninhabited Phoenix Islands with land-poor families from the southern Gilberts and a few of the Ellice Islands that were in similar straits. Each colonized island, it was hoped, would in time become economically self-sufficient through the then-profitable trade in copra (dried coconut meat).

In preparing the PISS proposal, Maude naturally had to visit the islands he proposed to colonize. As a result he, his colleague Eric Bevington, and nineteen I Kiribati ("Gilbertese") delegates visited the Phoenix group in October 1937, about three months after Earhart's disappearance. They arrived on Gardner Island on October 13 and spent the following two days looking it over. The delegates were enthusiastic about the island, associating it with Nei Manganibuka, a legendary ancestress who had come from an island with many buka trees that lay somewhere in the direction of Samoa. That island was called Nikumaroro in the legends, and thus Gardner Island received its new—and ancient—name.

> Once ashore, we proceeded on the work of the expedition: the island was thoroughly examined from end to end; holes were dug and the soil examined; wells were sunk and the water tasted; the flora, fauna and fish were studied from the point of view of future settlers; the lagoon was explored in the canoes which we had brought with us . . .

The island turned out to be eminently suitable:

> I shall always remember that first night in the Phoenix Islands. We lay in a circle under the shade of the giant buka trees by the lagoon, ringed by fires as a protection against the giant robber crabs, who stalked about us in the half-light or hung to the branches staring balefully at us. Birds were everywhere and for the most part quite tame. . . . Unfortunately for them, both the crabs and birds were very good eating, and we gorged ourselves on a diet of crabs, boobies and fish.[7]

In due time, the PISS was approved by High Commissioner Sir Arthur Richards and his superiors in London. The first colonizing party was assembled in December 1938, and landed on Nikumaroro Island five days before Christmas, less than eighteen months after Earhart's disappearance.

Although the would-be colonists were enthusiastic about Nikumaroro's prospects, it was not the initial focus of PISS settlement. The island had only 111 coconut trees, the remains of plantings started there in the 1890s by John Arundel, a notable Pacific entrepreneur.[8] Arundel's modest plantings had been untended since their abandonment before the turn of the century, and had not spread.[9] So Maude and his associate, the young cadet officer Gerald B. Gallagher, left a working party on Nikumaroro to clear land and plant more coconuts, while they sailed on with the majority of the colonists to Sydney and Hull Islands.

Sydney and Hull—renamed Manra and Orona (the latter after Honor Maude) by the colonists—had substantial stands of producing coconut trees. So Maude landed Gallagher and several colonizing families on Sydney/Manra, and more families on Hull/Orona. Consideration was given to colonizing the largest of the Phoenix Islands—Canton Island—but Canton was caught up in international economics and the impending war, becoming a base for Pan American Airways' transpacific Clipper flights and then a joint British-U.S. military base.

So as the British and Americans vied for Canton, and the PISS established itself on Sydney and Hull, Gardner (Nikumaroro) remained something of a backwater. The working party on the island was charged with finding water, establishing a village, clearing buka forest, and planting coconuts, and was headed by a redoubtable I Kiribati leader named Teng Koata,[10] from the island of Onotoa. It was an all-male working party, as in the Kilts account, but there were only ten men.

The first few months were tough and chancy. As TIGHAR researchers later learned, some descendants of the working party members—who live today in a village called Nikumaroro in the Solomon Islands—still sing of the "great search for water" that preoccupied their ancestors. But eventually ground water was found, wells were dug, trees were planted, and the colony looked to become a going concern. Some of the working party members went home while others—including Teng Koata, now officially island magistrate—remained and were joined by their families, bringing the total, for a while, to twenty-two.

Kilts had said twenty-three.

Other colonists arrived, so that by late 1939 the population of the island was fifty-eight men, women, and children.

Meanwhile, Maude had turned mostly to other duties, and his assistant, Gallagher, had become acting officer-in-charge of the PISS. Gallagher first established himself on Manra (Sydney Island), but when the colony there was up and running he relocated to Nikumaroro, which he set out to make "the model island of the Phoenix."[11]

"The Most Wonderful Master"

By all accounts Gallagher was much respected, even beloved, by the Nikumaroro colonists, and the year he spent on the island was a time of high accomplishment. A "Government Station" and a "Rest House" were built; a 1941 photo of the latter shows an impressive thatched building with high peaked roofs. Land clearing and planting proceeded, and Gallagher began dividing up the productive land and assigning it to colonial families to have, to hold, and to grow coconuts on.

Gerald Gallagher. TIGHAR
Collection from Dierdre Clancy.

But in May 1941 Gallagher went on leave to Fiji. When he returned in late September aboard the colonial vessel HMFS *Viti* in the company of colonial physician Dr. "Jock" MacPherson, he was deathly ill with some sort of serious stomach problem. Shortly after their arrival on the island MacPherson was forced to operate. The precise nature of Gallagher's illness wasn't specified in the published record, but whatever it was, MacPherson's operation came too late, and the young officer died.[12] He was buried on the island with great sadness by his I Kiribati colleagues. His servant, Aram Tamia, wrote a letter of condolence to Gallagher's mother:

> I have lost the most wonderful, kind, good and thoughtful master that any servant ever had. . . .
>
> Mister Gallagher is laid to rest at the foot of the flag-mast, and the flag he taught us to love and respect waves over him every day.
>
> We, the people who dearly love him, are going to tend his resting place. It is also for that reason, and a custom of my people, that I am remaining here for some time with my master.
>
> Please will you, his mother, accept from me, his sorrowing servant, my deepest sympathy in your sad loss of such a good son and man.
>
> Your obedient servant,
>
> Aram Tamia[13]

Reading the Gallagher story, it was impossible not to be struck by—besides its pathos—how it echoed the Floyd Kilts account. Gallagher was not an "Irish magistrate," but he presumably was of Irish extraction,[14] and he *was* in charge of the colony. He didn't die en route to Fiji, but he *did* die shortly after returning. He didn't try to row the 1,000-plus miles to Fiji in a four-oared boat, but it turned out that there *was* such a boat on the island—a whaleboat named Nei[15] Manganibuka after the ancestress. Was there something to the Kilts story? If so, what? At the time there was no way of judging, but the parallels seized everyone's imagination and became the sources of endless speculation.

Shortly after Gallagher's death World War II erupted across the Pacific. Japan seized Kiribati, and the British fell back to Fiji. Nikumaroro was never invaded, but it was left in a backwater, visited only occasionally by

British administrators from the joint British-U.S. military base that was established on Canton Island. In 1944 the U.S. Loran station was built, and it operated until the end of the war. Then it was closed by a Coast Guard team that presumably included Floyd Kilts.

A New Deal for Nikumaroro

After the war, a new official of the Gilbert and Ellice Islands Colony, Paul Laxton, spent time on the island and wrote an important account of it. It appears that while the colonial village—now named "Karaka," the I Kiribati rendering of "Gallagher"—had survived the war, and been lovingly maintained by its residents, it had stagnated economically. In other words, it wasn't producing copra. Part of the problem was that by the time of his death, Gallagher had not yet finished dividing up the land and assigning parcels to permanent colonists. The colonists, one reads between the lines of Laxton's article, didn't see themselves as landowners but as government employees, responsible for maintaining the village's assets while eking out a subsistence living, but with little investment in the coconut plantations. Laxton's mission was to change all that.

> [I] flatly presented this hard, realistic, Gideon-like policy. The weaker members should pack up and go: if they proved to be a great proportion of the island community then the whole settlement would be given up and a copra plantation formed. Otherwise, new blood would come in on a system of leaseholds, receiving a block of planted land in return for which they should clear and plant speci-fied areas for government. After three years the future of the pioneer settlement would be reviewed. This brusque challenge is what Nikumaroro needed . . .[16]

The colonists responded positively to Laxton's pitch, and in short order the coconut land of the island was divided into plots and assigned to fami-lies. More colonists came in from Manra, and the village itself was relo-cated. One gets the impression that Laxton was intent on getting the residents away from the Government Station that Gallagher had overseen, with his grave and all the other reminders of the time before the war, and focus their attention on cultivating coconuts. Apparently this worked; the

Gallagher-era village was effectively abandoned, and the colony's center of gravity shifted south along the southwest side of the island.

An Island of Parts

By this time the colonists had taken thorough possession of the island, naming its parts. These place names became ingrained in the team members' own brains as they pored over maps at the University of the South Pacific.

The northwest part of the island—the bulbous head of the fetus—was and is called Nutiran after New Zealand for—most likely—a party of New Zealanders who did a survey on the island in 1939. It is pronounced "Nusiran" with a soft, rather slurring "s" for the same reason Kiribati is pronounced "Kiribas." The passage that cuts through to the lagoon at Nutiran's south end—the major passage in from the sea—was called Tatiman Passage, said to be a reference to the Tasman Sea.

Southeast of Tatiman Passage is Rititai, named after High Commissioner Richards, and it is on this land that the Government Station and the village known as Karaka were built. Next down the southwest side of the island came Noriti, named for the wreck of the *Norwich City* up on Nutiran, clearly visible from the Noriti shore.

Nikumaroro's most notable landmark, the *Norwich City* ran aground in a 1929 storm.[17] She caught fire and burned, while her crew scrambled for shore. Eleven of them didn't make it—six Arab firemen and five English sailors lost their lives in the wreck.[18] The survivors were taken off by a rescue ship after several days marooned. Pictures of the *Norwich City* taken in the 1940s showed a looming steel hulk with a single funnel, her back broken on the reef and her bow pointing toward the beach. Virtually every visitor to the island commented on the wreck, and most ships tied off to her

Eric Bevington took this photo of the *Norwich City* from the northwest in 1937. TIGHAR Collection from Eric Bevington.

stern, sending landing parties picking their way across or around her toward shore—the anchorage off Nikumaroro is marginal at best.

Southeast of Noriti is Tekibeia, and then a small passage known as Baureke. East of Baureke Passage the land is known as Aukaraime, stretching clear around the southeast tip of the island and up the northeast, windward side. When the United States established the Loran station on the southeast tip, though, this parcel was renamed Ameriki for obvious reasons, thus splitting Aukaraime into north and south segments. Along the windward side, the north limb of Aukaraime merges with Taraia, which borders Nutiran.

The Lady and the Kiwis

There were other intriguing things about Nikumaroro that popped out of the books, though they didn't seem to have much to do with Earhart. Take Nei Manganibuka, for example. The ancestress is an important figure to the I Kiribati. In their traditions she came to Kiribati from her island—Nikumaroro—bringing the first buka tree, and she taught the people the all-important arts of navigation. Nikumaroro, it was said, was a beautiful island covered with buka trees.

It was also said that Teng Koata's wife—we later learned her name was Nei Aana[19]—encountered Nei Manganibuka one day while walking alone near the village

> The wife of Teng Koata, the first island leader, had been walking one afternoon and saw a great and perfect "maneaba," and sitting under its high thatched roof Nei Manganibuka, a tall fair woman with long dark hair falling to the ground around her, with two children: she conversed with three ancients, talking of her island of Nikumaroro, and the happy future when it would surely grow to support thousands of inhabitants.[20]

A *maneaba*, in Kiribati, is a meetinghouse, the social and religious center of the village. According to Laxton, the site of Nei Manganibuka's ghost maneaba was on the border between Ritiati and Noriti, on a peninsula in the lagoon between pools in which *baneawa* fish congregated.

This location, it later turned out, coincided with Kanawa Point, named by another group of explorers who spent time on the island from December

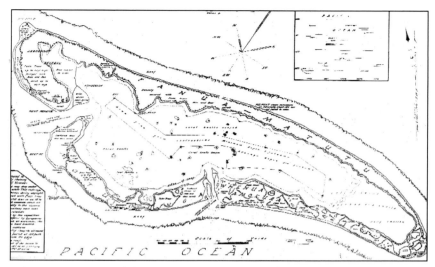

Nikumaroro map made by the New Zealand Pacific Islands Survey, 1938. New Zealand National Archives.

1938 into February 1939, overlapping the arrival of the PISS working party. This group was sent out by the Royal New Zealand Air Force to reconnoiter Gardner Island for possible use as an air base. As we have mentioned, the British Empire and the United States at the time were in competition for possession of the Phoenix Islands, which were valued as potential refueling points on the emerging flying boat routes between North America and Australia. The "Kiwi" survey was part of the Britain's contribution to this competition.[21] The names the surveyors assigned to the parts of the island hadn't "stuck" in the memories of the colonists, but the names Nutiran and Tatiman were apparently assigned in recollection of the New Zealanders. Kanawa Point had been named for the large stand of kanawa trees—*Cordia subchordata* to biologists, a tree with dark, fine-grained wood, prized for use in handicrafts and furniture. TIGHAR would have occasion to get very familiar with kanawa wood.

Leith, Leander, Bushnell, Pelican, and the Coasties

The "Kiwis" hadn't been the only ones to make an official survey on Nikumaroro not long after the loss of the World Flight—or even before. On

February 15, 1937, about six months before Earhart's disappearance, a shore party from HMS *Leith* erected a plaque and a flagpole, hoisting the Union Jack and claiming the island for the Crown.[22] In December 1938, a plane from HMS *Leander* flew over the island and took photographs. In November–December 1939, USS *Bushnell* spent a week mapping Nikumaroro as part of a geographical exploration. Towers were set up at various points from which sightings were made. In late April 1939 USS *Pelican* visited and sent up a plane to take aerial photos. And then there was the Loran station, established in 1944 at the southeast end of the island and home, for almost two years, to a group of twenty to thirty bored U.S. Coast Guardsmen. None of these visits and occupations had been reported extensively in the published literature, but there were records of them in various archives, which were beginning to turn up as TIGHAR prepared to set sail for Nikumaroro.[23]

So, with All These People . . .

TIGHAR was heading for an island with a considerable history, which had had quite a few people on it starting not long after Earhart's disappearance. Was it reasonable to think that evidence of her presence, and Noonan's, and the Electra's, wouldn't have been noticed by all these folks, and duly reported?

Those few who had looked at the matter in the past thought not. Goerner, for example, said:

> The apparent point is that both McKean and Gardner have been surveyed and occupied extensively since 1937, and it would seem obvious that if the wreckage of Earhart's Electra is in the vicinity that it must be underwater.[24]

And Maude, after all, had said of his 1937 visit:

> Once ashore, we proceeded on the work of the expedition: the island was thoroughly explored from end to end . . .[25]

Talking it over, Gillespie and King agreed that Goerner had dismissed the island far too easily, and that Maude's comment should be taken with a large grain of salt. After all, they reasoned, the island is not a tiny one, and it is heavily wooded. Maude and Bevington had been there for fewer than three days in 1937, and between 1938 and 1947 the colonists had cleared only a small part of its dense buka forest. There had been only a few dozen residents for most of the island's colonial history. For much of that time no one had been in an authority position to whom a discovery *could* have been reported. Perhaps, most importantly, no one on the island had been looking for Earhart. The colonists had plenty of other things to do—like finding water and planting coconuts—and the New Zealanders had been focused on assessing the island's potential as an air station.

When the team kicked the problem around in one of its regular evening meetings, in the cavernous lobby of the more or less abandoned Grand Pacific Hotel in Suva, King was particularly dismissive of the notion that the island had been "surveyed." There's a big difference between just *being* someplace and doing a deliberate survey to *look* for something.

"When we do archaeological surveys in the States," he said, "or in Micronesia or anyplace else, it's not uncommon—hell, it's perfectly normal— to find all kinds of sites that local people don't know about, because they just haven't been looking for them, and didn't much care whether they were there or not. Or they may know they're there but not bother to tell anybody until somebody asks them. Up in Chuuk, for example, when we were surveying in advance of airport construction, the villagers had lived among World War II remains for so long that they were just commonplace. They didn't think anything of them, so they didn't tell anybody about them until you came up and asked, 'Say, isn't that an old gun barrel you're sitting on in your cookhouse?'"

"It's the same with airplanes," Gillespie said, with nods all around from the other airplane enthusiasts. "People are still finding old airplanes tucked away in barns. Everybody on the farm knew the plane was there but it was just that old thing that Uncle Clem put in storage back in the twenties."

As for the visits by *Leander, Bushnell,* and *Pelican*—well, they'd been brief, and their surveys relatively cursory. The Coast Guardsmen had had their own jobs to do at one extreme end of the island. Maude's statement that he and his colleagues had "thoroughly" inspected the island had to be understood in context. In their short time on the island he and Bevington could hardly have "thoroughly" inspected it for dead aviators and airplane parts, and, of course, that wasn't their mission. They had "thoroughly" inspected it as a possible colonial settlement and coconut plantation; that's all.

At least, that's what everyone hoped, as TIGHAR's first Nikumaroro expedition crowded *Pacific Nomad*'s fo'c'sle and rails for departure from Suva on September 11, 1989. Clearing the harbor, the battered old trawler turned her bow to the northeast and took the first long rollers of the open sea. Seven days to Nikumaroro, which by now everyone rather affectionately called "Niku."

CHAPTER 8

First Time on Niku

Once a crazy lady
Vanished in an aeroplane.
Crazy, but not near as crazy as we.
For we sing as we search
'Mid the black tip sharks and buka trees,
You'll come a-finding Amelia with me. *
          —TIGHAR TUNES

*P*ACIFIC NOMAD WAS A STURDY, NO-NONSENSE SHIP, A former Japanese fishing boat converted for use by dive tours: A high fo'c'sle dropped into a midships waist, low to the water and equipped for scuba operations. Next came the superstructure with its wheelhouse and a spacious wood-paneled saloon where meals would be taken and Whitehouse would set up his radio rig, opening onto a comfortable fantail, open to the stars and suitable for parties. Above, a helo deck sans helicopter provided work space and opportunities for the sunbathing clinic that DeWitt and Williams conceived with glad cries. Inflatable zodiacs—universally called rubber duckies—and an aluminum skiff (the "tinny") were ready to be launched for transport to and around the island.

Captain Victor Jione, from the island of Rotuma, commanded his ten-man Fijian crew with a light but authoritative hand. Lots of laughter, singing, consumption of *yongona*[1] by the plastic washtub-full in the

---

*Sung to the tune of "Waltzing Matilda," by Banjo Paterson.

77

evenings, but the work got done, the ship went where she was pointed. Everybody put up with the crazy Americans, and the expedition's dive team quickly bonded with Ili, known as "Fiji Bear," the ship's massive divemaster. Kotuna Kaitara, the Kiribati representative, fell into an easy working relationship with both the ship's crew and the Americans. The island would be as new to him as it was to his shipmates, but he said he felt that it would be like going back in time, to the village where he had grown up.

The anti-seasickness patches that Love had procured for everyone worked like charms, and the weather was good. The Americans learned to drink yongona, with its accompanying hand-clapping ritual. DeWitt and Williams ran their tanning clinics with iron hands—"One-two-three; roll over *now*!" The divers tested their gear; Gillespie, Clauss, and Fenlason made sure all the metal detectors were in order. King built wire-mesh screens for sifting whatever they might excavate; Whitehouse tested radios and communicated with his network of Hams back home, and with the Toms in Suva. The Toms, in turn, communicated with the media. Everyone sharpened bush knives.

And everyone talked, theorized, argued, and speculated. Where were the most feasible places to land a plane? Where could the plane have wound up where it would remain undiscovered? What made sense in the Kilts story and what didn't? How would an I Kiribati colonist have known anything about American shoes? The days were bright, the nights full of stars, the Southern Cross burned, and *Nomad* rolled on toward the answers—maybe—to some of the questions.

Coming to the Island

Niku rose over the horizon at 11:17 A.M. on September 18, 1989—a low series of gray mounds, higher to the northwest, growing greener as they grew closer. These were the buka forests of Nutiran, which tapered off through coconut groves and scaevola to the southeast tip where the Loran station had been. Clouds of birds circling the trees, narrow white beaches all around, behind a wide reef flat. As *Nomad* steamed up the lee side—the southwest side—the team's airplane types looked with (at least hypothetically) knowledgeable eyes on the reef flat, exposed by a dead low tide, and agreed that from the air it might have looked to Earhart like a pretty good place to land. How well she would have fared doing so was another matter.

"Niku" rises on *Pacific Nomad*'s starboard bow, 1989. TIGHAR photo by Mary DeWitt.

Baureke Passage brought the first glimpse of the lagoon—startlingly bright aquamarine, with brightly lit trees and circling birds beyond. *Nomad* coasted along the Noriti and Ritiati shores, everyone looking in vain for the large concrete monument said to mark a landing channel blasted through the reef. Then came the mouth of Tatiman Passage, where a broad reef flat was littered with huge coral boulders tossed there by storms, and the *Norwich City* hove into sight: a colossal jumble of pipes, pistons, and boilers, huge hull plates, the bow broken off and upended, pointing skyward. Recalling the photos taken in the 1940s, showing a relatively intact ship, the TIGHARs were pretty quiet as their own puny little tub steamed past this testament to the power of the sea.

As *Nomad* rounded the northwest cape and came out of the lee she began to take long swells and water over the bow, but everyone stayed on deck, transfixed by the changing scene and dripping spray. The windward side was a long, straight, coral-armored shore with forest behind.

"What I want to know is," Williams deadpanned as she swept the shore with binoculars, "where's the mall?"

"Suburban Karaka," Kluge advised, "hang a left on Sir Harry Luke Avenue . . ."

"Big island," Gillespie murmured to King.

"Helluva lot bigger than it seemed by the map."

About halfway down the windward side a school of dolphin—there must have been fifty at least—began frolicking around the ship, accompanying her around the southeast end and back up the lee side to the anchorage off the mouth of Tatiman.

The anchorage, however, wasn't. There was just nothing to which the anchor could be set, and the expedition ended up, like Maude and Bevington and so many others before it, tying off to what remained of the *Norwich City*. In trying to set the anchor, the divers had their first look at Niku's underwater world. They came back, video in hand, extolling its wonders, and when they popped the tape into the VCR in *Nomad*'s saloon, everyone had to share their enthusiasm. Fish of every description, turtles, sharks, swimming around as though the divers were just pieces of floating debris, through a garden of variegated corals.

They also reported—bad news—that the reef face appeared to drop off sharply from the edge of the broad flat surrounding the island, into abyssal depths below. This not only eliminated hope for a reliable anchorage; it also made it likely that an aircraft that ran off the edge of the reef would be far, far down the face, beyond the reach of divers.

The Village

Moored to the wreck, the TIGHARs boarded *Nomad*'s tinny and rubber duckies, and made their first venture ashore. The landing channel was easily enough spotted, and once the TIGHARs splashed ashore they found the monument, looming out of the scaevola just back from the beach. It was quite an impressive structure about ten feet high, a steep-sided pyramid that flared out at the top, built of reinforced concrete over coral blocks, plastered to gleam white in the sun.

Very quickly, too, they began to see evidence of the colonial village. First a small frame building with a sign on the front: "Gardner Cooperative Store—1940." Inside were bottles, cans, a steel frame bed, and a cat, dead perhaps a couple of months. Nearby were house sites—scatterings of bottles, cans, enamel pans, fifty-five-gallon drums—sometimes with standing corner posts and col-

The Gardner Cooperative Store was one of the few colonial buildings still standing in 1989. TIGHAR photo by Mary DeWitt.

lapsed roof beams. In one of these sites was the first piece of aluminum—a box about eighteen inches on a side, ripped apart at the edges and flared out, probably with the idea of flattening it. Gillespie tipped it up with his machete, King squinted at it, and they let it lie. This was only a reconnaissance; it wouldn't be time to pick things up until their locations could be properly mapped.

From Tom King's journal:

> An occasional bird called; the crabs scuttled; otherwise the silence was total but for our footsteps. What a strange thing for a twentieth-century person to be somewhere where no one lives but that's full of life and the whispering ghosts of prior human inhabitants. Whatever else happens, we're privileged to be here.

They worked their way across the old village, through dense, quiet rain forest and a litter of fronds and rotting coconuts hiding coral slab foundations, rusting sheet metal, lumber, bottles, pipes, and barrels. Finally they broke out onto the lagoon, fringed with a sandy beach, birds circling over the green-gold trees on the other side.

> I came out on the lagoon shore, a fresh breeze blowing in my face and baby black-tip sharks cruising along the smooth, sandy shore. Seized by the sheer beauty and loneliness of the place, I stood for a while and offered a silent prayer to the spirits of the place—asking their welcome and hospitality and apologizing, I suppose, for our violation of the island's sanctity.

In his professional life back in the United States, King does a lot of work with Indian tribes, trying to use the federal environmental and historic preservation laws to protect historic places the tribes value from indiscriminate destruction. Many of these places are valued because people consider them spiritual—the homes of spirit beings, places of supernatural power. However much King respected these beliefs, and was willing to work to get government agencies to respect them, he had never really felt the power of a place until he stood on that beach on the Nikumaroro lagoon, looking at the sun-gilded trees across the lagoon and the white birds soaring. It sent goose-bumps running through the sweat on his back.

"Dammit," Williams swore, swinging her machete. "Why can't they keep the streets clean around here? And where's the mall?"

Birgus latro and His Brothers

The ground was alive with land crabs. Most impressive—and delightful to the Fijian crew—were the coconut crabs. The Americans had read about them, but weren't prepared for their size—bodies about the size of footballs—and their monstrous strong claws. Excellent eating, as Harry Maude's delegates had said, as Fijian colleagues confirmed, and as the TIGHARs learned when a few of the crabs got cooked in *Nomad*'s galley. In their juvenile form they go through hermit stages, so there were lots of *Birguses* of various sizes scuttling around in other people's shells. Hermit crabs that weren't *Birgus latro* were racing around, but no one could tell the difference without close study. Then there were the garden-variety land crabs, about six to eight inches across the shell, who dug burrows in open areas that made the ground treacherous to walk. Feisty little guys, they would rise up in their multitudes when anyone approached, brandishing their pincers defiantly.

A small convention of Nikumaroro's hermit crabs, many of them juvenile coconut crabs. TIGHAR photo by Pat Thrasher.

Other than the crabs, a fair number of largish rats, the single dead cat, and a whole lot of insects and spiders, there was no evidence of ground-dwelling animals. The colonists had left dogs; that was in the records. It was also recorded that wildlife management parties from Tarawa had been to the island at least a couple of times on extermination missions. They'd apparently succeeded. There were lots of birds, of course—Frigate birds, gannets, the snow-white terns called *kiakia* by the I Kiribati—soaring overhead, perching in the trees, and in the case of the kiakia, stooping down to hover in the faces of anyone passing by, apparently defending nests or territory.

The TIGHARs worked their way northwest through an open sandy area that came to be called "Crab City" for the host of land crabs that made their burrow-homes there, then cut back to the landing and gunned the zodiacs back to the ship through the red-orange sunset. The divers had made their own reconnaissance and came up in raptures. They had ridden on a turtle, swum through huge schools of fish that, they said, just swam up and asked to be speared. And they had found that although the reef did drop off quickly, it had shelves where airplanes could get hung up. And the water was clear enough to allow a highly efficient visual survey.

In council that evening, though, everyone agreed that Niku was a lot more to contend with than anyone had thought when looking at maps and reading reports. One mile by three seemed a lot bigger, up close, than it had on the map. The vegetation was denser than expected, the whole place just more complex. Perhaps more impressive than anything else was the fact that the whole island was so alive—just bursting with biology, new plants springing out of the decay of old ones, old ones relaxing into humus on which new ones could live. A complex, dynamic environment in which it would be very easy for things to be lost. Even quite large things.

It wasn't going to be possible to look at all parts of such a complicated island in equal detail; it would be necessary to prioritize.

Sun, Spiders, Sharks, and Scaevola

The first step was to establish a track across from the landing to the lagoon—they called it the "Gallagher Highway"—and a base camp on a sandy lagoon beach—promptly named "Club Fred." On the Club Fred beach John Clauss, to the admiration of all, shinnied up a coconut tree and tied a length of PVC pipe to the top with a red flag attached. In theory this would be something to sight on when mapping discoveries around the upper lagoon. Theory and reality didn't converge, as it turned out; the distances were too great. But the flag was a brave symbol. Bill Decker waved his bush knife at the crowd of watching crabs:

"Workers unite! Join the Popular Front for the Liberation of Nikumaroro!"

The crabs all clacked their claws, to everyone's satisfaction.

From Club Fred, the idea was to conduct systematic surveys of what seemed to be the most likely areas—"likeliness" determined by deduction from what it seemed likely that Earhart and Noonan might have done, and what might have happened to them and their airplane after they'd done it. "If one were trying to land into the wind in an open area, one would land at a place like X, and if one landed there, then the airplane should have wound up at location Y. So, let's look at location Y."

It didn't seem likely that an airplane would have gone unnoticed in the colonial village, so it was an easy decision not to look there—however

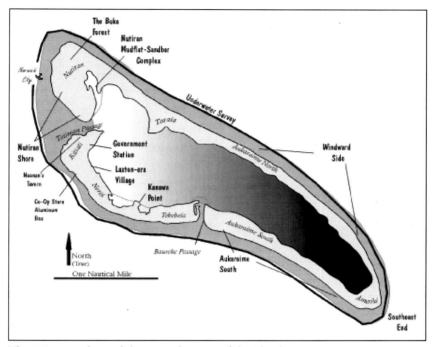

The 1989 expedition did a general survey of the island.

tempting it might be to poke around in the leavings of the PISS and pay respects to Gallagher's grave. Instead, the plan was to focus on areas somewhat away from the village where a landing might have been attempted and a wreck might not have been found promptly by the colonists, the Coast Guardsmen, or other visitors. This led first to a large, open, sandbar-mudflat complex that started just inside Tatiman Passage and extended up into Nutiran. Open enough to land on, but distant enough from the village that a plane wreck back in the surrounding bukas might not have been noticed until the forest was partly cleared for coconuts. Clearing didn't happen until the late 1940s and early '50s, by which time, it seemed reasonable to assume, an airplane wreck might be taken for wartime debris.

Archaeological survey isn't just a matter of walking around looking for stuff. It has to be done systematically, so you're sure when you have finished looking at an area that you have really finished looking at it—that you haven't left some big chunk of ground uninspected. Usually this is done by spreading people out in a line, each person a standard distance from the next, close enough that they can see all the ground between them. Then everybody walks forward, on a compass heading, looking and checking what he or she sees until the line comes to the end of the survey area. Then the whole line swings over and walks back again to cover the next swath of ground, or transect. The evidence worth looking for on the sandbar-mudflat, Gillespie and King reasoned, were small parts that might have been left by a plane in a rough landing, or the breakup of a plane in the surrounding jungle. Such pieces were likely to be metallic, so the field strategy featured controlled walking transects, sweeping the area not only visually but also with metal detectors.

The hapless Americans spent several sun-struck and rain-washed days scanning and metal-detecting on the sandbar-mudflat, falling into crab burrows, getting soaked by passing squalls, drying out and steaming. Aside from scattered pieces of steel barrel and heavy ferrous metal, doubtless from *Norwich City*, all they found was "Coralhenge"—a series of coral-slab alignments along the edges of the mudflat. Some kind of marker? "Help! Amelia and Fred"? It finally dawned on Kaitara and King, more or less

Scaevola, pretending to be benign. TIGHAR photo by Pat Thrasher.

simultaneously, that they were looking at land parcel boundary markers established by Laxton when the area was allocated for coconut growing.

Beyond the sandbar-mudflat were thick walls of scaevola that could have hidden almost anything. The stuff was impressive—thick, intertwined stalks about two inches thick, so interwoven that you couldn't see more than a few feet into the mass. When green it cut easily, but when it dried—and the guts of every clump were dry—the stalks hardened to resemble seasoned pine lumber. Machetes went *boing* and bounced off. It was much the same story with tournefortia, a kind of small tree that cohabited with the scaevola.

Gillespie and King looked at the mass of foliage and decided that if they could cut lines through it about every five meters (about fifteen feet), they'd be able to see enough to find at least large airplane parts. So they tried.

From Tom King's journal:

> We deployed on a skirmish line south of a thicket of scaevola that marks the south end of the sandbar, and moved out on a course of 330 degrees at five-meter intervals. "Moved" in this case means "hacked," "chopped," "beat our way," and words to that effect. Scaevola is unpleasant shit in which to work. Or, to quote a song that got composed as we hacked along:
>
> *Scaevola 'n tournefortia, I don't care which is which.*
> *One's tall, the other's shortia; together they're a bitch.*
> *They grab you by the throat and then they fall upon your head.*
> *They clutch you by the crotch and make you wish that you were dead.*
> *Oh, scaevola, oh won't you part for me?*
> *'Cause if I don't find Amelia, Ric will never set me free.*[*]

Hard work, hot work. Hard to keep a compass heading; no landmarks, easy to get disoriented. As a machete-wielder tired of hacking, it was a natural tendency to begin climbing over the stuff, and soon you would be a couple of meters up in a mess of scaevola, unable to see the ground below or much of anything in any direction. The temperature soared; Gillespie recorded well over 100 degrees on the beach, and no one wanted to know what it was back in the 'vola where the cooling breeze was cut off. You couldn't drink water fast enough. Doctor Love and Nurse Williams—universally called "Nursie," expert at fixing "owies"—were constantly after

---

*Sung to the tune of "Oh, Susannah," by Stephen Foster.

87

The divers surveyed the reef face down to 100 feet and more. TIGHAR Photo by
Mike Bowman.

everyone to stay hydrated, and some didn't listen well enough. There were
some hard days.

On the reef face, Latvis's strategy was much like the one on land, though
a bit more straightforward. The divers would deploy at regular intervals
down the face of the reef to the maximum depth they could safely go, and
they would then swim their way in stages clear around the island, inspecting the reef face and doing selective metal detector sweeps. Ili would work
with them, and the ship would move along to support them as they went.

The divers didn't have scaevola to contend with, but they were plagued
by equipment breakdowns and mobbed by sharks. Most of these were of
the relatively innocuous black-tip and white-tip varieties, but occasionally
a nastier gray reef shark would cruise by, and the sheer numbers of sharks—
half a dozen in the immediate vicinity wasn't uncommon—generated a certain nervousness. Another song appeared on the saloon bulletin board, to a
tune nearly as old as Earhart, "It Had to Be You."

It had to be sharks;
It had to be sharks;
Not guppies or goldfish
Nice young and old fish;
Had to be sharks.
We're here on a lark;
A shot in the dark;
But out on the reef,
They cried "Here's the beef!"
When we disembarked.

It had to be sharks,
Not sturgeons nor snarks.
They'd all think it grand
If we gave 'em a hand,
Or some other parts.

And so we're getting back in our zodiac
And in the lee we'll be parked.
If one comes abeam,
We'll join the land team.
It had to be sharks.

Nights were spent aboard *Nomad*, after supper writing up daily notes and meeting to discuss progress and to plan for the next day. The ship would drift until the predawn hours, then motor back to lie in the island's lee when the sun began to rise. Into the rubber duckies and off to the island then, and to wherever the divers had left off the day before along the reef face. A long day of beating the bushes or communing with the sharks, and then back aboard as the sun set, to shower, line up at the door of Williams's cabin to have "owies" repaired with disinfectant and antiseptic, then dinner, work on field notes, and another meeting to figure out where each team had been, what it had done, and what to do next. King put together a wall-sized map of the island and each evening marked off areas surveyed at different levels of intensity. They weren't very big areas.

By about the fifth day of work, the expedition leadership was beginning to wonder if TIGHAR had bitten off more than it could chew. And nobody

*"It Had to Be You," by Gus Kahn and Isham Jones.

was finding anything. An old barrel hoop here, a steel bolt there, a hunk of pipe the other place. Of course, in the 'vola it was easy to conclude that you could stumble and clamber within six feet of a T-rex and not notice if he didn't. But that was frustrating in itself; maybe the plane was out there—or the bones, or the shoes—and they just couldn't be seen for the vegetables.

Everyone began getting tense—from not finding anything, from the unexpected complexity of the work, from feeling as if they could easily be missing stuff, and from the personality conflicts that always come out when a bunch of disparate people are cooped up together. Cliques began to form— the divers and Ili forming one, much of the land team forming another, Gillespie, Thrasher, and a few others, unfortunately, falling into a third. "Workers" began to grumble about "management" and the divers supported Ili—some might say egged him on—in a long-standing grievance against Captain Victor. Gillespie and King had repeated fallings-out over field strategy, and over who was really in charge. People grew snappish. They'd been on the island less than a week, and the situation was already deteriorating.

In retrospect, many of the problems seem to have come from different attitudes toward the work and the island. Gillespie was—and is—focused on solving the Earhart mystery, and saw the island as a challenge to be overcome in solving it. King wasn't all that interested in Earhart as such, and had fallen in love with the island. The divers were having a macho good time. Not that everyone wasn't applying their intellects and muscles full time to the work, but the differences in attitude led to different definitions of just what the work *was*. For Gillespie it was finding indisputable evidence that Earhart and Noonan had been there. For King it was searching the island as thoroughly as he could, regardless of what turned up. For the divers it was seeing how thoroughly they could cover the reef, and to what depths, while enjoying its beauty and bounty and keeping the beer supply under control. Everybody had his or her own schtick, of course, and some of them seemed pretty frivolous to the leadership.

Clauss, Fenlason, and Knoll, though ready to do whatever needed doing, tended to share and even exceed King's passion for just exploring the island. It wasn't long before Clauss and King began promoting the idea of camping on the island. It would be so much more efficient, they argued, never admitting to anyone but themselves that what they really wanted to do was just see what the place was like at night, and see the sunrise over the lagoon. Gillespie and Thrasher said no way; too dangerous. If anyone got hurt, *Nomad* would have to take the wounded party to Canton Island for evacuation, and the whole expedition would be down the drain. Clauss and King couldn't deny that this was true, but wondered why camping on the island was more dangerous than clambering ashore every day from rubber ducks over sharp coral. No resolution was reached to this or to any of the other festering conflicts, but nobody camped ashore. The ducks took everyone in every morning and brought everyone back in the evening. The scaevola got hacked, the reef got swum, everybody bitched, and nothing got found.

Yongona for the Spirits

Kaitara and Victor politely suggested that a serious mistake had been made by failing to propitiate the spirits of the island properly. Whether it was Nei Manganibuka or somebody else, they felt, somebody or something on the island was not sending good fortune the team's way, and was fomenting discord. It was time to stop, back off a bit, and give the spirits of the place their due.

The next morning everyone—all the Americans, Kaitara, and all the off-watch crew—assembled on the beach near the landing monument, by now cleared of brush and shining in the fresh sunshine. They sat cross-legged and bare-headed; most of the crew wore sulus—the wrap-around skirts traditional in Fiji—as did Kaitara, who was also adorned with a string of pandanus leaves around his neck. He and the bosun, Tiko, sat on green palm fronds rather apart from the rest; another cluster of crewmen, with Victor, also sat apart, stirring a big wooden bowl of yongona with a palm frond.

Ili, son of a chief on his home island, began with a rather lengthy speech, delivered softly and with a slightly chanting cadence. Tiko occasionally responded with a word or phrase, then spoke briefly himself. After a little more talk by Ili, John the oiler circled carefully around the yongona bowl, accepted a half-coconut shell cup of the mildly narcotic drink, and crossed to Kaitara. Kaitara received the cup and drank solemnly, with a ritual clap to which John responded. Then in sequence, he brought a cup to each of the Americans, who drank with similar exchanges of claps.

Kaitara stood and offered a few words in I Kiribati. He then asked everyone to honor his people's custom by lining up behind him and walking to a spot closer to the monument, on the wet sand. He reached down and pressed the sand with his hand, then applied it to each of his cheeks. Each of the others did the same.

Kotuna Kaitara shows the TIGHARs how to apply sand to their cheeks to become people of the island to its spirits. TIGHAR photo by Mary DeWitt.

"We're all safer now," Tiko muttered.

As Victor explained later, Ili's presentation was addressed to the spirits of the island, for whom Kaitara sat as representative. He asked forgiveness for the team's failure to make a presentation at the time of arrival, and asked that everyone be made welcome, protected from harm, and given success. Kaitara's action with the sand represented a separate but compatible tradition. When an I Kiribati arrives on an island for the first time, he pats sand on his cheeks so the island's spirits, coming up and smelling him, will know he is of the island and make him welcome.

The yongona ceremony certainly didn't change everything. It didn't bring the Electra or Earhart crawling out of the bush, and it didn't even cure the tensions between Gillespie and King or the Ili/dive team axis and Captain Victor. But Gillespie and King agreed to reassign responsibilities, with King taking charge of the land team's systematic survey while Gillespie and Thrasher searched the island more informally with one or two team members, exploring and checking out hunches.

Spacemen and Flip-Flops

Having—he thought—exhausted the Nutiran sandbar-mudflat complex and its environs, King's first act as leader of the land team was to head for the southeast end of the island and the adjacent windward shore along Aukaraime North. This was Clauss's idea, reasoning that the long beach on the windward side might have been a good place to land, and ground-loop up into the scaevola. And it was an area that had not been substantially planted by the colonists, and accordingly probably hadn't been visited much.

From Tom King's journal:

Leaving Russ, Mary, Ric and Pat to get a handle on whether the village in which Club Fred lies is the Laxton-era or Gallagher-era village, the rest of us motored southeast in the tinny. At the southeast end we divided up—John, Leroy and Kaitara to work over the Loran site, Veryl, Bill and Jess to work the windward beach/scaevola interface with metal detectors, Julie, Victor and me to whack bush along the windward side.

The SE end looks like a moonscape badly reclaimed as a scaevola plantation. Ridges and piles and hot, searing plateaus of blackened coral shelves and white coral rubble, with mostly patchy but sometimes quite dense scaevola. At one point there's a dump of jet fuel drums—apparently a helicopter landing. At another, John's team found a trash dump full of containers with 1985 expiration dates. At the very tip there's an aluminum mast with a plaque bearing the insignia of the "Space and Missile Test Center."

"Center," not "Centre." It wasn't until years later that they learned what *that* was all about, but it was clear that someone American in recent years had used the old Loran site as a base for some kind of space-related—well, something.

We made an easy 300 meters or so through light scaevola—excellent visibility but no airplanes. Lots of recent flotsam, and enough rubber flip-flop to equip a smallish Japanese village. Then the scaevola got nasty—very thick and impenetrable both visually and physically. By about 1430 we were beat—even Victor feeling it, and stung by a wasp to boot. I was really impressed by how well Julie held up—complaining all the time about wanting to find the mall and go shopping, but soldiering on and ministering promptly to our not infrequent wounds. Victor suggested that I, at least, klutz that I am, should establish an account at the local blood bank.

We straggled back down the beach, checking on the "beachcombers" en route. Bill had found a substantial deposit of metal-bearing charcoal buried about 20 cm. deep, and Jess had located an odd piece of what at first looked like aluminum but turned out to be lead. Otherwise it was all flip-flops, bottles, and fishing floats.

Surveying on the southeast end taught King some things—notably that there had been some kind of activity on the island, somehow related to a space and missile center, in the 1970s or thereabouts. Gillespie thought—correctly, as it turned out—that this probably reflected some U.S. Air Force visits to the island that Smithsonian Institution biologist Roger Clapp had told him about. Clapp had accompanied the visits to do environmental studies, but he'd been vague about their purpose.

Another piece of new, if unwelcome, information was that the scaevola on the southeast end of the island was really, really dense. Since there was no particular reason to think that the airplane or Earhart had wound up there, it only made sense to look elsewhere. In retrospect . . . But let's not get ahead of ourselves.

CHAPTER 9

Can't Find That Train

The cook below makes luncheon to sustain us.
He sends it up to the ducky in a box
The cook below makes luncheon to sustain us
And
About every other day,
About every other day,
It tastes better than our shoes and socks.[*]
                              —TIGHAR TUNES

T HE "ELSEWHERE" NEXT VISITED WAS THE HIGH BUKA
forest of northern and eastern Nutiran—certainly the
part of the island least modified by human beings, and
hence probably least explored. The idea was to check out the possibility that
Earhart had put the Electra down in the trees. Nope. Nothing there but irri-
tated snowy-white kiakia that swooped into the searchers' faces and
screamed. As the buka tapered off into scaevola along the northwestern
windward shore, everyone got lost; it was impossible to see more than a
meter in any direction, and the coral shelves that made up the backbone of
the island made for rough going. Unable to get through to King with his
hand-held radio, Decker called *Nomad* for a patch via the ship's more powerful transmitter.

"We're having trouble with the terrain," he said tersely.

*Sung to the tune of "With a Little Bit of Luck," by Alan Jay Lerne and Frederick Lowe,
from *My Fair Lady*.

The wag Gillespie was at the base station aboard *Nomad*. "Train? Train? We're looking for a *plane*!"

After a short silence in which Decker no doubt counted to ten or muttered curses into the vegetation:

"Oh, is *that* what we're looking for? Hell, I've seen half a dozen of them; I thought she'd come by *train*."

With no sign of steam engines in the buka forest, attention shifted to Noriti, southeast of the landing, on the premise that it must have been cleared fairly early in the island's history and might tie into the Kilts story of bones and a shoe. It had been cleared, all right, but as usual . . .

From Tom King's journal:

> The scaevola got thicker, and eventually squeezed us out on the lagoon side near the Ghost Maneaba site. Deciding we had no choice but to cut through to our planned oceanside rendezvous with Ric and Russ, we did, but it took a long time and was hot, nasty, sweaty work. Bill took the point, cursing and threatening to frag Ric if he ever found him. Jessica (who heretofore has never said anything more adventurous than "gosh darn") experimented with obscenities and asked every five minutes or so to be left to die. I tried to make up new songs, but to little avail. Meanwhile Ric, Russ and Veryl had worked their way down the beach from the landing. Ric tried to give us directions, and we tried to follow his voice. Tried.
>
> Ric: "Steer for the palm tree on the beach."
>
> Jessica: "Palm tree on the beach shit! Here we are dying and this son of a bitch is trying to sell a romantic south seas adventure. I want to go home!"
>
> Finally breaking out, light-headed and weak, we collapsed in the meager shade of a scraggly tournefortia and lay there on the hard, sharp coral cobbles, swigging water from the recently chlorinated water jug, while Russ and Ric videotaped us. After advising Ric to engage in impossible sex acts with himself, Jessica sagely noted that it was a testimony to the power of scaevola that after a struggle with it one could feel good lying on sharp coral and drinking bleach. Bill just lay there saying "ow, ow, ow."

No train on Noriti, though Gillespie and Matthews, metal-detecting along the shore, came up with a Ronson cigarette lighter of the right vintage to be Noonan's—or some Coast Guardsman's, or Gallagher's, or Laxton's. Gillespie was enthusiastic; King was sarcastic. Ronson lighter indeed. Where was the train? Or the bones? Or the shoe?

Aukaraime South

The leadership had run pretty far down the priority list of places to look, and just randomly walking around and hoping to stumble over something began to look like as good a strategy as any. Clauss took a boatload down the lagoon to Kanawa Point, where Koata's wife, according to Laxton, had seen Nei Manganibuka in the ghost maneaba. No kanawa trees left—just a few palms and a lot of 'vola. No ghost maneabas visible to jaded American eyes. Along the shore, next to the cove where the baneawa fish hid out from the lagoon's sharkettes, was a litter of giant clamshells—not *that* giant, maybe eight or nine inches across, but of the giant clam genus *Tridacna*—thoroughly cemented into the coral. No man-made objects in sight, but the clams hadn't crawled up on the coral from the lagoon. Perhaps a prehistoric site, King thought as he sketch-mapped and photographed it.

Having worked their way from north of *Norwich City* clear around the island to the mouth of Tatiman Passage without finding a thing, the divers finally struck pay dirt with a three-cell battery on the bottom—the kind found

Joe Latvis brings up the pipe that turned out to be brass. TIGHAR photo by Mike Bowman.

in cars, or airplanes. This was exciting for a while, until Gillespie found more than a dozen just like them at what remained of the village wireless station. Then the divers found a pipe—an aluminum pipe, from the looks of it—but when it was duly mapped in and brought to the surface, it turned out to be copper. Off a ship, no doubt; certainly not off an airplane. Or a train.

King led a sweep up from Ameriki to Baureke, across the south part of Aukaraime. Much of the area northwest of the old Loran station, like the station site itself, had clearly been bulldozed. There were extensive areas of moonscape, sun-blackened, devoid of vegetation. Then came heavy scaevola, and then a lovely grassland reminiscent of the African veldt, studded with pandanus trees. The team staggered through five abreast, singing "No Scaevola! No Scaevola!" to the tune of the Hallelujah Chorus and wondering if they'd finally all gone mad. But then it was back into dense coconut jungle, bordering the lagoon east of Baureke Passage.

According to Laxton, the colonists had had "weekend houses" on Aukaraime South, some of which they moved back to the village when he prevailed upon them to reorganize and focus their attention on coconuts.[1] The team found scattered evidence of human occupation—an occasional fifty-five-gallon drum, a bottle, a pipe, a small grave.

Graves were common in the village at Ritiati, but this was the only one that had turned up anywhere else. Like other I Kiribati graves, it was marked by a low platform lined with small coral slabs. Unlike most others, it had rather high coral head and footstones. And it was small, only about four feet long. The team wrote it up, took pictures, puzzled a bit about it, and moved on.

Back to the Village

Having reasonably concluded that it was unlikely a great big silver airplane could go undetected if it were standing around where the colonists built their houses, the expeditionaries had shied away from the village site on Ritiati except for an occasional "recreational" foray during downtimes. But as time and likely places to look ran out, Gillespie and King agreed to give it a look. After all, it was possible that the villagers had found the plane somewhere else, and scavenged pieces to bring home. And there was that half-flattened aluminum box. And, Gillespie insisted and King grumped, that Ronson lighter on the beach.

So everyone regrouped at Club Fred and spent a few days in systematic survey of the village—not detailed mapping, but walking transects across it and sketch-mapping what crossed their paths. The expedition wasn't equipped for detailed mapping, but it was important to keep track of where things were found. If there were airplane parts or other Ameliana in the village, the locations where such things turned up might yield clues to what the colonists were doing with them. This in turn might—in theory—lead to some ideas about where they were getting them.

Ritiati presented its own problems for fieldwork. Starting out as a coconut plantation, it had of course gone to riot—a jumble of trees and fallen fronds, the ground covered two and three feet deep in rotting palm-parts and slippery coconuts. Someone proclaimed "Cakewalk with Bushknife" the official dance of the Ritiati survey party.

And spiders! It seemed like every space between two fronds in the coconut jungle had a spider web. Everyone took to cutting little branches and palm fronds to wave in front of them as they stumbled around in the nuts and fronds, to clear paths through the webs. Anyone watching—the crabs, maybe—must have thought they were seeing some kind of demented

Gerald Gallagher was buried under a monument modeled on Robert Louis Stevenson's grave in Samoa. TIGHAR photo by Richard Gillespie.

religious procession. The spiders were little guys, luckily, that didn't bite; the intruding humans just had to get good at waving a branch with one hand and wielding a machete with the other, put up with a lot of tiny crawly hitchhikers and their sticky filaments, and ignore how stupid it all looked.

But there was stuff to see, poking up through the vegetation, once you brushed the spiders aside and kicked the crabs away.

Up toward Tatiman Passage were the ruins of what had obviously been the Government Station of Gallagher's day: dead-square parade ground with a fallen flagpole in the middle, and at its base, the fanciest grave on the island—Gallagher's. A traditional I Kiribati grave, with a little coral slab-sided platform and a coconut tree at its head, but on top of the platform, a little house-shaped coral and concrete monument. Designed by MacPherson, said Sir Harry Luke's book, it closely resembled the grave of Robert Louis Stevenson in Samoa. Gillespie offered a graceful Gaelic toast: spilled a drop of Irish whiskey on the grave and everyone knocked back a shot.

Around the parade ground were neatly laid-out roads, seven meters wide and lined with coral slabs. Along the east side of this quadrangle were three concrete platforms that once had held buildings, and at an angle to these, the concrete foundations of the Rest House where Gallagher, Laxton, and visiting dignitaries had laid their heads. On the south side a low coral wall, dubbed the Great Wall of Karaka, clearly marked the border of the Government Station. Around and about, what were probably the remains of the dispensary and hospital, house sites, big pits dug down to the water table to cultivate taro and other water loving food plants like taro. Both the plants and the pits are called *babae*.

It was possible to identify some of the structures and sites, because Laxton, in his 1951 article, had described a walk around the Government Station. Photocopy in hand, DeWitt and Decker guided the others in following his footsteps from the Rest House to the wireless station, from there to the carpenter's shop—a half-standing structure loaded with tools and machine parts—then to the boathouse where the whaleboat Nei Manganibuka had been kept, and so on. And based on Sir Harry Luke's account they located and followed Sir Harry Luke Avenue, a fine if now overgrown road lined with coral slabs, running from the parade ground to the landing.

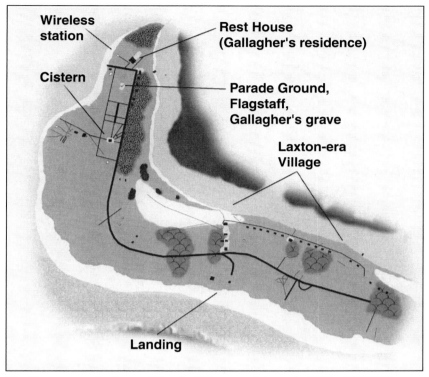

The Government Station and Karaka Village as of the early 1950s. TIGHAR map based on airphotos and archaeological observations.

Southeast from the landing and the crude cross-island track—the Gallagher Highway—the village's organization sort of broke down. House sites were strung out along a central road, but there was no organized center as there was at the northwest end. And everywhere here were things that obviously came from the Loran station. A pile of creosoted poles, galvanized tanks, even an industrial-size sink. Clearly the remains of the Laxton-era village, where the colonists had lived from the late 1940s until the colony failed, for lack of water or nerve, depending on what you read, in 1963.

As for airplane parts . . . Well, there was that box, which might or might not be from an airplane. King mapped the house site where it was found and collected it as Artifact 2-1. Elsewhere they picked up an aluminum wheel, a few aluminum fragments, and parts of the face of a radio. And one

Veryl Fenlason and Bill Decker metal-detecting along the Ritiati shore. TIGHAR
photo by Mary DeWitt.

day, working along the Tatiman Passage shoreline of the village, a couple of
wanderers came upon a house site with a substantial scatter of beer and
whiskey bottles. Naturally it was dubbed Noonan's Tavern. Among the bottles was a piece of aluminum—rectangular, about seventeen by seven inches,
with rivets and folded-over aluminum edging. Gillespie and King looked at
it, wondered what it was, and collected it as Artifact 2-18.

A word here about artifacts, collecting them, mapping them, numbering
them. Archaeologists can learn as much from the *context* of artifacts—that is,
where they lie relative to one another, and relative to other things—as they do
from the artifacts themselves. It's exactly like a crime scene investigation—where
the weapon lies relative to the corpse may be just as important as the weapon
itself. So archaeologists don't pick stuff up and toss it around, they make at least
sketch maps of every place they look, and when they do collect something, they
locate it on a map and give it a number so they can keep track of what came
from where. Another reason for keeping close track of artifacts in the case of
Nikumaroro is that TIGHAR's agreement with the Kiribati government provides that anything it takes off the island that proves to be historically significant

Rough landing on McKean. TIGHAR photo by Mary DeWitt.

is to be held in trust for Kiribati. The Earhart project is TIGHAR's second field operation (the first having been the *l'Oiseau Blanc* quest in Maine), so each artifact collected was given the initial number "2," followed by the order in which it was collected. The box was the first artifact chosen to be taken back; the rectangular thing was the eighteenth. Between them were sixteen pieces of aluminum and other items that no one was particularly enthusiastic about but that might, just might, be worth closer examination back home.

For the Birds

Having made no major discovery on Nikumaroro, the TIGHARs and their doughty ship steamed up to McKean and spent an exciting day with the birds. They could hear and smell the island long before they saw it—wall to wall goonies, terns, gulls, all sitting on eggs and screaming.

The divers, supported by *Nomad*, set out to circumnavigate the island, while the land team headed ashore in the tinny. The landing was rough, over the reef through heavy surf. The skiff kept trying to go

The birds of McKean. TIGHAR photo by Mary DeWitt.

broadside to the beach and overturn, but Tiko managed to avoid running over the blundering Americans trying to help fend off, and made good his escape.

The maps of the island, such as they were, suggested only two likely places to land an airplane—the beach on the northeast side, and the shallow, guano-filled lagoon.

From Tom King's journal:

Hiking toward the northeast shore, we were completely enveloped in birds, riding the wind all around us, keeping pace, and shrieking at the top of their tiny but collectively quite powerful lungs. Boobies and Frigates, Kiakias and a smallish black and white bird I didn't recognize—tens of thousands blackening the sky and filling the air with their cries and the beating of their wings. We had to shout to make ourselves heard even a few feet away, or over the radio.

Picking their way through the birds—at least there was no scaevola to contend with, or any plants at all that came above the ankles—the land

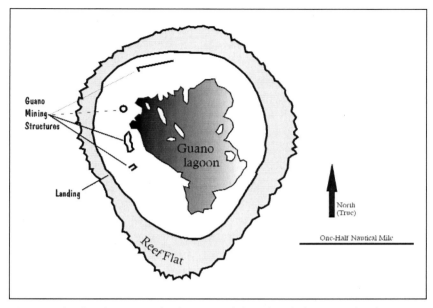

McKean Island is almost circular, barren, and dotted with the ruins of 19th century guano mining structures.

team reached the northeast beach and found it gone, eroded clean down to the coral. Spreading out, they swept southwest about twenty meters apart, recording the ruins of the nineteenth-century mining operation as they went along—not because they had anything to do with Earhart, but just because they were there. The intrepid Gillespie and a small team took on the lagoon, covering themselves with glory and guano.

From Tom King's journal:

> Down on the "lagoon," Ric took a few steps out and then almost vanished into the noisome ooze. Backed up by Russ and Bill, however—the latter sending up his complaints to compete with the birds—he was able to poke at about half the thing, finding that it's significantly deeper than the Smithsonian's records had suggested and that it's virtually *all* hot to a metal detector. Probably because the guano diggers left their draglines, rail cars, and other paraphernalia at the bottom. The Electra could be down there, too, but we sure aren't likely to find out. Ric and Bill tried to dig a shovel test pit, and it promptly filled up with ooze.

So, lots of metal in the lagoon, but since there were also the beds of narrow-gauge rail lines running into the muck, the likelihood was high that the metal represented rails, "ore" carts, and the like. Not worth digging for, considering the incredible difficulty (to say nothing of discomfort) of trying to dig in semicongealed excreta on an environmentally sensitive island. And especially considering that nobody could quite picture Earhart and Noonan landing in a lagoon full of bird poop. The tabloids, someone said, would have a field day, but that aside, it probably wouldn't have looked like much of a place to land, and if the Electra had landed there it would either have been easily visible to the *Colorado* pilots, or have sunk out of sight too quickly to get off any radio messages.

Leaving the island was not much more fun than getting ashore had been. First it was necessary to peel Fenlason off the top of a coralstone ruin where he'd begun flapping his arms and squawking like a bird. He later said he'd been kidding, but everyone else was convinced that he'd been driven mad. Then as Tiko brought the boat in, everyone was surprised to see him duck down below the gunwales. More or less prone, he navigated on in and collected everyone. Fenlason, who had more or less recovered his composure after the squawking episode, asked him why he'd suddenly lain down on the job. Tiko explained that a large Tiger Shark had been bumping the skiff with his nose. "I hit the deck," he explained, "because those sharks jump up out of the water and snatch people." Everyone quietly removed their hands from the gunwales and moved a little closer to the centerline.

So, that was it for McKean—lots of mining debris and stone-walled ruins (not "adobe" as Lambrecht had thought), a couple of wrecked fishing boats that probably represented insurance scams, and a few thin campsites with recent debris that probably had been left by passing ornithologists. No evidence of airplanes or aviators on land (though the ore-cart rails did raise some questions about trains), and the reef face was just as clean. Lots more sharks than at Niku, though; the divers were glad to get back aboard *Nomad*. As was everyone.

Pardon Me, Tin

Back on Niku, it was time to wind down. Time was running out, and supplies were running low. Lai, *Nomad*'s adaptable cook, began sending ashore lunches made up of leftover bean and spaghetti sandwiches. And though the expedition was hardly out of things to do, its members were running low on hot ideas about where to look.

Another mapping sweep through the village, to get a record of its layout, a few more spot checks. Clauss, Fenlason, and Knoll went walking about on western Nutiran, previously unvisited—breaking through the scaevola wall and finding a lot of unusually large babae pits and some structures that looked like they dated from the 1950s. And then it was time to go.

"So I stood by Gallagher's grave," Gillespie told the group on the last night, "and I asked, 'Gerry, we came all this way and we busted our butts and all for what?' And he said: 'So tell me about it!'"

From Tom King's journal:

So, it's the last Niku sunrise. A quiet, pink one, the island now just resolving itself out of grayness into the shapes of individual trees and groves. Bosun Sela leaning over my shoulder as I write.

"So, Tom, it's the last scaevola morning!"

"I dunno, Sela, maybe no scaevola today. Or maybe we'll chop some just for practice."

"Ayieee! Not this one!"

"I think I'll miss scaevola, Sela. Maybe I should take some home and plant it. Let my son hack on it—make him strong."

"Ayieee! Not this one!"

Gear and notes gathered together, and the paltry few artifacts. Clauss, Fenlason, and Knoll gathered coconuts for the ship's crew. A jet—Clauss thought it was an F-111—soared overhead at about 25,000 feet, rocking the island with two sonic booms; first sign of the outside world, must mean something. Then out to *Nomad* for the last time, and on the sun-washed afternoon of October 7, Victor pointed her bow south and left Nikumaroro astern. Most of the team looked back on the island with regret, not only because there hadn't been a great discovery but also because it was likely they'd never see the place again.

"Sure would've liked to spend some nights ashore," King grumped, leaning on the fantail rail. Clauss, Krakow, and Decker agreed; Williams said she was really sorry she'd never found the mall. Somebody offered a thin train joke. Victor broke out the rum.

After the captain's free-flowing "Farewell to Niku" party, it was six sober days' sail back to Fiji with a stopover in Pago Pago. Time to examine what had come off the island and assess what had been learned. The results weren't encouraging.

No Electra squatting in the bush, of course, or an obvious Earhart–Noonan campsite. Some aircraft aluminum, notably the funny rectangular piece and the box, but all these pieces were from the village site— picked up elsewhere by the colonists and transported there. Had they been scavenged from the Electra, or from some World War II wreck? Although no aircraft was recorded as crashing on Niku during the war, the colonists had contact with the other Phoenix Islands, and with Kiribati proper, so they could have brought in the aluminum from elsewhere.

And then there was the Loran station. The villagers had gotten a lot of manufactured stuff from the station when it closed—even a kitchen sink, for heaven's sake! Aluminum, radio parts, wires—lots of stuff that looked like it might have come from an airplane—might well have come from the Loran station.

Another song appeared on the saloon bulkhead as *Nomad* rolled on south.

Pardon me, tin,
Are you a piece of Earhart's choo-choo?
Or just a can,
Or something made for Loran?
Oh dear oh dear,
I think I've really made a boo-boo.
You're just a bore.
Should have left you ashore.

We had been hacking through scaevola fields for day after day,
Fighting sharks and manta rays down under the waves,
Still we couldn't sight her
Growing much up-tighter,
Best thing that we found was an old Ronson lighter.

Then I found you,
I said, 'Now, here's a piece of choo-choo!'
Good as they come,
It's made of aluminum.
But now I see
A manufacture date of nineteen-sixty-three!
Oh little piece of tin stuff,
*I'm throwing you in the sea!**

*Sung to the tune of "Chattanooga Choo Choo," by Harry Warren and Max Gordon.

Still, there were things to wonder about, things to analyze further back in the States. The box, the flat piece. . . .

And then there was the grave at Aukaraime South.

"Think about the Kilts story," Gillespie proposed, leaning against the ship's roll. "Suppose they found bones like the story says. Suppose most of the story's BS, but the core is true; they found bones. Gallagher died, they did something with them. What would they do with them?"

Nobody knew, of course. Kaitara, the ethnographic literature, and King's experience elsewhere in Micronesia all indicated that I Kiribati would be very respectful of bones, concerned about the *anti* (pronounced *ans*—ghosts) of the dead people they represented. But there was no telling what that might have compelled this particular group of I Kiribati to do with this particular set of bones, under this particular circumstance—if the whole Kilts story wasn't garbage.

"What if they buried them someplace safe, away from the village, where the *anti* wouldn't bother anyone?" Gillespie proposed. "Someplace where nobody lived or had land, like Aukaraime South? In a bundle, so it only took a small grave?"

"Well, sure," King replied, "they could have. But we also know from Laxton that the villagers had 'weekend houses' down at Aukaraime. The grave's probably a little kid who died there and got planted on his parents' land."

Gillespie was not dissuaded, and as it turned out, that was a good thing.

CHAPTER 10

Hope Springs Eternal

You might say that TIGHAR's crazy;
You might say they've lost their rocks.
But TIGHAR's got what no one else has,
An aluminum box. *

—TIGHAR TUNES

THE EXPEDITION'S TROUBLES DIDN'T END WITH DEPARTURE from Niku. The divers and Ili fell into open conflict with Victor, including a fistfight and its drunken aftermath. Gillespie and King scarcely spoke except to argue. Dispersing to homes and families was a relief to all, though some—Clauss and King, notably, who would happily have retired there—remembered the island in wistful fantasies. Gillespie was more hard-boiled about it. The island had licked him this time, but he'd be back, he assured everyone; he'd be back. By unspoken agreement, King would not be, though he would continue to be a member of TIGHAR and provide advice when asked—and sometimes when not.

Back at TIGHAR Central in Wilmington, Delaware, Gillespie and Thrasher returned to the quest for *l'Oiseau Blanc*, focusing now on a lake in Newfoundland. The White Bird was just as elusive as Earhart's Electra, however, and Gillespie still hoped that the artifacts from Niku would have something to say. He and Thrasher went to work, closely inspecting the artifacts and arranging for technical analyses. As often happens during the analysis phase of an archaeological project—because you can't possibly

---

*Sung to the tune of "Imagine," by John Lennon.

know everything about an artifact when you first see it on the ground—the results were surprising.

That Stuff from the Village

Artifact 2-1, the aluminum box, obligingly had a part number on it—28F4023—that identified it as a Consolidated Aircraft "Box-Furn., Navig. Book & Paper Stowage." In other words, an air navigator's bookcase. It hadn't been designed for an Electra, but then, there weren't any navigator's book cases designed for Electras.

Actually it had been designed for a Consolidated Model 28 PBY Flying Boat, but it had been modified; there were rivet holes where rivet holes didn't exist in the original design. In other words, it had been rejiggered to fit another airplane. An Electra? Well, surely Noonan had needed someplace to put his paperwork. A search of the records gave no clue as to how Noonan's navigator's station may have been equipped, but in one photograph of the Electra, on the ground at Darwin, Australia, with its door open, there was a shadowy rectangular thing inside that looked an awful lot like Artifact 2-1.[1]

The navigator's bookcase. TIGHAR photo by Pat Thrasher.

Earhart, Noonan, and the Electra in Darwin. The shadowy rectangular object inside the plane resembles the navigator's bookcase. TIGHAR collection from Elgen Long.

There was a small deposit of what looked like paint on the artifact, and a strip of black material. Either might help identify the origin of the artifact, so off went 2-1 to the FBI Crime Lab's Materials Analysis Unit. They concluded that the apparent paint was indeed paint, but not of a type that could be used for identification, while the black stuff was adhesive, possibly the remains of some kind of tape. Their conclusion: that there was nothing that would "disqualify this artifact as having come from the Earhart aircraft."[2]

Then there was Artifact 2-18, the rectangular piece from Noonan's Tavern. A dado, said experts at the Completions Division of Atlantic Aviation.[3]

No, not dodo, *dado*. In airplanes with finished cabins, dados run along where the cabin wall meets the deck, kind of like molding at the base of your wall at home, but usually angled out to cover the wiring that runs along the wall. Military aircraft seldom have dados, because a dado is trim, a finishing touch to make things look sharp. Lockheed Electras were reported to have had them, at least in their airliner configuration, but the reports weren't detailed enough to indicate whether they were much like the one from Nikumaroro. Had the dados in Earhart's Lockheed Electra—or indeed any Lockheed Electra—been like the one now in hand? It was impossible to tell, but in any event, it looked like TIGHAR had a piece of a civilian airplane here.

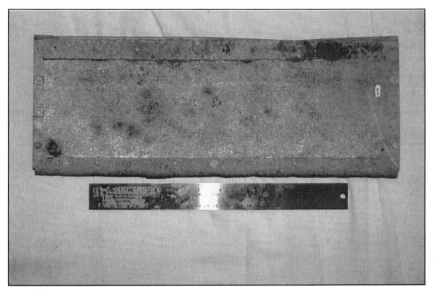

The dado. TIGHAR photo by Pat Thrasher.

The dado naturally had to be attached to the wall and floor somehow; this was done using mounting holes along its reinforced edges. On the Noonan's Tavern piece, these holes are fifteen inches apart, precisely matching the standard distances between stiffeners in the fuselage of an Electra Model 10. And finally, stuck around a rivet poking out of the piece was a tiny bit of bluish woven fabric—apparently kapok. Specifications for the Model 10 call for the cabin area to be insulated with .15 inch kapok, under the trade name "Seapak." Seapak was often blue.[4]

Several other pieces were definitely aluminum alloy, known as "Alclad," of the thickness used in airplanes. Some had rivet holes, or rivets, that were consistent with the spacing and rivet type used in the Electra, others did not. So the villagers had apparently had access to more than one airplane. Some aluminum pieces weren't Alclad, suggesting they had come from something other than an airplane—most likely containers and fixtures at the Loran station.

So what did all this say? That there were airplane parts on the island that had clearly been collected by the colonists, someplace, and brought to the village for reuse. That some of these were consistent—or at least not *inconsistent*—with being parts of the Electra. That others were clearly not from the Electra, but from some other airplane. As often happens, the stuff raised more questions than it answered. Did Noonan have a bookcase? What was it like and where did it come from? Where did the villagers get the airplane parts? If the parts weren't from the Electra, what airplane were they from? Or if some of them were from the Electra, where did the *rest* of them come from?

The Maudes and the PISS Papers

This kind of situation is typical in archaeological—or any kind of scientific—research; you seldom get your answers all at once, in the field, in some kind of defining moment. You get your data, come home, and spend months in analysis—which often leads to the conclusion that your hypothesis was wrong. This hadn't happened; the Niku hypothesis was neither confirmed nor proven false; the first expedition had simply produced ambiguous results.

This meant doing more research, and there was plenty to do before another trip to the island was seriously considered. TIGHAR needed to know more about the island, and more about the colony whose residents had been mucking around with pieces of airplane.

This brought King back into the picture. One of the most basic of any archaeologist's responsibilities is to "write up" what he or she finds—to prepare a report on it to share with colleagues and whoever else is interested. Though convinced that he was through flirting with the Earhart mystery, King was beginning work on a report covering the non-Earhart results of the 1989 expedition—notably the village. This required more research into the PISS, and King soon learned to his delight that Harry and Honor Maude were still alive and quite willing to correspond. They were living in Australia, cranking out books on central Pacific ethnohistory even though, as Harry put it, "my blindness is a handicap."[5] Maude himself didn't believe that Earhart had landed on Niku; he was quite sure the Japanese had captured her, but that didn't keep him from sharing information freely. He also put King and TIGHAR on to a number of important documents, many of them in the H. E. and H. C. Maude Collection at the Barr Smith Library at the University of Adelaide: Maude's 1937 official report on the inception of the PISS,[6] for example, and his 1940, then-secret appraisal of the historical bases for British and U.S. claims to the Phoenix Islands.[7] His quarterly reports on PISS progress, and Gallagher's.[8] Each quarterly report was several pages long, typed, and outlined what their authors knew and wanted to report about what had happened during the prior three months on each island. Data on Nikumaroro were scarce until Gallagher relocated there in September 1940. At this point sixty-nine settlers were on the island, but twenty of these were members of a working party Gallagher had brought with him from Manra. Supervised by Jack Petro (or Pedro), the colony's foreman of public works and a Tuvaluan-Portugese craftsman of remarkable skill to judge from the records, they set about with vigor to develop the place—clearing and building the Government Station, organizing the village, building the landing monument. Petro also worked to ease the island's chronic water problem, constructing a 10,000-gallon cistern to catch rainwater and using dynamite to dig wells.

A few quotes from Gallagher's progress reports convey the flavor of the period:

> During the quarter, work was commenced on the construction of the skeleton of the Government Station. . . . Work was also commenced on the rather formidable task of clearing away the rocks and tree roots which have to be removed before the Station site can be leveled . . . (and) on construction of the Rest House which, it is hoped, will be completed before the end of November. . . . It is hoped to furnish the main living room of the Rest House with furniture constructed entirely from locally grown "kanawa"—a beautifully marked wood which abounds on the island and is being cut to waste as planting proceeds.[9]

> The second half of the quarter was marked by severe and almost continuous North-westerly gales, which did considerable damage to houses, coconut trees, and newly planted lands. Portions of the low-lying areas of Hull and Gardner Islands were also flooded by high spring tides, backed by the gales, and, it is feared that many young trees have been killed.[10]

> Work on Gardner Island has been directed mainly towards the completion of the clearing and leveling of the Government Station area, the construction of roads and paths and the erection of a properly constructed latrine wharf to replace the sundry temporary structures

swept away by the December gales. . . . Work was also commenced on the demarcation and plotting of landholdings on the South-west side of the island and some twenty of these lands have been taken over by labourers who intend to remain on the island as settlers.[11]

Bones Again

As word of the expedition and its results began to get out, people began to come forward with information, anecdotes, and recollections. One of these was Bauro Tikana.

Tikana's son-in-law, Virgil Stennett, a shipping agent on Tarawa, saw an article on TIGHAR's work in *Pacific Islands Monthly*, and wrote a letter that found its way at last to Wilmington.

> My father-in-law . . . was Mr. Gerald B. Gallagher's clerk during this time and was with him when he died. According to Bauro there were bones found when they started clearing the island . . .

Whoops! Off went a letter to Mr. Tikana; back came a fax.

> When we first arrived I saw the ship wreck, and asked Mr. [Gallagher?] about it. He told me that it was the *Norwich City*. Later when the labor[er]s were cleaning they told me that they found bones near the ship. I do not know if Mr. Gallagher knew about the bones as I didn't tell him about it. The labor[er]s also told me they found bones at the other end of the atoll when they were cleaning the land in that area. I don't believe Mr. Gallagher knew of these as he was the only white man there and most of the labor[er]s didn't speak English and were afright to talk to him and Mr. Gallagher didn't speak Gilbertese.[12]

So here once again, a bones story—workers finding bones in the bush, but now two sets of bones, at opposite ends of the island. What to make of it? Well, it seemed likely that the bones Mr. Tikana reported on Nutiran represented some of the lost crewmen of the *Norwich City*, but what of those found at the other end of the island? On Aukaraime South? Awfully close to that little grave, Gillespie thought.

The Wire and the Water Catcher

Another person who came forward with a story was Dr. John Mims, who had flown PBYs between Kanton and Nikumaroro in 1944–1945, servicing the Loran station. He said that one day he had seen colonists using what turned out to be an airplane control cable as heavy-duty fishing tackle. When Mims asked them where it had come from, he said, the fishermen said it had come from a plane that been there when they first came to the island. When Mims asked where the plane was now, they just shrugged.

It was an interesting story; the first—and for quite a while the only—account of colonists reporting aircraft wreckage, albeit second hand. But nothing that could be checked on; no way to turn it into a testable hypothesis.

It was a different story with Dr. Richard K. Evans, who had been a member of the Coast Guard crew that ran the Loran station during the war. Evans remembered that he and some of his buddies had found "a small structure . . . designed to collect rainwater" in the bush on Aukaraime North, not far from the station. "We assumed the natives had built it," he reported, "but when we mentioned it to them a few months later they didn't know anything about it."[13] Evans said the structure consisted of a water-collecting cloth rigged on poles, hung above a metal tank, and his description of the tank sounded a lot like one of the 149-gallon fuel tanks that had been mounted in the Electra's fuselage. It wasn't long before one of Evan's former station mates, Herb Moffitt, corroborated the story and elaborated on it, saying that there was a very old campfire site nearby, together with a rusty five-gallon can and a pile of bird bones. The two were able to narrow the location of the structure down to a fairly definite stretch of the windward shore near the southeast end of the island.

What was this? Laxton, in describing a 1949 walk around the island, said of the Ameriki area:

The "buka" trees rise here sixty feet high, and were partly cleared to accommodate the neat gray iron [Q]uonset huts of the U.S. radio installation, neatly sealed, awaiting dismantling and transportation. Turning the tip to return along the northern rim, narrow, thundering with surf driven by the northeast trade winds, the path ends in a house built for Gallagher on a strip of land cleared from lagoon to ocean beach so that the fresh winds blow easily through.[14]

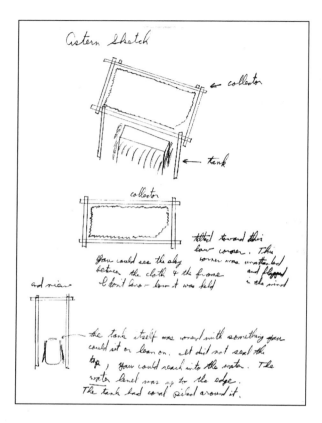

Cistern Sketch

← collector

← tank

collector

Dr. Richard Evans's sketch of the water catching device he and Herb Moffitt saw on Aukaraime North. TIGHAR collection from Richard Evans.

So maybe the remains of this house were what Evans and Moffitt had seen. But then again, maybe not. Why would they have seen it as only the remains of some kind of structure in 1945 or so, when Laxton unhesitatingly called it a house in 1949? Maybe it was a campsite, Gillespie thought, where a couple of castaways had looked wistfully out to the north, whence—they hoped against hope—would come their salvation, probably in the form of the *Itasca*. Maybe. It was worth checking.

Finally, there was the unresolved question of the reef. The 1989 dive team had scanned the reef face to as deep as 150 feet—deep for scuba—but had seen it slope off into the far, dim distances beyond and below. There was lots of room for an airplane to hide on the face of that reef, far deeper than a diver could explore. A robotic survey was in order, together with a good hard look for the Evans–Moffit water catcher and, Gillespie decided, an excavation of the Aukaraime grave.

CHAPTER 11

The Grave, the Skin, and the Shoes

Come back whenever life starts to get gray,
And troubles won't let you free.
Come back to old Club Fred, my friends,
Sweat is our only fee.[*]
                              —TIGHAR TUNES

Return to Niku

So Gillespie and Thrasher set out to raise money for another expedition, and by October 1, 1991, they'd done it, more or less. On that date, after a frantic last-minute scramble for the last contributions, ten TIGHAR members sailed from Honolulu aboard the research ship RV *Acania* for a bumpy nine-day cruise to the island. The team was made up mostly of veterans from the '89 trip—Clauss, Fenlason, Matthews, Love, Knoll, Gillespie, and Thrasher. Others were new to Niku—Kristin (Kris) Tague, Aysa Usvitsky, and Alan Olson. With them were an underwater remote sensing team under contract from Oceaneering International and a small press corps—videographer Sam Painter from NBC News and *Life* magazine correspondent Frank Fournier. Customs Inspector Manikaa Teuatabo represented the Kiribati government. Among other things, Teuatabo had the authority to permit TIGHAR to excavate the Aukaraime South grave, provided the work was done in a proper way.

---

*Sung to the tune of "Cabaret," by John Kander and Fred Ebb.

In the Wake of the *Colorado*

Acania wasn't long out of port before everyone concluded that this was not the time of year to be traveling to Niku. The steady, gentle trade winds of 1989 had been replaced by gusty squalls from all directions; the seas were high and confused. *Acania* more or less followed the path taken by the *Colorado* fifty-four years before, but *Acania* is no battleship, and October in the South Pacific is different from July. The die was cast, however, and finally the research ship hove to in Niku's lee. It was a shaky group of Americans that went gratefully ashore.

At the landing beach, something was missing—the landing monument, several tons of coral and reinforced concrete. From John Clauss' diary:

> There has been a hell of a storm somewhere along the line since we left (in 1989). It leveled the monument; only the foundation is left. And the vegetation has been destroyed for about 30 feet. The scaevola on the perimeter of the tree line is pretty much gone. We could see evidence of storm wash 150' back in the trees. The store in the village is collapsed. It must have been an extremely violent storm. . . .

The storm must have hit sometime in 1990, coming in from the west. It had torn away large pieces of *Norwich City* and chewed up the Ritiati shoreline. Noonan's Tavern couldn't be found. But in the tangle of coconut fronds and driftwood northwest of the collapsed cooperative store, Pat Thrasher stumbled on a piece of aluminum. A big piece, and if it wasn't skin from an airplane, nobody knew what it could be.

2-2-V-1

Artifact 2-2-V-1[1] was—and is—roughly rectangular, about twenty-three by nineteen inches. It was the right kind of aluminum, of the right thickness, to have come from the Electra. It looked like it had been cut off an even bigger piece. Marks along one edge suggested either crude tin-snipping or perhaps hacking with a machete. It lacked the zinc chromate paint that's typical of (though not universal on) military airplanes of the period, and it had rivets that matched those on the Earhart plane. Naturally the TIGHARs searched its neighborhood vigorously, noting that it wasn't far from where the aluminum box had been recovered in '89. A few more small pieces of aircraft aluminum—nothing definitive—turned up.

The Windward Side and the Reef

Inspection of the village and what the storm had done to it was only a side-light, though. The expedition had three main purposes. Oceaneering was to do a side-scan sonar search of the reef face to a depth of about 2,000 feet, with a remotely operated submersible standing by to take a close look at any suspicious "hits." Meanwhile the TIGHAR team would split into two groups. One would hit the bushes and beach along the windward side, look-ing for the Evans–Moffitt water catcher. The other—with Teuatabo's care-ful supervision—would see who was in that little grave at Aukaraime South.

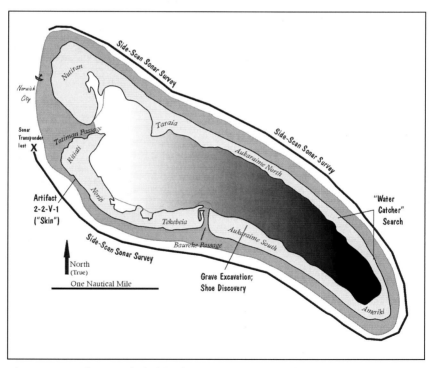

The 1991 expedition included a side-scan sonar search of the reef face and excava-tion at Aukaraime South.

Deploying the side-
scan-sonar array. TIGHAR
photo by Pat Thrasher.

In both the side-scan survey and the search for the water catcher, TIGHAR was skunked again. Something that looked a lot like part of an airplane showed up in one sonar sweep, but after a couple more sweeps it disappeared, resolving itself into an irregularity in the coral. Then the sonar "fish" (value $5,000) hit a reef-ridge that juts out near Tatiman Passage and was broken beyond repair. That was the end of the side-scan. Luckily Oceaneering had scanned most of the reef face to about 2,000 feet deep before the fish got away. The area not swept, though—the area from Tatiman Passage north to the tip of the island—is an area that, as luck would have it, we'd come to want very much to know more about. Much of it hadn't been inspected by the divers in 1989, either, because it was so full of *Norwich City* debris that they didn't think they'd have been able to see aircraft wreckage even if it were there.

While the sonar sweeps were going on, the land team divided what should have been the vicinity of the Evans–Moffitt structure into ten meter squares, and began to search each square systematically with metal detectors. They worked their way some distance back into the scaevola, which was as thick and nasty as it had been in 1989, but had no reason to penetrate deeply—they thought. Unfortunately—though they did manage not to break any equipment—they came up with no more than the reef team did.

Aukaraime South was a different matter, though not in the way Gillespie had hoped.

The Shoes

The Aukaraime grave lies in a relatively clear area amid coconut trees, scaevola, and small trees called *ren* by I Kiribati and tournefortia by European and U.S. biologists. It's three to four meters—nine to twelve feet— above sea level so it's pretty stable; there's no evidence of the sort of overwash that the Baureke Passage area farther west gets. The place is crazy with coconut crabs in all stages of development—from the little finger-sized fellows who run around in other people's shells to the huge, long-clawed guys who look like they would gladly decapitate you if you get in their way. If

The Aukaraime grave, shown here after excavation, reburial of the bones, and reconstruction, was a typical I Kiribati grave but for its small size and big head and foot stones. TIGHAR photo by Tom King.

you sit still for a while at Aukaraime South—or even if you don't—soon the ground will seem to start moving as juvenile coco crabs and other hermit crabs, most of them wearing the shells of large sea snails, start rambling around. A spooky kind of place, but well above the tide line, shady and breezy—a nice enough place to dig, a nice place to camp, perhaps as nice as any place to die.

Manikaa Teuatabo's permission to excavate the grave—and standard archaeological practice—required that the work be done with care and respect, and that the remains be promptly reburied and the grave monument rebuilt if it turned out not to be worth analyzing them as possible Earhart or Noonan remains. The team laid out a two- by two-meter area around the grave, and excavated it in ten-centimeter levels. They carefully dismantled the structure of coral slabs that marked the grave on the surface and set them aside to be reassembled. Tommy Love took charge of the digging, looking forward to examining, perhaps, some famous bones. He and his crew troweled and shoveled the soil into buckets to be carried down to

Grave excavation underway at Aukaraime South. TIGHAR photo by Pat Thrasher.

the lagoon, where Kris Tague and others sat with fine-meshed screens. Everything was washed through the screens as the workers looked for small objects of interest that, unfortunately, weren't there.

Tension was high by the time the trowels approached the bottom of the grave, where a mass of rootlets preserved the rectangular shape of a long-rotted box. It dissipated quickly when the bones came into view, however. To Tommy's practiced eye—and indeed to everyone else's unpracticed ones—they were obviously those of a very small child. So much for Gillespie's burial-of-dangerous-bones hypothesis.

But in the meantime, serendipity had stepped in. Literally.

Coming ashore on October 16, Love had gotten his boots wet. This was nothing new; it happened every day, and he carried a dry pair with him. He sat down on the ground under a tree about twenty yards from the grave to change his footgear. This naturally entailed looking down at his feet, and as he did so a young coconut crab scuttled by and turned over a leaf. There was something black under it—the heel of a shoe bearing the name "Cat's Paw Rubber Co USA."

Gillespie's notes for October 16 are surprisingly—or perhaps carefully—laconic:

> About 8:30 Tommy, in getting ready to resume digging grave, said, "There's the heel of an old shoe over here." A crab had moved a leaf off of it. Aysa [Usvitsky] and I spent the morning inspecting the immediate area and found a total of 8 pieces. 1–5 appear to be rubber. 6, 7, & 8 appear to be leather. Also found some bits of charcoal.

But the possible significance of a shoe, its heel apparently made in the United States, on a relatively remote part of an island where few people who wore shoes had ever lived, was not lost on him. Kilts had said:

> What attracted him to it was the shoes. Woman's shoes, American kind. . . . The shoes were size nine narrow.

While Love and the others continued work on the grave, Gillespie and Aysa Usvitsky cordoned off the area and began carefully "cleaning" the surface. This meant picking up each piece of surface litter by hand, looking at it to make sure it was just natural litter, and putting it in a white plastic

Kris Tague screens debris at Aukraime South. TIGHAR photo by Pat Thrasher.

bucket. Everything that wasn't natural they left in place, and then photographed it where it all lay. Once this was done they shot in the location relative to the grave and other immovable surface features of the site, and swept the area thoroughly with metal detectors, turning up a tiny fragment of a very small nail (which turned out to be, most likely, from the heel). Then they skimmed the first couple of centimeters of surface material—mostly organic detritus and coral rubble—and put it in buckets. These went to the lagoon shore, where Tague washed it through her screen. Only a little more charcoal and a small brass eyelet turned up in the screen; apparently all the pieces of leather and rubber had been lying right on the surface, not even slightly embedded.

By the end of the following day—the day the grave excavation was finished and the poor dead child left in peace—the team had fragments of rubber that apparently represented most of a shoe sole, the brass eyelet, the nail fragment, and a few fragments of what looked like leather. All were tightly clustered in an area about six feet across and associated with small flecks of charcoal. They'd cleared an area of about twenty by thirty feet, though, and were pretty sure they had found all there was to find, when *Life* magazine's

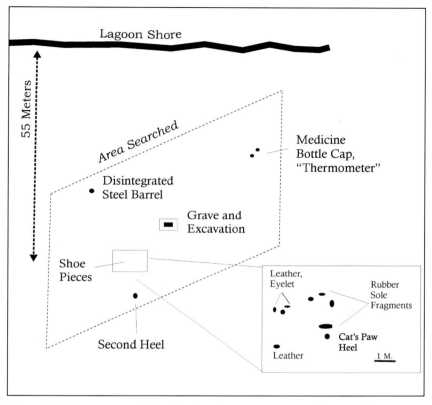

Most of the shoe parts at Aukaraime South were concentrated in a small area.

photographer Frank Fournier came back from shooting atmosphere and asked what they were doing.

"Looking for the other heel," Gillespie said tersely.

"Oh," Fournier said, brightly and reaching down to pick something up, "like this one?" Standing just outside the search area, he had looked down and seen another shoe heel.

This heel didn't look at all like the first one; it wasn't quite the same size, and it had no "Cat's Paw" marking. Whatever kind of shoe the second one came from, searching revealed no more of it. General ground searching between the "shoe site" and the lagoon turned up what looked like a broken thermometer and the lid of a medicine bottle with manufacturer's markings on it. These were duly mapped in and collected. Then time ran out. It was a long trip back to Honolulu, much of it spent assembling and pondering over shoe parts, and rereading Kilts's account.

"Woman's shoes." Was the Aukaraime shoe a woman's? That should be ascertainable, Gillespie thought.

"American kind." Well, the "USA" on the crab-delivered heel made its origin, if not the whole shoe, pretty much a no-brainer. But had Cat's Paw been around in 1937?

"Size nine narrow." Surely it should be possible to figure out the size of the Aukaraime shoe.

But how had Kilts's informant known about American shoes versus anybody else's? Women's shoes? Shoe sizes? What did those terms even mean to the "native"?

And what alternative sources were there for the shoes? Certainly few if any of the colonists would have worn shoes, but there was always Gallagher, Maude, Laxton, and other Europeans who'd doubtless visited at one time or another. And the surveyors from USS *Bushnell*. And the Coast Guardsmen, and. . . . Well, who else?

No way of telling while *Acania* plowed her way back to Hawaii, but Gillespie intended to let no grass grow under his feet, or under the Aukaraime shoe, when he got back to Wilmington.

CHAPTER 12

"We Did It!" or Not

We can now say with confidence that we have the proof.[1]
— TIGHAR TRACKS, March 1992

Gillespie's case doesn't stand up.[2]
— *LIFE* MAGAZINE, April 1992

Amelia Earhart's Shoe(?)

Once back at TIGHAR Central in Wilmington, it didn't take long for Gillespie to find out that Cat's Paw Rubber was a division of the Bilt-Rite Shoe Company, and to inquire about whether Bilt-Rite had experts who might be interested in taking a look at TIGHAR's discoveries. Although the company didn't have a historical forensics laboratory or anything of the kind, it did have a couple of knowledgeable and interested employees— William F. Foshage Jr. and Robert L. Ogintz—who were willing to volunteer their services. Fosage and Ogintz set to work on the two heels and the other shoe parts, and shortly were able to give Gillespie some observations that he found very thought-provoking, to say the least.

The heel the crab had kindly given to Dr. Love was a Cat's Paw replacement heel, they said, manufactured in the United States in the mid-1930s for a left shoe. It could have been attached to either a woman's or a man's shoe, but the shoe it had been attached to was almost certainly represented by the apparent sole fragments, because when reconstructed the sole matched the heel in size and nail spacing. The reconstructed sole was about 277 millimeters long—about 10.9 inches.

The Cat's-Paw heel. TIGHAR photo by Pat Thrasher.

Then came the really interesting part. Fosage and Ogintz indicated that to judge from the tightness of the stitching, the sole was most likely that of a woman's shoe.

A woman's left shoe, reconstructed sole length a bit under eleven inches—about a size eight and a half to nine in contemporary American sizing. The Bilt-Rite experts could infer the type of shoe, too, based on the tight stitching pattern and the small brass eyelet that had turned up in Tague's screen: most likely an oxford, they said—that is, a low lace-up shoe rather than one with straps or some other means of holding it on. Probably a

The sole of the shoe. TIGHAR photo by Pat Thrasher.

"blucher" oxford, they told Gillespie—the "blucher" referring to the way the tongue and other parts of the upper were put together.

The other heel—Frank's heel—was an original (not a replacement) heel from a completely different shoe, rather larger than the first one, perhaps a man's shoe. Beyond that, and that it exhibited about the same amount of degradation as the Cat's Paw—suggesting that both heels had been around for about the same length of time—the experts couldn't say much.

A probable woman's shoe, size eight and a half or nine, very likely from the 1930s—though of course it could have been lost on the island later—with a replacement heel made by a U.S. company. Plus another shoe that had to be from a different pair since it was larger and original; shoes are almost always reheeled in pairs. And on an island where few people wore shoes, in the 1930s or thereafter.

The I Kiribati colonists hadn't ordinarily worn shoes—almost nobody does in the Pacific even today, except when required to by business. Gallagher doubtless wore shoes, but hardly a woman's blucher oxford. The same could be said for Maude and Bevington, Laxton and the other WPHC people. Laxton did refer in his 1951 article to an American woman who had visited the island during his sojourn there, but that was all he provided—a passing reference. While she, or some other post-1930s visitor, could have lost a shoe on Aukaraime South, was it likely that it would have been a shoe

Earhart on the wing of the Electra
in Bandoeng, Java, during fueling.
The placement of her foot on
the rivet line permits accurate
calculation of shoe size. TIGHAR
Collection from Purdue University
Special Collections.

from the 1930s? If not, was there a woman wandering around this part of
the Pacific in the 1930s? Well . . .

The next natural question was, did Earhart wear blucher-style oxfords,
and if so, what size?

Gillespie and Thrasher had looked into this question earlier because
of the Kilts account, and found that like George Washington's teeth,
Earhart's shoe size had become rather the stuff of legend. It was generally
thought that Earhart had quite small feet. The physical evidence most
often cited to support this assumption was a pair of size six and a half bro-
cade dancing slippers that once belonged to her, now in the Atchison
County Historical Society Museum in Atchison, Kansas. No one seemed
to know just when Earhart owned these slippers, however, or how old she
was at the time.

Earhart's friend Helen Hutson Weber had loaned TIGHAR a pair of
leather dress shoes she said had been made in Paris and purchased by
Earhart while she was in Europe in 1932. An undated handwritten note
signed by Mrs. Weber reads in part:

She gave them to me in Nov. (1932) when I was her guest for 8 months—not for sentimental reasons but because they hurt her.[3]

The Sterling Last Corp. on Long Island analyzed Mrs. Webber's shoes and found them to be "about a size seven AA or AAA."[4]

Then there are the recollections of retired U.S. Customs Inspector Peggy Sledge. In her 1988 book *The Littlest Smuggler and Other True Stories*, she relates a series of anecdotes about famous people who passed through her Rio Grande customs office. One of them—identified in a contemporary newspaper article as referring to Earhart—reads:

A woman flyer, internationally known and believed to have been lost at sea on a 'round the world trip was known . . . in Customs for her extra large feet. She laughed about them too.[5]

As it turned out, TIGHAR had a much more direct source of information on what kind of shoes Earhart *did* wear on the World Flight—photos taken at the time.

From the many photos taken during both the first and second attempt, it appears that Earhart had three pairs of shoes with her. When not flying, she sometimes wore a pair of two-tone saddle shoes with light colored soles and heels. The other two pairs, apparently worn when flying or working around the airplane, were blucher-style oxfords.

Comparing pictures taken during the World Flight with those taken earlier in Earhart's flying career, it looks like sometime before the World Flight began, Earhart had had her oxfords reheeled. One of these photos—the one taken in Bandoeng, Java, just ten days before takeoff from Lae—show especially clearly that the heel of at least one shoe is lighter-colored at the bottom, suggesting a replacement heel. Among the many pictures showing Earhart wearing blucher-style oxfords, the lighter-colored heel is first visible in shots taken just before the launch of the first World Flight attempt.

And the size? The foot in the apparently reheeled shoe in the Bandoeng photo is up on the wing of the plane, angling across a neat pattern of rivets. Gillespie measured the spacing of the equivalent rivets on a surviving Electra, and found them to be 2.5 inches apart. So all he had to do was count the number of rivets between the tip of the toe and the back of the heel, and multiply by the rivet spacing, to get the apparent size of the shoe. It worked out, he found, to a bit over ten inches, indicating an American woman's size of eight and a half or nine. It looked like whatever her foot size, the shoe Earhart was wearing shortly before she launched for Howland Island was very, very similar to the shoe from Aukaraime South.[6]

Earhart's Medicine?

The bottle lid found at Aukaraime South was interesting, too. Experts from the Warner-Lambert Company found that it came off a bottle of patent medicine manufactured by their parent company, William R. Warner & Company of New York. Beginning in 1932, Warner used the logo on the lid—ironically enough a world globe—on the caps of three products: a laxative called Agoral, a stomach-settler called Cal-Bisma, and an indigestion remedy called Alka-Zane. The logo continued in use into the 1950s.[7] A number of anecdotal accounts told about Earhart having had stomach trouble during the World Flight. Had she taken something like Cal-Bisma or Alka-Zane to ease the pain? There was no way to answer that question, and it wasn't even possible to verify the anecdotes.[8] As for the "thermometer" found nearby, it turned out to be a broken psychrometer—an instrument commonly used in measuring humidity when making weather observations.[9] Conceivably, it was something that would be aboard the "Flying Laboratory," but more likely it had been broken and discarded by the Kiwi surveyors, or the *Bushnell* party, or Gallagher, or Laxton, or a Kiribati government party that had mapped the Aukaraime South coconut grove in 1978.[10]

But however equivocal the other artifacts might be, the shoe looked good. And in the presence of the other shoe, it suggested that two people had been there. It was hard not to think that Aukaraime South was Earhart's and Noonan's campsite—maybe their death site.

The Skin

Then there was Artifact 2-2-V-1, the skin: a big piece of Alclad airplane skin with no zinc chromate. Having made a Mylar template showing the rivet pattern, Gillespie crawled all over, under, around, and through an Electra at the Western Aerospace Museum in Oakland, California, and pored over

Artifact 2-2-V-1 as found on the edge of the village. TIGHAR photo by Pat Thrasher.

Lockheed construction drawings, looking for a match.[11] There wasn't one—quite. The overall spacing of the rivets was consistent with the belly of the Electra, and the surviving rivets themselves were consistent with those used in Earhart's plane. The problem was that 2-2-V-1 had two *additional* rows of rivet holes between two of those that matched the construction specs and the belly of the Electra in Oakland.

By the time Earhart's Electra disappeared, had its belly experienced any changes? Of course it had, as the result of that ground-loop and belly-skid in Hawaii. Repair orders retained by the Lockheed Corp. showed that the crash had destroyed the right side of the belly, doing less damage to the left.[12] The right side had been replaced in total, but only the damaged portion had been replaced on the left. That damaged portion was crossed by three stiffeners that matched three of the rivet lines on 2-2-V-1; if there had been enough damage to require additional stiffeners, it would have been reasonable to add them precisely where the additional rivet lines lie on the Niku artifact.[13]

Another discrepancy between 2-2-V-1 and the specs for Earhart's airplane might also account for the additional rivet lines. The original specs called for 0.040-inch Alclad skins on the center belly of the plane, but 2-2-V-1—like the original tail section belly plates and the upper fuselage—is only 0.032-inch thick. If for some reason it had been necessary to use 0.032-inch skin to patch the damaged part of the Electra's belly, then additional stiffeners might have been appropriate.

The repair orders didn't document anything like this, unfortunately, but they also didn't foreclose the possibility that it had happened. It was a plausible thing to have been done as part of the repairs, and there was no evidence to indicate that it hadn't happened. All in all, a highly suggestive artifact. Suggestive enough, in fact, to tempt. . . .

Succumbing to Temptation

Piled on top of the dado and the navigator's bookcase, the shoe and the skin created a bit more enthusiasm than, in retrospect, was really a good idea. The headline on the March 1992 issue of *TIGHAR's* newsletter, *TIGHAR Tracks,* was "We Did It!"[14] And in the April issue of *Life*—in an article whose first page featured Artifact 2-2-V-1 alongside a smiling Earhart striding past the Electra, Gillespie flatly stated:

> Every possibility has been checked, every alternative eliminated. There is only one possible conclusion: we found a piece of Amelia Earhart's aircraft. There may be conflicting opinions, but there is no conflicting evidence. I submit that the case is solved.[15]

Others quite immediately disagreed—starting, indeed, in the same issue of *Life*. Sure, TIGHAR had some physical evidence that was interesting, but it didn't have the "smoking gun." Nothing with Earhart's name on it, no ID plate from an Electra's engine.[16]

An awful lot to ask for, Gillespie rejoined—in any court of law, or any normal archaeological study, he would have made his case. But TIGHAR wasn't in a court of law, nor was it doing normal archaeology. It was dealing with one of the twentieth century's famous mysteries, about which there were lots of theories, about each of which many people felt strongly. As Carl Sagan said about contacts with extraterrestrials, "extraordinary claims require extraordinary evidence."[17]

"The Things We Do for England . . ."

While Gillespie was fending off attacks, serendipity struck again. Eric Bevington, Harry Maude's compatriot in the 1937 reconnaissance of Niku, contacted TIGHAR after reading the *Life* article. Not only was he alive and well, he had even published a book about his career in the colonial service, called *The Things We Do for England, If Only England Knew.*[18] It wasn't long before Gillespie and Thrasher were on a plane for England, equipped with video recorder and tapes.

Mr. and Mrs. Bevington were gracious hosts, patiently putting up with extensive videotaped interviews and sharing Bevington's detailed diary of the 1937 reconnaissance.[19]

When they arrived at the island, the diary revealed, Harry Maude had been suffering a severe case of lumbago and had been barely able to move. He had dispatched Bevington with several I Kiribati delegates to circumnavigate the island. Just as TIGHAR had, they found the island to be much bigger than expected—they had a better excuse, though, since at that time there were no accurate maps. The walk turned into something of an epic, but all arrived safely back in camp on what was to be known as Nutiran. The next day the I Kiribati set to work digging test wells. Bevington and Maude worked with them in the morning, but . . .

> In the afternoon we got a canoe and Maude came in it, his lumbago being better, and I took him to all the points of special note I had visited the day before. It was a deluxe way of doing it, in a canoe gliding across the lagoon with natives paddling. We found many interesting things including signs of previous habitation.

What?

"Oh," Bevington said, trying to remember, "there wasn't much as I recall. It looked as if someone had bivouacked for a night."

Gillespie rolled out a map. "Can you mark the place where this was?"

"Yes. I believe it was somewhere in this area." Bevington drew a question mark on Aukaraime South, in the neighborhood of the "shoe site."

Try as he might, Bevington couldn't remember anything more about what the place had looked like; he thought he remembered low, linear mounds of some kind. Gillespie dispatched a copy of the tape and diary to

King, who zipped off a letter to Maude. The father of the PISS answered promptly:

> Yes, curiously enough I do seem to remember the low pile of rubble that you mention. As far as my fickle memory of small events 60 years ago, it was in an open space at the other end of the lagoon to the village. I would describe it as a little pile of debris, not much higher than the surrounding earth, and after scratching around and on it I came to the conclusion that it was a rubbish dump used by Arundel's labourers when they spent some years on Nikumaroro planting coconuts for him.[20]

So there had been something at Aukaraime South, in the vicinity of where the shoes had been found in 1991, that looked like somebody had camped. Low mounds, perhaps, or a "little pile of debris." In response to further questions, Maude said he couldn't recall just what kind of debris it had been.

Aukaraime South, it appeared, needed some more study.

The Other Airplane

Meanwhile, there was that aluminum, and although some of it looked like it came from an Electra, some of it quite clearly did not. In fact, one of the aluminum pieces found in 1991 had a part number that showed it was from a B-24.[21] Much of the rest could have come from an Electra, but could also have come from something else. Gillespie needed to find out what he could about the "something elses"—try to understand all the plausible *non*-Electra sources that might have been mined by the colonists for aluminum. To do that, he needed to figure out, if he could, just how many airplanes, of what kinds, the colonists had had access to, and how they might have gotten hold of the pieces.

Kanton (then Canton) Island was the closest place where there had been substantial aircraft activity during World War II, and it was certainly possible that travel between Niku and Kanton had occurred during the war, resulting in the possible movement of aluminum. Gillespie set out to find records on every kind of aircraft that ever operated on or through Kanton. The list wound up looking like this:

Prewar:
Sikorsky S-42B

Wartime based at Canton:
Douglas A-24
Douglas C-47 (DC-3)
Douglas B-18
Consolidated PBY
Consolidated PB2Y Coronado
Lockheed PV-1 Ventura
Curtiss P-40 Warhawk
Bell P-39 Airacobra
Douglas A-20 Havoc

Wartime operating through Canton:
Douglas C-47
Consolidated PB2Y Coronado
Douglas C-54 Skymaster
North American B-25 Mitchell
Martin PBM Mariner
Consolidated Model 32 (B-24, PB4Y-1, C-87, etc.)
Curtiss C-46 Commando
Boeing B-17E

Lots of other airplanes, including B-24s. And any that were wrecked, or whose damaged and replaced pieces were discarded, could be sources of aluminum to I Kiribati and Tuvaluan workers, who could have transported or traded them to Niku.[22]

Another source, definitely wrecked within range of transport by the colonists, and in fact documented as used by the colonists, came to light as King was doing background research in the Library of Congress for his archaeological report on the village. *Titiana*, a 1964 anthropological study of the Manra colony by Kenneth Knudson,[23] was loaded with good historical information about the PISS, and what it said about the colonial villages on Manra—their social organization, values, beliefs—probably applied to Karaka Village as well. There was also a good deal of information on interactions among the Phoenix Island colonies during World War II and thereafter.

Lots of movement, lots of traveling. Lots of people going to Canton to work for the Americans and British. And then there was this:

> During the late war years, a large four-engined aircraft from Canton Island crashed on Sydney. . . . [I]t circled the island once before attempting to ditch in the lagoon. The approach was made too low, however, and the airplane . . . crashed just inland from the village. It burned on coming to rest, but the islanders hastened to pull the crew members from the wreckage. One man lived for a short time, but succumbed after an hour or so as he was badly burned. . . . The next day a ship arrived from Canton and the bodies were removed and taken aboard. After the ship left for Canton, the wreck became the chief source of aluminum for the islanders, who had learned on Canton to make combs and other ornaments from this material. Eventually almost nothing remained of the aircraft.

So a large four-engined plane—perhaps a B-24?—had gone down on Manra and been scavenged for pieces of aluminum. And then Laxton had brought five leasehold families from Manra to the reorganized colony on Niku. And then during the 1950s there had been lots more movement. Quite likely, Gillespie and King thought, they'd discovered the aluminum Mother Lode, and the way to account for the non-Electra-like pieces of aluminum in the village. But was it the only source? And had the plane really been a B-24? Gillespie couldn't find any official record of the crash, so it became, for the time being, just another unresolved question.

In Nikumaroro Village

When the Nikumaroro colony was abandoned in 1963, many of its residents were relocated to Wahgena (also known as Vahgena) Island in the Solomons. Here they settled down in a village that they nostalgically named Nikumaroro. And here they were visited in 1995 by Dr. Dirk Ballendorf of the University of Guam's Micronesian Area Research Center. Ballendorf had volunteered to make the trip on TIGHAR's behalf to see if he could learn anything from the survivors of the colony and their descendants.

Ballendorf and his colleague, Jul Hoehl, flew by small plane from the capital, Honiara, to the town of Ghizo and then traveled by canoe across the New Georgia Sound to the village. They were warmly welcomed by the village leader and Protestant pastor, Aberaam (Abraham) Abera, and were able to make interview arrangements, with Aberaam's daughter Teewa serving as interpreter.

None of the original colonists were still alive; most of the people in Nikumaroro Village today were children or infants when they left Nikumaroro Island. But a few people were old enough to recall stories that their elders had told them. Their collective articulation of past events was given, for the most part, by Teinamati Mereki, the most educated man in the village. He is a medical officer trained at the Fiji School of Medicine. Their method was to talk in their native dialect together after hearing a question from Ballendorf, and then Mereki would testify for everyone.[24]

Dr. Mereki, sixty-one years old, is the son of two of the original 1938 colonists. As transcribed by Ballendorf, he said:

> The few people here who remember Gardner all know the story of the skeletons that were found there. These skeletons were found, some say, laying side by side. They were of white people because they were wearing shoes. Some say they were not laying side by side. They said that one was a woman because it was smaller than the other. They were found, they say, in about this spot [points to Aukaraime South, but southeast of the shoe site and apparently on the ocean side]. The whereabouts of these skeletons now are not known. Nobody knows what happened to them [queries all those in the group; no one knows]. Some of the early people thought the skeletons were from the shipwreck.

Mereki said no one had knowledge of any airplane wreckage on Nikumaroro, though they knew there had been a wreck on Manra. Abera said the same thing, and also said he had heard of the bones. Both also commented on relations with the Coast Guardsmen at the Loran station, saying that there was no fraternization but that the Americans shared water with them when the village was short.[25]

One other resident gave Ballendorf direct testimony. According to Ballendorf's report:[26]

> [Erenite Keron was] more than sixty years old, but I don't know exactly how old I am. I was born on Gardner Island and went to

elementary school there. . . . I have heard the others talk about the bones that were found on the island, but I don't know anything about them. I never saw them. But I did see a ghost once on the beach near the lagoon. The ghost was that of a woman without a face. She came right up to me and I saw her. I told my mother about it, and other people. I saw this ghost only once.

Ghosts aside, here was the bones story again. Bones of a man and a woman, with shoes. Shades of Kilts. And on Aukaraime, albeit not specifically at the shoe site. The plot was thickening.

CHAPTER 13

The Skeptic and the Kiwis

Misstatements can do much harm to your credibility.
—RANDY JACOBSON TO RIC GILLESPIE, MARCH 1992

O
N MARCH 16, 1992, GILLESPIE MADE A PRESENTATION at the National Press Club in Washington, D.C. In the audience was an intrigued but skeptical Randy Jacobson. Jacobson has degrees in engineering sciences and oceanography, and a Ph.D. in earth sciences, as well as decades of experience in oceanography. At the time, he managed research programs in oceanography and related fields at the Office of Naval Research. (He has recently moved to Panama City, Florida, to work at a navy laboratory.) As he said in a letter introducing himself to Gillespie after the Press Club presentation, "My position demands a fair degree of skepticism and scientific rigor." An avid amateur historian, in part because of his father's role as a World War II fighter pilot involved in the shoot-down of Admiral Yamamoto, he was intrigued by TIGHAR's work, but unconvinced, and critical of what he regarded as sloppy thinking and even sloppier reporting. In his questions at the Press Club, and in correspondence thereafter, he raised questions about assumptions and picked at inconsistencies in reports of TIGHAR's work.

Gillespie was undaunted by Jacobson's challenges, and invited Jacobson to join the organization and the search. Jacobson has been TIGHAR's friendly critic and skeptic ever since, and promptly plunged into his own independent research. This included an investigation into the

Dr. Randall Jacobson (right) visists with Rick Gillespie (left) and Katie Henderson of the Airhearts (see p. 261). TIGHAR photo by Barbara P. Norris.

possibility that Earhart had landed on Winslow Reef, or another uncharted reef in the Phoenix Group (conclusion: very unlikely),[1] and a Monte Carlo simulation of possible flight trajectories for the Lae-Howland flight.[2] He developed a database of pertinent radio messages and transcripts, and managed to decipher many of Earhart's and Noonan's flight segments using their original navigational charts and their notations. One major result of this work has been to clear up a number of persistent myths about Earhart, and to clarify somewhat how she dealt with the public and government officials. Jacobson's research is the major basis for chapter 25.

Alone among the authors of this book, Jacobson has never been to Niku—evidence of his intellectual superiority, he sometimes modestly suggests. Acerbic, opinionated, and ever ready to engage in debate, he concluded early on that he and Gillespie, however much they enjoy arguing, would probably not complement each other in the field. Besides, he's an avid smoker, and TIGHAR doesn't allow smokers on its expeditions. The rest of us regret his absence, sometimes.

The Kiwi Survey

Jacobson's contacts around the world brought in some hard data on the hitherto rather mysterious 1938–1939 New Zealand survey on Nikumaroro. One of his colleagues in New Zealand, Dr. Alick Kibblewhite, offered to take a look in his country's national archives. Jacobson faxed him the information he needed in order to seek records on the survey, and Kibblewhite went right to work. He and archivist Brent Parker tracked down the expeditions' official report.

The "Kiwi Survey"—technically the New Zealand Pacific Aviation Survey—had been headed by Squadron Leader E. A. Gibson, who had prepared a brief official report.[3] Engineer's Assistant E. W. Lee had prepared a more detailed report focusing specifically on the survey's Nikumaroro work.[4] The survey team consisted of ten men, but its second in command, J. A. Henderson, was injured on arrival at Nikumaroro and had to return to New Zealand.[5] Their chartered ship, MV *Yanawai,* arrived at Nikumaroro on November 30, 1938, several weeks before Maude, Gallagher, and the first I Kiribati working party, and tied off to the stern of *Norwich City.* Unloading their gear across the reef was apparently something of an adventure, but with the assistance of the warship HMS *Leander,* which arrived the following morning, they got everything ashore by December 6 and set up camp. *Leander* and *Yanawai* sailed, and the Kiwis got to work.

The field conditions they reported sounded familiar.

[S]urvey work started on 8 December. For the first fortnight all the party found the excessive heat almost impossible to work in and the first work, which consisted of cutting stadia lines through the bush, was carried out in sweltering heat—up to 120 degrees—at a consequently slow rate of progress. After this period of acclimatization, however, better progress was made though the heat remained practically constant.

The Kiwis were on the island when Maude, Gallagher, and the PISS working party arrived on December 21, and reported their coming without comment. Lee summarized the team's work as follows:

The survey work consisted of traversing an area of about 200 acres at the northwestern corner of the island and static profiles were taken at five chain intervals from which a contour map has been prepared. The

The New Zealand survey party manhandling gear ashore past the bow of
Norwich City, 1938. TIGHAR Collection from Wigram Air Force Museum.

lagoon and later the coast were traversed and a plan of the entire island
has been prepared. . . . Upon completion of the preliminary investigations on the aerodrome site, runways were buoyed in the lagoon in
water clear of obstructions for a minimum depth of 2 fathoms.

Yanawai returned on January 30, and on February 5 Lee and his colleagues left for Fiji. Their conclusion was that the island was unsuitable for
aircraft operations, either as the site of an aerodrome on land or as that of
a seaplane runway in the lagoon.

For TIGHAR's purposes, what was interesting about the expedition was
what its members had done, where they had been, and what they had seen—and
how likely it was that they would have seen aircraft wreckage or other Earhart-
Noonan artifacts if any had been around. Their camp had apparently been on
Nutiran, and their maps, which were appended to Lee's report, indicated that
they had looked at the island in some detail. The maps were a bit deceptive, however, as indicators of how intensively they had inspected the place

As Lee reported, the contour map of the "aerodrome" site—Nutiran—
was based on survey lines cut through the scaevola at five-chain intervals.

The New Zealand survey party's camp was on the Nutiran shore. TIGHAR collection from Wigram Air Force Museum.

In land surveying, a chain equals sixty-six feet, so the Kiwi transects had been more than 300 feet apart. Considering that in heavy scaevola you can't see much more than three or four feet in any direction, this sort of spacing meant that airplane parts and ephemeral campsites could well have been missed. As for the rest of the island, their map was much less detailed—though extremely valuable because it showed the natural forest cover before any cutting had been done for coconut planting. Lee's report suggested that it was based on "traverses" around the lagoon and ocean shores. They had plotted coral heads and taken depth soundings in the lagoon, but in those pre-scuba days had presumably not done much visual submarine inspection. They had apparently not had a lot of free time; Lee's report stresses the difficulties they encountered with heat, limited water, and slow progress in general:

> It was for us a fortunate circumstance that the relief ship was put into quarantine as we were thus enabled to complete the fieldwork which must otherwise have been left incomplete.

Another paper that Parker supplied from the New Zealand Archives was a photocopy of a whole album of photographs—the originals, he said, were housed at the Royal New Zealand Air Force Museum—that were taken by expedition members. It took a good deal more digging, over several years, but eventually Gillespie got a good copy of the original album as well.

The photos in the album confirm that the party's camp was on Nutiran, just inshore from the *Norwich City*. They show that the *Norwich City* deteriorated considerably during their stay; early shots show her looking almost undamaged, but by the end of the expedition her funnel has gone away and her stern is corkscrewed and dipping over the reef edge. Several photos show the members of the PISS party—old friends such as Koata and Jack Petro. A couple of the photos show a lifeboat from the *Norwich City*. And one intriguing shot shows a scatter of what seem to be cans and other containers in the bush, and is labeled "Remains of wreck survivors' camp." Such a laconic reference could hardly be to the camp of the Electra's survivors; it must mean the survivors of the *Norwich City* disaster. This photo was to become much more interesting some years later, as would others from the Kiwi collection.

CHAPTER **14**

Back to the Windward Side

Scaevolin', Scaevolin'
Scaevolin's been my ru-eye-in;
I'll go no more Scaevolin'
With you, dull blade.[1]
        —TIGHAR TUNES

THE BAURO TIKANA, BEVINGTON-MAUDE, AND WAHGENA Island data all made Gillespie think that Aukaraime South was worth another close look—particularly since the shoe parts had been found so close to the end of the 1991 expedition that there hadn't been time for a very extensive investigation. So planning began for a substantial return expedition, scheduled for 1997. But Aukaraime South had some competition for TIGHAR's attention.

A Mysterious Clearing

While all the hypothesis formulation and testing had been going on—to say nothing of the claims and counterclaims—TIGHAR had also been steadily gathering basic information, wherever and whenever it appeared. Gillespie was able to find several important stashes of airphotos;[2] it was surprising how often the island had been visited, and flown over, both early in its colonial history and later. The *Colorado* flyers had taken a picture in 1937 and a plane from HMS *Leander* had made two images in 1938 when it was assisting in deployment of the Kiwi survey party. A plane from USS *Pelican* had shot

*Sung to the tune of "A-Roving," a traditional sea chantey.

Aerial photo of Nikumaroro's southeast end in June of 1941, taken by a U.S. PBY on an intelligence mission, and detail of the cleared area. TIGHAR Collection from U.S. National Archives.

enough images to make a photomosaic in 1939. In 1941 a U.S. Navy PBY had shot seven views, and in 1942 an Army Air Force plane had taken two. Charles Sopko, the Loran station's commanding officer, had taken two pictures while flying in or out of his station in 1944. Then there was a gap until 1953 when someone—we're not sure who—took eight shots, apparently for mapping purposes given their high quality and direct overhead vantage point. Then in 1975 ten pictures were taken by Roger Clapp's Smithsonian Institution team in a U.S. Air Force helicopter, and in 1978 at least one view was taken by Geomarex, a minerals exploration company. Finally, in 1988 Royal New Zealand Air Force patrol flights got five more images.

All these photos were helpful in a lot of ways. Some showed the Gallagher-era village and Government Station clearly, so Gillespie could correct the crude sketch-maps that King had made in 1989. Some showed the progression of buka-clearing and coconut planting—important because it was such clearing and planting that would have most likely revealed airplane wreckage, and because Floyd Kilts's story associated the bones discovery with coconut planting. And the 1941 photos revealed a peculiar pattern of clearing on Aukaraime North—the windward side—in the area where the '89 expedition had swept the beach edge with marginal results and the '91 expedition had searched in vain for the Evans-Moffitt water catcher. There was a funny clearing, shaped kind of like the number seven, but it appeared in photos from a number of different years and was apparently natural. What was more interesting was that in the 1941 photos it looked like a broad area had been cleared inland from the ocean shore, near the "top" of the seven-shaped clearing and extending about 300 feet toward the lagoon. In this area were a couple of dark spots that appeared rather rectangular, not like natural features.

The 1937 photo by one of the *Colorado* plane crews was also intriguing. Though it had a "North" arrow marked on it that pointed west, it clearly showed Aukaraime North, including the supposed location of the water catcher. Why had Lambrecht or one of his colleagues taken this particular picture? Was this where he saw the "signs of recent habitation"?

Jeff Glickman of Photek Inc. was willing to apply state-of-the-art forensic imaging techniques to the photos—Photek does a good deal of work for the intelligence community. His analysis indicated that the dark spots in the 1941 photo might well be large metallic objects.

The house built for Gallagher that Laxton mentioned? The water catcher? Parts of an airplane? Worth another look? Matching the old airphotos with newer ones, it was apparent that the cleared area—now, of course, overgrown by scaevola—was inshore from the locations searched in '89 and '91. Whatever had been there in the early '40s might still be there, and would almost certainly have escaped notice during the '91 fieldwork. But, of course, this location meant that finding anything would take a lot of heavy cutting, and it might not be there—or not be important if it was. Time on the island would be limited, as always, by the support ship's schedule, by available funding, and by the time people could take away from paying jobs. Gillespie was reluctant to spread the expedition too thin over too many objectives.

But how about a reconnaissance? The windward side project was a simple one in its way—one straightforward goal that could be achieved, he hoped, in a short time. In and out, see what's there, if anything. If there was something that looked important, then the '97 expedition could focus on it; if not, TIGHAR could leave the windward side alone and go after Aukaraime South and the village. Gillespie posed the idea to Joe Hudson of

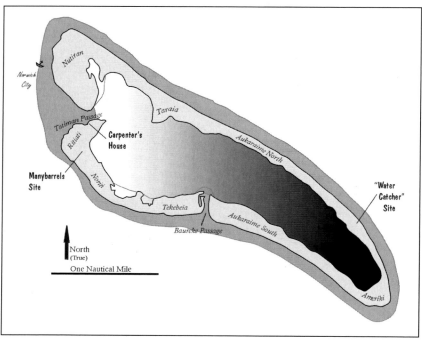

The 1996 expedition sought the water catcher on Aukaraime North, but also made discoveries in the colonial village.

Hudson Homes in Delaware, who agreed to put up the money for the reconnaissance trip.

So on January 29, 1996, a seven-person team sailed from Taveuni, Fiji, for Nikumaroro aboard MV *Matagi Princess II*. This time the team included the long-suffering Clauss, Fenlason, Matthews, Gillespie and Thrasher, and new recruits Don Widdoes and Joe Hudson, together with Kiribati customs agent Manikaa Teuatabo, back for more punishment. Four days later the *Princess* lay off the island.

In the 'Vola

Clauss and the ship's crew manhandled a launch through Tatiman Passage while the rest of the team reopened the "Gallagher Highway" from the landing site to the lagoon. Assembling there, the whole group motored down the length of the lagoon to the southeast end. Now for the scaevola.

It wouldn't do to just start hacking, though. So much scaevola, so little time. But as always, there was a plan. The two objects in the airphotos could be pretty securely located with reference to the width of the land—in other words, the searchers knew how far it ought to be from the lagoon to the ocean side near the objects, as opposed to everywhere else. So "all" that had to be done was to find the place where lagoon-ocean distances were right.

From John Claus's journal:

> To make a long story short . . . we finally got our charts somewhat straightened out—at least we know where our start points are and the measurements we took can be converted and laid on to a proper chart tonight. We cut transect lines approximately 150 meters each across the island. Scaevola all the way—it was brutal. Everyone sort of overdid it at one point or another. Just before lunch I had to force-drink a bunch of water and lay down and let my heart rate settle down. Veryl ran into the same problem in the afternoon. He came out of it too, after some rest. I barely touched my hand with my machete and sliced the knuckles. They bled pretty good but were okay after awhile. Joe recorded 108-degree temperature at one point. It was hot.

Hot, sweaty work, but by the end of that first day on the island the team had two transects cut, whose lengths approximated the width of the island in the neighborhood of the two strange images.

John Clauss communes with Scaevola on Aukaraime North. TIGHAR photo by Pat Thrasher.

Of course, one couldn't see more than about three feet into the masses of tangled greenery, so the next step was to open up the areas adjacent to the transects. They marked points at ten-meter (about thirty-five-foot) intervals along each transect, and then cut perpendicular lines into the 'vola at each of these points. Ten meters in, another cut was made perpendicular to the first, to create a "box" that could then be searched in detail.

Once again Manganibuka smiled, and after only about two hours the TIGHARs had found what they were looking for—though it wasn't quite what they expected.

The Catcher in the Scaevola

What they found was a steel tank three feet square and four feet high. It was painted white with the words "Police" and "Tarawa" dimly visible in blue. Inside and around it were six coconut shell halves—typical of drinking cups

The water catcher—a steel tank—and poles on the ground. TIGHAR photo by Pat Thrasher.

used throughout the Pacific. On the ground next to the tank were three wooden poles, each about six feet long, a few rusted scraps of corrugated metal, and the base of a light bulb. About ten feet away was a small tournefortia (*ren*) tree, at the base of which was a scatter of dry bird bones. In the other direction, about twenty feet away, was a hole about nine feet across and two feet deep. Lying at the bottom of the hole was a spent .30 caliber rifle cartridge. Between the tank and the shore there were a few pieces of fine copper screening, a brown button, a wooden stake, a can, a roll of asphalt siding, and a few other miscellaneous artifacts.

This closely matched the Evans-Moffitt description of the tank part of the water catcher, now too rusted-through to hold water, and with the canvas part gone, its supporting poles collapsed. The cartridge was consistent with an M-1 carbine like those carried by the Coast Guardsmen. In short, the site was almost certainly the one that Evans and Moffitt had observed, and it equally clearly represented one of the two mysterious airphoto images. With this location pinned down, it wasn't hard to navigate to the second image location, where there turned out to be the remains of a large dead buka—the only one in the neighborhood.

So Gillespie and his colleagues had found the water catcher, but it wasn't made up of Electra parts—Electras being very short on tarpaper and steel tanks attributable to the Tarawa police. Something built by the colonists, presumably.

"Turning the tip to return along the northern rim," Laxton had said, "narrow, thundering with surf driven by the northeast trade winds, the path ends in a house built for Gallagher on a strip of land cleared from lagoon to ocean beach so that the fresh winds blow easily through."

Houses need water, and the best way to get it on an island like Niku, especially in a place like the windward side, was to catch rain. So . . .

Funny place for a house, so far from the village. But nothing to do with Earhart, so the windward side and the Evans-Moffitt water catcher could be written off. With a few days left before the *Princess* had to sail, Gillespie decided the team might as well take another look at the village.

The Manybarrels Site

The objective in the village was to find Noonan's Tavern, but the watering hole continued to be elusive. Despite wishful thinking, it probably really had been eroded away by the 1990 storm. So the TIGHARs swung back to bushwhack their way through the residential area south of the Government Station and east of Sir Harry Luke Avenue. Here in a sort of clearing, Veryl Fenlason came upon a modest little house site with three fifty-five-gallon drums slowly relaxing into rust flakes—causing Russ Matthews to name it the "Manybarrels" Site. Here Gillespie noticed a couple of pieces of transparent plastic on the ground, but didn't pay much attention to them; after all, they weren't aluminum.

He showed them to Fenlason, however, who gently reminded him that the stuff wasn't entirely unlike what airplanes have in their windshields. Oops. The pieces were duly if unenthusiastically collected, along with a length of thin wire found nearby.

After a brief test excavation at the "Carpenter's Shop"—now collapsed by storms—the team boarded the *Princess* and sailed for Fiji. They were pleased at least to have found something they had gone out to find, a bit disappointed that it wasn't something left by the elusive flyers, mildly puzzled about what it *was*, and a bit relieved to have the windward side disposed of so the '97 expedition could focus on Aukaraime South.

Polymethyl Methacrylate

The artifacts from this trip to the village were a pretty paltry lot, but they needed to be analyzed, so off went the pieces of plastic from Manybarrels to the Winterthur Museum, not far from TIGHAR Central in Wilmington. Winterthur's analytical laboratory had agreed to perform compositional analysis. The two pieces were obviously from the same piece, matching neatly along a break; the larger piece was six by twelve centimeters (about two and a half by four and three-quarter inches), the smaller just a shard broken off the other.

Winterthur identified the stuff as polymethyl methacrylate. First marketed in Germany in 1927, it went into mass production in the United States in 1936 under the trade names "Plexiglass" and "Lucite." Roehm & Haas,

The plastic pieces from the Manybarrels Site in the village. TIGHAR photo by Pat Thrasher.

manufacturers of Plexiglass since the '30s, advised Gillespie that before World War II the material had been used almost exclusively in aviation and—tinted—in jukeboxes. During the war it was widely used in airplanes, for example in windows and windshields.[3]

So—most likely another airplane part. But it was better than that.

The piece of Plexiglass is an eighth of an inch thick, and it's curved. The curvature has to be original; to be formed, Plexi has to be heated to at least ninety degrees centigrade, far hotter than anything can get even in the sun on Niku. Gillespie compared the piece with the windows of every type of airplane known to have been in the neighborhood of Niku during the war. While some were curved, and some were an eighth of an inch thick, none were of that thickness and displayed the kind of curvature represented by the Manybarrels artifact. The curvature of the cabin windows in a Lockheed 10, however, exactly matched the artifact's curvature.

There was more. According to engineering drawings for the Lockheed 10, checked at the National Air and Space Museum, a change was specified in Part Number 40552—"Window Glass, Fuselage, Cabin"—on January 15, 1937. In this change, the thickness of the window was reduced from five-thirty-seconds of an inch to an eighth of an inch. It was at just this time that the cabin windows in Earhart's Electra were replaced and additional special windows were installed in preparation for the World Flight.

So the residents of the Manybarrels Site seems to have had a piece of Plexiglass that precisely matched the glass from Earhart's cabin windows, and didn't match the windows of any other airplane known to have been in the vicinity. They had apparently been cutting pieces out of it for use in some kind of handicraft; there are straight-sided cuts along the edges that look like places where rectangular pieces have been cut out. Perhaps they were making jewelry for family and friends, or maybe neat things to trade to the U.S. Coast Guardsmen.

The wire at Manybarrels was interesting, too. It turned out to be thin-gauge (about 0.5 mm) high-grade stainless steel wire, the strands twisted together in a manner typical of aircraft safety wire. Almost certainly another airplane part, though not necessarily from an Electra.

The Carpenter's Shop had also produced something: a couple of shielded cables consistent with those used on U.S. aircraft radio receivers. Connectors on their ends were made by the Howard P. Jones Company of Chicago. Known as "Part Number 101," they were first produced in the mid- to late 1930s and remained in use through World War II. Such connectors were used in some Bendix, Western Electric, and Sperry receivers.[4] Earhart used Bendix and Western Electric receivers, but of course, so did a lot of people.

Would It Take a Village?

It was beginning to look as if it had been a mistake to give the village such short shrift—to look around there only incidentally to looking elsewhere, or only when there was nothing else to do. TIGHAR now had eleven virtually certain airplane parts, at least two and perhaps four or five of which looked like Electra pieces, and they were all from the village. True, there was no intact airplane sitting there, and it was pretty certain that there never had been, but the people of the village had been getting airplane parts *somewhere*, and it looked like they'd been getting some of them from an Electra.

And just when the potential importance of the village was becoming clear, it turned out to be threatened—not only by the implacable forces of nature, but by the plans of humankind. Kiribati, said Teuatabo, was planning to recolonize the island.

From John Clauss's journal:

> It's pretty impressive how fast Nature has taken back this village. Right now you have to know there was a village there to be able to look around and figure out where things are or what they mean. The cistern, Gallagher's grave, and the house foundations are still there but they're deteriorating. This is a fairly fragile ecosystem. If the Gilbertese recolonize it, it will change everything. . . . I think we're coming to a time where we will lose what's left in evidence of AE. Most is already gone. But now that they are going to recolonize the island, things are really going to change—and forever. The problem for us is that we must come up with some kind of real plan and a way to approach the search. . . . If we had known what we know now in '89, we could have come up with a hell of a lot more.

But however fascinating the village, and however threatened,[5] it would take a major investment in serious archaeological survey to understand it, and meanwhile there was the "shoe site" at Aukaraime South. And maybe there was a way of shortcutting the search—finding the Electra without having to reconstruct it from parts found in the village.

CHAPTER 15

The Shattered Shores of Niku

Hey, Mister Ric Gillespie, sing your song for us.
One more time, we'll search the shattered shores of Niku.
Hey, Mister Ric Gillespie, sing your song for us.
*Through the buka and scaevola, we'll come following you.**
                              —TIGHAR TUNES

T HE 1997 EXPEDITION EVOLVED INTO A THREE-PRONGED attack—on Aukaraime South to look for more footwear (or whatever), on the village for plane parts (or whatever), and on the lagoon for (perhaps) the plane itself. The challenges inherent in going after the village led Gillespie to call back the world's second greatest expert on the archaeology of Nikumaroro (after Gillespie himself). It was—to King, at least—a gracious and much appreciated move. After only a little shuffling and mumbling, he agreed to be tossed into the briar patch. Hatchets were buried, goodwill was protested on both sides. Older and perhaps wiser, Gillespie and King took on another partnership.

Aukaraime International Airport

So, where was the Electra? Or more accurately, where had it been when—and if—the villagers had been scavenging parts from it?

*Sung to the tune of "Mister Tambourine Man," by Bob Dylan.

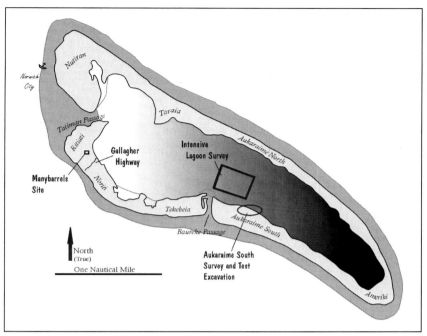

The 1997 expedition did archeological work in the village and at Aukaraime South, and detailed instrument and diving survey in the lagoon.

If Aukaraime South was where Earhart and/or Noonan had lost the shoes, and maybe left their bones, then it stood to reason the plane might have been nearby. At least, it stood as much to reason as any other proposition. And with this in mind, Gillespie noticed something peculiar about the landscape of Aukaraime South, just east of Baureke Passage.

It was flat, which was no big surprise—most of Niku is flat relative to, say, Montana. But it was *very* flat, and in all the airphotos that showed it, from 1939, 1941, 1953, and 1975, it was largely clear of vegetation. Just scattered scaevola, it looked like. It wasn't hard to see why this was so. It was low, and lay right alongside Baureke Passage, so it was regularly washed over by storm surges.

"Every time there's a nor'wester," Gillespie suggested, "the surf rolls right over this area and cleans it out, pushes everything into the lagoon."

"Like whatever's grown up in the interval since the last storm," King observed neutrally.

"And like any airplanes that are sitting around."

The fact that the area was so flat and clear, Gillespie argued, made it a likely place for Earhart to try to land. The same attributes would make anything parked on what, by now, they'd started calling "the runway," vulnerable to being washed into the lagoon by the same kinds of violent westerly storms that had destroyed the landing monument up on Ritiati.

"So if they land and leave it sitting out in the open," someone asked, "why don't the *Colorado* pilots see it?"

Gillespie had the answer to that one, in the map of the island drawn by the 1938–39 Kiwi expedition (see page 73). The map showed the distribution of vegetation, and at the west end of Aukaraime South it clearly showed the open area, bordered by buka forest on the east.

"You land on Niku in an aluminum plane. It's 110 degrees or so. Are you going to park it in the sun?"

"So you taxi up under the shade of the bukas . . ."

"And people flying over can't see you."

"Pretty dumb place to park it, then."

"Not really. They had no reason to expect an aerial search. There weren't any airplanes for thousands of miles, as far as they knew. They would have been watching the sea, looking for *Itasca*, and setting up signal fires, not leaving their plane out to be spotted by somebody they never expected to fly over."

"So the plane sits there long enough to be found by the colonists, and then washes into the lagoon?"

"Look at Gallagher's progress report for December 1940."

The second half of the quarter (just past) was marked by severe and almost continuous North-westerly gales, which did considerable damage to houses, coconut trees and newly planted lands. Portions of the low-lying areas of Hull and Gardner Islands were also flooded by high spring tides, backed by the gales, and, it is feared that many young trees have been killed.[1]

"So you're positing," King summarized, a bit pontifically, "that the airplane sat there from July 1937 until maybe late October 1940 and then the gales washed it into the lagoon. Which means that Bevington and the Gilbertese walked right past it."

"You've been there. You know that if you're a hundred feet from something, even in light scaevola, you're not going to see it."

An awful lot of "ifs" strung together, King thought, but he had no better ideas, and stranger things had happened. If a crab could deliver a shoe that seemed to match Earhart's, there was no telling what further weirdness might reward another trip to Niku. Besides, there would be no use trying to deflect Gillespie once he had seized an idea—even if there had been anything that seemed worth trying to deflect him toward. King gave a metaphorical shrug and penned a few lines to a well-remembered melody from his college days in San Francisco:

> *Though we know that Earhart's airplane burrowed deep beneath the seas,*
> *Flew off to the Pleiades,*
> *Or fell prey to Japanese sent out to chase her,*
> *We're ready yet to speculate on where it might have been,*
> *And from there, just where it went,*
> *Long scenarios to spin,*
> *To Hell with Ockham's razor!*
>
> *Hey, Mister Ric Gillespie, sing your song for us.*
> *Through the wildest of hypotheses we're following you.*[*]

Call in the Corps

Testing the idea that the plane had washed off the "runway" would involve looking in the lagoon, and the lagoon is not an easy place to look. About twenty to thirty feet deep, the lagoon has a soft, silty bottom that's easily stirred up; visibility tends to be bad and quite unpredictable. It's studded with coral heads, and besides all that it's big—more than two miles long, and more than half a mile wide.

But the Electra probably wouldn't have floated far, the reasoning went, so priority could be given to the area just northeast of the "runway" and Baureke Passage, and if we had a crackerjack team with good technology . . .

Kenton Spading is an engineer with a penchant for technology, and a stickler for detail. He works for the U.S. Army Corps of Engineers in chilly St. Paul, Minnesota. In 1991, he had run across an article in his local newspaper about fellow Minnesotan Veryl Fenlason's participation in the then-recent expedition that had bagged the shoe and the airplane skin. He

*Sung to the tune of "Mister Tambourine Man," by Bob Dylan.

Kenton Spading rigs a magnetometer for the lagoon survey. TIGHAR photo by
John Clauss.

immediately called Fenlason to get more information. Intrigued by the
Earhart mystery and impressed by Fenlason's dedication to the cause, he
quickly sent in his membership dues and volunteered for the next expedition.

Volunteering, of course, is not enough to get you a berth on an expedition to Nikumaroro; if it were, every trip would have to be made in a substantial tour ship. You have to take a TIGHAR-sponsored class in aviation
archaeology and get some U.S. field experience under your belt. Luckily or
not, Spading had plenty of time for both before the next major expedition.
He shivered (perhaps less than volunteers from more southerly climes)
through four ventures into the wilds of Newfoundland in search of *l'Oiseau
Blanc,* helped excavate a World War II bomber in Delaware not far from
TIGHAR Central,[4] and undertook extensive documentary research into
Nikumaroro's colonial history before being tagged as head of the Lagoon
team for Niku-97.

The '97 expedition would be the highest-tech fieldwork to date. The
Lagoon team was equipped with a Geonics electromagnetic (EM) sensor and

Lonnie Schorer maps the
Manybarrels Site. TIGHAR
photo by Tom King.

an underwater magnetometer. Spading and Fenlason would sweep the lagoon
bottom in the area northeast of the "runway," following a carefully controlled
search pattern to make sure they had covered all the ground. Tommy Love
and Van Hunn, a retired Air Force pilot and diver from Texas, would provide
eyes below the surface to supplement the instruments. A Geonics EM sensor
would also be used to sweep the neighborhood of the shoe site on Aukaraime
South, searching for subsurface anomalies in the earth's electromagnetic field
that might indicate graves, firepits, or rubbish deposits. A two-seat ultralight
aircraft, piloted by John Clauss and Veryl Fenlason, would provide an aerial
observation capacity never before available. The team would keep track of
where everything was, using a laser transit operated by new recruits Lonnie
Schorer of Virginia and Gary Quigg of Indiana, and a suite of Trimble Global
Positioning Satellite (GPS) units linked to a base station under the command
of Don Widdoes. All this would, of course, be in support of Mark-One
Eyeball survey—lots of clearing and ground inspection.

It would also be the most stylish expedition yet—all hands (except Clauss,
who resolutely stuck with grubby shorts, and Fenlason, who would not be

parted from his worn-out dress shirts) were outfitted for free by Willis and Geiger, a company that had supplied Teddy Roosevelt and many other explorers, including Earhart herself. Willis and Geiger went out of business shortly after the expedition; no one, thankfully, has suggested a causal relationship.

There were three targets. Search the Aukaraime South Site as carefully and broadly as possible. Search the lagoon northeast of Baureke Passage, in enough detail to be satisfied that there was nothing there worth seeing—unless, of course, there was. And finally, take a good hard look at the village, for the first time doing a really systematic, intensive surface survey and small-scale excavation. Intended targets in the village were the Manybarrels Site and the carpenter's shop.

The whole business would be documented by ABC News, which sent along producer Howie Masters and a film crew. To the delight of Niku '91 veterans, ABC's videographer was Sam Painter, laid-back but highly professional, who had been NBC's man on the island when the shoe was found. The sound man was Kenny Kosar—a short, enthusiastic surfing nut who brought his board along, despite everyone's insistence that surfing into the edge of Niku's coral reefs would be a real bad idea. He also had his mike, of course—a hand-held boom affair with a fat, fuzzy end. Everyone refrained (most of the time) from calling it what it really resembled, and just called it "Kenny's dachshund."

Customs agent Tonganibeia (Tonga) Tamoa would represent Kiribati. We'd travel aboard *Nai'a,* a handsome 110-foot motor sailor out of Suva. Gillespie would be in overall charge, King would be chief archaeologist but would focus on the village, with Kristin Tague specifically responsible for Aukaraime South.

The best-laid plans of mice and TIGHARs . . .

Cyclone Season Is Past

If you go to Nikumaroro between about early May and the end of October, you can be pretty sure of calm, trade-wind weather, but it's going to be really hot—like 110 degrees or so. You don't want to go between about November and late March because that's cyclone season. Cyclones are the same as hurricanes or typhoons, only they're in the South Pacific. What you want to do, Gillespie figured, is to sneak in between the rough weather—which thus far had pretty much been missed—and the high temperatures—which definitely had not. But there were also personal schedules to be accommodated, and the smart money in Fiji said that the possibility of a late season cyclone between Fiji and Niku was slight. So TIGHAR wound up with a late February–early March expedition.

From Tom King's journal:

> I'm sitting in the waist, starboard side, watching a thin yellow sunrise through scattered stratus clouds. Course looks to be NNE, and there are islands off the port and starboard bows, gray shadows with heads in the clouds.
>
> As yesterday afternoon progressed, Lonnie and I tried to figure out the laser theodolite—made some progress with Kent's help. Then, right on time at 1730, two bagpipers showed up, engaged by Ric to pipe us away. Under the bemused looks of the Taiwanese fishermen on their grimy tub across the dock, the lines were let go, the engine came to life, and the *Nai'a* backed out of her slip. With a (small) crowd on the dock waving enthusiastically, the pipers tootling, the fishermen scarfing rice and looking skeptical, and the ABC crew circling in a runabout shooting, we were off again to search the Phoenix Isles.
>
> We took a turn around poor old *Nomad,* tied off to an equally decrepit whaler at anchor in the harbor, awaiting the shipbreakers—or whoever dismantles old ships around here. "We had some good times on that fantail," John murmured. And then we headed out the channel.

Nai'a stood out of Suva Harbor on February 22. Fiji had been hit by a cyclone just weeks earlier, and the seas were still rough, but the people who knew about these things were pretty sure that the worst of the cyclone season was over. Excellent prospects for good weather, everyone figured, and an opportunity to beat the heat.

They were right about the heat, anyway.

Nai'a was a fine ship, with a great crew, including First Officer Ravai, a refugee from the poor, rusting *Nomad* and a captain in his own right. *Nai'a* shipped three captains on this voyage—one the regular captain, one for deep-water sailing, plus Ravai, but there seemed to be no arguments about the command structure. The ship's co-owner, Rob Barrel, was aboard as well, with his marvelous lady, Cat Holloway of Australia. Rob and Cat are both divers, and Cat is an expert in the marine biology and ecology of the area. She also turned out to be an accomplished songwriter, and proselytized tirelessly but with absolute futility for Vegemite, a tarlike substance commonly consumed on toast in the strange world of the Commonwealth. With an extra-heavy keel and sails that served more as stabilizers than as driving forces, *Nai'a* was fast, stable, and comfortable.

Which was a good thing, because the sea still showed the effects of cyclone season—rough and choppy. King found that accupressure bracelets kept his stomach under control; Clauss was less successful with a high-tech gizmo called "No Vomit" that sent pulses into his wrist. It didn't live up to its name. The real sufferer, though, was Gary Quigg, who just hadn't experienced anything like this in Indiana, and spent the voyage in his bunk. Gillespie and King promptly took advantage:

If you'd like to have a logical explanation
How he came upon this life of regurgitation,
He will tell you this is certainly no vacation,
It's the TIGHAR bunch,
Makes him lose his lunch.

Gary Indiana
Here in Oceana
Feed him a banana or a spot of Vegemite.
Then Gary Indiana
Gary Indiana
*Gary'll have to plan ta be up all night.**

After five rollicking days, the TIGHARs were once again in Niku's lee, as usual unable to find safe anchorage. And it turned out that this year, at this season, it wasn't really the lee. The usual prevailing northeast trades had been replaced by fitful squally winds from the west, and long rollers pounded the usually quiet southwest shore. The *Norwich City* had taken some heavy hits in the last few years; little was left but its huge expansion engines, sticking up off the reef like some strange abstract sculpture. But the birds, the surf, the trees, the beach, the dolphins, were all there as they had always been, and as everyone hoped they always would be.

From Tom King's journal:

The tide was high, so we hustled. Boats over the side—the New Zealand version of zodiacs, appropriately called Naiads—and ABC ashore first, then us,

---

*Sung to the tune of "Gary Indiana," by Meredith Wilson, from *The Music Man.*

clunking into the boats with our knives and canteens. Easy landing in the channel, now marked by white-painted cocos and a crude cairn near the base of Jack Pedro's shattered monument. Great feeling of anticipation, elation—handshakes on the boat and the beach. Sand on cheeks—Lonnie looked like she'd rubbed her face in it, and it stayed on all day.

The Lagoon team pushed, dragged, and walked a boat in through Tatiman Passage and drove it down to Baureke, where Spading and Fenlason began placing buoys to mark the corners of search blocks. The rest of the group made for Aukaraime South.

First, of course, it was necessary once again to open up the Gallagher Highway. As the team blundered along on their sealegs, hacking down branches and fronds, brushing away spider webs, Sam Painter drew first blood.

"Hey, here's some aluminum," he said laconically.

It was indeed, a little square-cut piece of aircraft aluminum lying in the midst of a field of debris—biscuit tins, fifty-five-gallon drums, pipes, the remains of a bicycle, a sewing machine. They named the place "Sam's Site," flagged the aluminum for later mapping and collection, and moved on.

As they neared the lagoon, they heard an airplane. An airplane? Everyone stopped cold, fell silent.

"Piston engines," Gillespie said. "Sounds like a twin."

"An Electra," somebody said. Nervous laughs. The engine noise passed overhead, its source out of sight beyond the coconut canopy, and faded away. Another minute, then a collective shrugging of shoulders, and back to the task of organizing to take on Aukaraime South. The "ghost Electra" lives on in TIGHAR folklore, though it was probably—well, maybe—a Royal New Zealand Air Force picket plane helping Kiribati enforce the Law of the Sea Treaty by nabbing pirate fishermen.

If I Only Had a Rake

At Aukaraime South, there was little to show that the 1991 work had ever happened, but thanks to the maps made at the time it was relatively easy to find the place where the shoe parts had been found.

From Tom King's journal:

We relocated the grave site and the shoe discovery location, and after much debate—well, first surveyed back west to Baureke, inspected the "runway" (no tire tracks), and came back along the lagoon shore for lunch. *Then* debated, decided to stake out a perimeter about four meters beyond the area cleared in '91, within which to work. This was Kris's suggestion, cutting through a lot of pointless dawdling and speculation about how shoes can move. Solid, sensible peasant stock, that Kris; much appreciated. She and I staked the perimeter while the others poked around. Flushed a coconut crab from its coco-fiber lined nest in a pile of fronds. It went up a tree and became an instant ABC star as Howie, Sam and Kenny prevailed upon it to do tricks.

After building a protected "office" out of green tarps (dubbed "the Green Room" by Kris), we spent much of the day pitching cocos and dragging fronds to clear the site. Well, Gary, Howie (who pitches in, as it were, like a trooper), Ric and I pitched while Kris filled up the canvas garden bags and dragged them away. Grist for her mill about us testosterone-soaked hackers and slashers and pounders of everything around us. Meanwhile Tommy and Lonnie tried in vain to locate the reference stake from which Russ surveyed the site in '91 (Never did find it, but nailed its location within about 50 centimeters by shooting back from the grave)—a frustrating but relatively low-impact activity. This left Lonnie, who had started the day looking like a Willis and Geiger fashion plate, still looking thus at day's end, while Kris looked like she'd been wallowing in rotten coconuts. Which, of course, she had.

Clearing the site of its dense litter of fronds and rotting coconuts took awhile, and was a rather self-limiting activity since it created huge piles of debris that had to be moved to clear more space. When an area about 2,000 feet square had been cleared, the bulk of the team laid out grids four meters on a side and began a close visual search of the surface. At the same time, Spading and Fenlason walked the EM over the site and plotted anomalies.

Nothing much showed up on the surface—a cluster of nails and a pair of Gillespie's gloves left from 1991, and a nondescript small washer. The EM revealed only two rather vague subsurface anomalies. King laid out one- by two-meter excavation units on these locations and began to dig.

Meanwhile, Spading and Fenlason had begun the lagoon search. This involved first setting up search "boxes," located with reference to fixed points on shore by Schorer with her trusty laser transit. Then Spading and Fenlason drove transects, up and down, back and forth, across each box towing the EM and magnetometer. Fenlason said that his long experience plowing fields on the vast plains of Minnesota equipped him well for steer-

Veryl Fenlason and Kenton Spading sweep Aukaraime South with an electromagnetic sensor. TIGHAR photo by Pat Thrasher.

ing straight, making sure the mag and EM swept the entire bottom of each box. Spading was amazed at his ability to hold a heading. Hunn and Love then followed up with visual survey, joined in the water by Rob Barrel and Cat Holloway from *Nai'a*, riding "manta boards" towed behind the boat. Despite everyone's best efforts, however, they found nothing but coral heads and silt, and one piece of steel chain that the EM sensed and the divers found—showing, at least, that the equipment wasn't malfunctioning.

Back at Aukaraime South, the test excavations had gone to sixty centimeters with no results whatsoever; it looked like the anomalies had been caused by filled in crab holes, or perhaps rotted-out tree stumps. The surface search went slowly—picking up every twig and leaf fragment by hand and dropping it in baskets to be carried away, then scanning the ground.

Quigg, quite recovered from the miseries of the sea voyage, and cheerful despite his subject, sang:

Test excavations at Aukaraime South mostly came up dry. TIGHAR
photo by Pat Thrasher.

> *I've spent hours on my knees,*
> *A-pickin' at the leaves,*
> *And thinkin' there's some mistake.*
> *When I find I am dreamin'*
> *Of a tool with tines a-gleamin,*
> *How I wish I had a rake.**

Using fingers rather than rakes was an effort to avoid disturbing shoe
parts, of course, but as it turned out this was no problem—there wasn't a
piece of leather or rubber to be seen. No bones, either, and no rings,
watches, or bracelets inscribed "To Amelia with love from George."

Just a little charcoal—little flecks here and there. Tague and Gillespie
dug and screened a series of shovel test pits[3] across the site to see if they
could trace its distribution and find a concentration. No luck.

*Sung to the tune of "If I Only Had a Brain," by E. Y. Hasburg and Harold Arlen,
from the *Wizard of Oz*.

Gary Quigg plots artifacts at Manybarrels. TIGHAR photo by Tom King.

Aluminum Everywhere

Deciding to leave Aukaraime South to sit for a time while they thought about it, the team shifted attention to the village. This was at least more rewarding—there was *lots* of stuff. They cleared Manybarrels of fronds and nuts, and swept it with metal detectors. Schorer and Quigg located each "hit," and each visible artifact and feature (house foundation, cookhouse charcoal pit, and so on), with the laser transit; Gillespie, King, and the rest of the team troweled to expose whatever the metal detector had detected, recorded what they found, and collected whatever looked like it might have anything to do with an airplane—and some stuff that didn't, but that they just weren't sure about. Lots of aluminum, all in small pieces, usually more or less rectangular, cut from larger pieces with tin snips or maybe a machete. Some pieces were in an area more or less between the house—marked by the remains of a stone-lined platform—and the dense charcoal and bone deposit left by the cookhouse. With one of the aluminum pieces were pieces of pearl shell and a glass bead. It looked like someone at Manybarrels had been making handcrafts with aluminum decorations.

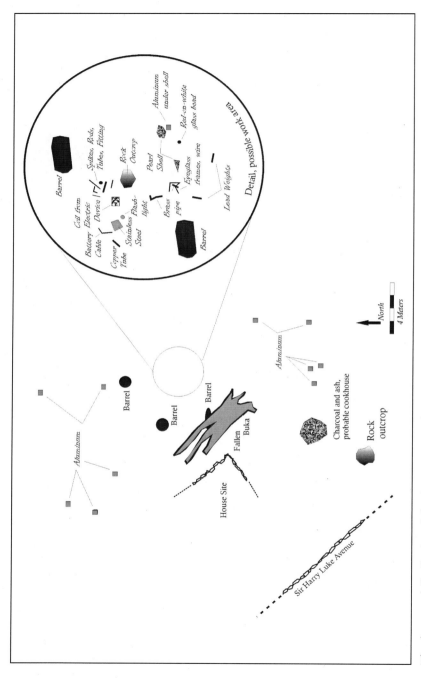

The shapes and distribution of aluminum pieces at the Manybarrels Site indicate that they were probably being used in handicrafts.

Walking back and forth from the landing each day, people kept seeing aluminum along the Gallagher Highway and on Sam's Site, so Schorer, Quigg, and King spent some time mapping, locating, recording, and collecting there. Quite a bit more aluminum, some of it in pretty big pieces, a lot of little pieces, and a few other items that looked like they might be aircraft-related.

The weather was a lot cooler than usual, and the seas a bit higher—high enough, in fact, that the Flying TIGHARs couldn't get the ultralight over the side and into the water to take off. This was a disappointment, though every evening the collective wisdom was that tomorrow would be calmer and the Clauss-Fenlason aircrew would be able to fly. Otherwise life settled into the usual Niku routine. Nights were spent aboard *Nai'a,* with the usual evening meetings and time for note-writing—together with dinners to which Gillespie decreed that all males must come shaved and bathed. Dinner was often accompanied by off-key renditions of whatever ridiculous songs Quigg, Gillespie, King, Holloway, or others of musical bent had thought up to commemorate the day's events. Off to the island by Naiad in the sunrise, and days spent tossing coconuts, hauling fronds, picking over the ground, bobbing about in the lagoon with sensors and divers, digging test pits, making maps. Back to the ship as the sun set in the glory that's reserved for day's end at sea.

It was a bit odd to be taped full time by the ABC crew, and Masters— who joined Love and King in a sunrise kaffeeklatsch every morning aboard the ship—had fascinating stories to tell about his adventures around the world. The "ABCs" were careful not to get in the way—though some team members grumbled when they found "Kenny's goddam dog" stuck in their faces while dragging fronds or tossing nuts. Masters was intent on not influencing the direction of research, and Gillespie voiced his appreciation:

We're uninvolved observers.
Forget that we are near.
Just go about your business,
But do it over here!

Wait for the camera,
Wait for the camera,
Wait for the camera,
And we'll see what we will see.[*]

[*] Sung to the tune of "Wait for the Wagon" (adapted from a traditional folk song), in *How the West Was Won,* score by R. Bishop Buckley.

CHAPTER 16

Harassed by Hina, Favored in Funafuti

I've just seen a wave
Crash on a reef
Who's gonna save
Me from that skiff
It's gonna sink
And I will fly
Into the drink
As sharks swim by
Ooh ooh ooh when's high tide?[*]
                    —TIGHAR TUNES

Cyclone Season Is Not Past

Then the rains began, and Barrel said that a late-season cyclone, named Hina, was forming up east of Fiji. The seas got higher and rougher; it was never calm enough to get the ultralight over the side for takeoff, so the air force was permanently grounded. The navy wasn't doing real well, either; getting on and off the island each day became trickier and more dangerous. Barrel usually piloted the Naiad rubber boat, with the mighty Felipe Kamakorewa, able seaman,[1] giving hand-signal directions from the bow. Rob had to choose his wave just right for the run-in up the channel, and

*Sung to the tune of "I've Just Seen a Face," by John Lennon and Paul McCartney.

176

Felipe had to be precise in his warnings, to avoid smashing against the rocky channel's end or being swamped by the returning surf. At the end of the channel the team members would all pile out onto the coral and struggle ashore, while Barrel spun the boat around and found the right wave to ride back out.

Things were getting depressing. Yes, they were finding aircraft aluminum, but nothing that shouted "Electra," and some pieces shouted "Not." Zinc chromate paint, not found on the Electra. Rivets flush with the surface—the Electra's rivets were not flush. And nothing at Aukaraime South, nothing in the lagoon, the divers getting tired of bouncing off coral heads.

The crew threw a party on the beach—steaks, fish, chicken, taro, bananas, yongona, beer, and music. As everyone relaxed, the waves grew higher and higher. Clauss sidled up to King.

"I don't think we're going to get ashore tomorrow."

"You might be right. What are you thinking?"

"Maybe some of us should stay ashore tonight—get some work done . . ."

Clauss and King had wanted to stay ashore overnight ever since 1989—experience the island at night, get a better feel for the place. But there had never been an excuse. Now there was—let at least a few people not waste a day rolling around on the ship—and there was leftover food and beer. With surprising (to King and Clauss) ease, Gillespie agreed, and asked for volunteers. In the end Clauss, King, Quigg, and Schorer, who came to call themselves "the sand people," stayed ashore for a rather magical two days and nights.

Sunrises over the lagoon and sunsets over the storm-tossed sea. *Nai'a* coming in with the morning sun after a night spent drifting, white and gleaming like a great sea bird. Bathing in the lagoon, sleeping on a mat by a beach fire. Munching cold steaks and tossing back warm Fiji bitter beer. Gamboling on the beach at night, with phosphorescence flying around the feet. And working, too—finishing most of the testing and surface inspection at Aukaraime South, mapping in the village, observing how the high seas affected water levels in the lagoon, and as it happened, rescuing some pretty pricey equipment.

From Tom King's journal:

Aboard *Nai'a*, the stranding of four ashore had apparently been whipped up into a major crisis. ABC was on the bridge, taping the worried leader receiving situation reports from his beleaguered troops.

Ric: "Shore party, please advise as to your condition."

Nai'a stands in to check
on the "stranded" island
team. TIGHAR photo.

Me: "Shore party to *Nai'a*. Never better. Happy as clams. Getting lots
done. Interesting experiences. Lots of water, food's getting low, beer's gone.
Would appreciate a resupply when possible."

Ric: "I read you in good condition but needing food."

Me: "Yeah, but no big deal. Tomorrow night we'll be catching crabs,
but . . ."

At that moment there was a shout from down the beach where waves
were beginning to shove up under the $40K GPS base station. John, Lonnie,
and Gary were lifting cables to keep them dry, but it was apparent that the
thing would soon be underwater.

Me: "Uh, *Nai'a*, shore party, be advised that the base station's about to
get real wet. What do you want us to do?

Ric: "Let me check with Don. There may be some shut-down procedure."

Five minutes later:

"*Nai'a*, shore party. Be advised that we've lifted the whole station up
and are holding it in the air awaiting your direction."

Waves were now breaking over our knees. The twenty-foot antenna whipped in the wind. Don eventually got on the line and began detailed unplugging instructions. After awhile . . .

Me: "You're basically saying unplug everything from everything else and drag it up the beach, right?"

Don: "Right."

Me: "Got it. Shore party out."

The near loss of the base station drove home an unwelcome fact. The situation was becoming plain dangerous, not just to equipment but also to people. Hina was moving, and it looked like she was going to slip in between Niku and Fiji, blocking *Nai'a*'s escape. And at the island the rain was intensifying, the waves getting bigger. Every trip in and out was an adventure.

We got swells,
We got waves.
There is nothing to do but be brave.
Starting here,
Starting now,
*Honey everything's coming up coral.**

Barrel and Gillespie conferred and decided it was time to start packing up. One last day at Aukaraime South, Tague insisted they drop a shovel test pit in the exact middle of the 1991 shoe site. Voila! Just a few centimeters down, a concentration of wood ash and charcoal. They troweled around it and then removed the whole block of coral rubble, sand, ash, and charcoal into plastic bags to be taken back for analysis. Screening around the edge, Tague found a tiny piece of paper with printing on it. What was this? Carefully pressed like a leaf between sheets of dry paper, it went back to the ship.

Taking a break, Spading, Quigg, Schorer, and Gillespie went for a short walk to the east to see what the next clearing held. They found some mounds of sand and coral rubble next to holes in the ground. Were they the mounds of rubble that Maude had mentioned in his letter to King, or the

---

*Sung to the tune of "Everything's Coming Up Roses," by Stephen Sondheim and Julie Styne, from *Gypsy*.

remains of clearing and coconut planting in the 1940s? No time to find out—another end left loose.

One last day in the village, mapping between Manybarrels and Sam's Site in drenching rain. A property marker on the edge of Sir Harry Luke Avenue showed that Manybarrels was on either Ritiati parcel 15 or 16, which Laxton's 1949 memo and map showed had been assigned respectively to Teng Banibai and Nei Tebea and to Teng Maraki and Nei Kantaraa.[2] It was nice to have names for the people responsible for the place, but Laxton provided no further data on them.

From Tom King's journal:

We wore life vests for the first time—even Felipe, which Rob said made him "somewhat concerned." We roared up the channel on the back of a swell and nosed in to the port side. John, Gary and I disembarked to port and got out safely. Lonnie, going over the starboard bow, went into the channel and began being sucked under the boat. Ric jumped in after her and went into a hole.

"Rob," Lonnie called over the roar of the surf and the engine. "I don't think I can hold on."

"Felipe," Rob asked politely, "please pull Lonnie out."

Which Felipe willingly did, with one of his huge arms, passing her bodily to John, who put her on her feet with the rest of us. Then he did the same for Ric, who had a nasty coral cut on his knee.

We stumbled ashore and watched Rob and Felipe, and Sam, who'd come along to film, successfully negotiate the exit over a half dozen white-cresting swells. Lonnie bandaged Ric with sodden Band-Aids from the sand people's erstwhile camp, and we got on with the sad business of packing up and out.

Gear, artifact bags, the bagged-up ash and charcoal from Aukaraime heaved into boats; gunning down the channel and up the wave front, cresting it and out. Up Nai'a's pitching ladder and underway, with everything piled on the deck in disarray. The Sand People and Holloway lined the taffrail, watching the island fall astern under lowering clouds, wondering if they'd ever see it again. Painter and Kosar tried to record the poignant moment. King growled.

"Get your goddam dog out of my face, Kenny."

If the rest of the team felt rotten about fleeing, once again without anything that felt like a smoking gun, Gillespie felt *really* rotten. But he flipped the island the bird, assured it he'd be back, and retired to the saloon to gaze

We got swells. Rob Barrell pilots a Naiad out the channel as Cyclone Hina approaches. TIGHAR photo by Tom King.

moodily out at the growing swell and increasing whitecaps. *Nai'a* and her several captains tried to outrun the storm.

They failed. Three hours out, as several of the team members worked securing gear in the ship's waist, a strange vacancy appeared off to starboard—like the world ending in a sort of gray, fast-moving mist. A white squall—a violent little patch of wind holding tons of water in suspension—rushed at the ship with Electra-speed.

From Tom King's journal:

> The squall hit, Rob estimates, at over fifty knots, pushing a solid wall of rain. *Nai'a* took it on her starboard bow with thrice-reefed mainsail and no jib,[3] going over on her beam ends but saved, Rob says, by her extra-heavy keel. We were all instantly soaked, and tumbled into the saloon pushing and pulling the gear that remained in the waist. Ric was peering moodily out the window, with the *Indiana Jones* theme on the CD player. He barely acknowledged our—or the squall's—arrival.

If Gillespie was depressed, he—and everyone else—would get a lot more so in the days to come. Hina was coming, and they weren't going to outrun it to Fiji. After a day trying to fight steadily rising wind and seas, Barrel altered course to the west, running for the atoll lagoon at Funafuti.

Three days then of twenty-, thirty-, forty-foot seas, walls and sheets of rain, lightning, thunder. Impossible to feed anyone, hardly possible to move around the cabins, no one allowed on deck. But finally the seas began to calm, and *Nai'a* picked her way through Funafuti's reef into the sheltered lagoon of the capital of Tuvalu, formerly the Ellice Islands.

Serendipity was waiting. King, Thrasher, and Quigg found seats on the Air Marshall Islands flight to Fiji the day of their arrival, but the next day the airplane broke and air service was cut off pending its repair. It was a couple of days before the seas quieted down enough to let *Nai'a* safely get underway. The ocean wasn't all *that* quiet, however, and after contemplating the prospect of several days bouncing around on it some of the team members put their faith in the return of Air Marshall Islands. This faith was misplaced; as it turned out they arrived in Fiji at almost the same time as *Nai'a* did, with Clauss, Schorer, and Tague tanned and happy after a pleasant crossing. However, stranding on the shores of Funafuti turned out to be another of those fortuitous circumstances that makes it seem, sometimes, like Nei Manganibuka takes care of foolish Americans.

There's not much to do in Funafuti if you aren't either part of the community or deeply interested in drinking Foster's and shooting pool in the Vaiaku Lagi Hotel. So Gillespie and Spading began asking around to see if anyone there had ever lived on Nikumaroro. It wasn't long before they found themselves talking with Risasi Finikaso, manager of the very hotel where they had tired of tipping warm beers. Ms. Finikaso, it turned out, had been born on Nikumaroro in 1959. Not only that, she said; she was also regarded, and regarded herself, as the granddaughter of Nei Manganibuka.

The Wing on the Reef

Ms. Finikaso had been just a toddler when Niku was abandoned, but she had a somewhat older friend who had also lived on the island, and whose father—the schoolmaster in the late '50s—was also alive and living on Funafuti. With Ms. Finikaso's introductions and help, Gillespie and Spading were soon interviewing Pulekai Songivalu, the former schoolmaster. Mr. Songivalu was somewhat older than seventy in 1997.[4]

Gillespie and Spading had talked with Ms. Finikaso about what TIGHAR was interested in, so there was the danger that she—and through her influence

Songivalu—could be tempted to tell his interviewers what they thought they wanted to hear. The two TIGHARs were alert to signs of this kind of influence, and tried to avoid it by not asking direct questions about airplanes or bones on the island. They asked more general questions, and questions about other things, exploring to see what their interviewees would volunteer.

The interview took place in the main room of Songivalu's house, a modest island home with a corrugated steel roof. After establishing when Songivalu had arrived on Niku and what he had done there, Gillespie (with Spading taking notes) turned to questions about fishing, to see if anything would come out about the use of aircraft aluminum for lures, or control cable for line. It didn't. Next he prospected for knowledge of stories about the early days of the colony.

Pulekai Songivalu was a teacher on Nikumaroro in the 1950s. TIGHAR photo by Kenton Spading.

Songivalu: The old men would tell stories. They had no houses when they first arrived. There was lots of hard work and lots of sunshine. The sunshine could last as long as six months.

Gillespie: Do you mean a drought?

Songivalu: Yes, a drought.

Gillespie: Did they have a hard time finding water?

Songivalu: Yes.

Gillespie: [trying the direct approach] Did you hear any stories of bones being found when the land was being cleared?

Songivalu: No.

Oh well. Back to fishing lures for a while, and then to canoe travel among the Phoenix Islands. While on the subject of other Phoenix Islands, Gillespie asked if he had ever heard of an airplane crash on Manra. Songivalu looked thoughtfully at the 1943 map of Nikumaroro that Spading had spread out in front of him. "No, but I saw pieces of an airplane on the lagoon side."

Whoops! But airplane pieces in the late '50s? Gillespie asked where he'd seen them. Songivalu studied the map intently, and then indicated the point that sticks out into the lagoon right across from Tatiman Passage—Taraia.

Songivalu went on to say that the wreckage had appeared to be old, that people had made "plates and other things" from it, and . . .

> I think maybe it was a plane from Canton, I am not sure. I am trying to think of why it was there. I think the plane ran out of oil, or gas, maybe. They said the pilot was saved though. The people looked after him. I asked, "Where was the pilot taken?" They said he was taken by the Americans on a ship.

Huh? In its reference to the pilot being taken care of by the people, and the plane having come from Canton, this sounded a lot like the Manra crash, though of course in Knudson's account the pilot hadn't survived that one. Gillespie went on to explore how people used metal in cooking fish, and was puzzling over where to go next, when Ms. Finikaso, who had been in the next room, came in with Songivalu's daughter, Tapania Taiki. Ms. Finikaso later told Spading and Gillespie that when they had arrived, Ms. Taiki had been too shy to come into the main room and meet them. So Ms. Finikaso had asked her two questions. Ms. Finikaso insisted that these were the only questions she had asked, and that she had given no indication of what a "correct" answer might be:

Tapania Taiki remembers a wing on the reef. TIGHAR photo by Kenton Spading.

Ms. Finikaso: Have you ever heard of an airplane wreck on
Nikumaroro?
Ms. Taiki: Yes.
Ms. Finikaso: Have you ever heard of skeletons on Nikumaroro?
Ms. Taiki: Yes.

At this point Ms. Finikaso had become more insistent that Ms. Taiki talk with Spading and Gillespie, and Ms. Taiki had finally agreed. The conversation now went like this:

Gillespie: When did you arrive on Nikumaroro, how old were
you?
Ms. Taiki: I arrived there in 1958 or '59. I was five or six years old.
Gillespie: Can you tell us what you saw on the reef?
Ms. Taiki: I saw a piece of airplane wing on the reef. I could see
the ship wreck from there. It looked far away.
Ms. Finikaso: I suppose it would look far away to a child.
Gillespie: Can you show us where you saw it?
Ms. Taiki: [looking at the map] It was along here somewhere
[pointing to an area along the Nutiran reef about
halfway between Tatiman Passage and Norwich City].
Gillespie: What color did you say it was?
Ms. Taiki: [pointing up at the exposed bottom of the dull, silver-
colored corrugated steel roof on the house] It was
that color only much thicker. There were also a few
other pieces of things laying around on the reef. It
was not complete.
Gillespie: You also mentioned skeletons. Can you tell us about
that?
Ms. Taiki: The older people said they saw the skeletons of a man
and women, one each, the elders said, "Do not go to
where the plane is, there are ghosts there." They were
trying to scare us to keep us away from there.

She also said that other people had interest in the wreckage. A good deal of conversation followed, in which Ms. Taiki said there had been a "European style" house not far from the wreckage, that she and her friends used to play with the wreckage despite the warnings of their elders.

Ms. Taiki: Some white people came once in a government boat. They were taken in canoes to here [tracing a path with her finger from the village area across Tatiman Passage along the shore toward *Norwich City*] to take pictures of the airplane parts.

Spading: What did they take the pictures with?

Ms. Taiki: A camera.

With that established, it was time to hightail it to the airport.

CHAPTER 17

After the Storm

Without corroboration, the stories we heard on Funafuti are no more credible than are the tales told about the lady flier held prisoner on Saipan.

—RIC GILLESPIE[1]

Corroboration—of a Sort

Well, it was only anecdotal, but still, for the first time TIGHAR had living people who had lived on the island, saying they had seen airplane wreckage in specific locations—at Taraia and on the Nutiran reef. There was the peculiar stuff about the surviving pilot, and about the white people taking pictures.

But still . . . anecdotes are interesting, but they're good only for hypothesis formulation; they're not truth. Back at TIGHAR Central, Gillespie began to see if there was a way to corroborate—or disconfirm—the Funafuti stories.

He had good airphotos taken of the island in 1953. Gillespie reasoned that if there was really airplane debris on the reef flat in the late 1950s, it might have been there in the early '50s as well. So it was back to Jeff Glickman of Photek.

Using his state-of-the art digital imaging system capabilities, Glickman examined the images of the Nutiran reef flat. He could make out four objects that met the qualifications for being aluminum debris—light color, small size, linear orientation as though part of a distributed debris field, and presence in at least two photos to ensure that they didn't represent flaws in an image. Moreover, one of the light-colored objects exhibited the type of glint normally seen only from sunlight shining on metal.[2]

Glickman next examined the adjacent shoreline for any sign of airplane wreckage. No detailed photography was available of the Taraia shore, but on the Nutiran shore a 1988 aerial photo taken by the Royal New Zealand Air Force showed another reflection suggesting the presence of shiny metal—this time of a rounded, perhaps even capsular, shape. This photo didn't show anything on the reef that looked like aluminum.

So, something that might have been aluminum on the Nutiran reef in the '50s, gone by the late 1980s, but then something suspicious back in the bush. Which just might still be there. Something to think about, but not enough to justify another trip just yet.

The Stuff from the Expedition

Tommy Love performed a microscopic scan of a soil sample from what King noncommittally called "the Aukaraime burn feature" with negative results— nothing of interest. Cultural Resource Analysts of Lexington, Kentucky, ran

Lonnie Schorer catalogues artifacts from the village at the University of Maryland. TIGHAR photo by Tom King.

a much larger sample through flotation separation—pouring the soil through agitated water that causes material to sort out according to specific gravity, thus separating out the big stuff from the little, the heavy from the light. King then went through each fraction with a myopic eyeball, finding nothing but charcoal. So something had burned on Aukaraime South, right around where the shoe fragments had been, but were the shoes associated with the fire, or was it all coincidence? When had the fire burned, and why?

We're sometimes asked if we couldn't have gotten a radiocarbon date on the feature—if we couldn't have had some of the charcoal reduced to gas and its radioactive carbon 14 content determined, which is a measure of age. The answer is, it wouldn't have done us any good. Radiocarbon age determination isn't fine-grained enough to distinguish between something that lived thirty years ago and something that lived sixty.

The charcoal *could* be used—maybe—to find out what kind of wood had burned in the fire, and that might indicate something of its age. If it was coconut palm, then it would almost have to have burned after Aukaraime South was planted with coconuts in about 1941. If it was something else—well, then maybe the fire burned earlier. But there wasn't very much charcoal, and it was in tiny pieces. Biologist Rachel King (Tom King's older daughter) at the University of Miami in Florida examined a small sample and said she thought it resembled a dichot—that is, not a palm—but she needed a larger sample. Looking at *all* the charcoal sorted out by the flotation technique, she concluded that it was mostly from monocots—the huge division of the plant world that includes palms. This didn't look much like charcoal from a pre-1941 fire.

But then there was that little piece of paper that Kris Tague had found screening around the burn feature. When a color photo of this little scrap was blown up to about ten times actual size, things could be seen on it—letters spelling out "ROWER PRODUCE" and some kind of a tropical scene with what looked like banana leaves in the foreground. "Grower Produce"? A label, maybe off a vintage can of bananas? Something Earhart would have had as emergency supplies aboard the Electra? Maybe. TIGHAR launched an extensive search for produce companies to whom the apparent label might mean something. There's a Grocery Hall of Fame in Canada and a Museum of Packaging and Advertising in England with extensive comparative collections, and people who specialize in historic tin cans, but no one recognized the Aukaraime label.

Then at an Earhart search symposium at the Hiller Museum in California, TIGHAR member Walt Holm noticed, way down in a ragged corner of the scrap, something that looked an awful lot like a bit of a bar code. Research by Holm, Bob Perry, and Vern Klein showed that this was exactly what it was, and that bar codes have been around only since the early 1970s. Whatever the can label was, it hadn't arrived on the island in the 1930s. That meant the burn feature probably didn't have anything directly to do with Earhart. In 1978, a government survey party had inspected Aukaraime South and other parts of the island, in support of planning for another settlement attempt (which didn't happen).[3] It didn't seem likely that a member of this all-male, I Kiribati party would have been wearing a woman's shoe from the 1930s, or even a small, narrow man's shoe. But perhaps the shoe had been lying around in the deadwood on the ground, and as a result had been thrown into the fire. One could dream up lots of possibilities, but none of them featured Earhart and Noonan scarfing the contents of a bar-coded can.

If anything, 1997 at Aukaraime South had raised more questions than it had answered—and most of them still aren't resolved. Why were the remains of a fire that must have burned in the 1970s and the remains of a 1930s-vintage shoe in the same location? Why had so much of the shoe been found in 1991, and never a vestige of it in 1997? Had the shoe—and the heel of the other one—walked in, or floated, drifted, or been dragged by crabs—from someplace else? If so, where, and how had it wound up in the fire? Or did it?

All that aluminum from Manybarrels and Sam's Site didn't turn out to be very informative either. Ultrasound scanning by systems engineer Tony Mucchiardi showed that the collection of aluminum fragments broke down into two general groups based on their internal structure. It looked like one group represented parts of airplanes, while the other was made up of nonaircraft stuff—parts of mess trays, for example, doubtless from the Loran station. Of the aircraft aluminum some was clearly not from an Electra—it had the wrong kinds of rivets, for example, or was painted with zinc chromate. Other pieces could have been from an Electra, or could have been from any other airplane. No smoking guns. A brass casing from some sort of instrument, found at Sam's Site, turned out to be the remains of a nautical barometer, or perhaps a chronometer. Built by the famous English instrument makers Negretti and Zambra, it was probably off *Norwich City*. A fire extinguisher briefly gave King a start because it resembled those recorded in the inventory

Most of the aluminum pieces from the village had been cut into small squares. A few had been made into combs. (Scale in centimeters.) TIGHAR photo by Tom King.

taken after the Luke Field crash as being aboard the Electra, but it turned out to be different—probably from the Loran station. Lots of stuff, some of it intriguing, none of it identifiable as being from the Electra.

The Bookcase Bombs

Meanwhile, the navigator's bookcase had become very shaky as a possible addition to an Electra. Remember that its consolidated part number was 28F4023; the "28F" part meant that it was built for a PBY flying boat. In trying to identify some of the other pieces of aluminum, Gillespie noted that artifact number 2-2-V-8—a rather heavily reworked four-inch square of heavily corroded aluminum—had a faint design that appeared to be a part number, most likely 32B 108. The style of the numbering looked like the number on the bookcase. Model 32 was the B-24 Liberator, PB4Y-1 series; B meant a structural component of the fuselage. Trying to nail down the part's identity— in which he never succeeded—Gillespie went through a B-24D/PB4Y-1 parts catalog, and kept running into parts numbered "28F," that is, parts desig-nated for installation in a PBY. Most of the items were interior furnishings, doubtless adapted to their new use in the efficiency bred of war.

"Oh, my God," Gillespie says he thought, "I wonder if . . ."

On through the catalog, and there it was: 28F4023 "Box—Navigator's book and paper storage." Following up at the National Archives, he found a photo showing a navigator's bookcase identical to the Niku case—fasten-ers, mounting holes, the works—mounted in a B-24. The bookcase, once so promising, had to be abandoned as an Electra association.[4]

The Other Airplane

So what about that B-24 that seemed to be responsible for so much or the alu-minum in the village? Research by TIGHAR member Craig Fuller finally turned up the identity of the "four-engined airplane" that Knudson's 1964 paper said had gone down on Manra. It turned out not to have been a B-24—or four-engined at all—but a two-engined C-47A. Its crash was a story in itself.[5]

The plane, with a four-man crew headed by Army Air Force Second Lieutenant William Prater, had arrived on Canton Island in November 1943, where it stopped for repairs to its wing tip. It took some weeks to get the repairs done, by which time Prater and his crewmates were probably pretty bored.

Pilots were allowed to take their aircraft out on local flights with little formality, and jaunts to Manra and Orona—said to be interesting to look at—were not uncommon. On December 17, Prater and two of his crew, together with visiting USO entertainer Bob Ripa and five other would-be tourists, took off on such a jaunt.

The only recorded first-hand account of what happened next was later provided by Manra's native magistrate:

> The plane was crashed on land. Flew around the island more than four times. At last during the time flying it slide wheel down and flew off at a distance of not more than a mile and then return per-haps ten or twenty feet above sea level. When reached above there be fit [sic] flew up of all a sudden it bumped the palm with right wing. During that time the plane get in fire and at the last the body fell down beyond the Maneaba [meeting house]. All the crew found

dead except one of the lot get breath not fifteen minutes later, then died again.

The I Kiribati colonists wrapped the bodies in white sheets and covered them with woven mats in graves six feet deep. The next day an Army Air Force investigation team exhumed and recovered the bodies, and examined the crash site. The resulting accident report by Major W. C. Cotner, commanding officer of the Air Transport Command unit at Canton, describes a horrific crash, with the plane more or less disintegrating and burning completely but for the tail and a portion of wing. Cotner went on to report:

> The wheels were retracted and . . . the throttles and controls were in full flight or cruising position. All evidence indicates that the pilot came in a right bank, struck the tree, careened on over the village and other trees and finally hit ground with all power on. Both propellers were badly bent and broken off. One occupant was said to have been thrown clear of the plane but died a few minutes later. The remaining eight were said to have been found in the plane after the fire. The natives stated that the plane made several circles over the island and kept coming lower and lower and finally came in over the water quite low just before the crash occurred.

Cotner put the cause of the accident to "low flying." A review board later found that "it appears that the pilot may have been attempting a forced landing."

The C-47 so tragically lost on Manra could certainly be the source of a lot of the Niku aluminum, but it wasn't a B-24. The parts specific to that type of aircraft, most likely, had come from Kanton, but a specific source could not be identified.

Where Things Stood

As 1997 came to an end, TIGHAR had almost ten years of Earhart research to look back on, and the view was foggy. With four expeditions to Nikumaroro under its stripes, and a vast amount of historical, oral historical, and other research completed as well, the Nikumaroro Hypothesis still looked good, but the evidence for it wasn't getting any better.

There was still what the Toms had started with: the navigational logic of the hypothesis. It still made sense that Noonan would have had Earhart head south along the LOP, and if they started south of Howland, the most likely places to wind up were McKean and Niku. We felt confident that we had eliminated McKean as a good possibility—though there *were* those metal detector hits in the guano lagoon—but Niku still made sense. And the post-loss signals still seemed to point toward someplace in Niku's neighborhood.

There was still the Floyd Kilts bones story, and a bit more information that was consistent with it. Other stories of bones, the numbers of people on the island at key times, the fact that Gallagher not only was of Irish extraction, but—as we now knew from some of the documents that Spading and others had gleaned—carried the nickname "Irish."

It was now clear that there was aircraft aluminum on the island, and that it had been salvaged by the colonists from someplace. Most of it couldn't be traced to specific airplanes, and some of it—including, it now appeared, the bookcase—clearly came from things other than an Electra. But some of it looked more like Electra parts than it did like anything else: the Plexiglass, the dado, the piece of aluminum numbered 2-2-V-1.

And then there were the shoe parts, notably the remains of the blucher-style oxford. The shoe certainly could have been left by someone other than Earhart, but there were no very high-profile candidates. It was possible that the shadowy American woman mentioned by Laxton had worn 1930s-style blucher oxfords, had visited Aukaraime South, and had for some reason left a shoe there, but that complex chain of circumstances seemed at least as improbable as the association with Earhart—who certainly had worn such shoes, and had been in the neighborhood. Some other, totally unknown, woman might have left the shoe—some passing yachtie, perhaps, some tran-sient military woman, some donor to a missionary relief package—but Aukaraime South is a pretty out-of-the-way place for a casual visitor to drop in, or for a contributed item to wind up. As for the Coast Guardsmen, none of them were female, and their use of women's footwear seemed a rather remote possibility. The testimony of station veterans and the log of the station itself both indicated that footwear of *any* kind had been in short supply. And of course, there was the coincidence of the shoe site with Bevington's 1937 "bivouac."

But the 1997 work at Aukaraime South, if anything, had confused the shoe situation by showing that for some reason, the shoe parts seemed to be associated with a fire that had most likely burned in the 1970s. It wasn't clear what to think about Aukaraime South.

On the other hand, the work to date had eliminated a number of possibilities. The plane clearly wasn't anyplace around interior Nutiran. There was no reason to look further for it—except in small, relocated pieces—between Baureke and Tatiman Passages. There was (it seemed) no reason to think that the water catcher on the windward side was associated with Earhart and Noonan. A chunk of the lagoon had been closely inspected with negative results, though by no means the whole thing. Most of the upper reef face looked clean, as did the lower face from the northwest end of the island around clockwise to Tatiman Passage. The area where a search appeared fruitful was narrowing.

The whole reef area from the passage north, though, through the *Norwich City* debris field and on to the northwest cape, remained essentially unsearched. It was precisely here that the anecdotal accounts from Funafuti reported airplane wreckage, and where aerial imagery suggested such wreckage both on the reef flat and back in the bush.

So there clearly was some work to be done along the Nutiran shoreline and reef, and there was more to be done on Aukaraime South—though it wasn't quite certain what. And there were undoubtedly still airplane parts to look for in the village.

And then, adding a new wrinkle, along came Bruce Yoho.

CHAPTER 18

Kanton in the Rain

Where the hell's that stupid engine?
Where the hell's that stupid engine?
Where the hell's that stupid engine?
Let's throw some rocks around![*]
    —TIGHAR TUNES

ICBMs and a Radial Engine

Bruce Yoho teaches aviation maintenance at Long Beach City College in California. Reading in the newspaper about TIGHAR's work, he found the e-mail address and got in touch about a radial engine he said he'd airlifted off a beach in the Phoenix Islands. He thought it might have been a Pratt & Whitney R1340—the kind of engine that drove Earhart's Electra.

An engine on a beach? In the Phoenix Islands? Airlifted? Who was this guy?

Consulting with Yoho, checking his story against independent sources, and follow-up research at Vandenberg Air Force Base in California by John Clauss and Kris Tague, provided the story. The research also put Roger Clapp's Smithsonian environmental survey in context and accounted for that aluminum mast we'd seen on Ameriki in 1989, with the "Space and Missile Test Center" plaque on it.

---

[*]Sung to the tune of "The Battle Hymn of the Republic," by Julie Ward Howe.

The U.S. Air Force's Space and Missile Test Center (SAMTEC) was set up at the newly developed Vandenberg launch facility in 1970. Its purpose was to test intercontinental ballistic missiles (ICBMs) by lobbing them into the Pacific. The Phoenix Islands were chosen as one of the target areas. The program required downrange tracking stations, so temporary facilities were erected on Kanton, Orona, and Enderbury Islands. Predevelopment environmental surveys were carried out on other islands of the group including Manra, Nikumaroro, McKean, and Birnie. The survey, construction, and maintenance operations were carried out by a civilian contractor.

Three Sikorsky HH-3 helicopters supported these operations from the test program's base at Kanton. The helicopters were flown and maintained by contract pilots and mechanics. Yoho was one of the mechanics; he worked on the project for several months in late 1970 and early 1971.

During its use as a major U.S. and British military base during World War II, Kanton—then called Canton Island—had seen a good deal of development. After the war, its 6,000-foot, paved runway became a refueling stop for U.S. and British transpacific airline traffic, but the advent of nonstop jet service in the mid-1960s ended its usefulness, and it was abandoned. It was reoccupied for the missile test program by about 300 men, mostly contract employees with a few Air Force and other military people. As Yoho described life on the island—and as he documented in home movies he shared with TIGHAR—the civilians had quite a lot of free time and not a whole lot to do. This, he said, is what brought him to collect the engine.[1]

We would take cargo and workers to the other sites. Sometimes to other islands for, I suppose, some kind of research. Normally on long flights when we arrived at the destination all we [flight crew] had to do was scout around and look for glass fishing balls that may have washed up on the shore. They were popular souvenirs. At times it got purely boring out there as SAMTEC had not set up entertainment or R & R distractions as yet. Therefore, one made or found his own.

This is how the engine came to be retrieved. As we were flying off of an island, I sat in the cargo door and watched the beach and coral reefs go by under the helo. One could see large sharks and stingrays swimming from time to time. One day we were leaving and I saw this engine on the coral reef. I talked the pilot into retrieving it and we all agreed (although the pilots thought I was nuts). So we slung the engine under the helo for the return to Canton.

Yoho wasn't, and still isn't, sure which island he found the engine on. He thinks it was Niku, on the western reef, but he doesn't recall seeing *Norwich City*. In any event, he said he collected the engine just as something to kill time with, intending to clean it up and see what it was.

> The engine was placed alongside our hangar where our work was done when we were not flying. I would tinker with it from time to time. It was very corroded and the top cylinder heads (those that stuck out of the water on the reef) had corroded away. The cylinders were there and coral sand was packed into the cylinders. I could not dislodge it easily. I suspect that the chemical residue of corroding aluminum, mixed with the sand, turned it into a concrete type substance. Bolts that I attempted to turn were frozen and shoulders were corroded to the point that you could not get a good bite with a wrench. I recall there being a hole in the case and I could see gears. . . .

However . . .

> I got bored very soon with the engine as I was a young man and my attention span was only as long as the excitement. I could, however, watch the World Airways stewardesses stand on the ramp for hours trying to determine what they were wearing or not wearing and after ten minutes they normally were not wearing much in our eyes.
>
> Okay, a two-star general was to do some kind of inspection and the boss wanted the area cleaned up so I was told to hide the engine. Well, totally bored with it, I took it to a salvage area and dumped it.

A story that was weird enough to be true, and Yoho's credentials checked out. If it *was* true, it was *very* interesting. Bruce knows his engines, of course, and as he discussed what he remembered with Gillespie and other TIGHAR airplane experts, it was clear that what he had seen had looked an awful lot like an R1340. Though the R1340 and the similar

R985 are probably the most common radial engines in the world, no airplane known to have operated in the area before, during, or after World War II was equipped with them, with three exceptions. The *Colorado*'s float planes had R1340s, but none of them were lost, or came home missing an engine. The Vought Kingfisher, carried on U.S. cruisers and battleships during the war, was powered by the Pratt & Whitney R985, but none of these are known to have even been in the Phoenix Islands, let alone lost there. And then there was the Lockheed Electra 10E Special flown by Amelia Earhart.[2]

Worth a check, and although Kanton Island—like Niku, a part of Kiribati—isn't exactly a bus ride away, it's not nearly as hard to get to as Niku, or as expensive. One could fly in, and Yoho was quite sure that he could walk right to the spot where he had left the engine, so it could be a quick trip.

Maybe. On the *l'Oiseau Blanc* search there had been so many instances of engines found in the woods someplace, to which people thought they could easily walk, that "the engine in the woods" had become a sort of TIGHAR trademark for fruitless endeavors. Not that the people who had seen the various engines weren't telling the truth as they remembered it, or that they couldn't walk right to the spots where they had seen or thought they had seen an engine, but things change, and engines in the woods have a strange habit of disappearing. So some skepticism was in order, and some checking on what had happened to Kanton Island since the 1970s.

After the Air Force

The U.S. Air Force had been gone from the island since the late 1970s. A few phone calls gleaned the news that the runway was still serviceable, and that a few I Kiribati families lived on the island, taking weather observations and maintaining an aviation fuel farm in the hope of future air service. Clauss and Tague's research at Vandenberg provided quite a lot of data on how the air force had left the place.

Between 1974 and deactivation of SAMTEC's operation on the island in 1976, the records showed, there was much official discussion as to how Canton should be cleaned up. Only a few years after passage of the National Environmental Policy Act, environmental cleanup was a bit of a new concept for the air force, but SAMTEC seemed sensitive to its responsibilities. Report after report stressed the fragility of the island's ecological balance and the need for procedures to protect plant and animal life.[3]

Earlier, some scrap metal had been dumped at sea but this was determined to be expensive and dangerous. A November 1974 report stated, "Most bulky noncombustibles are deposited in an area adjacent to the landfill, but there are other scattered areas with minor accumulations."[4] The junkyard where Yoho dumped the engine was apparently one of the latter "minor accumulations." The report continued, "Although the disposal areas may appear unsightly, they are not causing any apparent environmental problems or health hazards." Consideration was given to building a jetty out over the reef edge from which to dump "bulky noncombustible wastes" into the ocean, but a January 1975 report titled "Environmental Protection" rejected the idea as "not feasible."[5] It appeared, then, that the disposal areas for noncombustible waste—such as old Pratt & Whitney airplane engines—had been left alone. So this particular engine in the woods—or rather, in the "minor accumulation"—might still be there.

On February 14, 1998, a thirteen-person TIGHAR team,[6] including Bruce Yoho and the long-suffering Sam Painter of ABC, took off from Honolulu aboard a chartered Gulfstream 1 for the flight to Kanton Island. Without a ship to live on, and unsure what would be available on the island, Tommy Love had been able to supply the party with boxes and boxes of U.S. military MREs—"meals ready to eat." They looked a good deal more appetizing than the C-rations that King remembered from his navy days in the early '60s.

A Funny Kind of Cleanup

Kanton's long, once well-maintained runway is cracked and weed grown, but serviceable. Landing was an odd experience, like landing on the set of a movie about the aftermath of nuclear holocaust. A huge, modern hangar stood near one end of the runway, burned out and half-collapsed. A radar dome, draped in vines, poked out of the jungle. Nobody was there. But before long there was the sound of an engine, and a tractor appeared pulling a wagon loaded with women and children. It stopped and they piled out,

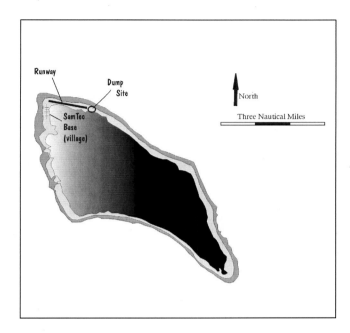

Kanton Island. Bruce Yoho's dump site was near the end of the runway.

but stood shyly at a distance. Gillespie's daughter Heather, the expedition photographer, had collected leis in Honolulu. She went up and passed them around, and the ice was broken.

A small flatbed truck roared up (it had no muffler), fenders hung on with wire, one door akimbo, with a uniformed official who proved to be the customs agent/policeman. With landing fee paid, the two vehicles rented (the only ones on the island), and arrangements made to spend the night, the team went to work.

It was fairly late in the afternoon, and the best the TIGHARs could hope for before dark was to locate Bruce's dump site at the far end of the runway from where the plane was parked. Some walked, some rode. Yoho, with King and Clauss, walked along an old access road that paralleled the runway, getting reacquainted. At the end of the runway everyone but Yoho deployed across the landscape and swept the area; Yoho continued to follow his memories.

The place resembled some ancient city, with pyramids and palaces collapsed into rubble; high mounds of coral with concrete wall stubs poking

The dump site, before the rain. TIGHAR photo by Heather Gillespie.

out of them; deep holes between; strange mounded heaps covered with networks of vines. It soon became apparent that they were looking at the results of what the air force, in the 1970s, had defined as "environmental cleanup"—bury everything. Here was part of a truck sticking out of a mound; there a hole opened up, down into the engine compartment of a buried bulldozer. It was beginning to look less than promising, and to make matters worse, the blue tropical sky was clouding over and it was starting to look like rain. Enough for the day; they had a sense of the lay of the land.

They camped on the lagoon shore—at least the dumb ones did. The smart ones made for the concrete floor of a still-standing hangar, and never mind the drums of avgas stored there.[7] It was a lovely evening on the beach, with a companionable fire and plenty of MREs, but then it started to rain. By daybreak everyone was congregated in the hangar, soaked and shivering. Cold in the Phoenix Islands, for heaven's sake! Cold MREs for breakfast.

The rain slackened as the light grew, and before long the surveyors were headed down the runway again. Yoho began to recognize landmarks, and before long gladly announced that they were on the site of the dump where he had left the engine. It was a dump, all right. A more or less open area around the rusted hulk of a bulldozer, relaxing into the ground. Scattered all around were old engine blocks, heads, pistons, differentials, pieces of airplanes. Windrows of bulldozed coral rubble surrounded the site, and the whole mess was largely covered by a mat of ground-creeping vines.

For the next couple of hours everyone searched, poked, prodded, cut, and rolled up the vine matting, and tried to ignore the steadily increasing rain. By noon it was pouring, and the wind had picked up. By this time, too, they had narrowed down the search area, based both on Yoho's recollections and on their failure to find any radial engines anyplace else. Unfortunately, the prime target was a filled-in trench.

From Kenton Spading's notes:

Raining, fairly hard-driving rain, windy, everyone is soaked. People are scrambling to get into bushes for cover—no use—soaked to the skin. Ric announced that anyone who wants to go back can (the truck is here now). Only Ric, John C., Russ M., Tom K., Johnny Johnson, and I stayed behind. I ate an MRE. Chicken stew.

The rain let up, so we went to a pile of coral rubble just east of the bulldozer. The pile has chunks of iron sticking out. Motors, rear ends, etc. We started uncovering some of the stuff by hand. John C. recovered some airplane parts. I looked around some. It is clear that the bulldozer has been all over this area. You can see where the blade has left ridges and low berms of coral. Other than the rusty bulldozer, 99 percent of the stuff is half buried. It is obvious that someone came in here to purposely bury the junkyard/dump.

It was easy to see where bulldozers had scraped up everything on the surface, pushed it into a trench, and then covered it with rubble. Lots of stuff was sticking out—airplane parts, truck parts, pipes, pieces of engines, but none of them radial. Many, many tons of coral covered who knows what—quite likely covered a radial engine, but if so it was well covered and nobody was going to find it without a whole lot more serious excavation than anyone on the island that day was prepared to do. It was a disheartened bunch that slogged and dripped back up the runway that afternoon.

> Still raining, so we gave up and are heading back to the airplane. Very wet out. Sat around in the fuel shed and wrote notes. Ate another MRE.

They weren't leaving until the morning, and the rain had stopped, so there was time to look over a bit more of the island. The sense of having fallen into a postapocalyptic movie grew as they walked the streets of the old SAMTEC community. Radar dishes frozen in mid-sweep, cables hanging down, vines growing up. Roads and streets, still with signs reminiscent of U.S. suburbs, evolving into paths through the scaevola. A fire truck standing in the middle of a road, rusting into a heap. Apartment buildings with windows blown out, holes in walls, jungle creeping in and through. Once neat suburban-style houses, sagging and abandoned, or taken over by cheerful I Kiribati families.

"You certainly have a lot of kids," Spading remarked to one of the young I Kiribati men.

"There's not much to do here," the man replied with a grin.

Yoho found his old house, now occupied by an I Kiribati family. The house next door was vacant and the TIGHARs considered staying there, but it was buggy, and in the end everyone opted for a return to the avgas hangar. Next to the hangar were a couple of old transformers, leaking PCBs into the coral sand. John Clauss, whose real-life work is in environmental remediation, found a collapsing paint storage building loaded with toxic chemicals in cans that were coming apart, forming puddles on the floor. All in all, the air force seems to have had a funny idea of how to turn its environmental rhetoric into reality.[9]

The I Kiribati community invited the team to the village maneaba that evening—a capacious new building where everyone sat in their appointed places around the edges while food was served, speeches were made, and the people sang and danced. A couple of the young men were going off to school soon, and this was a farewell party for them, so the TIGHARs left early to let them get on with it, back to the avgas shed with conflicted feelings about these cheerful, hard-working, friendly people, living in a toxic waste dump. At least TIGHAR could leave them some untoxified MREs in indirect thanks for their help and hospitality. Lots and lots of MREs.

The U.S. Air Force made a mess of Kanton Island, and the leftovers from its mess are probably shortening the lives of the I Kirabati people who now live there. It put the team's inability to find Yoho's engine in some perspective, as the Gulfstream took off the next morning for the flight back to Hawaii.

From the standpoint of TIGHAR's narrow interests, it clearly wasn't going to be possible to get at Yoho's engine without a major excavation requiring heavy equipment, a whole lot of people, or both—and certainly requiring a lot more time. Wherever the engine had come from, and whatever it was, it would remain another loose end for the time being.

CHAPTER 19

Bones for Real

Skeleton discovered by working party six months ago—
report reached me early in September.
　　　　　　　—GERALD GALLAGHER, OCTOBER 17, 1940

Remains Found on Nikumaroro

Not every TIGHAR member is focused on the Earhart search. Peter
McQuarrie, for example, is primarily interested in World War II.[1] In pursuit
of this research interest, he journeyed to Tarawa, capital of Kiribati, in the
spring of 1997 to review documents in the Kiribati National Archives. A
regular user of the Internet, McQuarrie was off-line while in Tarawa, but
when he got home to New Zealand he dropped an e-mail to TIGHAR to let
Gillespie and Thrasher know that he had returned to cyberspace. At the end
of the note he said:

> In Kiribati I had a good look at the Government Archives and found
> the file on the remains found at Nikumaroro by Gallagher. It turned
> out they were the remains of a Polynesian man more than 60 years old
> when he died and the remains had been exposed to the atmosphere
> for at least 20 years. The sole of the shoe was a woman's all right.

What? Gallagher found remains? With a woman's shoe? Kilts was right?
But it was an elderly Polynesian? With a woman's shoe? Who'd been
around how long? What *was* this?

TELEGRAM.

From The Officer-in-Charge, Phoenix Scheme, Gardner Is.,

To The Ag. Administrative Officer, C.G.I.D., Tarawa.

No............ ①   (Date) 23rd Sept. 1940.

Please obtain from Koata (Native Magistrate
Gardner on way to Central Hospital) a certain bottle
alleged to have been found near skull discovered on
Gardner Island. Grateful you retain bottle in safe place
for present and ask Koata not to talk about skull which is
just possibly that of Amelia Earhardt.   ·

Gallagher

Gallagher's "bottle" telegram. TIGHAR files from Kiribati National Archives.

With trembling fingers, Gillespie asked for more information. McQuarrie promptly put him in touch with Joe Russell, an American living in Tarawa. Russell was able to photocopy and fax the file McQuarrie had found. As soon as he'd looked at it, and caught his breath, Gillespie called King.

"Are you sitting down?"

"Yup. What you got?"

"Let me read it . . ."

The file contained copies of wireless traffic between Gallagher on Nikumaroro and various other WPHC officials, notably High Commissioner Sir Harry Luke and his immediate staff in Suva. The first—dated September 23, 1940—was to a colonial officer at Tarawa. It read:

Please obtain from Koata (Native Magistrate
Gardner on way to Central Hospital) a certain bottle alleged to have been found near skull discovered on Gardner Island. Grateful you retain bottle
in safe place for present and ask Koata not to
talk about skull which is just possibly that of
Amelia Earhardt [sic].

Gallagher

Oh my, oh my. But that was only the beginning.[2]

The same day, Gallagher sent a longer telegram to the resident commissioner of the Gilbert and Ellice Islands Colony on Ocean Island:

Some months ago working party on Gardner discovered human skull—this was buried and I only
recently heard about it. Thorough search has
now produced more bones (including lower jaw)
part of a shoe a bottle and a sextant box. It
would appear that

(a) Skeleton is possibly that of a woman,
(b) Shoe was a womans [sic] and probably size 10,[3]
(c) Sextant box has two numbers on it 3500 (stenciled) and 1542—sextant being old fashioned [sic]
and probably painted over with black enamel.

Bones look more than four years old to me, but
there seems to be very slight chance that this may
be remains of Amelia Earhardt [sic]. If United
States authorities find that above evidence fits
into general description, perhaps they could supply some dental information as many teeth are
intact. Am holding latest finds for present but
have not exhumed skull.

There is no local indication that this discovery is related to wreck of the "Norwich City."

Gallagher

TELEGRAM.

From The Officer-in-Charge, Phoenix Scheme, Gardner Is.,

To The Resident Commissioner, Ocean Island.

No. 71. (Date) 23rd September, 1940

Some months ago working party on Gardner discovered human skull - this was buried and I only recently heard about it. Thorough search has now produced more bones (including lower jaw) part of a shoe a bottle and a sextant box. It would appear that

(a) Skeleton is possibly that of a woman,

(b) Shoe was a womans and probably size 10,

(c) Sextant box has two numbers on it
3500 (stencilled) and 1542 - sextant
being old fashioned and probably painted
over with black enamel.

Bones look more than four years old to me but there seems to be very slight chance that this may be remains of Amelia Earhardt. If United States authorities find that above evidence fits into general description, perhaps they could supply some dental information as many teeth are intact. Am holding latest finds for present but have not exhumed skull.

There is no local indication that this discovery is related to wreck of the "Norwich City".

Gallagher.

Gallagher describes the discovery. TIGHAR files from Kiribati National Archives.

Not surprisingly, Gallagher's speculation drew the attention of his superiors. The resident commissioner replied on October 1:

Your telegram No. 71. Information has been passed
on to the High Commissioner particularly with
a view to identifying number of sextant box.
Information on following points, where possible,
would be of interest:

(a) How deep was skeleton buried when found,
(b) How far from shore,
(c) In your opinion does burial appear deliberate
or could it be accounted for by encroachment of
sand, etc.
(d) Is the site of an exposed one (i.e. if the body
of Mrs. Putnam had lain there is it likely that it
would have been spotted by aerial searchers)?
(e) In what state of preservation is shoe,
(f) If well preserved does it appear to be of modern style or old fashioned [sic],
(g) Is there any indication as to contents of bottle.

Do you know anything of wreck of "Norwich City"—
e.g. when did it takes [sic] place, where [sic]
any lives lost and how long were survivors
marooned at Gardner Island?

Resident

Gallagher replied on October 6, paragraph by paragraph:

(a) Skeleton was not buried—skull was buried after
discovery by natives (coconut crabs had scattered
many bones),
(b) 100 feet from high water ordinary springs . . .

"[H]igh water ordinary springs" would usually be taken to mean the average
high tide line.[4] Gallagher skipped paragraph (c), presumably because the body
hadn't been buried by anything, and went on, seemingly referring to the likelihood that the body would have been "spotted by aerial searchers":

```
(d) Improbable,
(e) Only part of sole (of shoe) remains,
(f) Appears to have been stoutish walking shoe
or heavy sandal,
(g) "Benedictine" bottle but no indication of
contents,
```

```
There are indications that person was alive when
cast ashore—fire, birds killed, etc.
"Norwich City" wrecked and caught fire 1930 or
1932. Number of crew sailed to Fiji in lifeboat,
remainder picked up later at Gardner by "Ralum."
Think Board of Enquiry held Suva—loss of life not
known. This information derived from gossip only.
```

Gallagher

Gallagher's "gossip" about the *Norwich City* wasn't very good, as we'll see later. But that didn't detract from his first-hand observations. Suddenly there was documented, contemporary confirmation of the core of Kilts's story, as well as Bauru Tikana's recollections and the Wahgena Island stories. Bones *had* been found on Nikumaroro, they *had* been reported to Gallagher, and he *had* associated them with Earhart. They had even been associated with a shoe—probably a woman's shoe! So it was maybe size ten, rather than size nine; don't sweat the small stuff. And so Gallagher thought the bones had lain around for more than four years; was there any reason to assume he knew anything about how fast bones weather?

The wireless traffic went on. The High Commissioner's Office became involved on October 15, telegraphing more questions and directing that the matter be kept "strictly secret for the present." Gallagher responded on October 17, describing the eleven bones that had been found—skull, lower jaw, thoracic vertebra, half pelvis, two femurs, and so on—and further reported that:

```
Bones were found on South East corner of island
about 100 feet above ordinary high water springs.
Body had obviously been lying under a "ren" tree
and remains of fire, turtle and dead birds appear
to indicate life. All small bones have been removed
```

by giant coconut crabs which have also damaged
larger ones. Difficult to estimate age bones owing
to activities of crabs but am quite certain they
are not less than four years old and probably
much older.

Only experienced man could state sex from
available bones; my conclusion based on sole of
shoe which is almost certainly a woman's.

So—eleven bones, most of them among the larger, less fragile parts of
the skeleton, lying under a tournefortia tree with the remains of a fire and
bird and turtle bones, and what was "almost certainly" the sole of a
woman's shoe. The bones had been scattered and chewed by *Birgus latro,*
on the "southeast corner" of the island, a good distance back from the
water. They were at least four years old in Gallagher's on-the-spot but not
necessarily authoritative opinion.

The description raised a lot of questions. Do coconut crabs eat people?
We had seen one at Aukaraime South, up in a tree, casually peeling a rat like
an orange, eating the meat and dropping the skin, so they certainly weren't
the innocent coconut eaters they are sometimes thought to be. But would
they carry off bones? Or gobble them up completely? And what kind of
shoe was it that was found with the bones? Why was Gallagher so sure it
was a woman's? Was it a blucher-style oxford? Was he right about the bones
being more than four years old at the time? How could one find out? And
most of all, where, oh where was the "southeast corner" of the island?
Ameriki is the absolute southeast end; if the site was there, it had probably
been wiped out a few years later by the Loran Station. But was this where
Gallagher meant? And was the shoe he found the same one TIGHAR found,
or had he found one and TIGHAR the other?

And why had the high commissioner—Sir Harry Luke, whose *From a
South Seas Diary* we'd pored over back in 1989—decided to keep the matter secret?

And what had become of the bones? The sextant box? The shoe?
Gallagher's October 17 telegram went on to report that:

We have searched carefully for rings, money,
and keys with no result. No clothing was found.
Organized search of area for remaining bones would

```
take several weeks as crabs move considerable
distances and this part of island is not yet
cleared. . . . Bones at present in locked chest
in office pending construction coffin.
```

On October 26 the WPHC Secretary—Henry Harrison Vaskess, we later learned—directed that:

```
Organised search should be made in the vicinity
and all bones and other finds, including box, sex-
tant and shoe, should be forwarded to Suva by the
first opportunity for examination.
```

Then there was a two-month gap in the messages; Gallagher didn't respond until December 27. His response took the form of a letter, which probably accompanied the bones on the journey they were then beginning. It said:

> I have the honour to acknowledge the receipt of your confidential telegram No. 2 of the 26th October, 1940, and to state that two packages are being handed to the Master, R.C.S. "Nimanoa," for eventual delivery to the High Commission Office in Suva. The larger of these packages is the coffin containing the remains of the unidentified individual found on the South Eastern shore of Gardner Island; the second package is the sextant box found in the immediate locality and contains all the other pieces of evidence which were found in the proximity of the body.

He went on to discuss the condition of the bones, and to report that "an intensive search" had failed to turn up any more bones, rings, coins, keys, or other items. But, he said:

> . . . it is possible that something may come to hand during the course of the next few months when the area in question will be again thoroughly examined during the course of planting operations, which will involve a certain amount of digging in the vicinity.

Finally, he suggested that:

Should any relatives be traced, it may prove of sentimental interest
for them to know that the coffin in which the remains are contained is
made from a local wood known as "kanawa" and the tree was, until a
year ago, growing on the edge of the lagoon, not very far from the
spot where the deceased was found.

So everything had been shipped to Fiji, with the bones in a kanawa box.
Then what?

The next document was a February 6 telegram to Gallagher from
"Isaac," who turned out to be Dr. Lindsay Isaac, the acting senior medical
officer at Tarawa:

> I understand from the Master R.C.S. Nimanoa, that
> he has certain human remains on board consigned to
> Suva. As I am in charge of Medical and forensic
> investigation of such objects throughout the whole
> colony and have no knowledge of the matter, I pre-
> sume that the package was intended to be consigned
> to myself.

At this point the wireless messages became a bit unclear about what was
happening. On February 7 the resident commissioner on Ocean Island
advised Gallagher that he was "informing him [Isaac] of position and there
is no need for you to take further action." On February 11 Isaac informed
Gallagher that:

> For your information remains taken from "Nimanoa"
> part skeleton elderly male of Polynesian race and
> that indications are that bones have been in shel-
> tered position for upwards of 20 years and possi-
> bly much longer.

So there was the source of McQuarrie's observation that the bones had
been those of an elderly Polynesian, and that they'd been exposed on the
ground for a long time. Was there any reason to accept Isaac's conclusions
as authoritative? Apparently Gallagher had; his response on February 11
noted that Isaac's conclusion was "rather an anticlimax."

But what had Isaac done with the bones? What "position" had the resident commissioner taken, and what had Isaac done about it?

Notwithstanding the resident commissioner's implied direction not to take further action, Gallagher apparently considered further discourse with Isaac on the subject, but then thought better of it. On his "anticlimax" telegram, several lines of text had been typed in but then crossed out by hand:

```
Personal should be delighted if you keep box but
matter has been mentioned in private letter to
High Commissioner who is interested in timber used
and may ask to see it. It would be fun to make you
one for yourself or perhaps a little tea table—we
have a little seasoned timber left. Please let me
know whether you prefer box or table and if former
give any particular inside measurements.
```

It seemed as if Isaac had been more or less sitting on the bones and that Gallagher was trying to persuade him to let them travel on to Fiji, bribing him with his own kanawa box or tea table, while the resident commissioner was telling Gallagher he could back off and the authorities would prevail on Isaac to let the bones continue their journey. But it appeared that some correspondence was missing—otherwise how could Gallagher know that Isaac had liked the box?

The fact that the text was marked out—by pen or pencil—provided a clue as to how the file had wound up in Tarawa. Most likely it was Gallagher's own file of wireless messages, and the February 11 document was Gallagher's draft, parts of which he'd thought better of before giving it to the wireless operator to be sent. The file had probably been collected on Niku sometime after the war, and eventually deposited in the Kiribati capital, whose occupation by the Japanese during the war, and violent liberation in 1944, make it unlikely that the file originated and survived there.

In any event, Isaac's last telegram is dated February 14 and says:

```
Matter became somewhat tense and complex after
guillotine conversation between us. As I had
(and still have) no information save presence of
remains and therefore . . . quarantine from . . . no
```

```
danger infaction [sic], I am still wondering how
wretched relics can be interesting.
```

It's not clear what had happened. How could Isaac and Gallagher have had a "conversation"? There's no evidence that Gallagher had the capacity for voice transmission from Niku. And what did a guillotine have to do with it?[5] The gaps in the message were consistent with the idea that the file was Gallagher's; these probably represent gaps in Isaac's transmission as received by the wireless operator on Niku. In any event, apparently one way or another Isaac had been persuaded to let the "wretched relics" go, and they were off to Fiji at last.

But *Nimanoa* must have had a few more ports of call; it wasn't until April 28 that the WPHC Secretary telegraphed Gallagher confirming that the "remains and sextant box" had been received. He also asked where the sextant itself was. Gallagher immediately responded that:

```
No sextant was found. Only part discovered was
thrown away by finder but was probably part of
an inverting eyepiece.
```

And with that, the file ended.

The WPHC Archives

So bones had been found, with a shoe, as Kilts had said. And the bones did leave for Fiji, doubtless on the island's "four-oared boat," from which they were loaded aboard the *Nimanoa*. But they didn't leave in a bag; they left in a kanawa box, and they weren't thrown in the water en route to Fiji. They got there.

Which, of course, raised some obvious questions: What had happened to them next? And where were they now?

The answers—and answers to other questions, such as why the discovery had been kept secret, what the shoe had looked like, why Isaac had thought they were Polynesian and had spent at least twenty years on the ground, and what Gallagher had meant by the "South East corner" or the "South East shore"—might well be in the files of the WPHC. But where were those files?

Fortunately, Kenton Spading knew. Back in early 1996 he had embarked on a quest for the WPHC's documents by corresponding with the New Zealand National Archives. After almost a year of explaining his mission to one archivist after another, he finally received a fax asking why he was not corresponding with "the British in Hanslope, England."

"Hanslope" meant Hanslope Park, the Foreign and Commonwealth Office records center about sixty miles northwest of London. Spading fired off another letter—by now able to describe what had been found in Tarawa—and asked about relevant documents. His letter found its way to the Archive and Library Section, where Kenton found a willing and capable accomplice in Maria Simpson. On February 2, 1998, she wrote:

> I have found a file entitled "Skeleton. Human: - Finding of, on Gardner Island" reference WPHC 4 Vol 2 IV MP 4439/1940(G&E). Most of the papers . . . are duplicates of the ones you have already. However, there is a report by Dr. Hoodless of the Central Medical School, it appears it was this gentleman who examined the bones. I enclose a copy of his report.[6]

Bingo. And here was what Dr. Hoodless had said:

> 1. I have today examined a collection of bones forming part of a human skeleton. These bones were delivered to me in a closed wooden box by Mr. P. D. Macdonald of the Western Pacific High Commission.
> 2. The bones included: (1) a skull with the right zygoma and malar bones broken off; (2) mandible, with only four teeth in position; (3) part of the right scapula; (4) the first thoracic vertebra; (5) portion of a rib (? 2nd right rib); (6) left humerus; (7) right radius; (8) right innominate bone; (9) right femur; (10) left femur; (11) right tibia; (12) right fibula; and (13) the right scaphoid bone of the foot.
> 3. From this list it is seen that less than half of the total skeleton is available for examination.
> 4. All the bones are very weather-beaten and have been exposed to the open air for a considerable time. Except in one or two small areas all traces of muscular attachments and the various ridges and prominences have been obliterated.

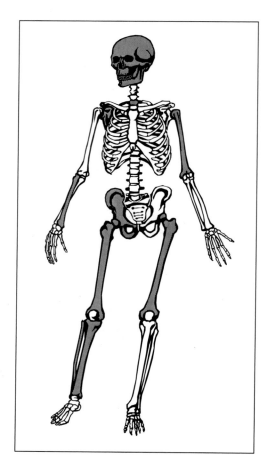

The shaded bones were listed by
Dr. Hoodless in his report of
skeletal remains found
on Nikumaroro in 1940.

5. By taking measurements of the length of the femur, tibia and
the humerus I estimate that these bones belonged to a skeleton of
total height of 5 feet 5½ inches approximately.

6. From the half sub-pubic angle of the right innominate bone,
the "set" of the two femora, and the ratio of the circumferences of
the long bones to their individual lengths it may be definitely stated
that the skeleton is that of a MALE.

7. Owing to the weather-beaten condition of all the bones it is
impossible to be dogmatic in regard to the age of the person at the time
of death, but I am of the opinion that he was not less than 45 years of
age and that probably he was older; say between 45 and 55 years.

8. I am not prepared to give an opinion on the race or nationality of this skeleton, except to state that it is probably not that of a pure South Sea Islander—Micronesian or Polynesian. It could be that of a short, stocky, muscular European, or even a half-caste, or person of mixed European descent.

9. If further details are necessary I am prepared to take detailed and exact measurements of the principal bones in this collection, and to work out the various indices (e.g., the platymeric index for the femur or the cnemic index for the tibia) but if such a detailed report is required the obvious course to adopt would be to submit these bones to the Anthropological Dept of the Sydney University where Professor Elkin would be only too pleased to make a further report.

Thirteen bones now, where Gallagher had noted only eleven. The immediately interesting part, though, was that Dr. Hoodless didn't support Isaac's dismissive conclusion that the bones were those of an elderly Polynesian. Rather, he thought they might have belonged to a European, or maybe to a person of mixed descent, maybe as old as fifty-five but quite possibly younger, somewhere around Noonan's age. . . .

So was this "stocky, muscular, European male" Noonan? The "European male" part fit, but not the "stocky, muscular" bit.

But if Isaac's conclusions about age and race weren't reliable, how reliable were Dr. Hoodless's? What could we find out about Dr. Hoodless, and the basis for his decisions?

Kris Tague began looking for information, and soon found a biography of the doctor written by his daughter, Margaret Guthrie of New Zealand.[7] It turned out that Dr. Hoodless was another memorable member of our developing epic's cast. He had come out to Fiji as a teacher in 1911 and then retooled himself as a doctor in the 1920s, finally receiving his formal qualifications in 1935. In the meantime, combining his talents, he presided over the expansion of Fiji's local medical school into the Central Medical School, servicing the whole western Pacific. The CMC—and Dr. Hoodless—pioneered the education of native medical practitioners, who provided the backbone of health care in Britain's western Pacific colonies. As a result of this, Dr. Hoodless's name is understandably and justifiably revered in Fiji and the surrounding islands.[8]

However, that didn't necessarily mean that he was an expert bone man. In fact, it was hard to see why he would be; there is no reason for osteology

Report on portion of a human skeleton.

I have today examined a collection of bones forming part of a human skeleton. These bones were delivered to me in a closed wooden box by Mr. P. D. Macdonald of the Western Pacific High Commission.

2... The bones included:- (1) a skull with the right zygoma and malar bones broken off: (2) mandible with only four teeth in position: (3) part of the right scapula (4) the first thoracic vertebra: (5) portion of a rib (? 2nd right rib): (6) left humerus: (7) right radius: (8) right innominate bone: (9) right femur: (10) left femur: (11) right tibia: (12) right fibula: and (13) the right scaphoid bone of the foot.

3... From this list it is seen that less than half of the total skeleton is available for examination.

4... All these bones are very weather-beaten and have been exposed to the open air for a considerable time. Except in one or two small areas all traces of muscular attachments and the various ridges and prominences have been obliterated.

5... By taking measurements of the length of the femur, tibia and the humerus I estimate that these bones belonged to a skeleton of total height of 5 feet 51/2 inches approximately.

6... From the half sub-pubic angle of the right innominate bone, the "set" of the two femora, and the ratio of the circumferences of the long bones to their individual lengths it may be definitely stated that the skeleton is that of a MALE.

7... Owing to the weather-beaten condition of all the bones it is impossible to be dogmatic in regard to the age of the person at the time of death, but I am of the opinion that he was not less than 45 years of age and that probably he was older: say between 45 and 55 years.

8... I am not prepared to give an opinion on the race or nationality of this skeleton, except to state that it is probably not that of a pure South Sea Islander-Micronesian or Polynesian. It could be that of a short, stocky, muscular European, or even a half-caste, or person of mixed European descent.

9... If further details are necessary I am prepared to take detailed and exact measurements of the principal bones in this collection, and to work out the various indices (e.g. the platymeric index for the femur or the cnemic index for the tibia) but if such a detailed report is required the obvious course to adopt would be to submit these bones to the Anthropological Dept of the Sydney University where Professor Elkin would be only too pleased to make a further report.

S. W. Hoodless

Principal,
Central Medical School
Suva.

4th April, 1941.

Dr. Hoodless's report. TIGHAR files from Foreign and Commonwealth Office, Hanslope, England.

to be given much priority in a school where tropical medicine was the specialization. And the forensic study of human skeletons wasn't a terribly advanced science in 1940.

Ms. Simpson and the quality of the WPHC archives came through again. It turned out that the archives contained Dr. Hoodless's original handwritten notes on the bones, including his measurements of the cranium and long bones. Fortuitously, it turned out that Dr. Hoodless had taken some of the same measurements that are used in modern skeletal analyses. The result was that it was no longer necessary to worry about Dr. Hoodless's ability as a bone analyst. With the measurements taken in 1940 in hand, TIGHAR could run its own analysis using modern forensic anthropological methods, provided the expertise could be found to do it. As it happened, that expertise was not hard to find.

But what else was in the WPHC archives? It wasn't fair or productive to lean any more on Ms. Simpson's indulgences; TIGHAR would have to look for itself. After raising more funds, Gillespie and Spading headed for England.

CHAPTER 20

Flesh on the Bones

Pl[ease] ask CMA [Central Medical Authority] to convey my thanks to Dr. Hoodless for his effort and the trouble he has taken in this matter, and request him to retain the remains until further notice.
— SIR HARRY LUKE, APRIL 1941

HANSLOPE PARK IS A HIGH SECURITY FACILITY—A compound of about a dozen modern brick buildings, with a chain-link fence topped with razor wire and a second tier of high-voltage electric fencing. One well-armed gatekeeper cleared Gillespie and Spading for entry while another went around the car with a mirror on a stick, making sure its underside carried no bombs. They parked at the security building and were issued passes to wear at all times—not that they could go anywhere; they had to wait for escort. Down corridors then, through doors opened with swipe cards, to the appropriate section of the Library and Archives Section of the Foreign and Commonwealth Office. Once there they couldn't go anywhere else unescorted, even to the loo.

But everyone was friendly and helpful. Maria Simpson had moved on to another job, but the section director, Joan McPherson, did all she could to help Gillespie and Spading glean records from the massive WPHC files. In the end they emerged with some 600 photocopied pages. None of these was a "Eureka" page—no secret memo revealing a cover-up, no map of the bones discovery site. But the trove that Gillespie and Spading brought home is a rich body of data on a wide range of subjects, all still being productively mined in ongoing research. Among the topics that the documents discussed in considerable detail was the bones story itself.

"Human Skeleton—Finding of"

File number M.P. 4439-1940, as advertised, contained most of what we'd already seen in the Tarawa bones file, plus correspondence among WPHC officials, Dr. Hoodless, and others in Fiji. Each item was numbered and cross-referenced to a running, mostly handwritten, chronological log of the file's growth as it passed from hand to hand within the WPHC.[1] Each annotation—known as a "minute," with the whole log known as the "Minute Paper"—bears the dated initials of the person doing the annotating; in most cases this was Henry Harrison Vaskess, WPHC Secretary.

The first item in the file was a telegram dated October 1, 1940, from Francis George Holland, acting resident commissioner on Ocean Island, to Sir Harry Luke, summarizing Gallagher's report and noting that:

```
Possibility of this being Mrs. Putnam is naturally
remote but Your Excellency will probably wish to
make enquiries concerning numbering of sextant box.
```

After the initial flurry of telegrams already seen in the Tarawa file, Vaskess sent a note to Sir Harry on October 9, suggesting that:

A communication might be addressed to the U.S. Consul in Sydney, but, before doing so, I suggest that Mr. Gallagher should be asked by telegraph for full details. . . . If Your Excellency concurs, Dr. MacPherson would no doubt advise as to points which might be put to Mr. Gallagher. . . .

Dr. Duncan Campbell McEwan ("Jock") MacPherson, who would try in vain to save Gallagher's life the following year, turned out not only to be a WPHC medical officer, but also the Central Medical Authority's forensics expert.[2]

Gallagher was asked for details and supplied them in the telegrams found in the Tarawa file. Sir Harry sent the package to MacPherson with the note:

What do you make of 4 [Gallagher's description of the bones]. Would it in yr opinion be consistent with the ascription of the remains to Mrs. Earhardt [*sic*]?

MacPherson replied at length on October 17, holding out little hope for positive identification without a complete pelvis, dental work, or associated artifacts. He suggested that the bones be sent either to the University of Sydney or to Fiji for further study, and "that the search be continued with a view to discovering farther [*sic*] bones, personal trinkets, etc."

He also suggested that further study of the sextant box would be in order, together with the sextant itself, which Holland had erroneously led Sir Harry and his colleagues to think had been found as well.

"Thinnest Rumours . . ."

Vaskess passed along MacPherson's note to Sir Harry on October 26 with a draft of the telegram directing Gallagher to make a further search. He also suggested that:

> Perhaps a carefully worded letter should now be sent to the U.S. Consul-General in Sydney asking him to obtain a description of the sextant carried by Mrs. Putnam and any number or distinguishing mark on it?

Sir Harry replied the same day, approving the telegram to Gallagher but saying:

> Yr Para. 2: better I think await the arrival of the remains etc. Thinnest rumours which may in the end prove unfounded are liable to be spread.

The telegram to Gallagher went out the same day. Aside from the cryptic handwritten annotation "B.U." and a date that had been corrected several times and that could be November 21 or December 21, 1940, or February 21, 1941, the file remained unchanged until February 13, 1941.

The Box's Travels

The Tarawa file had indicated that Gallagher put the bones in the kanawa box aboard *Nimanoa* in late December, and that it took more than a month for them to reach Tarawa and almost another two months to reach Suva. WPHC List No. 4, IV, M.P. No. 3775/1940 (G&E) revealed what happened: On December 10, *Nimanoa* was in a westerly gale near Abemama Island, unable to make headway and running low on fuel. To complicate the situation, a German raider was reported to be in the area. RCS *Kiakia* was dispatched to render assistance, and by December 11 both vessels were lying safely in Abemama's lee. *Nimanoa* arrived at Tarawa on December 16 in a storm-battered condition, and on December 20 began repairs. She had lost copper from her bow, her sails were torn, and a lifeboat, davit, and windlass were damaged. The acting resident commissioner estimated that she would not be ready for sea until about January 10, and recommended that *Kiakia* be sent to the Phoenix settlements with "radio batteries and essential stores."

A record of *Kiakia*'s movements was not among the papers that Gillespie and Spading copied from the WPHC archives (since they had no idea it might be of interest), so it's not clear whether she visited Nikumaroro.

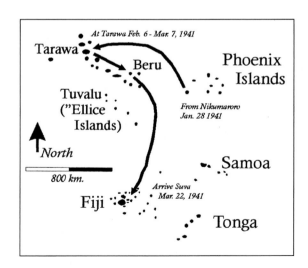

The bones had an adventurous trip from Nikumaroro to Suva.

A Kanawa *(Cordia subchordata)* box from Nikumaroro, acquired by Dr. John Mims during World War II from the colonists there. The inlay is aluminum. The "bones box" may have been similar, though there is no report of inlay. TIGHAR photo by Pat Thrasher, courtesy of Dr. John Mims.

However, No. 3775/1940 goes on to record that *Nimanoa* left Tarawa on January 15, 1941, bound for Beru and the Phoenix Islands. She visited Nikumaroro on January 28. Isaac's February 6 telegram to Gallagher doesn't mention *Kiakia* but indicates that he had learned that the bones were aboard *Nimanoa*, which had apparently just arrived at Tarawa. Therefore Gallagher must have put the box of bones aboard *Nimanoa* when she visited Nikumaroro on January 28, not on or about December 26. After her return to Tarawa on February 6, *Nimanoa* remained there "decarbonizing," that is, having carbon cleaned off her cylinder heads and pistons,[3] until March 7, then sailed to Suva via Beru, arriving there on March 22.

The file also documents that the radio on Nikumaroro failed on about December 20. Gallagher's quarterly report indicates that it was back on line on January 11. This suggests that *Kiakia* in fact visited Niku early in January, bringing batteries. Why Gallagher didn't put the bones aboard her isn't clear, but the late December date on his transmittal letter suggests that he prepared

226

it before the wireless went down—when he was still expecting *Nimanoa* any day—and then held it with the bones until the ship finally appeared.

The Escape from Tarawa

The WPHC file also fleshed out the curious incident of Isaac's seizure of the bones in Tarawa. On February 11, 1941, Holland reported to Sir Harry:

> Confidential. Acting Senior Medical Officer has taken objection to presence on Government vessel of human remains consigned to Suva. Circumstances indicate that these are those referred to in correspondence ending with your telegram No. 500, 1940, Confidential [the telegram directing Gallagher to search the site and send the bones to Suva].
>
> Acting Senior Medical Officer appears to be acting in unorthodox fashion and is detaining all ships calling at Tarawa (at present four) on health grounds on account of this incident. I am enquiring as to authority under which he presumes to do so but in the meantime should be grateful for definite instructions from Your Excellency to pass on to him.

Vaskess didn't equivocate. On February 13, he gave Sir Harry a draft telegram, which went out on February 14, directing Holland to:

> instruct acting Senior Medical Officer that ships must not be detained without good reason and then only in accordance with Regulations or higher instructions. He should be directed to report reasons for action taken referred to in your telegram and instructed that if human remains are those they are assumed to be he is not to detain shipping.

In the meantime, as the Tarawa file documented, telegrams were flying between Gallagher, Holland, and Isaac. By February 17, Isaac had decided the bones were those of an elderly Polynesian male that had been lying around for about twenty years. Holland reported this conclusion to the high commissioner, and followed up with a telegram announcing that Isaac had now lifted the quarantine on Tarawa. It was March 7 before *Nimanoa* sailed, however, and she didn't arrive in Suva until March 22. On March 24, Gallagher's cover letter was logged in at the WPHC. The bones in the kanawa box, and the sextant box—now containing the shoe and other artifacts—had arrived in Suva.

The Hoodless Analysis

On March 31, Assistant Secretary Patrick MacDonald sent the file to the director of the Central Medical Authority. The director passed it on to the principal of the Central Medical School—Dr. Hoodless—indicating that the bones would follow for inspection and report.[4] The next entry, on April 4, added Dr. Hoodless's report to the file—the one Ms. Simpson had supplied to Spading earlier. The doctor's transmittal minute said, "My report on these bones is enclosed. I will take charge of these bones until it is decided what to do with them."

End of the Trail?

Vaskess duly passed Dr. Hoodless's report to Sir Harry, noting that it "appears definitely to indicate that the skeleton cannot be that of the late Amelia Earhart."

He also noted that Sir Harry might want to follow up on Dr. Hoodless's suggestion that the bones be sent on to the University of Sydney, "although it does not seem possible that any useful purpose will be served by proceeding further."

Sir Harry must have agreed that there was no point in sending the bones on to Sydney. On April 12, he asked Vaskess to ask MacPherson "to convey my thanks to Dr. Hoodless for the trouble he has taken in this matter [and] to request him to retain the bones until further notice."

MacPherson passed on the high commissioner's thanks and request, and on April 17, Dr. Hoodless responded: "Noted—thank you."

And with that, the bones in their kanawa box disappear from the written record.

The Unfortunate Castaway

There was one postscript on the discovery, however. On July 3, Gallagher, now in Fiji preparing for his last, fatal mission, added a handwritten minute to the file:

I have read the contents of this file with great interest. It does look as if the skeleton was that of some unfortunate native castaway and the sextant box and other curious articles found nearby the remains are quite possibly a few of his precious possessions which he managed to save.

There was no evidence of any attempt to dig a well and the wretched man presumably died of thirst; less than two miles away there is a small grove of coconut trees which would have been sufficient to keep him alive if he had only found it. He was separated from those trees, however, by an inpenetrable [*sic*] belt of bush.

Curious image—a native castaway wandering around Niku with a woman's shoe and a sextant box. But Gallagher provided some useful information, too—less than two miles (but presumably well over one, or he wouldn't have said "less than two") to the nearest coconut grove, through an impenetrable belt of "bush"—doubtless TIGHAR's old friend scaevola. The only bearing coconut trees on the island in 1940 were those planted by Arundel's workers back in the 1890s, and Gillespie knew where those had been; the most easterly had been in the vicinity of the future colonial village on Ritiati. Hence the bones discovery site should have been more than a mile but less than two miles from the village.

The Other Parcel

When Gallagher readied the bones and artifacts for shipment from Niku, he had put the shoe parts and other items found with the bones into the sextant box. The WPHC file showed that the box's contents had been removed about June 7, 1941, and repackaged. This parcel was examined by Dr. K. R. Steenson, the senior medical officer on Tarawa, who was on temporary assignment in Suva. Dr. Steenson added the following note to the file on July 1:

I have examined the contents of the parcel mentioned. Apart from stating that they appear to be parts of shoes worn by a male person and a female person, I have nothing further to say. Those corks on brass chains would appear to have belonged to a small cask.

Male person? Two shoes, then; one male, one female? Shades of Aukaraime South! And corks on brass chains? Why hadn't Gallagher mentioned them before? And where was the Benedictine bottle?

What about the Sextant Box?

```
Sextant box has two numbers on it 3500 (stenciled)
and 1542—sextant being old fashioned [sic] and
probably painted over with black enamel.
```

Thus Gallagher reported in his September 23, 1940, telegram to Holland. This was an odd thing for a castaway to have, unless the castaway were a navigator, or closely associated with a navigator.

So what about the numbers? Would they lead anywhere?

It turned out that Sir Harry and Vaskess had shared the idea that the box might help identify the castaway. On April 11, Vaskess wrote the high commissioner noting that he now had the box, and thought that "Captain Nasmyth might be willing to examine it." Sir Harry responded that Vaskess should "ask Captain Nasmyth orally if he can throw any light on the origin of the sextant." Commander G. B. Nasmyth was in charge of the recently formed Fiji Naval Volunteer Force.[5]

Somewhat belatedly, it would seem, Vaskess wondered what had happened to the sextant itself, which, based on Holland's original inaccurate report, he still thought Gallagher had found. He asked Gallagher about it, and Gallagher responded on April 28 that no sextant had been found—only part of an "inverting eyepiece " that had been "thrown away by finder." An inverting eyepiece is a sextant attachment that flips the user's perceived image of the sky and horizon upside down—useful in making certain observations. Such an eyepiece would normally be kept in the sextant's carrying case.

Nasmyth and Gatty

With this clarified, Vaskess sent the sextant box to Nasmyth in early June, but Sir Harry himself apparently retrieved it in early August to show to "Mr. Gatty"—almost certainly the famous Tasmanian-born aviator Harold Gatty. In an August 8 note that accompanied the box on its return to Vaskess, Sir Harry said:

Mr. Gatty thinks that the box is an English one of some age and judges that it was used latterly merely as a receptacle. He does not consider that it could in any circumstances have been a sextant box used in modern trans-Pacific aviation.

This no doubt comforted Sir Harry in his decision not to bother the Americans with the discovery. But it also made sense to us. Bubble octants, not old-fashioned nautical sextants, were the navigational instruments of choice in Pacific aviation at the time; Noonan, in fact, was documented to have had a bubble octant aboard the Electra. So the sextant box apparently wasn't linked to the Earhart flight.

With the box back in his hands, Vaskess pursued Nasmyth's opinion, which the commander rendered on August 11, saying that "the make of the box—that is—the dovetailing of the corners—makes it appear to be of French origin."

This was the last document in the file dealing with the sextant box.

Playing the Numbers

So the box had dovetailed corners. Nice piece of work, but hardly unusual in boxes holding fine instruments. It was hard to believe that only French instrument makers would have used them, and, of course, Gatty had thought the box was English.

Gatty had dismissed the idea that the box could be associated with transpacific aviation, but as usual Gillespie wasn't about to take anyone's unsubstantiated opinion as gospel. TIGHAR members Peter Ifland, David Charlwood, and Lou Schoonbrood began visiting museums in the United States and in Great Britain and other Europe nations that held collections of old navigation instruments. They found quite a few boxes with dovetailed corners, but none with numbers on them: serial numbers on the instruments themselves, yes, but numbers on the boxes, no.

Meanwhile, a search of documents about Noonan's use of instruments turned up a note from Noonan to Commander P. V. H. Weems of the Weems School of Navigation. Noonan was describing the methods he used in navigating a Pan Am Clipper flight in 1935:

Two sextants were carried. A Pioneer bubble octant and a mariner's sextant. The former was used for all sights; the latter as a preventer.[6]

So Noonan, the longtime ship's navigator fairly recently turned aviator, at least sometimes carried a nautical sextant with him as a "preventer," by which he probably meant a backup to whatever fancier equipment he may have been using. The idea, presumably, would be to prevent getting lost if the more complicated gadgets didn't work. So it wasn't improbable that he would have had a sextant aboard the Electra in addition to the octant. And he would have had to keep it in something . . .

Ifland, Charlwood, and Schoonbrood continued their inspection of the instrument cases—close to 500 boxes. However, they still found no numbers on any of them.

What did the numbers on the Niku box mean, anyway? Apparently Gatty hadn't known, Nasmyth hadn't known, and nobody else seemed to know, either. Serial numbers? Inventory numbers? The 3500 had been stenciled, Gallagher said, but he hadn't said whether the 1542 had been inscribed on an attached plate, scribbled in ink, or burned in by a fiery finger. Had Pan Am used stenciled numbers in keeping track of its instruments? Although many of Pan Am's files are housed today at Florida's University of Miami and available for research, nothing could be found there about sextant numbering systems, and contacts with Pan Am veterans didn't yield any useful recollections. It appeared that no instrument boxes that had been preserved had used such a system.

The Pensacola Ludolph

Then Buddy Macon, deputy director of the National Museum of Naval Aviation in Pensacola, Florida, reported that his museum had a sextant box with numbers on it—albeit not stenciled. The box had dovetailed corners, the number 116 handwritten on the front, and the numbers 3547 and 173 handwritten on the bottom. It held a sextant manufactured by W. Ludolph of Bremerhaven, Germany, in 1919, with the serial number XIX 1090, painted black.

Well, 3547 was only 47 away from 3500, so the two boxes might represent parts of a series. Where had the Pensacola instrument come from? The Museum of Naval Aviation naturally keeps meticulous records on everything in its collection. The Ludolf, in its box, had been donated by W. A. Cluthe, a retired Pan Am captain. The file included a certifying note from Cluthe:

6 June 1968

TO WHOM IT MAY CONCERN:

I, hereby, certify that the accompanying Navigation Sextant was the property of Mr. Frederick J. Noonan, who was copilot-navigator on the World Flight with Amelia Aerhardt [*sic*] when their plane was lost in the Pacific Ocean.

The instrument was borrowed by the undersigned who at that time was studying navigation under Mr. Noonan in preparing for service in the Pacific Division of Pan American Airways, for use in practice praticle [*sic*] navigation. Identification marks are not in evidence, however the undersigned hereby certifies as to the authenticity of the above remarks.[7]

The Pensacola sextant box. TIGHAR Collection from National Museum of Naval Aviation.

So did Noonan have a collection of sextants, perhaps acquired during his career at sea, that he loaned to students, like a college professor loans books? Did he keep track of them with some kind of catalog system that featured numbers written—or stenciled—on their boxes? There's no way of knowing—as yet. But three things are sure: out of some 500 boxes examined by TIGHAR, only one had numbers on it; one of those numbers was similar to one of the numbers on the Niku box, and the box with that number once belonged to Fred Noonan.

CHAPTER 21

Whose Bones, and Where?

The morphology of the recovered bones, insofar as we can tell by applying contemporary forensic methods to measurements taken at the time, appears consistent with a female of Earhart's height and ethnic origin.
— KAREN R. BURNS ET AL. 1999

The Forensic Anthropologist

Dr. Karen Burns is a forensic anthropologist—or to be precise, a forensic osteologist.[1] That means she studies the skeletal remains of dead people to figure out who they were and what made them the way they are.[2] Dead, that is, and reposing however they're reposing in or on the ground (or elsewhere). She is at the University of Georgia, but she has spent much of her professional life working crime scenes, clandestine burial sites, cemeteries, and disaster scenes in the United States, Guatemala, Tunisia, Iraqi Kurdistan, and Haiti. She has also been involved in more historical, less stressful research, like figuring out whether the remains sealed up in the Pulaski Memorial in Savannah, Georgia, are in fact those of the Polish military strategist Casmir Pulaski, a major contributor to the American Revolution.

In 1997, after reading news stories about TIGHAR's search of Aukaraime South for Earhart's bones, Burns contacted Gillespie to ask how he expected to find such things when he didn't know what they looked like.

Karen Burns at
Nikumaroro, 1999.
TIGHAR photo by
Ric Gillespie.

"I was only curious about the logic," she says today; "I was not curious about Earhart." Luckily she did not contact King, who—though no forensic osteologist—probably would have said something off-putting about having dug up a fair number of dead people himself over the years and knowing perfectly well what human bones look like.

Gillespie was more gracious, and knowing a good thing when he saw one, asked if Burns would talk to an upcoming meeting of current and would-be expeditionaries about what bones look like in the wild. Burns brought along a collection of the human body's less obvious pieces (knee cap, hand and foot bones, fragments of long bones), put on a show that was well-received, and stayed to talk about the project with the rest of the gang. Gillespie promised that the next time TIGHAR went to the island to look for bones, it would definitely equip itself more fully with appropriate expertise, and encouraged her to stay in touch. She agreed, though there wasn't much at the time to command her attention.

This changed with the arrival of the Hoodless report and measurements. Gillespie asked if Burns would be interested in looking at them, and though deeply engrossed in Guatemalan genocide at the time, she agreed. As soon as her schedule let her, Burns began to pore over what Dr. Hoodless had said and measured—and soon was as hooked as everyone else. Plus she noticed some intriguing things.

The Stocky European

Dr. Hoodless, of course, had opined that the bones from Niku were those of a "short, stocky European or half-caste," and definitely those of a male. This description didn't fit either of the Earhart saga's key *dramatis personae* very well; Noonan wasn't short and stocky, and Earhart certainly wasn't a male. But the science of osteology has come a long way since 1941, and no one knew how thoroughly versed Dr. Hoodless had been even in the osteology of his day. Burns confirmed that there was no reason to take his interpretations at face value.

Looking at Dr. Hoodless's report, Burns noted the doctor's statement that less than half the total skeleton is available for examination. He also had noted that only thirteen bones were present, and there are not twice but fifteen times that number of bones in the adult human body. Not a big deal, but enough to raise questions in Burns's mind. These led her to focus on the statement that:

> Except in one or two small areas, all traces of muscular attachments and the various ridges and prominences have been obliterated.

All well and good, but if there were virtually no muscle attachments, how could he tell whether the person represented by the bones had been "muscular"? Another thing that raised Burns's eyebrow was Dr. Hoodless's certainty that "it may be definitely stated that the skeleton is that of a MALE."

Skeletal biologists learn to be cautious about stating anything "definitely." Things like male-female variation, limb proportions, and muscularity vary from one population to another. Therefore, it's never wise to leap to conclusions about a single subject without knowing a good deal about the skeletal characteristics of that subject's population. But this sort of caution is the product of lots of research; forensic anthropologists have learned to be cautious because there have been so many cases in which first impressions—or second,

237

Dr. Hoodless's measurements. TIGHAR files from Foreign and Commonwealth Office, Hanslope, England.

or third—have been wrong. Dr. Hoodless couldn't be expected to be anything other than the product of his time—a time when experience with human skeletal variation was still limited, but people were willing to make unequivocal statements on the basis of evidence that modern anthropologists know is inherently equivocal.

As for Dr. Hoodless's conclusion that the bones were those of someone between forty-five and fifty-five years old, Burns noted that this ten-year interval in the middle of life is a narrow range. To be at all certain about it, Dr. Hoodless should have had some definite indicators with which to work, but if he did, he didn't report them. There was no way of knowing whether he based his judgment on cranial suture closure, dental wear, osteoarthritis, or some other indicator—none of which is completely reliable by itself.

Burns's conclusion: there was no reason to accept Dr. Hoodless's conclusion at face value. The bones, she said, were definitely worth another look. Of course, TIGHAR didn't have the bones; all it could supply were Dr. Hoodless's measurements of them. But beggars can't be choosers.

FORDISC Says Different

Burns analyzed the measurements using a computer program called FORDISC 2.0,[3] developed by S. D. Ousley and R. L. Jantz. FORDISC is an interactive program used to classify unknown adult human skeletons according to "race,"[4] sex, and stature. It uses discriminant function analysis (DFA) to sort through and compare the wide variety of measurements possible from a human skeleton. DFA is a statistical method for determining the importance of each factor (in this case a measurement) when compared or combined with others. Each factor is weighted according to its actual value as a predictor.[5] Using DFA, FORDISC takes any set of standard osteological measurements and compares them with a large database derived from skeletal measurements of people of known age, sex, and ethnic background. It then classifies the individual represented by the measurements in terms of closeness to the various populations represented in the database. One of FORDISC's very useful traits is its ability to recognize and characterize the "atypical" (also known as "mixed race"). If the cranium measured by Dr. Hoodless had indeed been that of a "half-caste, or person of mixed European descent," it should not fit neatly into a particular category.

Even when interpreted by experienced anthropologists, FORDISC cannot tell you with absolute certainty that the skull you have measured is, say, that of an Irish male. What it offers is probabilities. Burns found that FORDISC did not suggest a high probability for the "stocky, muscular European or half-caste male" identity that Dr. Hoodless had ascribed to the skeleton. They suggested something quite different.

This time it was Burns's turn to call Gillespie and ask him if he was sitting down. The best match for the skull Dr. Hoodless had measured, according to FORDISC, was with a female of northern European ethnic origin.

The results were so startling that Burns suggested that she share the measurements with her colleague, Dr. Richard Jantz of the University of Tennessee at Knoxville. Jantz has been doing and teaching forensic anthropology since the 1960s, and has written a number of the key publications in the field.[6] Burns knew that Jantz was continually upgrading the FORDISC program with new data and hoped that he would have even more information to apply to Dr. Hoodless's measurements. Jantz looked at the data independently— and arrived at the same conclusions.

Jantz also gave the skeleton's stature special attention, and concluded that the individual had most likely been 5 feet 6 inches to 5 feet 7 inches if a female, about 1.5 inches taller if a male. He then turned the question around and asked what bone lengths would be expected in a woman of Earhart's height. According to TIGHAR records, Earhart gave her height as 5 feet 8 inches, but some other sources suggested that she might have been closer to 5 feet 7 inches. Regression predictions of bone length for a woman of 5 feet 7 inches to 5 feet 8 inches fit well with the lengths of the bones Dr. Hoodless had measured.[7]

In a nutshell, then, Burns, Jantz, and FORDISC concluded that—to the extent Dr. Hoodless's measurements could be relied on—the individual represented by the bones was more likely female than male, more likely of European than of Pacific Island origin, and most likely somewhere between 5 feet 6 inches and 5 feet 9 inches tall. In other words, the castaway of Nikumaroro probably looked a lot more like Earhart than he or she looked like a stocky European male.[8]

In finding fault with Dr. Hoodless's analysis nobody is accusing him of anything but having been in keeping with his times. He measured the Nikumaroro bones and analyzed the results in a responsible and professional way, using the analytical tools available to him—including, apparently, the

Artist's reconstruction of the skull found on Nikumaroro in 1940, based on Gerald Gallagher's and Dr. Hoodless's descriptions. The "right zygoma and malar [are] broken off"—in other words, the entire right cheekbone is missing. The bone is pitted and finely cracked, as it would become if "weather beaten" as a result of being "exposed to the open air for a considerable time." Consistent with Dr. Hoodless's measurements, the drawing is based on a skull typical of a European-type female. The four teeth that Hoodless indicates were in the mandible (Gallagher mentions five) are assumed to have been molars, because molars tend to remain in the skull longer than other teeth due to the configuration of their roots. This drawing is also based on the assumption that anything not described by Hoodless as missing was actually present. Drawing by Joanna Wallington.

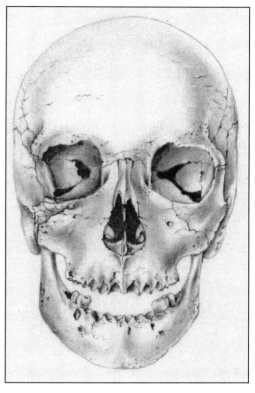

cranial indices published by the anatomist Karl Pearson (1857–1936), an entirely appropriate source for an anatomist at the time. Interestingly, Dr. Hoodless actually wrote "European" repeatedly in his notes, but he seems to have been unwilling to believe the conclusions suggested by his own measurements and calculations. He didn't go any further than to say that the skeleton was from a "mixed race" individual. Apparently recognizing his own limitations, he went on to suggest it might be well to send the bones on to Professor Elkin, a specialist at the University of Sydney.[9] Sir Harry Luke apparently chose not to do so.[10] Had the High Commissioner taken that single next step, the fate of Amelia Earhart might not be a mystery today.

Though of course, it's also possible that Dr. Hoodless was right and Burns and Jantz are wrong; Burns often bemoans the fact that she has not yet been able to take her own measurements. It's a chancy business to try to classify a skeleton based on sixty-year-old measurements taken by someone else. In the absence of other measurements, just a few millimeters make a difference, particularly when the errors are inconsistent. Burns and Jantz had no choice but to assume—and there doesn't seem to be any reason not to—that Dr. Hoodless measured the bones at the same points they are measured today, but if he didn't, then analysis based on his measurements isn't reliable.

In short, FORDISC provided another piece of suggestive evidence that—combined with everything else—tended to support the Nikumaroro hypothesis. Dr. Hoodless's own conclusion, on the other hand, left one to wonder what a muscular European or mixed-race male was doing on Nikumaroro with a sextant box and a woman's shoe.

How Long Had They Been There?

But what about Gallagher's, and Isaac's, and Dr. Hoodless's observations that the bones had been lying around for—respectively—"more than four years," "upwards of twenty years," and "a considerable time"? The bones were found only about three years after Earhart's disappearance. At a team meeting to discuss what to do next, Spading played devil's advocate on that one with Burns, who was not impressed.

Spading: So assuming for a moment that this was Earhart—who couldn't have been dead more than about three years when the bones were found—why did Gallagher say that the skeleton looked as if it had been there at least four years?

Burns: He probably felt he had to come up with an estimate. The first thing someone is going to ask him is, "How long has it been there?" He's suggesting that this might be someone important; people are going to want to know whether it's possible, timewise. Trouble is, he has no experience to base his estimate on except maybe that dead cow he saw in a back field somewhere in England.

It's not so strange. How many people have experience with dead bodies lying in open tropical environments? Most people don't stick around to watch anything decompose. They've seen road kills, of course, but they don't get out of their cars and keep track of how fast the thing rots.

Spading: Okay. But Gallagher had to have some basis for his estimate, and Isaac, after all, thought it had been lying around for twenty years or more. And there weren't many bones left. Why did the skeleton look so far gone? Why had it lost its muscle attachments, for instance?

Burns: Because it was on the surface of the ground on an equatorial island.

Spading: So? What's the big deal about being on the surface?

Burns: The conditions are less stable than they are underground. Things are always changing—day and night; storm and sun. And there's a greater array of diners. One hundred-plus pounds of food is a real treat—bring on the molds, algae, mosses, insects, birds, crabs, and rats. They find the body quicker, and they change places quicker. The shade-lovers can work under the body, those that don't mind the sun can work on the upper surface, the moisture lovers can work inside, or the inside can just decompose anerobically and produce a really bad stink. The work is done efficiently and in short order.

Spading: Uh . . . yeah, Okay, you can skip the details. Just tell me this: how long do you think it takes for a body to decompose on Niku?

Burns: If you really want to know, take a body out and record its decomposition! Start your own experimental station. You'll need a couple of people to stay on site and record the changes. Volunteers. John?

Gillespie: Oh yeah, there'd be volunteers, but we can't do it. There must be some other way.

Burns: If you can't do it yourself, use comparative data. When I think about hot places, I think about cases I've worked in Haiti or Georgia. Bodies in Georgia don't deteriorate quite as quickly as in Haiti, but skeletonization can take place in two weeks in the summertime—even without the help of large animals like dogs. In Haiti, I've worked with bones that were exposed for no more than a year, but most of the organic material was leached out. The bones were chalky white, cracked, and beginning to crumble.

Spading: Which could suggest to Gallagher or Isaac that they'd been around for a really long time. But aren't bones white anyway, unless they're stained by soil?

Burns: Bone is more or less yellow—when it is alive.

Spading: So why were the bones in my college anatomy class white?

Burns: They were processed by the supplier. Bone is organic matter within an inorganic matrix—living cells inside a "hard sponge." The cells maintain, repair, and replace bone, just like they do in any other living tissue. The bone doesn't turn white until the organic part of the bone breaks down and leaches out of the bone. Cleaning agents and bleach can do that. Decomposition does it too. The cells lyse— that is, they break and release their contents—such things as proteins, nucleic acids, and lipids. Actually, it's nice to get rid of this part, because it tends to be greasy and it gets rather smelly. When the cell contents are degraded more by microbial activity, they release various fatty acids and amines. The acids actually etch the inorganic part of the bone as they are being leached out of the bone.

Gillespie: He asks about the color and she gets gross.

Burns: But I was just getting to the important part! You see, without all the organic material, the bone becomes brittle and easy to damage. You leave it on a coral rock island with pounding rain, strong winds, and occasional storm waves, and the bone's going to move around at least a little. Pretty soon the bone surface is going to wear off, muscle attachment areas and all.

Spading: So, a big animal doesn't have to chew on the bone? It can still lose surface features such as muscle attachment areas and begin to crumble, even without big animals around?

Burns: Yes.

Spading: Okay, so maybe the muscle attachments can disappear without chewing, but why were most of the bones missing?

Burns: You mean you were expecting the bones to be lying there like some picture out of *National Geographic*? I can't say I know exactly why, but I do know that a complete skeleton is the exception, not the norm, especially on the surface. Police crime scene investigators don't even manage to bring in everything. I rather suspect that the crabs and the weather were enough to move the bones around.

Gillespie: Well, it still seems like something had to eat and scatter the bones, and unless there were dogs or pigs on the island . . .

Burns: Are you always thinking about your dog?

Gillespie: I don't have a dog. I do horses. And I'm not volunteering my horse.

Where Is the Southeast End?

Another question about the bones was, of course, "Where did they come from?" Gallagher said the site was at the "South East corner of island" (October 17, 1940) or the "South East shore" (December 27, 1940). The true southeast corner of the island was Ameriki, which raised the rather awful possibility that the U.S. Coast Guard may have destroyed the site where Earhart breathed her last. But the true southeast corner may not be what Gallagher meant. Study of the literature indicated that the term was used in a variety of ways by the island's visitors and residents.

Paul Laxton, in a memorandum report on April 6, 1949, says:

The *southeastern and southern rim* is again generally narrow, being broken by a shallow tidal passage named Bauareke Passage, the land up to this passage being named *Aukaraime*. [11]

So Aukaraime South might be considered to be on the "southeast end." Since this was where TIGHAR found the shoe parts in 1991, it was tempting to think that this was the place Gallagher had in mind.

But in the same memo, Laxton also says:

Fish are plentiful, and fishing is possible on most days off the ocean reef on the sheltered eastern end of the atoll, *particularly off the southeastern corner, near the "Neriti" village site.* The "baneawa," a fish which it is possible to "farm" in brackish water ponds on the tidal flats, abounds in the lagoon and on the ocean reef.

But "Neriti" or Noriti is the land parcel just below Ritiati, on the northwest side of Baureke Passage. And the location Laxton had in mind is nailed down more certainly by the following from his 1951 article in the *Journal of the Polynesian Society:*

> Nearby, on either side of the peninsula, two large pools form on the lagoon flats, filling on the high springs, when tens of thousands of young baneawa fish take refuge in them . . .[12]

The peninsula he was referring to is Kanawa Point. He goes on:

> Further along the atoll's southern rim is the land known as Tekibeia and then, beyond the shallow reef passage of Baureke the land called Aukaraime.
>
> Further east from the end of Aukaraime the atoll rim narrows . . .
>
> At the eastern tip the wedge-shaped area is taken up partly by great pools . . .
>
> Turning the tip to return along the northern rim . . .

It seems that Laxton envisioned the island as oriented with its long axis running more or less east and west. All of Noriti, Tekebeia, and Aukaraime made up the "south" part of the island, and Ameriki was the "east" end.

But even so, how could he have envisioned Kanawa Point as being at the "southeast" end? One possibility was that Laxton, and hence perhaps Gallagher, thought of Nikumaroro overall as an atoll made up of two islands—one between Tatiman and Baureke Passages made up of Ritiati, Noriti, and Tekebeia; the other comprising the rest of the island. Kanawa Point would be on the "southeast corner" of the former island.

Believing that Kanawa Point was the site of the bones discovery was tempting because it's Nei Anna encountered Nei Manganibuka in the ghost maneaba (see page 72). Does this story somehow relate to the finding of the bones? And at Kanawa Point, too, there are all those clam shells cemented into the coraline ledge (see page 97). Somebody at some time ate a lot of clams there. At first, King had figured that their firm attachment to the coral ledge on which they were found meant they had been there a long time—maybe since sometime in prehistory—but consultation with colleagues in the Pacific had shown him that calcium carbonate cementation can happen in a matter of decades or less. Those clams could have been harvested in the 1930s, or '40s.

But Harry Maude confused the matter with the following, in a 1937 report on the PISS proposal:

> On the *south-west corner of the lagoon* a natural lake had formed which teemed with "baneawa" fish . . .[13]

The only such "lake" that fits this description is the pond Laxton describes at Kanawa Point—actually two shallow coves separated by the point, and partly cut off from the lagoon by a reef. So here Maude seems to see Kanawa Point not as being on the southeast corner but the southwest. And in his second PISS progress report, Maude says:

> [I]t is estimated that all of these [coconuts] can be planted around parts of the lagoon and on the *savanna country in the south-east part of the island.*[14]

The only savanna country on the island is at Aukaraime South.

So, was it Aukaraime South or Kanawa Point? Or someplace else? Gallagher provided a few more clues in a telegram sent October 17, 1940:

```
Body had obviously been lying under a "ren" tree
and remains of fire, turtle, and dead birds appear
to indicate life.
```

So it was someplace with tournefortia trees, perhaps close to someplace where turtles and birds can be had. Not much help there, though we had seen the most evidence of turtles hauling out to lay eggs on the windward side. The telegram continued:

```
All small bones have been removed by giant coconut
crabs. . . .
```

Birgus latro likes to live in the shade, so the place probably was wooded.

```
This part of the island is not yet cleared.
```

So the site hadn't yet been cleared for coconut planting. However, as he stated in a letter, dated December 27, 1940, that accompanied the box of bones:

[S]omething may come to hand during the course of the next few months when the area in question will be again thoroughly examined during the course of planting operations.

So it was supposed to be cleared soon. Kanawa Point has been cleared—it no longer has kanawa trees, and does have some coconuts—and airphotos taken in June 1941 by U.S. Navy PBYs doing an aerial survey show that Aukaraime South was cleared and planted by that time.

In the same letter, Gallagher mentioned that the box in which the bones would travel was made from a kanawa tree that "was, until a year ago, growing on the edge of the lagoon, not very far from the spot where the deceased was found."

This suggested that the site may have been on or at least near the lagoon shore, that kanawa trees grew nearby, and that someone had been cutting them down a year earlier. This implicated Kanawa Point, but Laxton's article refers to kanawa trees elsewhere[15] and Bevington's diary suggests that they were common on the island.[16] They are rare at best today, though John Clauss found one in 1996 near the water catcher site on the windward side.[17]

Finally, there's Gallagher's note to the file dated July 3, 1941:

There was no evidence of any attempt to dig a well and the wretched man presumably died of thirst. Less than two miles away there is a small grove of coconut trees which would have been sufficient to keep him alive if he had only found it. He was separated from those trees, however, by an inpenetrable [sic] belt of bush.

Kanawa Point is less than a mile from the Arundel-period coconut groves at Ritiati. Aukaraime South is more than a mile but less than two miles from the same groves.

So there seemed to be three "candidate" bones sites—none of which entirely fit Gallagher's description: Kanawa Point, Aukaraime South, and the "true" southeast end, including Ameriki and the eastern parts of Aukaraime North and South. No one was especially enthusiastic about the last, since Ameriki had been churned up by the Coast Guard and the southeast end of Aukaraime North had been searched in 1991 and 1996 during the water catcher expeditions.

CHAPTER **22**

Meanwhile . . .

The PEOPLE will find Amelia!
—NOTE ON THE EARHART FORUM, 1998

T HE WPHC FILES YIELDED A WEALTH OF CLUES, AND—AS such discoveries always do—showed that a lot more research was needed. Luckily TIGHAR had a spectacular new research tool to use that not only made it possible to run down some of the leads developed in the archives, but pointed in some new directions as well.

The Earhart Forum

TIGHAR had launched its World Wide Web site—www.tighar.org—in 1997, and by the beginning of 1998 it had received a "Best 100 Aviation Sites" award and was getting about 100 visits per day.[1] The site's success led to the creation of the Amelia Earhart Search Forum, a Gillespie-moderated discussion group open to TIGHAR members and nonmembers alike. Though generally organized around testing the Nikumaroro hypothesis—people who want to speculate about Japanese spy plots or alien abductions can go elsewhere—the forum is open to reasoned dissent and alternative hypotheses, and it's pretty free-wheeling. In many ways it's revolutionized the project, expanding TIGHAR's research capacity immeasurably. Individuals take on special research projects, and groups form to work on complex problems.

People all over the world participate—the "international" in TIGHAR's full name has taken on new meaning—and this opens the door to cost-effective research in England, New Zealand, Australia, and other countries having something to do with Earhart, Noonan, and Niku.

What Was Noonan Up To?

Chapter 3 presented some of the results of one forum-based study—the Noonan Project, organized by Jerry Hamilton of Berkeley, California. Jerry and his colleagues, scattered all over the United States, have made the previously mysterious navigator into a more or less known quantity, though there are still intriguing questions about his life and his involvement in the World Flight. Notable among these is his relationship with Eugene Pallette, a then-popular if now little-remembered actor in Hollywood. Noonan apparently arranged to report to Pallette at regular intervals as the World Flight progressed. In a letter to Pallette sent from Dakar in West Africa, dated June 9, 1937, Noonan wrote:

> Having trouble sending messages such as I promised you but I am doing the best I can. Facilities are not always available, and therefore I am sending one message when possible, naming stop made since last message.[2]

Why was he reporting to Pallette? What happened to his other messages, assuming there were some? Did they say anything useful about Noonan as navigator, as participant in the World Flight, about what might have gone wrong on the night of July 2? Perhaps someday we'll know; the Noonan Project is an ongoing study.

Gallagher's Goods

Besides the information on the bones, the WPHC Archives contained a wealth of documentation about the PISS and Gerald Gallagher—greatly fleshing out the poignant story of Gallagher's career and how it ended.[3] Following up on the Gallagher data, a Gallagher Project was put together by Earhart Forum members Simon Ellwood and Phil Tanner in England, John Thompson in Ireland, and Vern Klein in the United States, among others.

According to an inventory taken on Nikumaroro after his death, among Gallagher's possessions on Niku were a camera, photographs, and negatives. The photos and negatives would be great to find, as would any letters he wrote home about the time of the bones discovery. Sir Harry Luke and Harry Maude had arranged for Gallagher's effects to be sent to his mother, Edith, in care of her sister Miss Julie Clancy, at Clanmere, in Malvern, Worcester.[4] The Gallagher Project has found that in 1940 Clanmere—now an office building—was a retirement home, established between the World Wars by Julie Clancy, Edith Gallagher's sister, and a partner. Edith's and Julie's mother (Gerald's grandmother) apparently lived at Clanmere at the time of Gerald's death. Julie Clancy's daughter was able to supply some recollections about the family, and the photo of Gallagher reproduced on page 68, but had nothing more in the way of documents.

More Shoes

The WPHC archives also yielded inventory records of the Gardner Cooperative Store, and to their considerable surprise, Gillespie and Spading found that the store had stocked—shoes!

The inventory for 1940 listed ten pairs of shoes, with a total listed value of £1 9s 2p—that's one pound, nine shillings, and two pence for readers who use the dollar, the euro, or some other newfangled currency. The inventory didn't say what kinds of shoes they were, or why they were stocked.

Gillespie and Spading each looked into the price of shoes in 1940, to see whether those available from the Gardner Cooperative Store might have included American blucher-style oxfords. A rather surprising number of variables have to be considered—the value of the pound in U.S. dollars in 1940 as compared with its value today, the buying power of the pound at that time in Australia, where the inventory indicates the shoes originated, and the wholesale price of blucher-style oxfords in the United States at that time. Spading's investigation is incomplete at this writing, but tentatively, it looks like the shoes in the store were probably a good deal cheaper than blucher-style oxfords with American replacement heels would have been.

Gillespie has argued that no matter what they may have cost, there is no plausible reason for the store to stock relatively narrow American-style women's shoes. After all, the colonists certainly went barefoot, and as a result, like most Pacific islanders, had broad, heavily callused feet. If anybody would have worn shoes, he suggests, it would have been men on working parties in moonscape areas, where they would have had to contend with a lot of sharp coral underfoot. They would have wanted wide, loose shoes, not narrow ones, and certainly not women's shoes.

Without disputing Gillespie's logic, Spading has countered that Gillespie must not know much about the ways of government quartermasters if he thinks they would stock only things that the store's customers might actually use. The argument goes on, while Spading patiently gathers data. The bottom line, though, is that there were shoes for sale on the island in 1940. They were probably quite inexpensive shoes, possibly manufactured in Australia (some anecdotal evidence suggests China), quite likely used on rare occasions when people had to work in moonscape terrain—or perhaps worn by local officials, such as Koata, on ceremonial occasions. The likelihood that the stock included women's blucher-style oxfords with American-brand replacement heels seems very small, but shoes *were* available.

The debate about the Gardner Cooperative Store as a possible shoe source stimulated a broader discussion, on and around the Earhart Forum, into the whole question of where—other than from Earhart's foot—a woman's blucher oxford with a Cat's-Paw replacement heel could have come from. There *are* alternative sources. Members of the Woman's Army Corps (WACs) during World War II wore blucher-style oxfords, so it's conceivable that a WAC found her way to Nikumaroro and lost a shoe. The survey party from USS *Bushnell* made observations from the lagoon shore at Aukaraime South (probably accounting for the psychrometer found there in 1991); it's conceivable that there was an unreported woman aboard *Bushnell* who lost a shoe during the survey. It's possible that someone came by in a yacht. But then, it's possible that the shoe was washed up in a storm wave, dropped from an airplane, or coughed up by a whale; there's really no end to the possibilities. None of the alternatives identified so far are very persuasive, but research continues.

The Wreck of the *Norwich City*

The Earhart Forum has been a great way for interested people, and people with useful information, to learn about TIGHAR's work and to make contact. One such person, who has a fascinating story to tell, is Janet Powell, grandniece of Daniel Hamer, master of the *Norwich City*.

Before Ms. Powell contacted TIGHAR, forays into various archives had netted a number of documents about the wreck, including the findings of the Naval Court that investigated its circumstances.[5] The documents associated with this investigation included fairly extensive accounts by members of the ship's company. Ms. Powell was able to flesh out the story considerably, based on a manuscript Hamer had prepared and that had been passed down in the family.[6]

The ship went up on the Nutiran reef during a westerly storm on the night of November 29, 1929. She caught fire, and as dawn approached it was obvious that the ship would have to be abandoned. Lowering boats amid fire and explosions in the dark, in high winds and breaking seas, was no small feat, and in trying to lower the port lifeboat Hamer was washed overboard. Remarkably, he managed to make it to shore alive.

A lifeboat with all remaining hands aboard left the ship, but capsized in the surf. Eleven men were killed. Only three bodies washed up while the survivors were on the island, and those were buried on the beach. Both lifeboats washed ashore, with considerable gear aboard, and the survivors

By 1989, there wasn't much left of the *Norwich City*. TIGHAR photo by Pat Thrasher.

improvised a shelter about 100 yards into the bush. Food and water were in short supply, several members of the company were barefoot, and the camp was subject to forays by rats and coconut crabs. One night the mate "was awakened by the playful nip" of an inquisitive *Birgus,* and nearly "jumped out of his clothes."

After two full days and nights on the island, the survivors were cheered by the arrival of SS *Trongate* of London and MV *Lincoln Ellsworth* of Oslo, responding to distress calls that *Norwich City's* radio operator had gotten off as the ship exploded in flames around him. A crew of Tuvaluans was able to get a boat ashore with provisions, and rewarded themselves with coconut crabs. It was impossible to get the boat back across the reef at that point, however, so a better place for embarkation was sought. The location found was about 1.5 miles south of the wreck, apparently on the ocean side opposite where Kanawa Point juts into the lagoon. Crossing the reef here was no picnic either, however; the seas were still high and a number of sharks had gathered. It took two days and several unsuccessful attempts before the entire party of survivors was extracted and the two rescue ships sailed.

One event that Hamer mentioned, rather in passing, was of special interest:

> Before leaving camp all provisions etc., were placed in the shelter, but I sincerely hope that no one will ever be so unfortunate as to need them.

Ten years later the New Zealand survey party photographed the "remains of wreck survivors' camp"—a collection of what appeared to be containers of various kinds in the bush. Certainly not neatly "placed," but scattered around. Scattered by rats and coconut crabs, or through use by the castaways for whom the stockpile was intended? If the latter, were they our castaways? And what would castaways have found in the stockpile? What would have been left? A bottle of Benedictine? A cask with corks on chains?

The Wreck Photo

Meanwhile, the thing that Jeff Glickman's photo enhancement suggested was in the bush along the western shore of Nutiran in 1988 made Gillespie begin to rethink another photograph that had fallen into TIGHAR's paws almost ten years earlier. The photo was that of a two-engine aluminum airplane, badly broken up, with tropical vegetation in the background. Its story went like this.

Sometime around 1978, retired navy Captain George Carrington brought the "wreck photo" and another picture to officials at Lockheed Aircraft. He said they had been given to him by a former British seaman who had served aboard the submarine tender HMS *Adamant* in the western Pacific in late 1946 and early 1947. Carrington said that the seaman, who insisted on anonymity, had given him the pictures because the wrecked airplane in one of them reminded him of Earhart's airplane as shown on the cover of a book Carrington had published describing his own theory (in which Earhart is portrayed as a spy).[7]

The seaman's other photo showed the beach of a tropical island from just offshore. A group of perhaps forty men in shorts are standing about on the beach and in the shallow water. Most are shirtless. The level beach extends several hundred feet inland and is bordered by a few tall palm trees,

The mysterious wreck photo. TIGHAR Collection from U.S. National Air and Space Museum.

behind which the vegetation and terrain rise steeply to high jungle hills in the distance. According to Carrington, HMS *Adamant* had put these men ashore on the uninhabited island to gather sand, which was used for fighting engine room fires, and also to enjoy a little recreation. The seaman did not recall the name of the island, if he had ever known it. Supposedly he walked along the beach with a friend until they noted a couple of large coconut palms that had been knocked down. Back in the bush they found the wreckage of a twin-engine airplane and took the photo.

First Lockheed, then the Smithsonian Air & Space Museum, and ultimately TIGHAR (with some hi-tech photo-analytical help) tried to determine:

A. Did the photo show a Lockheed Model 10 Electra?
B. If it was an Electra, what version was it?
C. Where might the photo have been taken?

The results were inconclusive. Most agreed that the aircraft was an Electra Model 10, although there were dissenters. No compelling case could be made one way or the other as to whether it was a 10A (with 450 hp Pratt & Whitney R985 engines) or a 10E (with 550 hp Pratt & Whitney R1340 engines). Earhart's aircraft was, of course, a 10E.

Botanists at the Smithsonian's Museum of Natural History confirmed that the vegetation was appropriate for a Pacific island, but they pointed up some problems with the story. The mature coconut palms visible in the wreck photo appear to be very sick trees—perhaps because of an infestation of rhinoceros beetles, perhaps from drought—while the trees in the photo of the men on the beach are healthy. The two photos, said the Smithsonian botanists, probably could not have been taken on the same island at the same time. Further investigation also showed that HMS *Adamant* had been docked in Hong Kong during the entire period when the sand-gathering visit to the mysterious island was supposed to have taken place.[8]

It appeared there was nothing anyone could do with the wreck photo at that time, so it went into TIGHAR's growing file of shoulder-shrugging quasi-data. But when the "thing" on the Nutiran coast showed up, Gillespie began to wonder. He dredged up the wreck photo and sent it to Glickman to have a go.

Glickman's analysis, and Gillespie's report of its results, were very technical, but in essence confirmed that the airplane in the photo probably was an Electra. Further, even more fine-grained analysis led to the conclusion that some key features were consistent with a 10E and not with another kind of Electra.[9]

So, maybe it was a plane like Earhart's, but of the fifteen Electra 10Es that Lockheed manufactured, eight couldn't be accounted for and could have crashed in tropical environments. So even if it *was* a 10E it wasn't necessarily the *right* 10E.

Gillespie called Carrington to see if he could provide any further information. He declined. The picture would have to stand on its own.

What intrigued Gillespie was that the background in the Carrington photo looked a lot like what the background of the Nutiran shore should have looked like if one had photographed it from the beach sometime in the 1940s. The mature coconut palms shown in the background would be from one of Arundel's groves from the 1890s. The grasses and sedges in the foreground were right for the Nutiran strand, as were the bushes and low trees—probably scaevola and tournefortia—in the middle distance. And in the background were tall trees that look for all the world like buka.

The Cruciform

So, Gillespie proposed a new scenario: Earhart lands on the Nutiran beach—not a bad place at least to try to land, and perhaps attractive because of the *Norwich City,* which she might have thought indicated a settlement nearby or at least a source of stuff useful to castaways. Landing safely, she gets out of the sun by taxiing into the shade of the trees along the shore, where—just as in the Aukaraime "runway" scenario—the plane is invisible to the *Colorado* pilots. She and Noonan find the *Norwich City* survivors' campsite and live off the provisions there for a while before dying. Storms push the plane back into the scaevola and tear it up, leaving it in the condition in which it was photographed—by whomever—in about 1946 or 1947. Colonists cannibalize it for aluminum, but the remains are still there, accounting for what Glickman could see in the 1988 photo.

Looking more at that photo, and others taken in the 1950s, Gillespie made another intriguing observation. In these shots, clearing and planting had gotten under way on western Nutiran, and a large building had been constructed. Not far from the building, and close to—though not precisely at—the location of the "thing" in the 1988 airphoto, was something that

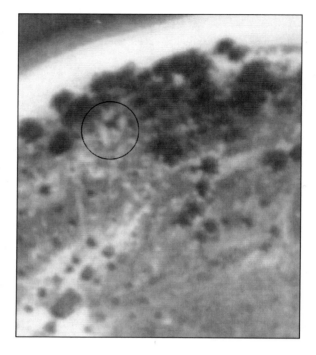

An aerial mapping
photo of Nikumaroro
taken in 1953 revealed
the "cruciform" on
the Nutiran shore.
TIGHAR Collection
from the New Zealand
National Archive.

attracted people, but that hadn't been cleared of vegetation. It showed up as a dark area from which paths radiated; it was roughly cruciform in shape, and about the right size to be the remains of an airplane.

This was getting almost scary. The Funafuti account, the airphotos, the Carrington wreck photo, and now the cruciform all suggested something very much like an airplane wreck on the western Nutiran shore—an area that for all practical purposes, TIGHAR had never looked at. Some of the 1989 team had walked the beach in the vicinity, and John Clauss, Veryl Fenlason, and LeRoy Knoll had taken a quick sashay through the scaevola on the day before departure. They had noted house remains and agricultural pits, but that was all, and they hadn't done a real survey. Lots of room for things to be there. Big things. Airplane things.

CHAPTER 23

Where the Plane Came Down

It's them thirteen bones; where could they be?
Not walkin' down the street or up in a tree.
Home and family don't you call me 'cause my soul is in hock
To them thirteen bones in a kanawa box.*

—TIGHAR TUNES

An Embarrassment of Possibilities

There were almost too many leads to check out. Never mind "almost"; there *were* too many leads to check out, at least within the limits of TIGHAR's perennially stressed resources.

With the documentation from the WPHC and Tarawa files on the travels of the thirteen bones[1] in their kanawa box, there was every reason to throw a lot of effort into finding them. They could well be in Fiji, where the documents last put them, but they could also have been passed back to Tarawa when the WPHC closed up shop and Kiribati achieved independence. Or they could have gone to England. Or they could have gotten lost in the shuffle of World War II. Or . . .

Fiji was clearly the place to start, and there was quite a bit of research that could be done there without even buying plane tickets. Kris Tague, Kenton Spading, and Tom King started corresponding with people, narrowing possibilities. By early in 1999 the Fiji Museum had agreed to cooperate in the search; Tarisi Vunadilo, head of the archaeology department,

---

*Sung to the tune of "Sixteen Tons," by Merle Travis.

259

was enthusiastic about the possibilities, and her boss, Kate Vusoniwailala, agreed to the museum's full involvement. They put out a press release and began contacting government ministries, asking for information and seeking permission to search likely places.

"Likely places" naturally included the old Central Medical School, now absorbed into the massive Colonial War Memorial Hospital and Fiji School of Medicine, in Suva. The school's original building was now the hospital's dental clinic; the school itself had moved to a new building on a leftover World War II military base in nearby Tamavua in 1954. Later, part of the school had moved back to a modern building at the hospital, built for the purpose and called, naturally, Hoodless House after the school's pioneer principal. The anatomy department was based in Hoodless House; if it had a collection of bones, it was another place to look. However, it was reported that its bone collection had been "disposed of" some years before when instructional philosophy had changed. No one was willing or able to say what "disposed of" meant. The museum itself was another possibility, and then there was Government House, Sir Harry's residence in 1940, in 1999 the residence of the president, His Excellency the Right Honorable Ratu Sir Kamisese Kapaiwei Tuimacilai Mara. Government House has a covey of outbuildings, including those in which the WPHC had had its offices. And these weren't the only possibilities. Suva is a city of about 90,000 (400,000 in the metropolitan area), with a rich colonial architectural tradition—in other words, it has *lots* of old buildings that were in use before World War II, many of them by the government.

Lots of places to look, and it quickly became apparent that despite the museum's best efforts, the bones weren't going to walk in the door or pop into some Fiji citizen's head in an epiphanic flash of inspiration ("Oh, *that* kanawa wood box full of bones!"). Some on-scene TIGHAR participation was needed. A visit would also provide the opportunity to dig into the National Archives for information we hadn't known to look for before, to talk with people who had lived on Niku or been affiliated with the WPHC, and perhaps to let serendipity strike again.

And then there was Niku. If the cruciform was the wreck, then TIGHAR had a major excavation and recovery operation in store, but it would be really unfortunate to pull together the couple of million dollars such an operation would require, only to find out that it *wasn't* the wreck. There were also the three candidate bones discovery sites—Aukaraime South, Kanawa Point, and eastern Aukaraime North. Each was a big area to search for very small stuff—stuff that had been searched for by Gallagher and his colleagues to no avail when the site—wherever it was—was a lot fresher. Searching any one of them would be a major archaeological project, and we had little idea how to establish priorities, boundaries, methods, and so on.

So a reconnaissance was needed: Check out the cruciform and the west side of Nutiran generally. Take a hard look at the possible bones sites. Once again Gillespie and Thrasher went into fund-raising overdrive, and by June 1999 there was enough in the coffers, barely, to support a two-pronged expedition.

One small team—two to three people in staggered groups—would spend a month or so in Fiji—working with the Fiji Museum to accelerate the bones search, do archival work, and interview people—while another team would go on to Niku. The Niku work had two purposes: check out the western side of Nutiran, especially the cruciform site, and apply Karen Burns's expert forensic eyes to the three candidate bones discovery sites.

Burns's expert eyes were first needed to look at the collections of bones we already knew about, in the museum itself and—we hoped—in the School of Medicine's anatomy department. She and King would comprise the first Fiji team, arriving about a week before the rest of the group. When the main team arrived in Fiji it would embark with Burns aboard *Nai'a* for Niku, while Kris Tague and TIGHAR's newly named education director, Barbara Norris, would work with King to continue the search in Fiji.

The Airhearts

Barb Norris had come to TIGHAR in 1998. A teacher at Uwchlan Hills Elementary School in Downingtown, Pennsylvania, she and her fifth grade class read about TIGHAR and found Gillespie's phone number. With some trepidation they called, and soon had him in the classroom for a typically spellbinding account of the project. Before long the entire class had joined TIGHAR, Norris had become education director, and she had developed a whole curriculum built around "The Search." The kids called themselves the Airhearts, and began an ongoing e-mail correspondence with Gillespie and King.

Norris found that the project had all kinds of advantages as a focus of study. Earhart herself was an inspirational figure, particularly for girls. The project exposed the kids to a wide range of academic study topics—history and archaeology, of course, but also oceanography, navigation, aeronautics, meteorology, even tropical ecology. Most important, it provided a vehicle

for encouraging organized problem solving. Like everybody else involved in
the search, the Airhearts developed and evaluated hypotheses and figured
out how to test them. They put on a special presentation to their school, in
which Gillespie took part and that was taped and broadcast by the History
Channel. They also raised money for the project. And in the summer of
1999 they formed a cheering section for Norris as she embarked to join the
Fiji team in the search for the bones.[2]

Collections and Crawl Spaces

Burns and King arrived in Suva on June 26. Working around press confer-
ences and meetings with ministries, they focused first on known bone collections, to which Burns could apply her calipers and laptop-loaded
FORDISC. First, Tarisi Vunadilo arranged for Burns to inspect all the bones
in the museum's collection that weren't from documented archaeological
sites. None matched Dr. Hoodless's measurements. Then up to the School
of Medicine's anatomy department at Hoodless House. As they had heard,
the school's leadership had decided to "dispose of" the bone collection when
changes in teaching methods rendered hands-on manipulation of bones
passé, but it turned out that a dedicated lab manager, Satya Deo, had hidden the collection and saved it—boxes and boxes and boxes of bones. A
good thing, since hands-on instruction has come back into favor, and a good
thing for TIGHAR. Unfortunately, however, no matches were found, and
most of the bones were from recorded cadavers that had been rendered
down when the students were through with them.

Vunadilo: What's in that big tank?

Deo: [opening the lid and stirring with a paddle] Let me show
you.

Vunadilo: [turning almost as gray as the floating corpse] Oh—er—
thank you so much.

While Burns measured bones, King and three Fiji Museum volunteers
began searching attics, basements, and crawl spaces. Luckily Faiz Ali,
Elaitia Vakarau, and Steven Brown were an agile trio. They made short
work of the attic of the old Medical School, the attic and basement of Dr.

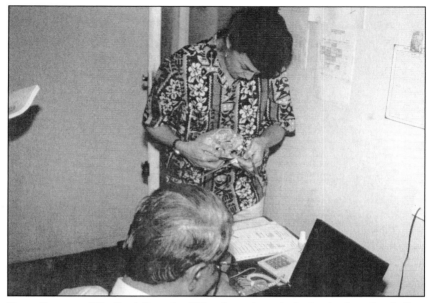

Karen Burns and Dr. Roel Cayari, a Fijian forensic pathologist, analyze the skull measurements from a Fijian forensic case with the FORDISC program. TIGHAR photo by Tom King.

Hoodless's residence, and a number of other high, low, hot, dusty, slimy, and generally uncomfortable places where bones might have been stashed. Lots of stuff *had* been stashed—wheelchairs, file cabinets, dental records—but the only bones that turned up were those of a bird, more or less mummified among the dusty dental tools in the old Central Medical School's attic.

Ever the responsible professional, Burns felt obligated to volunteer her services when an unidentified skeleton was brought in by the police from the rain forest in nearby Navua. It had been found by farm kids and their dogs, on a ridge facing the sea. The skeleton was of a big, strong guy, Burns opined as she sorted through the bones on a hospital gurney, probably of European racial background.

> Burns: I'll bet he smiled or squinted a lot.
> King: Give me a break; how can you tell that?
> Burns: See these little muscle attachments on the maxilla—very well developed.

It was out to the discovery site then, through a mile or so of mud and marsh grass, up and over several slippery, jungle-clad ridges. A vigorous search turned up a few more bones, gnawed by dogs or pigs, and in the process elicited more information from the kids who had discovered the body and the police who had searched the site before. The site was no place for a homicide, but an excellent place for a suicide—pretty, serene view out to the sea, over rain forest and grassland.

The skeleton turned out to be almost certainly that of an American who had been missing for a few months, and who had probably committed suicide. The proprietors of the hotel where he'd been staying when he disappeared had a photo of him—a big, healthy looking guy with a broad smile and tightly squinted eyes.

What was interesting to Burns and King from an Earhart point of view was that the body had been completely skeletonized in a matter of months, and that all that had been found in the way of clothing were the tattered remains of a backpack. It made one wonder what the basis was for Gallagher's opinion that the bones on Niku had been there for several years, and Isaac's that they'd lain around for a couple of decades. Of course, the Navua suicide's bones still showed clear muscle attachments, and the Niku bones apparently had not—but then, the muscle attachments on a woman's bones tend not to be as prominent as those on a man's, so if Gallagher and Isaac had been looking at a woman's skeleton. . . . And Navua's environment isn't as unfriendly to bone preservation as Niku's. Navua has pigs and dogs, but the site isn't made up of coral rubble, the sunlight is nowhere near as intense as on Niku, and there are no coconut crabs.

By the time Burns departed with the rest of the Niku team on July 5, the Fiji team had exhausted known collections. Barb Norris took over working with the volunteers, focusing on exciting places like the tunnels under the medical school campus at Tamavua, while King dealt with diplomatic issues. The government, not surprisingly, hadn't been wild about a bunch of Americans searching Government House, and word of this had leaked to the opposition media, whose implications that government was standing in the way of historical research were not appreciated by the President's Office.

While this flap was being delicately worked out by Vunadilo and her colleagues at the museum, Norris, Tague, and King began to interview people—retired doctors who had been medical students under Dr. Hoodless, the head of the Fiji Intelligence Service, the head of maintenance for all government buildings. Sir Leonard Usher, who'd worked with the Fiji Defense Force during World War II and knew everyone on Sir Harry's staff.

"Oh yes," he said, thumbing through the WPHC file. "That's vintage Vaskess. See how everything's cross-referenced. The Prince of Bureaucrats, was Vaskess." But Sir Leonard knew nothing about the bones.

During a press conference at the museum, a reporter told King that there was a box of bones secreted away in the Suva Masonic Lodge; it had been seen by a worker making modifications in the building for use by a local TV station. Well, maybe Dr. Hoodless had been a Mason, King thought, and had figured the bones would be safe there. The Masons proved entirely cooperative. Of course they had a box of bones; it was used in certain rituals. No, no one had any idea where it had come from; it had been there for as long as anyone could remember. Would the searchers like to see it?

The box was dark wood—it could have been kanawa—but it had a sliding door, which when opened revealed a skull and crossed leg bones, rather chewed around the ends by—well, maybe coconut crabs, but who could tell? The skull looked like that of an elderly male, and most significantly it had both malars intact. Dr. Hoodless had been quite clear that the right malar had been missing on the Niku skull. So much for the Masonic connection.

The President's Office eventually gave permission to search the basement of Government House and its associated bomb shelters—a remarkably open attitude, when you consider how the U.S. government would react to a Fijian expedition wanting to search the White House. The building contained lots of junk, like you would find in any basement or abandoned tunnel, but no bones, and no kanawa box. The Fiji Intelligence Service opened its building, formerly the WPHC's bachelor officers quarters, it was said (imagine a Fijian party asking to search CIA Headquarters!), but there was nothing there either. The Colonial War Memorial Hospital denied permission to search beyond the limits of the old Central Medical School ("Crikey, what a waste of time!"), but the hospital is so enormous, with so many nooks and crannies, that King couldn't imagine making a dent in it anyhow, within the time available.

It was beginning to feel like a replay of 1989 on Niku—running out of possibilities, beginning to just wander around hoping something would turn up. And as it happened . . .

Foua Tofinga

One person King very much wanted to interview was Foua Tofinga, a retired government executive originally from Tuvalu. Peter McQuarrie had told Kenton Spading how knowledgeable Tofinga was about the latter days of the WPHC, and how he'd been in charge of disposing of WPHC assets back in the 1970s. It turned out that Intelligence Director Metuisela Mua knew him well, and soon he was sitting in the archaeology department office at the museum.

Foua Tofinga is a charming, cultured, and careful gentleman. He began by explaining that when he worked for the WPHC he had sworn certain oaths of secrecy that he would have to honor. He said he would let them know if they were blundering too close to anything he couldn't discuss. "You've worked for government, Dr. King; you know how these things are," he said. Then he proceeded to provide a wealth of information about Sir Harry, Vaskess, Gallagher, and—to King's surprise—Nikumaroro.

"There is just something about that island," he mused. "I would like to go back there . . ."

It turned out that as a young man in the 1930s, he had gone from his home in Tuvalu to Tarawa for schooling. He recalled being called out to search the reef for anything that might have washed up after Earhart's disappearance. He was then summoned to Suva to work for the WPHC, and had become, in his words, "the only brown face" in Sir Harry's office. He looked at the bones files and shook his head.

"Those English," he said. "I was right there in the office, and they never told me about this."

He recalled seeing the sextant box on a table with other curios in Henry Vaskess's office. He had helped Gallagher load supplies aboard *Viti* for the voyage that was to be Gallagher's last.[3] He talked of how hard Gallagher had worked, how he had not placed himself above his I Kiribati, Tuvaluan, and Fijian colleagues, what a fine gentleman he had been. How shocked he, Vaskess, and Sir Harry had been by Gallagher's death, and how he, like Aram Tamia, had written a letter of condolence to Gerald's mother. He spoke of Dr. Isaac—Dr. Verrier, as he was known during and after the war. He, too, was a good man, Tofinga said, and like Gallagher very much in sympathy with the people.

Tofinga had traveled to Niku with Sir Harry a month after Gallagher's death; he had seen Gerald's grave, stayed awhile in the village, and then sailed on with Sir Harry on his inspection tour. This tour had been cut short by the Japanese attack on Pearl Harbor; they had run for Canton so Sir Harry could board a Pan Am Clipper and fly back to his duties.

He had been responsible for disposing of the WPHC's furniture when the operation in Fiji had closed down; he didn't recall a kanawa box. He would have recognized it, because in fact he had one of his own, made on another island and given to him and his wife as a wedding gift. He brought the handsome piece to the museum, carved with an adze out of a single block of wood, inlaid with an elaborate pattern of—naturally—cut aluminum.

And Tofinga had been responsible for dividing up the commission's papers and sending some off to Tarawa, some to Funafuti, some to England, among other places. He didn't recall anything about bones.

"But," he said, "you know, the daughter of the man who must have built that box lives here in Suva."

What?

"Oh, yes, she's Tuvaluan. Her name is Emily Sikuli. Her father was the carpenter on Nikumaroro. Sir Harry Luke and I brought her back here to work as a nurse, when we visited that time after Mister Gallagher died. Would you like to talk with her?"

Does *Birgus latro* poop in the scaevola?

The Carpenter's Daughter

A few days later Tofinga reported that he had spoken with Mrs. Sikuli and that she clearly remembered her father building the box for the bones. He had set up an interview with her, at his home. Mrs. Sikuli spoke only Tuvaluan, so Tofinga would serve as interpreter.

The Tofinga residence, where Tofinga lives with his wife, Selepa, is a pleasant concrete-block home in a modest residential neighborhood. Selepa served tea. Mrs. Sikuli, a slight, smiling woman, sat on a couch with her daughter Sarah, who was fluent in English and helped with interpretation. Based on Barb Norris's notes, the conversation went like this:

Tom King:	Your father is kind of a famous man to us, because we're trying to find that box he built.
Emily Sikuli:	[smiles, gets photocopies out of a folder] Here is his picture, and a picture of my mother.

Emily Sikuli. TIGHAR photo by Richard Gillespie.

The photos were from a magazine or book of portraits, professionally done, perhaps sometime in the 1950s or 1960s—possibly on Niku and possibly in the Solomons or in Kiribati; we have not been able to locate the original. The pictures were of a handsome older couple. Mrs. Sikuli, who said her Tuvaluan name was Segalo, said her father had been Temou Samuela. The carpenter was a rugged guy with a stubbly lantern jaw. Norris took copies of the photos.

> King: We are all interested about the bones in the box. Can you tell us something about the circumstances of that day?
>
> Mrs. Sikuli: The bones were found in the sea on Nikumaroro. There was a boat that was wrecked, but that boat belonged to New Zealand and that part of the island was named for New Zealand. Where the boat was on the reef, not too far from there, is where the plane came down.

Plane? We hadn't said a word about airplanes, but Tofinga later said that he had explained generally what we were interested in. Still . . .

268

King picked himself up off the floor, pulled out a map of Niku, and asked her where this airplane had been. She pointed to the Nutiran reef north of the *Norwich City*.

> Mrs. Sikuli: Not far from where the ship was. Not toward the village but away from it. The struts were there.

It was Tofinga who used the word "struts," of course; we don't know exactly what Tuvaluan word Mrs. Sikuli used. She held up her hands in a circle, apparently indicating that the struts were round in cross-section, about eight inches or so in diameter. Then she went on:

> Mrs. Sikuli: It was around that area where the bones were found. Could be bones from the ship or the airplane. During the westerlies, heavy swells took the rest of the bones away. There were not many that we found. Maybe ten different people whose bones were found along that area. There were some with leather bottles and a pipe. I used to accompany my father to fish. Some people would not go to that area to fish because they were frightened. You would come up on the reef, then the beach comes up where the island shrubs start to grow.

She and Tofinga conferred, and indicated with gestures and words that she meant the first scaevola line in from the beach, inland from the low ridge of coral rubble that is thrown up by storms all along the Nutiran shore.

Ten people? This sounded like *Norwich City* victims. The conversation veered off for a while into a discussion of her father's carpentry and how he had fished for the village, taking her with him. She had walked all the way around the island three times, she said. King then brought the discussion back around:

> King: Did you see the plane fall?
> Mrs. Sikuli: No, it was already there when I came. I came in 1938–1939, when I was eleven years old. I left in December 1941. The steel of the plane was there sometime before we got there.

Steel. King asked about aluminum; she indicated a clear understanding of the differences between aluminum and steel, and said she'd seen no aluminum. She went on:

Mrs. Sikuli: Fishermen found the bones. They were frightened and they brought the story of them to the Onotoa man.

She seemed to be struggling to recall the name of the man from Onotoa, a person in authority. Here King made a serious mistake; trying to be helpful, and knowing that Koata, the magistrate, had been from Onotoa in Kiribati, he led the witness.

King: Was that Koata?
Mrs. Sikuli: [smiling broadly as in recognition] Yes.
King: What did Koata do?
Mrs. Sikuli: He sent people to bring the bones. People were frightened. Only people working for the government received the bones. My father had to look at the bones. Mr. Gallagher asked my father to make the box.

More discussion of her father's carpentry work, the dimensions and appearance of the box. Then . . .

King: Please clarify about the bones. Were the ten skeletons/bodies separate from the bones that were put in the box?
Mrs. Sikuli: The bones of the ten people were toward the shoreline, but these bones [the bones in the box her father made] were found on the reef near the remaining parts of the plane. People decided these bones were from the people from the plane. When I used to go to the place, the bones of the ten people were still there. People who found the bones near the plane were frightened to touch them. They told Tem Koata of the bones and he told Gallagher. Koata had them collect the bones for Gallagher. Until I left the island, I hadn't heard anything about what had happened to those bones. The government put restrictions that children were not to frequent that area.
King: Did people use parts of the airplane?

Mrs. Sikuli: I don't know for sure. When we got there only the steel frames were left, only the long pieces were there. We were frightened to go close to the plane. Where the shipwreck was—the remainder of the plane was not very far from there. The waves were washing it in low tide. The ten people had complete skeletons. Looking at those people, they could be tall people. They were very long. People were afraid of all the bones in both places.

When the interview ended the Fiji team hightailed it to the telephone to get a radio message off to *Nai'a* at Niku—*look on the reef edge north of the shipwreck!* Unfortunately, however, as with Earhart and the *Itasca* back in 1937, it was impossible to establish two-way communication. *Nai'a's* radio was down.

The next day King had to return to the United States. When he arrived at the Los Angeles airport he called TIGHAR central with the news, so Thrasher could pass it on to Gillespie in the event he called in. Norris and Tague carried on in Suva, interviewing, doing archival research, working more with Tofinga, exploring dusty attics and musty tunnels with the three doughty volunteers. No bones. Before he left, King put his faith in the market and put up a reward for information, but as this is written, nobody has claimed it.

Meanwhile on Niku

Nai'a had had a rough passage to Niku, with high seas and head winds. It took six days to get to the island, and once there, it was pouring rain. Gillespie and the team wrestled their gear ashore and reopened the Gallagher Highway, worked a skiff in through Tatiman Passage, and ferried themselves and the gear up to Nutiran.

As usual, the field team included both veterans and new recruits. Clauss and Fenlason made it once more, along with Hunn and Quigg from 1997 and Matthews from '89, '91, and '96. New to the island were Burns, expedition sponsors Chris Kennedy, Ron Rich, and Jerry Ann Jurenka, and TIGHAR directors and sponsors Skeet Gifford and Dick Reynolds.

From a base on the Nutiran shore, the laser transit made it an uncomplicated matter—though a tiring and soggy one—to lay out twenty-meter squares in the scaevola and begin examining the neighborhood of the cruciform.

The "cruciform" area was divided into blocks, cleared, and carefully searched.
TIGHAR photo by Ric Gillespie.

Where they found, in essence, nothing. No airplane. No airplane parts. Nothing at the cruciform location itself but an old oarlock, perhaps from a *Norwich City* lifeboat. A scatter of nails, wire, and cans at the site of the large building that had been so visible in the airphotos. A bit farther north, the ruins of a wood frame building with boards and corrugated metal siding— probably the European-style building mentioned by Tapania Taiki. One small piece of airplane skin here, the first one found outside the village, but it was painted with zinc chromate—of military origin.

But there was another grave—another isolated grave, marked in traditional I Kiribati fashion, near the shore. With the permission and supervision of the government's representative, TIGHAR's old friend from 1991 Manikaa Teuatabo, Burns, and her team—Gary Quigg and Skeet Gifford—excavated it.

Several things about this grave helped us to understand the dynamics of the island.

The grave was located in the midst of a thick clump of scaevola. This may not seem like much of a surprise, but in places like the Nutiran shore behind the wall of scaevola that tends to border the beach, the stuff becomes rather patchy. Some of these inland areas are made up of nothing but coral rubble. Even a hardy pioneer plant like scaevola can't find anything to suck out of such ground—imagine trying to grow a bush in a gravel pit. So when a hardy clump of scaevola is growing in the midst of a bare area, there's reason to be suspicious. The plant's food may be the contents of a grave.

The bottom of the Nutiran grave was more than two meters deep; Quigg had disappeared from view by the time he reached bottom. This was impressive to Burns; digging coral rubble is a lot harder than digging nice, soft dirt. Burns used to think that Georgia clay and 90-degree temperatures were terrible; now she embraces them. The walls of the excavation showed stratigraphic layers. The layers were composed of thick deposits of coral rubble defined by thin, dark bands of organic material. The coral was probably deposited by the wind and water of large storms. The organic bands resulted from the quiet times when rotting leaves, bird droppings, and algae could slowly accumulate on the surface of the coral. The layers were up to two feet in thickness—Nutiran has seen some really big storms.

Quigg continued to dig following the density and pattern of roots, which marked the boundaries of the original grave pit—kind of like following a dog on a scent. He stayed with the roots until they branched out over the little coffin. Just as in Aukaraime South, there was a mass of rootlets, reflecting the rectangular shape of a box.

And just as at Aukaraime South, inside the box were the fragmentary remains of a human infant. The bones went respectfully back into the hole and were reburied.

Aboard *Nai'a,* the "watermaker," which converts seawater to fresh through diffusion through membranes, hadn't worked since shortly after Fiji fell astern, and things were getting a bit dry and stinky. To make matters worse, the radio had gone out. Gillespie had an Iridium satellite phone, but had been reluctant to use it because he had no idea what it would cost (as it turned out, it wasn't expensive). However, at this point—midway through the expedition—he decided it was time to call Thrasher in Wilmington. He thus learned what Emily Sikuli had told the Fiji team, and King had passed on to TIGHAR central from the L.A. airport.

Gillespie didn't immediately redeploy everyone to the reef edge north of the *Norwich City.* There was time for that, and more work to be done in an orderly fashion. After completing a check of the Taraia shore where Pulekai

Songivalu had reported wreckage—nothing there but styrofoam and plastic flotsam, and *very* heavy scaevola—the team continued to work north along the Nutiran shore. The scaevola here was daunting; it formed a virtually impenetrable wall just behind the wave-built ridge of coral rubble that backed the beach. Transects were cut, boxes opened up, the ground inspected, and nothing was found but *Norwich City* debris—and another possible grave. It was marked by a single standing coral slab rather than by the typical little slab-lined platform, so perhaps—if it was a grave at all—it wasn't I Kiribati. Intriguing, but there was no time to excavate it.

While most of the team continued sweating and slashing in the scaevola, Gillespie, Burns, Matthews, and Clauss headed off one morning to reconnoiter the possible bones discovery sites. Kanawa Point was the first stop. The cove just east of the point turned out to have what amounted to a quicksand bottom, as Gillespie learned to his embarrassment and everyone else's

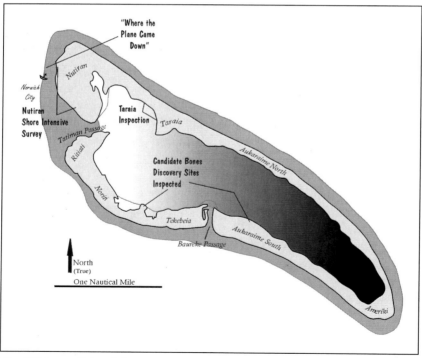

The 1999 expedition did an intensive survey on the Nutiran shore and reef flat, and inspected Taraea and two of the three candidate bones sites.

amusement when he was first person out of the boat. The point itself was devoid of kanawa trees, but well wooded in scaevola. On the lagoon shore east of the point, the scatter of giant clamshells recorded in 1989 turned out to be larger than King had thought—some 300 shells over an area easily sixty feet long and fifteen feet wide. As in '89, no artifacts were to be found.

Aukaraime South was next. In preparation for this visit, Spading had gone to work processing the EM sensing data from 1997. John Evaskovich, a TIGHAR member who processes remote sensing data for a living, had heard about Spading's work and offered to help. After a few late nights crunching data, Spading and Evaskovich had been able to crank out a contour map of EM readings, which they delivered just hours before the team departed for Fiji. The map showed two apparent subsurface anomalies that hadn't been detected in 1997. Using the map as a guide, the site-visit team swept the vicinity of the anomalies with metal detectors, but found nothing. Burns took a look, everyone noticed how the scaevola had grown up since '97, and that was that.

Time ran out before the group could make it to the third candidate bones site—the water catcher vicinity on the windward side. At the time, no one thought much of this; Burns had seen two of the three sites, and the prospect they presented wasn't encouraging. Far less than great conditions for bone preservation, and if any had been preserved, finding them among the coral fragments would be a serious challenge.

Time was running out generally, and so were evident possibilities for useful research. Finally at a very low tide the team spread out over the reef flat north of the *Norwich City*, but found nothing. Whatever Mrs. Sikuli had seen in 1940 wasn't there any more. However, there *was* a smooth area on the coral, about 700 feet long. A tempting place to land an Electra, perhaps.

On July 20, it was time to call it quits. They had accomplished a lot—inspected a lot of landscape, made useful observations. But they had found no airplane, no suspicious dead bodies, and whatever the cruciform had been, it wasn't detectable any more. *Nai'a* sailed for Fiji, and this time the crossing was smooth. And the watermaker was back on line, to the intense relief of all.

Mrs. Sikuli Again

Back in Suva, Gillespie and Tague, with Tofinga translating, interviewed Mrs. Sikuli again, this time with Matthews videotaping. Some key pieces of the transcript:

275

Gillespie:	When Dr. King and Kris talked to you before, you told them about an airplane wreck on Nikumaroro when you got there. I'd like you to tell me what you know about that. I'd like to hear your story.
Mrs. Sikuli:	When we went there, no plane came during that time. Until we came off, no plane had come. We only heard that there was a plane that crashed near that ship.
Gillespie:	Let me repeat this back to be sure I understand. No plane arrived or crashed while you were at the island. But people said that before the people came a plane had crashed there near the ship. And when you refer to the ship you mean the ship that was on the reef, that was aground.
Mrs. Sikuli:	It is true.
Gillespie:	Did you ever see any part of that plane?
Mrs. Sikuli:	Only the frame, a piece of steel.
Foua Tofinga:	It's not a piece. The term she uses "afiti." It could be this long or this long [moves his hands close together, then far apart]. But it's steel. Only the framework.
Gillespie:	And where was this piece?
Mrs. Sikuli:	Nearby that wrecked ship. It was not far from there. From about here to that house. [She points to a house across the road.]
Gillespie:	Okay. That's probably 100 meters. Was it on land or in the water?
Mrs. Sikuli:	On the rocky part. It was not far from where the waves break.

In answer to Gillespie's questions, Mrs. Sikuli went on to say that the airplane wreckage was near the edge of the reef but that she had seen it only from the beach. She drew a picture of what she had seen—a long line with a small solid circle at the end.

Mrs. Sikuli:	I do not know what part of the plane it was. We were forbidden to go there. I was following my father. When I went there my father stopped me.

She said she knew that what she saw was part of an airplane because those who were there before her family arrived had told them that it was. She had already said that they arrived on the island two years before she was taken off in 1941.

Gillespie:	Were there ever any bones found on Nikumaroro?
Mrs. Sikuli:	Yes.
Gillespie:	What can you tell us about the bones that were found?
Mrs. Sikuli:	Some Gilbertese went to fish, they saw in the shallows some pools, at the place where the plane crashed, some bones, and they knew these were human bones because of the skull bone. They went and reported to Teng Koata, there were bones. So from that they assumed that these must have been the bones of those who were in the plane when it crashed. These were under the plane, near the plane. This was near the top end of the steel.
Gillespie:	Did you see the bones?
Mrs. Sikuli:	I didn't see them. We were forbidden, but my father told us.
Gillespie:	Were the bones found while you were on the island or did this happen before?
Mrs. Sikuli:	These bones were found when we had already arrived on the island. These Gilbertese came and found bones and reported to Teng Koata. Then Teng Koata took them to the European. So it was arranged for a box to be made for the bones and the bones were brought. There were not many bones.
Gillespie:	Were any other bones ever found on Niku?
Mrs. Sikuli:	Only these few bones they found. They do a search around that area but they found no other bones. Only these big bones that they found. I do not know how many. My father knew.

As Gillespie wound up the interview, he thought he ought to check on something.

Gillespie:	Do you know the name Amelia Earhart?
Mrs. Sikuli:	What kind of person is she? Where does she come from?
Gillespie:	America.
Mrs. Sikuli:	Is she alive?

CHAPTER 24

Trying to Make Sense of It All

Now we're on a hunch,
A wild goose chase,
Researchers are trying to end the mystery,
And close the case.
　　　—MIKE BERTHA OF THE AIRHEARTS

COMING OFF THE 1999 WORK IN FIJI AND ON NIKU, AND with the active participation of the Earhart Forum, research in late 1999 and 2000 burst out in all kinds of directions. What had been learned needed to be validated and built upon, and it opened new possibilities that could be pursued. And, of course, there was always serendipity, producing things that were entirely unexpected.

Mrs. Sikuli's Coming and Going

Gillespie went through the WPHC files and found clear documentation supporting and clarifying Emily Sikuli's accounts of when she and her family arrived on Niku and when she left. Mrs. Sikuli told King that she and her family—father, mother, and two of her three brothers—traveled from Beru to Nikumaroro in roughly 1938–1939; she told Gillespie that she had arrived about two years before Sir Harry and Foua Tofinga took her off in 1941. Her comments to King suggested that her uncle, the redoubtable public works foreman Jack Kima Petro, had preceded them. The archives show that Petro was on Nikumaroro in 1939, constructing the 10,000-gallon cistern. She reported to Gillespie that her father built canoes; among other things. Gallagher's progress report for the first quarter of 1940 mentions the arrival of an "expert canoe builder and his family of four." Gillespie asked Mrs. Sikuli if she recalled Europeans coming to the island to "do things" and she said no; this suggests that she arrived after the November 29–December 5, 1939, survey visit by USS *Bushnell*. We feel confident, then, in placing Mrs. Sikuli's arrival early in 1940. As for her departure, the records of the *Viti* show that the ship was at Nikumaroro with Sir Harry, Tofinga, and others on Sunday, November 30, 1941, and departed with a nurse named "Sengalo" aboard. Mrs. Sikuli's Tuvaluan name is "Segalo," often pronounced and spelled with an "n."[1]

More Forensic Imaging

Mrs. Sikuli's account of wreckage on the reef naturally sent Gillespie back to photos of the Nutiran reef from the 1930s and '40s. One pertinent photo was taken by Eric Bevington in October 1937 from at sea, looking south toward the *Norwich City*. This photo shows objects in the breaker line on the reef edge north of the shipwreck. One is long, the other short, so they have come to be referred to as the "dot and dash." Another picture was taken through a hole in the hull of the *Norwich City* in December 1938 by a member of the New Zealand survey team. It looks north along the reef edge and shows what look like the same "dot and dash" that appear in Bevington's picture. The sketch of the wreckage that Mrs. Sikuli drew for Gillespie showed a long skinny object ending in a round fat one. Whatever parts of an airplane these might be (if they are airplane parts), they could easily look like a "dot and a dash" in a photograph.

There's a lot of aerial imagery of the Nutiran shore, too, and some of it is quite early. A plane launched by HMS *Leander* took a photo in December 1938; a floatplane from USS *Pelican* took photos in April 1939; U.S. Navy PBYs took more in 1941. In some cases TIGHAR has good copy negatives or first-generation positives of these pictures; in other cases it doesn't. Work is under way as this is written to get the best possible copies of these images, as well as those shot by Bevington and the Kiwis, and Photek has started analysis of those now in hand. The results remain to be seen.

Bones on the Reef

What about Mrs. Sikuli's report that the bones were found on the reef near the airplane wreckage? Completely at odds with Gallagher's account, of course, but was it even possible for bones to survive on the reef? Burns's inspection of the reef flat left her certain that it was not—or at least that the bones could not have been there long before they were discovered. The reef is a high-energy environment, and bones just aren't up to the task of surviving in such a place. So was Mrs. Sikuli misremembering, or had the discovery been misreported to her, or what? Had the bones perhaps washed out of the beach and been deposited on the reef flat shortly before they were found? And how did they relate to the bones reported by Gallagher? These are loose ends, impossible even to begin to tie up without some independent source of information—perhaps Mrs. Sikuli's brother, who lives in Tuvalu and has yet to be contacted. More work needs to be done on this one, too.

Navigation, Fuel Consumption, and Radio

Several forum participants with extensive knowledge of celestial navigation —they call themselves the Celestial Choir—began looking into questions about navigational challenges along the Lae-Howland route on the night of July 2, 1937—what problems might Noonan have faced, what factors could have driven him to miscalculate the Electra's position? Another forum group, made up mostly of pilots and aviation experts, is working on questions of speed and fuel consumption—given the time that elapsed between takeoff and the last radio message, how much fuel should Earhart have had by the time she reported herself on the LOP? No firm answers have been found yet, but research continues.[2]

Somewhat firmer results have emerged from a study conducted by retired naval officer and forum member Bob Brandenburg, who has been analyzing the reported post-loss radio signals. Using a computer model that computes the signal-noise ratio (SNR) of signals—which models the distance at which a signal can be detected—Brandenburg has concluded that two of the four signals he has analyzed thus far could *not* have come from a transmitter on Nikumaroro. Two others, however—one heard at Nauru on July 3,[3] the other picked up by the U.S. Navy at Tutuila, American Samoa, on July 5, could have originated on the island.[4]

The Kilts Quest

It's now clear that much of what Floyd Kilts said about the bones back in 1960 was correct—albeit a bit garbled. Kilts got his information—apparently from an eyewitness—only a few years after the bones were found, so it's quite possible that he got a lot more than appeared in the *San Diego Tribune* article. Kilts, however, is dead. But did he leave papers? King and one of Kilts's contemporaries, ex-Coast Guardsman Chuck Boyle of the Earhart Forum, set out to track down any that might exist. Through newspaper archives and California real estate records they finally found Dorothy K. Josselyn, Kilts's daughter, and King called her on the phone. Besides being rather amazed that TIGHAR had found her, Mrs. Josselyn was interested in TIGHAR's work and willing to help. She said her father had often talked of Nikumaroro Island and its Earhart connection, and that when he died he was writing a book on the subject. Unfortunately, however, he had died before the book was complete, and although Mrs. Josselyn had seen the manuscript she had no idea what had happened to it. He had been writing it, she said, in connection with a class supervised by the late Scott O'Dell.[5] O'Dell's widow, contacted by Barb Norris, could provide no useful information. Mrs. Josselyn said she had never seen a map of the island in her father's possession, and she had no information beyond what was in the 1960 newspaper article.

With this avenue seemingly a dead end, Boyle and King turned to Kilts's Coast Guard associates. Research at the National Archives in Washington, D.C., revealed that Kilts had arrived at Nikumaroro with six other men from Canton Island on February 26, 1946, aboard USCGC *Basswood*. Their job was to replace a "vertical radiator," one of the transmission antennae. There was no record of their leaving before the station was closed down several months later.[6]

With names and service numbers in hand, Boyle set out to find the other six men. The Department of Veterans Affairs reported two of them dead. Boyle was able to track down one veteran, John Powrzanis, with whom King talked on the telephone. Powrzanis remembered Kilts, and Nikumaroro, but nothing about a colonist telling Kilts about a bones find. Letters to the other three men, through the Department of Veterans Affairs, have gone unanswered. The search for more information about whatever it was that Kilts heard seems to be at a dead end.

The Seven Site

TIGHAR came away from Nikumaroro in 1999 daunted by the prospect of even finding the 1940 bones discovery site, to say nothing of excavating or otherwise studying it. Both Aukaraime South and Kanawa Point are size-able places, and there seemed no way to narrow the search to something that could be reasonably handled in the field.

Then while working on a comprehensive report of work to date,[7] Gillespie and King began to think and correspond about the water catcher on the windward side—now called the "Seven Site" because of the roughly seven-shaped natural clearing nearby.

Laxton, describing his walk around the island in 1949, said of Ameriki:

> The "buka" trees rise here sixty feet high, and were partly cleared to accommodate the neat grey iron Quonset huts of the U.S. radio installation, neatly sealed, awaiting dismantling and transportation. Turning the tip to return along the northern rim, narrow, thunder-ing with surf driven by the northeast trade winds, the path ends in a house built for Gallagher on a strip of land cleared from lagoon to ocean beach so that the fresh winds blow easily through.[8]

That house built for Gallagher—presumably represented today by the Evans-Moffitt water catcher found by the 1996 expedition, with the tar paper and bird bones . . .

Bird bones?

". . . and remains of fire, turtle, and dead birds appear to indicate life," Gallagher had said.

And the house, Laxton had said, was on "a strip of land cleared from lagoon to ocean beach."

Cleared in preparation for planting operations that never happened? Cleared for some other reason? Why had Gallagher needed a house at the opposite end of the island from the village, anyhow?

Let's put things in sequence. On October 17, 1940, Gallagher sent a long telegram to Vaskess answering questions posed by MacPherson, through Sir Harry and Vaskess, about the site. He indicated that:

> Organized search of area for remaining bones
> would take several weeks as crabs move consider-

```
able distances and this part of the island is not
yet cleared.
```

On October 26 Vaskess directed that:

```
Organized search should be made in vicinity and
all bones and other finds . . . should be for-
warded to Suva . . .
```

The bones file then goes blank until Gallagher's letter of December 27, transmitting the box of bones. But his quarterly report for October–December 1940 says:

The second half of the quarter was marked by severe and almost continuous North-westerly gales. . . .

No communication was available, during the quarter, with any of the islands of the District. . . .

Difficulties of communication were by no means alleviated by the failure of the wireless telegraph installation at Gardner Island in the middle of December and the Officer-in-Charge was completely cut off from headquarters for some five weeks until communication could be restored on the 11th, January, 1941.

So Gallagher was directed to make an organized search of the bones site, but then ugly weather intervened, and he was busy battening things down and coping with the damage. He didn't communicate with headquarters about it because his wireless went down. But at some point he must have undertaken some kind of organized search, resulting in the discovery of the corks on brass chains—mentioned in Steenson's note on his examination of the artifacts in Fiji, but not in any of the telegrams. The search probably also resulted in the discovery of the rib and foot bones not mentioned in his telegrams but noted in Dr. Hoodless's report, and perhaps the shoe parts from a "male person" mentioned by Steenson—and perhaps, too, the inverting eyepiece, which Gallagher said on April 28, 1941, had been "thrown away by finder."

So, does one have a house built—perhaps not much of a house, just a four-pole number with a water catcher—so that one can have shelter from passing squalls while thoroughly searching a site during a period of inclement weather?

Does one perhaps have this done so that one can stay there and do the searching when the lagoon is too rough to travel? Does one perhaps stay there and do the searching because one doesn't trust others not to throw stuff away?

Suddenly the Seven Site started to look much more interesting. It is more than two miles from the nearest Arundel-period coconut grove, but not much more; it's obviously on the southeast end, though on the northeast shore of the southeast end. It's about 100 feet or so from the high-tide line, and it's not far from the lagoon. There's a kanawa tree nearby now, so it's a safe bet that there were a few around in 1940. At that time it was apparently wooded mostly in buka, and hence was shady, a good place for *Birgus*. And the turtles come ashore to lay their eggs along the windward shore—in July.

And there's a hole in the ground at the water catcher site, which the 1996 team interpreted as a well. In retrospect, however, and on reviewing photos and videotape of the site, Gillespie realized that it didn't look much like any other well he or anyone else had seen on the island; it was much more like—well, just a hole. Was it, perhaps, a hole dug to retrieve a skull?

If so—Gallagher reported finding five teeth in the skull's lower jaw. Dr. Hoodless reported only four when the skull arrived in Fiji, but whatever had happened to one tooth in transit, what of the other twenty-plus that the whole mouth must have had to start with? Might they still be in the hole, or in the backdirt around it? Teeth come loose easily, and would be easy to miss in the coral rubble. They also preserve better than bones, and they're prime sources of mitochondrial DNA, which can be used to firmly link whoever they're from with his or her maternal relatives.

Finally, one of the aerial photos taken by a plane from HMS *Leander* in 1938, when enhanced through the magic of Photek, shows what very much look like trails across patches of coral "moonscape" between the Seven Site and the lagoon shore. *Leander* was there before the PISS work party arrived with Maude and Gallagher, so if what we see in the photo are trails, they were made by someone walking between the lagoon and site before the colonists were there to walk around. We don't know how much walking around it takes to create a trail like the one that seems to show in the aerial photo, but it's hard to believe that a single crossing by Bevington and his barefoot I Kiribati colleagues could have done it during their October 1937 reconnaissance. Bevington and his colleagues are, of course, the only people known to have walked around this end of the island in or before 1937, and if they didn't create the trail. . . .

CHAPTER **25**

What Happened on the Night of July 2?

The truth is I never took much trouble getting into all the technical detail of transmitter frequencies and so on. Even my Morse was limited, Fred's, too. It seemed to me that flying was all that mattered. Maybe it still is.
—AMELIA EARHART, AS IMAGINED BY JUNE KNOX-MAWER[1]

GOING BACK TO THE BEGINNING, A NUMBER OF TIGHAR researchers and participants in the Earhart Forum have worked over the many questions that surround the Electra's progress toward Howland Island on the night of July 2, 1937. It turns out—not unexpectedly—that a lot of folklore surrounds the World Flight's disappearance, folklore that's not always entirely consistent with the facts. Randy Jacobson, Ric Gillespie, and others have tried to cut through the myths, going back to original sources and rigorously reexamining assumptions. The results have been enlightening—and sometimes startling.

Did They Have Enough Fuel?

One much-debated question about the Lae-Howland flight has been whether the Electra had enough fuel aboard to give Earhart and Noonan a reasonable margin for error as they approached Howland—and specifically, enough to get to Nikumaroro.

We know from Bureau of Air Commerce records that the plane could carry 1,151 U.S. gallons of fuel, but how much gasoline was actually aboard when the flight departed Lae and struck out over the Pacific bound for Howland Island? James Collopy, in a letter to his superiors dated August 28, 1937, said, "They left Lae with a total of 1,100 U.S. gallons of fuel . . ." He further explains, "One tank contained only 50 gallons of its total capacity of 100 gallons. This tank contained 100 octane fuel and they considered the 50 gallons of this fuel sufficient for the take-off from Lae."[2]

Earhart's Pratt & Whitney "Wasp" engines could deliver their full 550 hp only when fed with 100 octane aviation fuel, but in 1937 the new high octane gasoline was not yet widely available. The fuel in Lae was 87 octane—fine for cruising, but to launch the overloaded Electra from Lae's 3,000-foot runway would require every possible pony the engines could muster. At some point earlier in the flight, probably in Java, Earhart and Noonan had topped off one tank with 100 octane specifically for takeoff use. With fifty gallons left, they were not about to dilute that tank with 87 octane gas. Hence the decision to leave with not quite a full load of fuel.

Back in California, Kelly Johnson, later famous for his leadership of Lockheed's "Skunkworks," had helped Earhart figure out how to get the best "mileage" out of the Electra, and we have his recommendations on fuel consumption as a function of power settings, altitude, and time aloft.[3] Based on a fuel load of 1,100 U.S. gallons, the plane should have had 24.15 hours of endurance at the nominal 130-knot airspeed. Since the flight to Howland was expected to be on the order of eighteen hours, this allowed a better than 20 percent safety margin—the accepted standard at that time for long-distance flights.

With an authoritative and perfectly logical description of the airplane's fuel load provided in a contemporaneous document by Collopy, an aviation professional who was present for the takeoff, it might seem that the Electra's fuel load wouldn't be at issue. Over the years, however, debate has raged about how much gas was actually aboard the plane.

Earhart's press release from Lae on June 30 said, in part, "Lockheed stands ready for longest hop weighted with gasoline and oil to capacity." This has been cited as evidence that the aircraft carried the full 1,151 gallons, but later reports confirm that the airplane was not serviced for the Lae-Howland flight until the morning of July 1, so Earhart's June 30 statement can hardly be regarded as precise. An argument has been made for a much smaller fuel load, based on an article that appeared in an Australian newspaper, *The Sydney Telegraph*, four days after the disappearance. This piece alleged that, on the eve of departure, Noonan had told a reporter that the aircraft would be carrying "950 gallons of petrol—sufficient to give a still-air cruising range of 2,750 miles."[4] The conclusion might naturally be drawn that there was only enough fuel to cover the 2,556 statute miles to Howland, with little or no margin for possible head winds, and certainly not enough to fly an additional 400 statute miles down to Niku. However, the article does not specify whether Noonan was talking about U.S. or Imperial gallons, or whether Noonan was speaking of nautical or statute miles.

No combination of the variables seems to make any sense when applied to Kelly Johnson's predicted performance figures. What would make sense is if Noonan, speaking in Imperial gallons for an Australian reporter, had actually said 915, not 950, gallons; 915 Imperial gallons is 1,100 U.S. gallons—the figure reported by Collopy—and might be expected to yield about 2,750 nautical miles of still-air range, providing a comfortable 500-nautical-mile reserve for the 2,223-nautical-mile flight to Howland. Whether that's what Noonan really said is, of course, anybody's guess.

What is not speculation is that further confirmation of the 1,100-gallon figure emerged rather dramatically in 1991 with the discovery of a long-lost letter. At the end of Collopy's report to his Bureau of Air Commerce superiors, he comments that "Mr. Chater . . . forwarded a comprehensive report . . . to Mr. Putnam." Eric H. Chater was general manager for Guinea Airways at Lae, and oversaw work done on the Electra while it was there—including its fueling. If any report should be authoritative, his should be, but somehow Chater's full report never made it into the official file and was long considered lost. Then in December 1991, attracted by the publicity surrounding TIGHAR's discoveries, Hugh Leggatt decided to telephone Ric Gillespie. Leggatt was manager of corporate communications for Placer Dome Inc., a mining company based in Vancouver, British Columbia. He thought TIGHAR might like to know about a document he had come across while going through the company's old files. It was an eight-page letter addressed to M. E. "Frank" Griffin, a Placer executive in San Francisco in 1937, from Eric Chater, describing events in Lae, New Guinea, leading up to Earhart's departure on her last flight.

Gillespie immediately realized that what Leggat had found was the lost Chater report and asked if TIGHAR might have a copy. Leggat did better than that. He sent one of the original carbon "flimsies" plus copies of all the supporting correspondence. Griffin, it turns out, knew Chater through the company's gold mining operations in New Guinea, and was also a buddy of

William T. Miller, the Bureau of Air Commerce liaison with Earhart. Following the disappearance and failed search, Miller was looking for information about what had happened in Lae. He knew that Griffin had contacts in New Guinea and asked him to see what he could find out. Hence, Chater's letter to Griffin.[5]

Eric Chater was a thorough fellow. His report provides details about what was done to the plane while in Lae, about the takeoff, and about radio messages received during the first few hours of the flight. On the matter of fuel, he is quite specific. He explains the same 100 octane situation described by Collopy and concludes:

> This would indicate that 1,100 U.S. gallons was carried by the machine when it took off for Howland Island.

One might be forgiven for thinking that the discovery of the Chater report would settle the fuel question once and for all, but one would be mistaken. It's been suggested that because the tanks were filled on the morning of July 1 and the airplane presumably sat in the hot sun all that day, the fuel expanded and caused as much as eight gallons to dribble out onto the ground through the fuel vents.[6] A recently fueled airplane parked in the sun will do that. To suggest that Earhart and Noonan and everybody else at Guinea Airways didn't know that such venting might happen, didn't notice fuel streaming from the vents, didn't smell eight gallons of gasoline on the ground, and didn't top off the tanks prior to departure the next morning presumes a pretty high level of negligence. In any case, eight gallons plus or minus does not create a material difference in range.

At 10 o'clock local time, which conveniently was 00:00 Greenwich time, the Electra made a successful takeoff from Lae with—it seems safe to assume—1,100 U.S. gallons of fuel aboard. By following Kelly Johnson's recommendations, Earhart and Noonan could expect to remain aloft for just about one full day—six hours longer than the anticipated eighteen-hour flight to Howland Island.

"Everything Okay"

Although little is known about what happened once NR16020 disappeared over the eastern horizon from Lae, enough information is available to draw some fairly safe conclusions that greatly constrain the possibilities.

Although no map of the intended route to Howland has surfaced, plans for the same trip—albeit in the opposite direction—were prepared for the first World Flight attempt and are on file in the Purdue University special collection of Earhart memorabilia.[7] They show a direct route with no deviations. Some fragmentary position reports, related secondhand by Chater, who got them from the radio operator in Lae, provide clues to the flight's early progress but also leave room for much speculation.

For example: about four hours after departure, Earhart reportedly was heard to say, "Height 7,000 feet, speed 140 knots" then some unintelligible remark concerning "Lae," then "Everything okay."[8] At this point, according to Kelly Johnson's recommendations, the Electra should have been cruising at 8,000 feet at an airspeed of 130 knots. "Airspeed" is how fast the airplane is moving through the air, while "ground speed" is how fast it is covering ground—airspeed plus or minus how much the wind is either helping or hindering its progress. When Earhart said "speed 140 knots" did she mean airspeed or ground speed? Airspeed is read from a cockpit instrument called, creatively, an "airspeed indicator." The one in front of Earhart read in miles per hour, so if she meant 140 knots airspeed, then she was looking at a reading of 160.5 mph and, for some reason, doing the arithmetic to convert that to knots before transmitting the information back to Lae. Airspeed of 140 knots would mean that Amelia was pushing the airplane along 10 knots faster than recommended. That's a lot—and the only way to do it would be to use a lot more power and, therefore, a lot more gas. Why would she do that? Three hours later, in another report, she reportedly said "wind 23 knots"[9] but, again, she failed to say whether she meant head wind or tailwind or crosswind. Could it be that she had a 23-knot head wind that she was attempting to overcome by carrying more power?

Perhaps, but Johnson's recommendations specifically say that, in the event of unusually strong head winds, she should further economize fuel consumption by reducing the amount of gas in the fuel/air mixture rather than by increasing her airspeed and trashing her fuel economy. Maybe it's more reasonable to assume that when Earhart said "speed 140 knots" she was reporting a ground speed calculated by Noonan in statute miles per hour. Noonan, like all navigators, could work in either statute or nautical miles and in miles per hour or knots. It is not difficult to imagine a minor communication problem between Noonan and Earhart resulting in her "140 knots" report when Noonan had calculated 140 mph. A 140-mph ground speed would indicate only a 10-mph head wind, which would go nicely with the comment "Everything okay." Alternatively, the "140 knots" report could be a correct calculation of ground speed with a 10-knot tail-wind—even better evidence that everything was, in fact, okay.

In any event, the same message in which Earhart said "wind 23 knots" also gave her altitude as 8,000 feet—right where she should be—and a lat-itude and longitude position that put her smack on the direct course for Howland Island. It does seem, therefore, that roughly seven hours into the trip everything was going pretty much as planned.

How Fast Did They Go?

If our conclusions about the progress of the flight are sprinkled with words like "roughly" and "approximately," it's because we've tried to resist the temptation to be more specific than the available information permits. For example, the position that Earhart reported at 5:18 P.M. Lae time (seven hours, eighteen minutes after takeoff), places the airplane on course and some 740 nautical miles from Lae. If they covered that distance in that time, it means that they made an average ground speed of only 101 knots. This suggests that they encountered significant head winds, doesn't it? Well, no it doesn't.

Randy Jacobson examined the original navigation charts used by Fred Noonan and Harry Manning during the flight from Oakland to Hawaii,[10] and compared the notes on these charts with the record of that flight's trans-missions. This examination revealed that in no case did Earhart provide a position at the time it was calculated. The smallest deviation between time calculated and time reported was twenty-five minutes, the largest forty-two minutes.[11] So why didn't Earhart report her position as soon as Noonan gave her the information? Because that was never the plan. Earhart made radio transmissions only at set times, as was the standard practice in the 1930s. For somebody to hear her they had to be listening on her particular frequency at the time she was talking, and any given radio operator had many different frequencies to listen to for messages from many different stations. There were no "scanners," as there are today, to monitor several frequencies at one time, and an operator could listen on only one frequency at a time.

The solution, naturally, was to set a schedule. As reported by Chater, Earhart's arrangement with the radio operator at Lae was that she would send her transmissions and listen for messages at eighteen minutes past the hour. It wouldn't do her any good to transmit at any other time because nobody would be listening. So the information heard at seven hours and eighteen minutes into the flight might be fairly current, or it might be nearly an hour old—there's no way to tell. Maybe it took the plane more than seven hours to cover 740 miles or maybe it took, say, only six and a half hours, which would present an average ground speed of 114 knots and no suggestion of unusually strong head winds.

The next indication of how the flight was progressing came later that night when the radio operator on the island of Nauru, just north of the mid-point on the direct route to Howland, heard Earhart say, "Ship in sight ahead."[12] Two ships are known to have been in the vicinity of Earhart's intended route that night. One was the U.S. Navy sea-going tug USS *Ontario*, which had been positioned midway in the trip specifically to provide a checkpoint for the flight. The other was the SS *Myrtlebank*, a commercial vessel inbound to Nauru to dock early the next morning. Unfortunately, we have no way to be sure if either was the ship that Earhart reported in the transmission to Nauru. The *Ontario*'s bridge logs indicate that at the approximate time that Earhart was in the area, the weather was clear with visibility at least forty miles, but they do not indicate that anyone heard or saw Earhart.

Many years later the *Myrtlebank*'s third mate claimed that he heard an airplane pass over that night.[13] We do not know the exact position of the *Myrtlebank* at that time, but we do know that she was east of the *Ontario* and a bit north of Earhart's intended flight path. If either ship was the one reported by Earhart to Nauru, then she was roughly on her intended flight path. In any case, this message represented a departure from her announced transmission schedule because it came not at eighteen minutes past the hour but on the half-hour, ten hours and thirty minutes into the flight. Because the content of the message describes a real-time event, it may be that Earhart was making the announcement just in case anyone happened to be listening. If, indeed, Earhart was in the vicinity of either the *Ontario* or the *Myrtlebank* at that moment, the flight had covered approximately 1,200 nautical miles for an average ground speed of about 114 knots.

The only clue to the flight's further progress during the long night is an alleged witness to it passing over the island of Tabituea, one of the islands in the Gilbert chain (now Kiribati). In 1940, Irving Johnson, captain of the schooner *Yankee*, sailed through the central Pacific islands looking for evidence of what might have happened to Earhart. He didn't search Nikumaroro

Island but he did report that a resident of Tabituea told him he had heard a plane overhead on the night of July 2.[14] That island just happens to be on the direct route from Lae to Howland so, if the report is true, it is another indication that Noonan was keeping the flight on course for Howland.

Regardless of what may have transpired en route, there has never been any real doubt that the flight reached the Howland neighborhood more or less on schedule. That conclusion was based in 1937, as it is now, on the signals received from Earhart by *Itasca* and described in chapter 4. These signals steadily increased in strength and clarity from the first unintelligible signal at 2:45 A.M. local time until her puzzled "We must be on you but cannot see you" message was heard at maximum strength some five hours later at 7:42 A.M.—just nineteen hours and twelve minutes after takeoff. With only fifty watts of power to the transmitter and much less than that actually emanating from the antenna, the strength of Earhart's last signals would seem to be a sure sign that she was close to Howland. Expert estimates at the time ranged from 50 to 100 miles. So there seems to be little doubt that Earhart and Noonan covered roughly 2,200 nautical miles in about nineteen hours and made an average ground speed for the entire flight of about 116 knots.

What Went Wrong?

With everything apparently gong so well right up until the last few hours of the trip, why did they fail to find Howland Island? Chater reported, "Both Captain Noonan and Miss Earhart expressed their complete satisfaction" with preparations for the flight, and Collopy wrote, "Mr. Noonan told me he was not a bit anxious about the flight to Howland Island and was quite confident that he would have little difficulty in locating it."

Noonan's confidence was undoubtedly based on his demonstrated ability to find tiny islands after long overwater flights when he had pioneered the transpacific route for Pan American Airways in 1935 and 1936. His technique was to use "dead reckoning"—following precalculated compass headings—and to monitor his progress using celestial observations—measuring the apparent height above the horizon of selected stars or the sun—to stay on course. Once he was within a few hundred miles of his destination he would fine-tune his approach with the aid of a radio navigation technique called "radio direction finding." In principle, this was a bit like finding someone you can't see by having them shout and noting the direction the sound comes from, except this was done with radio waves instead of sound waves. In Pan American's system the airplane would send out a signal (shout) and the ground station would note the direction the signal came from and tell the pilot which way to fly. The technique could also be reversed, in which case the ground station would send a signal (shout) and the pilot would determine what direction it was coming from by rotating a special circular or "loop" antenna on the airplane. Either way, the pilot would know what compass heading to follow to reach the intended destination.

Because it's clear that the flight got close to Howland Island it would also seem obvious that Noonan was able to apply his dead reckoning and celestial navigation skills with enough accuracy to keep the flight on course through the long day and longer night. But neither Earhart nor Noonan labored under any illusion that dead reckoning and celestial techniques alone would be sufficient to find Howland Island within the time constraints imposed by their fuel reserves. Unless they were phenomenally lucky, help from the plane's radios would be essential to successfully complete the flight. As it turned out, they received no help from the radios and the only luck they had was the bad kind.

After the fact, Collopy in New Guinea observed:

[I]t is very apparent that the weak link in the combination was the crews [*sic*] lack of expert knowledge of radio.

The more we have learned about what happened on July 2, the more apparent it has become that Collopy was on the right track, but didn't know the half of it. In the early morning hours, the radio operators aboard *Itasca* picked up Earhart's first faint attempts to establish contact with them and thus began a drama of frustration and growing alarm that culminated in disaster.

Radio in 1937

Because the radio messages heard aboard the *Itasca* are such important clues to what went wrong, let us briefly review what aviation radios were like in Earhart's time and what we know about how she used them.

By 1937, radios were standard equipment in most commercial and many military aircraft, but they were incredibly user-hostile by today's standards.

Many aircraft carried skilled radio operators whose sole job was to coax cooperation out of the cantankerous sets, tapping out and receiving messages in Morse code. Voice communications, or "radiotelephone" as it was known, had much shorter range and could be hard to understand through the distortion and static that plagued transmissions on the frequencies then in use. When actors in those old 1930s airplane movies talk on the radio in that corny flat monotone—"Flight Five from Chicago coming in for a landing"—they are imitating the way pilots really spoke in an attempt to be understood. For communication at distances of more than about 200 miles, Morse code was the standard.

Today's aircraft are equipped with lightweight, compact "transceivers" that provide reliable, noise-free, voice communication with both sides of the conversation—sending and receiving—using the same frequency: you just dial in one frequency on one radio and start talking. Antennas are short little wands or tabs. It was a lot more complicated in 1937. The radio system in NR16020 involved several different large, heavy devices that were, quite literally, scattered all over the airplane. Let's start with the transmitter.

The Famous "Trailing Wire"

Earhart's Western Electric Model 13C transmitter was a black box about the size of a small suitcase that was bolted to the floor in the rear part of the cabin and was connected via a long cable to remote controls in the cockpit. Earhart could select one of three "crystal-controlled" frequencies—3105 kilocycles, 6210 kilocycles, or 500 kilocycles. "Crystal-controlled" means that the frequencies were preset and could be selected by turning a knob; no need for tedious tuning by hand.[15]

The antenna for the transmitter was a long wire on the top of the airplane that ran in the shape of a V from a mast that stuck up just behind the cockpit to the top of each of the two vertical fins on the airplane's tail. This antenna was part of the problem. It's important that the length of a transmitting antenna match the frequencies to be transmitted. As it turns out, a 46-foot antenna works fine for 3105 and 6210 kilocycles, but the 500 kilocycle frequency really wants to have a much longer wire. As configured for the first World Flight attempt in March, the V antenna on NR16020 was 46 feet long and a separate antenna, known as a "trailing wire," was provided for use on 500 kilocycles. This was a 250-foot length of wire stored on a spool inside the airplane that could be played out and trailed behind

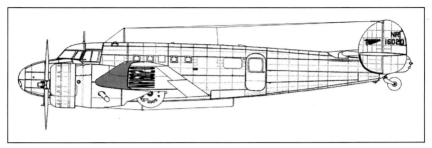

The Electra's antenna setup at the beginning of the World Flight. TIGHAR
Collection, based on drawing by William Harney.

the airplane in flight. Of course, 250 feet of wire and the mechanism for
reeling it in and out were heavy and you had to remember to reel it back in
before landing or—snap—good-bye antenna.

If the antenna was such a bother, why have the 500 kilocycle frequency
in the first place? There were a couple of good reasons. Five hundred kilocycles was the international maritime distress frequency and was monitored
by all ships at sea. That might come in handy. Also, most radio direction
finders could not "home in" on the higher frequencies—such as 3105 or
6210—so if you wanted someone to take a bearing on your position, you
would want to be able to transmit on a low frequency so they could tell
you where you were. Of course, virtually everyone who was listening on
500 kilocycles was using only Morse code, but that wasn't a problem on
Earhart's first World Flight attempt because Harry Manning was an amateur radio buff and a whiz at Morse.

After the wreck in Hawaii, several changes were made that, ultimately,
had disastrous effects. The accident had wiped out the trailing wire mast on
the belly and, during repairs, the decision was made to dispense with it.
Earhart folklore has the trailing wire being deleted in Miami but photos
taken in California the day after the airplane came out of the repair shop
confirm that it was simply never reinstalled. Instead, the V antenna on the
top of the airplane was lengthened to 54 feet. Unfortunately, this reduced
Earhart's transmitting capability on 3105 and 6210.

To understand why Earhart would do something so foolish, we have to
review her experience with radio. Incredible as it seems, neither Earhart nor
Noonan was adept at sending or receiving Morse code. According to Chater:

Miss Earhart and Captain Noonan spent a considerable time in the radio office and . . . it was learned that neither of them could read [M]orse at any speed but could only distinguish letters made individually slowly and repeated often; in that case their direction finding apparatus would be useless or misleading unless they were taking a bearing on a station using radiophone which could give the station position on voice.

Aboard the Pan Am Clippers, Noonan had always had the luxury of a trained operator to handle the radios so that he could devote his full attention to dead reckoning and celestial navigation. Earhart, for her part, had carried a radio on a long-distance flight for the first time in 1935 when she flew her single-engined Lockheed Vega from Honolulu to Oakland. On that flight she had used the radiotelephone to make periodic transmissions, but these were hardly formalized position reports; they were live press releases about her progress. Despite all the fuss about the radios installed aboard her "flying laboratory" Earhart seems to have had little patience for mastering the complexities of their use. Her technical adviser, Paul Mantz, complained that he could never get Amelia to take the time to practice with the radios, and she begged off taking a government-required radio navigation test, saying that it would put too many hours on her Electra's engines prior to her World Flight.[16]

Manning's departure from the crew after the debacle in Hawaii meant that nobody aboard could communicate effectively in Morse code, so the usefulness of the 500 kilocycles frequency for communicating with ships at sea was no longer a factor. The frequency might still come in handy for direction finding, however. Earhart's radio consultant, Joseph Gurr, suggested that by lengthening the V antenna on the top of the airplane they could get some transmitting capability on 500 kilocycles and therefore eliminate the weight and the hassle of the trailing wire altogether.[17] To Earhart, with virtually no expertise in radio, it apparently sounded like a good compromise—a little less transmitting capability for a big saving in weight and complexity. In fact, the lengthened V provided no meaningful performance on 500 kilocycles, and it degraded the aircraft's ability to transmit on the other two frequencies.

Despite these drawbacks, it's clear that at least some of Earhart's transmissions on 6210 were heard by the radio operator at Lae in the first few hours after her departure. Later, the operator on Nauru heard her on 3105.

There is also no doubt that her transmitter was successfully sending out her voice on 3105 as she approached Howland Island the next morning. Effective communication, however, is a two-way proposition and it was in the receiving department that the worst problems arose.

More Blessed to Receive?

Earhart's Electra was delivered with a Western Electric Model 20B receiver tucked under the copilot's seat. Unlike her transmitter, which could send signals on only a few preset frequencies, Earhart's receiver could pick up any of several thousand frequencies. These could be tuned in much in the same way you would tune an old-fashioned car radio: you turn a knob (or, in this case, a little crank) to move a needle to the right place on the dial while you listen for the desired station to come in. The procedure was complicated somewhat by the need to first select one of four "bands" of frequencies and then be sure you were tuning to the correct set of numbers on the dial. There was no speaker in the cockpit so the pilot had to wear earphones to hear what the receiver was receiving. Tuning in a station and listening for messages could be a difficult and unpleasant process because the high level of noise from the engines, and the cotton in your ears to protect you from it, made it necessary to have the volume turned way up. Frequencies in the range that Earhart was listening on are highly susceptible to atmospheric interference; any electrical activity in the clouds in the area will treat a listener to frequent crashes of ear-splitting static.

When delivered by Lockheed in July 1936, the Electra had no radio direction finding capability. The transmitter used a trailing wire (the V antenna on top came later) and the receiver almost certainly used the wire antenna that ran along the belly of the airplane supported on masts—the antenna's lead-in entered the fuselage just where the receiver was mounted. In October 1936, a prototype, state-of-the-art radio direction finder was installed in Earhart's airplane by its inventor, Frederick Hooven. The new device, known as a "radio compass," featured a completely separate receiver that was mounted on top of one of the fuel tanks in the plane's cabin. It was much easier to use than conventional radio direction finders but, of course, carrying a second receiver also meant carrying extra weight.

Early in 1937, as Earhart was preparing the plane for her World Flight, the Bendix company came out with a new device that permitted a circular direction finding "loop" antenna to be coupled with a conventional radio receiver such as the Western Electric unit aboard the Electra. Sacrificing advanced capability for less weight, Earhart had Hooven's rig removed and the new Bendix loop and coupler installed just two weeks before she left on her first World Flight attempt on March 17, 1937. This change is well documented in publicity photos taken at the time. Hooven, before his death in 1985, wrote that he felt sure that Earhart's decision to save thirty pounds by replacing his easy-to-use radio compass with an "old-fashioned" radio direction finder was a major contributing factor in the plane's disappearance.[18]

The loop radio direction finder's frequency band aboard the Electra was described at various times during the last flight as 200-1430, 200-1500, 200-1400, and 2400-4800 kcs. Of course, we have no actual information as to its capabilities for bearing determinations. Unfortunately, there are no photographs or diagrams that show the internal layout of the aircraft's radio system four months later, at the time of the last flight. With facts missing, speculation has quickly filled the void. The presence of a second receiver aboard the airplane has often been postulated; once postulated, its proposed characteristics have been described in detail.[19] Sometimes it's hard to remember that that there is no documented evidence that it ever existed.

Based on available documents and photos, it appears that when the Electra taxied out for takeoff at Lae, its radio setup probably consisted of:

- A Western Electric 13C transmitter with three preset frequencies; 3105, 6210, and 500 kilocycles.
- A dorsal V antenna connected to the transmitter that virtually negated any transmission capability on 500 kilocycles and was inefficient on 3105 and 6210.
- A manually tuned Western Electric 20B receiver with frequency capabilities in four bands; 200–400 kilocycles, 550–1500 kilocycles, 1500–4000 kilocycles, 4000–10,000 kilocycles.
- A ventral (belly) wire antenna, entering the fuselage near the receiver.
- Bendix loop antenna mounted over the cockpit.

It's not clear, however, how all this equipment was configured to work together to transmit, receive, and find direction.

During her flight around the world as far as Lae, Earhart's radios aboard the Electra were not essential to her success and their use was often fraught with problems. The flight from Lae to Howland was the first time in Earhart's career that her life depended on her radios. Noonan's navigation could get them close to their destination, but to find one tiny island in a very large ocean before their fuel ran out would require the assistance of radio direction finding. Both the Electra and the *Itasca* had loop antennas and there was a third direction finding radio set up on Howland, so there were lots of ways for the airplane to use radio direction finding to locate the island. Of course, proper prior coordination was essential.

What We Have Here Is a Failure to Communicate

Arranging for radio communication wasn't just a matter of picking up a microphone and pressing a button. It was necessary to have an agreed upon communications schedule so that when you were transmitting, the other guy would be listening on the correct frequency. In the days leading up to the Electra's departure from New Guinea, telegrams flew back and forth between Earhart and the U.S. Coast Guard trying to sort out just who was going to do what and when. The general plan was for Earhart to send voice messages on 3105 kcs during the night and 6210 kcs during the day at quarter-past and quarter-to each hour, at which times *Itasca* would be listening for her on the appropriate frequency. *Itasca* was to send messages, such as weather reports, on those same frequencies on the hour and the half hour. *Itasca* was also supposed to send the letter A in Morse code along with its own call letters (NRUI) on the hour and the half hour, presumably so that Earhart could use her loop antenna to take bearings. Earhart asked that these signals be sent on 7500 kcs until she got close to Howland, whereupon *Itasca* was to switch to voice on 3105 or 6210. Unfortunately, 7500 kcs was a frequency far too high for her direction finder to respond to. No one aboard *Itasca* questioned her request.[20]

Itasca personnel also apparently failed to note, or decided to ignore, two other important aspects of the plan. Earhart had specifically asked that *Itasca*'s reports be sent to her in "English, not code, especially when flying," and yet during the flight, most of *Itasca*'s transmissions to Earhart were in Morse code. *Itasca* had also asked what time zone Amelia would be using for her radio schedules. She replied that she would use Greenwich Civil Time (GCT), and yet *Itasca* persisted in its use of local time. This caused considerable confusion because the ship was using GCT plus eleven and a

USCGC *Itasca*. TIGHAR collection from U.S. National Archives.

half hours for local time. That half hour meant, for example, that when Earhart said at 18:15 (her time), "Please take bearing on us and report on half hour"—that is, 18:30 her time, the next scheduled time she would expect to receive a message from *Itasca*—the men in the radio room were looking at a clock that said 06:45 and thought she was asking for a bearing at 07:30, which didn't make any sense. They replied,

```
We cannot take a bearing on 3105 very well; please send
on 500, or do you wish to take a bearing on us? Go
ahead, please.
```

But there was no response from Earhart, probably because she had a much bigger problem with her radio. She apparently couldn't hear *anything*—no code, no voice, no nothing. *Itasca* was hearing her just fine; her transmissions were getting steadily stronger as she drew closer and closer but, of course, she didn't know that, and hence didn't know whether she was getting through to *Itasca* or not. At 19:12 GCT (07:42 local time), she said:

```
KHAQQ calling Itasca. We must be on you but cannot see
you, but gas is running low. We have been unable to
reach you by radio. We are flying at 1,000 feet.
```

The above was recorded in the original log of the primary Earhart tracking radio aboard *Itasca*. A second log, kept by the operator who was keeping track of other radio traffic on another radio and subsequently edited, includes some Earhart messages as well. This log reports that "Earhart said [she] had a half an hour of gas left and cannot receive *Itasca*'s messages." Setting aside the question of whether Earhart was talking about sending or receiving, many researchers have focused on the statement that only half an hour of gas was left. In fact, however, the original log of the primary Earhart tracking radio reports the transmission as saying only that gas was running low. Only the edited log of the second radio seat—the operator who was keeping track of other radio traffic—contains the words "half an hour."

Assuming Earhart was managing her fuel reasonably, at 19:12 GCT she would have been approaching the point at which she would need to tap her fuel reserves—amounting to about 200 gallons and allowing for perhaps four hours of flying time. Saying that her gas was low is consistent with this premise; gas was low and the need to go into the reserves would be cause for concern on Earhart's part. In point of fact, she did have more than half an hour's worth of fuel at 19:12 GCT, because her last transmission was at 20:13 GCT, an hour later. But, of course, the *Itasca* crew couldn't know how much fuel Earhart had, and the "half an hour" may have been a misunderstanding of her reference to "on the half hour."

At 19:28 GCT (07:58 local time) the *Itasca*'s primary radio log reports that she said:

```
KHAQQ calling Itasca. We are circling but cannot hear
you. Go ahead on 7500 with a long count, either now or
on the scheduled time on half hour.
```

Having apparently given up trying to get the *Itasca* to take a bearing on her signals, she was going to try to use her own loop antenna to take a bearing on them. The *Itasca* could not send the "long count" Earhart had requested because the ship had no voice capability on 7500, but they immediately sent Morse code A's (dit dah, dit dah, dit dah) on that frequency. For the first time, Earhart heard their transmission but reported that she had been unable to get her loop antenna to respond. No bearing. No help. She then asked again that they take a bearing on her and sent some long dashes on 3105. Then silence.

Itasca kept up an almost steady stream of calls on both 3105 and 7500, trying to establish contact with the plane, even broadcasting right through her scheduled 19:45 GCT transmission time—effectively blocking any attempt she may have been making to call them. Then, at 20:13 (08:43 local time), within two minutes of her regular transmission time, Earhart was on the air again.

```
KHAQQ to Itasca. We are on the line 157 337. We will
repeat this message. We will repeat this on 6210 KCS.
Wait.
```

The radioman thought the transmission was ended, but suddenly she was back saying, "We are running on north and south line" or something like that. It's clear from the log entry that the operator was not sure what he had heard.

Again *Itasca* bombarded the airwaves, urging Earhart not to change frequencies, assuring her that they had heard her on 3105, but again there was silence. Two hours later, convinced that the aircraft must be down at sea, the captain of the *Itasca* ordered the ship underway to begin a search.

The Last SNAFU

It's obvious that Earhart had problems receiving signals from *Itasca*. The only message we know she received was the one at 19:28 GCT, on 7500 kcs, through her radio direction finding equipment. So what was wrong with her receiver?

A difficulty that everyone who has examined this question has had to contend with is that although we know—more or less—what radio equipment Earhart had, we don't know precisely, and we don't know how it was configured. Several mechanics and technicians worked on the equipment

The Electra taking off from Lae, quite likely losing its belly antenna in the process. TIGHAR Collection from Neil Royes of Bardon, Queensland, Australia.

between the time the plane left Burbank and the time of its departure from Miami, and the work records are spotty. Clearly, though, something had to have been wrong with an important part of the receiving circuitry.

Analysis of film taken immediately before and during the plane's departure from Lae[21] suggests that the wire antenna that ran along the aircraft's underside was accidentally lost during takeoff. We can see that the short mast under the cabin area that is the aft terminus of the antenna is present as the airplane taxis out for takeoff. However, the airplane has never before been loaded this heavily and the tip of the mast is barely clearing the turf of the runway. It would be easy for the mast to be knocked off as the tail of the airplane was swung around at the far end of the runway to begin the takeoff.

When the film of the takeoff itself picks up the aircraft, the tail is already up and the machine is building speed. Early in the sequence, a small, concentrated puff of something—probably dust—appears abruptly under the plane. It could be the product of some odd eddy of wind, or perhaps something kicked up by the wheels. But it could also be a severed mast or antenna wire hitting the ground.

A suggestive sidelight to the photographic evidence is the recollection of Robert Fullenwider, who was in Lae during his service in World War II. Long before the photos were analyzed he told of hearing the "old timers" at Lae say that they hadn't been surprised when Earhart was lost because her wire antenna had been found after she left, out on the runway.[22]

Exactly what effect the loss of the belly antenna would have, of course, depends on what function it served, and about that there is still much debate. When delivered, the antenna's lead-in entered the fuselage just where the receiver is mounted—it almost certainly was the receiving antenna. Though the Electra underwent many poorly documented changes over the next year, it seems likely—though some of TIGHAR's radio experts aren't sure they agree—that the plane was still equipped with the receiving antenna on its belly when it left Lae—but that it apparently lost the antenna on the runway. Its loss, of course, could explain Earhart's inability to hear *Itasca* until she switched to her less powerful directional antenna. It would also explain why Harry Balfour, the radio operator in Lae, never received acknowledgment of the signals he sent her.

A Tragedy of Errors

So in summary:

1. The information provided *Itasca* before Earhart's takeoff said that Earhart wanted signals to be sent for her direction finding equipment that were outside the range her equipment could use. It is hard to think that *Itasca*'s radio personnel didn't know this, but if they did they didn't say anything to Earhart about it, and never asked for confirmation.
2. At the same time, Earhart expected *Itasca* to be able to take bearings on her on frequencies that were beyond the capacity of *Itasca*'s equipment, but this fact wasn't known until the flight was approaching Howland.
3. During takeoff the aircraft suffered unnoticed but possibly highly significant damage that deprived it of its belly antenna.
4. *Itasca* and Earhart appear to have been operating thirty minutes out of synchronization because of the half-hour time zone problem. This must have added to the confusion, even if it had no direct, specific result.
5. Compounding the problems, *Itasca*'s radiomen broke radio discipline by broadcasting at times when they weren't scheduled to, possibly blocking receipt of messages from Earhart. They used telegraphy despite Earhart's explicit request for voice transmission.

In his official report on the incident, *Itasca*'s captain, Commander Warner K. Thompson, laid the blame for her loss on Earhart herself, claiming that *Itasca* was on station only to provide signals for Earhart to home in on, not to provide bearings for her.[23] This is consistent with all directions provided from the U.S. Coast Guard Office in San Francisco, under whose jurisdiction *Itasca* operated, but it is curious for the ship's role to be so limited and passive. One also has to wonder why Thompson sent a team ashore to man the high-frequency direction finding equipment if he didn't plan to take bearings and do something with them. And even if *Itasca*'s role was supposed to be that of a passive beacon, this is no excuse for the confusion surrounding her communication, such as it was, with the flight.

Itasca's errors only built on those that made by the Coast Guard in San Francisco and by George Putnam himself before the takeoff from Lae, providing confusing information about equipment and communications protocols. Adding all this to the apparent loss of the belly antenna means that very, very large odds were stacked against Earhart and Noonan.

And, of course, Earhart and Noonan didn't help themselves by being so poorly conversant with Morse code. As Collopy dryly put it:

> I do think that had an expert radio operator been included in the crew the conclusion may have been different.

Some Earhart investigators have suggested that Earhart did not take the direct route from Lae to Howland, but instead deviated north to Nauru, south to avoid New Britain, or far north to spy on the Japanese in the Marshall Islands or in Chuuk (formerly Truk). While we don't have enough information to reconstruct the actual flight path with any precision, everything we do have is consistent with a path that was close to the direct, great circle route from Lae to Howland. There is no need to propose complex deviations and devious actions. The evidence supports the conclusion that Earhart and Noonan flew as directly as they could to Howland Island. But "direct" based on celestial navigation and dead reckoning wasn't good enough; they needed radio navigation to bring them safe to land. And thanks to confusion on everyone's part, and very likely the loss of an antenna, radio was precisely what they did not get.

CHAPTER 26

And Then? And Now?

Back to Scaevola, and sand in your socks.
Dance on your feet of clay.
Come back to old Club Fred, my friends,
Come back here any day.*
                    —TIGHAR TUNES

What Happened on the LOP?

So what happened once Earhart and Noonan were on the line of position
but not at Howland? We don't know, of course, but we think the evidence
is good for what we might call the Refined Nikumaroro Hypothesis.

When we started out in 1988, we had only the general idea that the
fliers, unable to find Howland, had flown down the LOP and wound up at
what was then called Gardner Island. Now we can be a good deal more
detailed in our hypothesizing, though we stress that what we're presenting
here is *only* a hypothesis, and it is subject to change as more information
comes in.

Having advanced one's LOP to the point where it should pass through
Howland, but being unable to find the island, a navigator who wants to live
is more likely to turn south than north, unless he or she is certain of being
south of the island. A navigator who doesn't know whether he or she is north
or south of the island and who directs the pilot to fly north has only a fifty-
fifty chance of finding something—Howland—before running out of fuel and

---

*Sung to the tune of "Cabaret," by Fred Ebb and John Kander, from *Cabaret.*

falling in the ocean. This, of course, is because there is nothing north of Howland for many, many miles. Turning south gives the navigator a much better chance of coming up on an island. If it turns out that the navigator's starting point is north of Howland, flying south will bring him or her up on Howland and Baker. If the starting point is south of Howland and Baker, the navigator will come up on Nikumaroro—which, incidentally, is a lot bigger than Howland or Baker and, with its bright lagoon and tall trees, a good deal more visible from the air.

So we think that Earhart and Noonan flew south along the LOP, and that they were either south of Howland to begin with (as Jacobson's Monte Carlo simulation suggests), or unable to see it for some reason. Such a reason isn't hard to imagine; a small island in the bright light of the low morning sun can be difficult to spot. One can argue endlessly about whether they *should* have been able to see the island, or the *Itasca,*[1] but they *didn't* see them, so such arguments are kind of fun but fruitless.

We think that they had enough fuel to make it to Nikumaroro. This too can be argued about endlessly, positing different head winds, course changes, speeds, altitudes, and so on to support different conclusions. There is absolutely no way to know for sure. What we do know, assuming Chater was telling the truth, is that 1,100 U.S. gallons of fuel were loaded on the airplane before it left Lae, and that should have been enough for about twenty-three to twenty-four hours in the air. Which should mean that they had about three or four hours of fuel by the time they got to the vicinity of Howland—plenty enough to get to Niku. And as discussed in the previous chapter, we think the reputed message about having only a half-hour of fuel left was a misinterpretation.

So we think they flew south, and came up on Niku with some but not much fuel in their tanks. At low tide, the long smooth reef flat north of the *Norwich City* would almost certainly be visible (we have yet to fly over the island to find out for sure, however). The *City* herself might have been a tempting landmark. "Let's land there; there may be something in it we can use, and we can tell *Itasca* we're close to the ship on the reef." Here there's a bit of a wrinkle in the hypothesis. Jacobson has made an effort to "hindcast" tidal conditions in the area, and the results suggest that when the Electra should have been over the island—at about 24:00 GCT, noon local time—the tide would have been high, and the reef flat underwater. Hindcasting is a risky business, however. It doesn't tell us with any exactitude when the tide came in that day, or how high it was, so we really don't know how much water, if any, covered the smooth surface of the reef flat. Nor, of course, do we know exactly when Earhart and Noonan arrived at the island, assuming they did.

Given only shallow water on the flat, they could have landed, wheels down, successfully enough that they would be able to crank the starboard engine, run the generator, and get enough power to put out at least the post-loss signals that Bob Brandenburg's analysis suggests are worth considering.

But the tide goes out and the tide comes in, and some tides are higher than others. It would be only a matter of time before the ocean would begin to have its way with the Electra. We think that eventually it was dragged out to the edge of the reef and more or less broken up. This could well have left the heavy undercarriage and perhaps an engine or two on the reef for the I Kiribati fishermen, and perhaps Bruce Yoho, to see years later, while the fuselage and wings went over the edge.

Assuming that Earhart and Noonan had survived the landing in good shape, they would now be marooned on an uninhabited island, but they wouldn't be entirely without resources. Not only was the island itself rich in plant and animal life; there was also the cache of supplies left by the *Norwich City* crew. We don't know what was in that cache—perhaps some small casks with corks and chains, perhaps a bottle of Benedictine, but almost certainly some food, and maybe some water. Water would be a precious commodity; remember how difficult it was for the colonists to find any by digging.

A few days later the *Colorado* pilots fly over. They see the *Norwich City,* so why don't they see the remains of the Electra? Again, we don't know, but if all that was left was the steel undercarriage and perhaps an engine or two, in the surf line—and this time, from the photo taken by one of the plane crews, we know that the tide was high—it might be hard to see anything that anyone would recognize as the remains of an airplane.

But if Earhart and Noonan are there, chowing down on the *Norwich City*'s supply cache, why don't they run out and wave their hankies to attract attention? Maybe they did. In 1989 while we were surveying on the Nutiran mudflat, a Royal New Zealand Air Force picket plane flew over at about 500 feet. We waved and jumped up and down and did everything we could to attract attention, just because it seemed like the thing to do, and there was no indication that anybody saw us at all. Little things like people are hard to see in the complicated visual environment of a tropical island.

Or maybe they didn't get out into the open to wave. Maybe they were back in the bush looking for food or water or a Man Friday or whatever, and couldn't get out to the beach before the *Colorado*'s planes flew away. Scaevola tends to impede one's scampering abilities.

So suppose they are not seen, and are left to fend for themselves. What then?

Well, they would probably decimate the *Norwich City* cache, accounting for its scattered condition when the Kiwis photographed it in 1939. And once these supplies run low, or maybe before, the reasonable thing to do would be to explore, figure out what was on hand to work with to survive.

So we hypothesize that they—or perhaps only one of them—set out to walk around the island and have a look, and made it as far as the bones discovery site. Catching a turtle and some birds along the way, carrying water in a Benedictine bottle and food, perhaps, in Noonan's sextant box. And at the bones site they, or one of them, died.

But why die on a paradisiacal tropical island? Because Niku isn't all that paradisiacal. There is plenty to eat, but most of it is on the fin, flipper, pincer, or wing, and you have to catch it. And to do that you have to scramble through some unpleasant bush or over a lot of hard, sharp coral. And water, of course, is another matter entirely. Coconuts and rain are the only sources, other than sucking on scaevola vines. Maybe you get lucky and get enough, but maybe you don't.

And suppose that as you charge around trying to catch a booby or a *Birgus latro,* or as you haul stuff ashore from the Electra, or as you shinny up a coconut tree, you happen to cut yourself? The wound is going to become infected quickly in the lush tropical environment, and if you don't have any way to stop the infection from spreading, the results can be serious, to say the least.

However one wants to embellish it, the hypothesis in simplest terms is, we think they landed, lived on the island for a while, and died.

Transformation Processes

A building or a battlefield or a campsite becomes an archaeological site through what archaeologists naturally refer to as "transformation processes." Reconstructing those processes is basic to figuring out what it was in the past that was responsible for what we see in the present. So after

Earhart and Noonan died, what do we think transformed them and the Electra into what Gallagher and his colleagues saw in 1940, and what we see today? Let's consider the airplane first.

The Electra on the Reef

If the Electra landed on Niku, then it was there for a time, and very likely is still there in some form. The dado and other Electra-like pieces in the village, assuming they did come from the Electra, suggest that it was someplace where the colonists could salvage pieces. The recollections of Emily Sikuli from 1940–1941 and of Tapania Taiki from the late 1950s suggest that the main body of wreckage was on the western Nutiran reef. It is possible that fragments are still on the reef flat, but if so they are not apparent.

But if they were visible to Ms. Taiki in the 1950s, and to Mrs. Sikuli and her father in 1940, they were surely more apparent in 1937, '38, or '39. Even accepting our premise that the *Colorado* pilots could have missed them from the air during their brief flyover, why did Maude and Bevington not see them in October 1937 when *Nimanoa* tied off to the stern of the *Norwich City*, when they made their way to shore across her decks? Why didn't the Kiwi survey party see them when they came ashore the same way and did their survey in 1938–1939?

We don't have answers to those questions, of course, but we also don't think that the fact that people didn't see things on the reef necessarily means they weren't there. If all that remained on the reef edge were some steel struts and maybe an engine or two, in the surf line, these would have been no more recognizable as airplane wreckage from the beach, or from the *Norwich City*, than they would have been from the air. Bevington's photo and the Kiwi photo that show the "dot and dash" suggest that there was, indeed, something at or near the location where Mrs. Sikuli reports the wreckage. If it was part of an airplane, though, was it recognizable as such to the casual observer, or readily distinguishable from *Norwich City* wreckage? Obviously it either wasn't recognizable or distinguishable, or it wasn't part of an airplane. We don't know which is true, but "there and not recognizable" is not an implausible proposition.

If this is the case, then why did the *colonists* find the wreckage—assuming Mrs. Sikuli is accurate in reporting that they did so? There's a plausible answer to this one, too. The reef edge is where you fish—right off the reef in a canoe, using line, net, or diving with a spear, or on foot along the reef edge itself, using a net or spear. It's where the fish congregate, and a fisherman will naturally go where the fish are. So an I Kiribati fisherman—or a Tuvaluan, in the case of Mrs. Sikuli's father—is going to be canoeing or walking around out there, getting up close to whatever the fish are swimming around.

And how would such a fisherman recognize the wreckage as that of an airplane, since aircraft were not exactly common in the area at the time? Well, here are excerpts from the deck log of the seaplane tender USS *Pelican*, during her visit to the island on April 30, 1939:

```
0938   hoisted out plane,
1120   Mr. Jack Pedro, Foreman of Gardner Island and two natives
       came aboard.
1240   hoisted in plane.
1242   three natives from Gardner Island came aboard.
1405   two natives left the ship.
1448   one native left the ship.
1513   Mr. Jack Pedro left the ship.²
```

So before 1940, but not long before, the colonists—including Jack Kimo Petro, the Tuvaluan/Portuguese PISS public works foreman who, according to Mrs. Sikuli, was her uncle—had gotten a good, close look at an airplane. If the wreckage on the reef included something like an engine, it's not unreasonable to think they would recognize it.

So the wreckage could have been on the reef, and might have gone unrecognized until a colonial fisherman noticed it. But if it was there, where is it now?

The Nutiran reef hasn't been as closely inspected by TIGHAR expeditions as some other parts of the reef. The dive team gave it short shrift in 1989 because they thought it would be impossible to find stuff amid the *Norwich City* debris, and Oceaneering broke its sonar fish just before getting there. However, aerial photos and more or less casual diver observations show that the reef face in this area drops at an angle of about 45 to 60 degrees for about forty-five feet, and then levels out in a shelf up to 300 feet wide. Then it drops off again into the abyssal depths. Airplane parts could easily have wound up on the shelf. In mid-2000, *Nai'a* visited the island with a group of reef biologists. Kenyan biologist David Obura inspected the

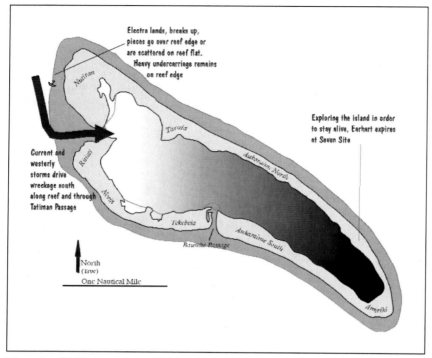

The refined Nikumaroro Hypothesis suggests three areas as the next targets for field investigation—the Nutiran reef ledge, the northern lagoon, and the Seven Site.

shelf, and reported the surface to be solid coral rock and rubble, partly covered by living coral and algae of various kinds.[3] Though Obura reports seeing no debris of any kind—even from the *Norwich City,* which should be thick on the surface—such debris could easily be covered by algae and coral, and could be found using metal detectors.

Of course, there is also the possibility that pieces went on over the lip of the ledge and down into the darkness, perhaps all the way to the bottom several thousand feet below. We can search there, too, but it will take much more expensive technology.

If the original landing/wreck site was north of the *Norwich City,* it's interesting that the aluminum wreckage reported in the late 1950s was said to have been south of the shipwreck. It's not hard to imagine pieces of the Electra bumping along the shelf on the reef face and then getting thrown up on the reef flat periodically by storms. The direction of movement is correct;

the current tends to flow southeast along the reef face here, as the tides pump water into the lagoon through Tatiman Passage. That's the direction that anything movable on the shelf is likely to go. Eventually it may well get thrown up on the reef flat and pushed in through Tatiman Passage, winding up in or around the lagoon.[4] We have evidence of this sort of process in a huge steel tank, which has to have come from the *Norwich City* and that is now on the lagoon shore down in Noriti near Kanawa Point. And of course, Pulekai Songivalu's report of wreckage on Taraia is consistent with the idea of stuff being washed in through Tatiman Passage, opposite the Taraia point.

So one answer to the question "Where's the plane?" is "Along the shelf, or in the northern lagoon, or both." This may or may not be the correct answer, but it's a possible answer that can be checked out, a hypothesis that can be tested. Ironically, the north end of the lagoon is the start of the sandbar that becomes the mudflat that extends up into Nutiran—the first place we searched in 1989, and wrote off thereafter. Perhaps we just didn't look deep enough, or get wet enough.

Of course, another answer to the question—not mutually inconsistent with the first—is "in little pieces in the village," picked up by the colonists and brought home to use in making things. This one's testable, too, through a lot more archaeological work in the village, and we might get lucky; there might be a smoking gun.

But this highlights another question: Why does Gallagher seem not to have known about the plane wreck, if it was there for Mrs. Sikuli's father to see, and for the colonists to collect stuff from? The second part of the question isn't too hard to posit an answer to; the aluminum wreckage that the colonists scavenged may not have been coughed up on the reef flat, or onto the Taraia shore, until after Gallagher died. The reports of aluminum wreckage and small plane parts we have—from John Mims, from Pulekai Songivalu, from Tapania Taiki—are all from well after Gallagher's demise. But why didn't he know about the heavy wreckage that Mrs. Sikuli's father reported? That's another story, and it involves the bones, so let's turn to them.

Which Bones Were When?

How Earhart—if it was Earhart—became the skeleton under the ren tree isn't hard to figure out, at least superficially. She died, of whatever cause, and her bones were gnawed upon and scattered by coconut crabs. But does *Birgus latro* scatter bones? The question is of some importance, because answering it might help us figure out when the individual represented by the bones died.

If coconut crabs don't scatter bones, then something else had to, to create the situation that Gallagher says he found—only about a dozen bones left, "damaged" to the point where Dr. Hoodless found that virtually "all traces of muscular attachments . . . have been obliterated." There are rats on the island, and they were almost certainly there in the 1930s (it's a rare Pacific island that *doesn't* have rats), but while they could certainly gnaw off muscle attachments, rats don't make off with large human bones. Half a pelvis, a tibia, and one whole arm were missing. Weather, wave action, plant growth, and gravity can erode bones and move them around, too, but would such processes have caused a number of bones to remain in place while lots more went missing?

Pigs and dogs are the culprits in many cases of bone reduction and dispersal; they are quite capable of both carrying bones away and splitting them into small fragments. It's not quite clear when pigs and dogs arrived on Nikumaroro, but it's pretty certain there weren't any around before the arrival of the colonists. So if *Birgus latro* doesn't scatter bones, or chew them up much, this might suggest that the bones in question were fresh enough to be interesting to a dog or a pig—who don't much go for bones in an advanced state of decomposition—when the colonists brought the creatures ashore. The person the bones represented would have had to have died not too long before. Before when? We're not entirely sure. In *Titiana*, Knudson tells us that Harry Maude brought pigs to Manra on May 1, 1939;[5] this may be when they arrived on Niku, too, but Mrs. Sikuli was pretty sure there were neither pigs nor dogs on the island when she lived there.

So it would be helpful to know whether *Birgus* scatters bones. It turns out, unfortunately—not surprisingly, really—that although there is substantial literature on the natural history of the coconut crab, nobody has done a systematic study of what they do with dead people, or dead creatures in general. We know that *Birgus* eats meat—the literature says so, and we've seen crabs peeling rats like oranges, dropping the empty skins out of trees—but do they drag bones around? If so, how far? Far enough to keep Gallagher and the colonists from finding them? Far enough to keep *us* from finding them, if we get the chance?

Crab experts we've consulted have generally opined that *Birgus* can and doubtless do carry bones around, and chew them up considerably, and might also carry them down into the burrows in which they shed their exoskeletons from time to time—about fifty centimeters into the soil.[6] But the only hard evidence we have suggests otherwise. This information comes from the 1999 discovery of the victims of a double murder on Saipan. The bodies had been deposited in an area frequented by coconut crabs, and although they were completely skeletonized when found (only a few months after their disappearance), the bones were not scattered.[7] But there are lots of people on Saipan, many of whom eat coconut crabs, so the crabs are a lot fewer and farther between than on Niku, and a lot shyer.

So we have an unanswered question; something scattered the bones of the castaway, and we don't know for sure what it was, or when it happened.

The fact that the sextant box was still intact when found, though, suggests that whoever the castaway was, she or he hadn't been lying dead for too terribly long—particularly since the box was in good enough shape to retain visible numbers, to serve as a packing crate when Gallagher sent the discoveries to Fiji, and to be something Vaskess would display in his office. However, we don't have any better experimental data on how long a wooden box will last in Niku's environment than we do on the dining habits of *Birgus latro*.

Then there's the fact that we have documentation indicating the discovery of only one skeleton. If it's Earhart, where's Noonan, and vice versa?

Of course, both Bauro Tikana and Teinamati Mereki gave us stories of two skeletons, and Mrs. Sikuli talked about one skeleton plus a concentration of up to ten others. Was there another skeleton, somewhere, that Gallagher didn't know about? And if so, was it one of the *Norwich City* casualties, or someone else, such as Noonan? Does the fact that we found the remains of two different shoes—one probably a woman's, the other more likely a man's—indicate that a man and a woman were present at Aukaraime South? Does the fact that Dr. Steenson mentions the shoes of a "male person and a female person" from the 1940 bones site indicate that a man and a woman were there? Or does it indicate that one person was wearing shoes from two different pairs, perhaps to accommodate an infected, swollen foot? Lots of room for speculation.

Mrs. Sikuli's story of the bones discovery is obviously at odds with what's documented in the WPHC files and the Tarawa file. In the documents, Gallagher says the bones were found on the southeast end of the island; Mrs. Sikuli says they were found on the Nutiran reef near the northwest end. And of course, Gallagher says nothing whatsoever about an airplane wreck. How are we to account for these discrepancies?

We don't know, of course, but there are currently two competing hypotheses.

One group of speculators suggests that the bones—one set and only one—were found at the southeast end, but associated in the minds of the colonists with the wreckage they had found at the northwest end. This hypothesis requires that the colonists refrain from telling Gallagher about the wreckage for some reason. Perhaps, it is speculated, having learned something about the Earhart flight from Gallagher in connection with the bones discovery, or perhaps from the *Pelican, Bushnell,* or *Leander* crews, and knowing of the competition between Great Britain and the United States for the islands, they were afraid that revealing the information could put the colony at risk. Supporters of this premise argue that the wreckage had to have been found around the same time as the bones reported by Gallagher, or earlier, or the site could not have been put off limits by Teng Koata, as Mrs. Sikuli says it was. We know from Gallagher's first telegram that Koata left Nikumaroro in September 1940 (Benedictine bottle in hand). As far as we know he never returned. According to a list of magistrates and their dates of service in Laxton's 1949 memorandum, he was replaced as magistrate in 1941 by Teng Iokina, about whom at this writing we know nothing.

The other school of thought is that the bones that went into the kanawa box were found on the southeast end, while another set of bones was found later near the wreckage on the northwest end (though almost certainly not on the reef itself), the latter discovery happening *after* Gallagher left for Fiji in May 1941. In this formulation, Gallagher's death on his return, after having dug up the skull and otherwise desecrated the first group of bones, caused the colonists to pack up the new batch and dispose of them in the ocean, thus tying up a loose end in the Kilts story. This argument requires that it be Iokina, not Koata, who put the wreck site off limits. This is possible if King "led" Mrs. Sikuli into misidentifying "that Onotoa man" with Koata, when in fact she had Iokina in mind.

King—who prefers the second hypothesis—argues that Iokina may well have been from Onotoa as well. Gillespie—who prefers the first—points out that Mrs. Sikuli described Koata in some detail in her interview with him, and seemed to know exactly whom she was talking about.

As of late 2000, we were trying to track down Koata's son, last heard from in the 1950s on Ocean Island, and contact authorities on Onotoa and in Tarawa about Koata and Iokina. At present, though, all we can say is that there are a lot of loose ends to be tied up where the bones are concerned.

Not the least of which is: where are they now? Whatever bones Gallagher and the colonists didn't find and the crabs (or whatever) didn't eat presumably are still on Niku, though quite likely reduced to dust by now (with a very interesting possible exception, discussed below). But what about those they *did* find, the ones that went to Fiji?

We obviously didn't find them in 1999 in our search of obvious places, and the reward we put up for information leading to their apprehension has yet to be claimed. But there are lots of places they could be. They could have been buried—or burned—by the medical school in the same way cadavers were disposed of. They could have gone into a storage cave during World War II, as the Fiji Museum's collections did, but unlike the collections the bones might not have emerged. Blocked up caves can be found all over Suva. The bones might still be in some dusty corner of some closed-up attic in some government (or nongovernment) building. They might have been packed up and sent to Tarawa, or Funafuti, or even England when the WPHC closed down. They might be somewhere in the huge complex of Victorian and modern structures that makes up the Colonial War Memorial Hospital. One story—which King is trying to check out—says that the bones were seen as recently as the 1960s, in the personal possession of a former colonial officer.

"Betty"

Late in 2000, a whole new line of inquiry opened up when Gillespie learned about a "new" post-loss signal report—this one far better documented than any previous example, though at first blush it seemed pretty far-fetched.

The report came from a woman TIGHAR refers to only as "Betty"; she has a heart condition and doesn't want to be besieged by the media. Now seventy-eight, at fifteen Betty was living with her parents in St. Petersburg, Florida, in July of 1937. One afternoon—she didn't record the exact date—she says she was listening to her parents' shortwave radio and was startled to hear a voice say, "This is Amelia Earhart."

Betty grabbed a notebook in which she kept track of popular songs and movies, drew pictures, and otherwise recorded her teenage world, and wrote out what she heard. The transmission was scratchy and broken, she says, but she recorded the words as she heard them. Lots of numbers, lots of obscure sentence fragments, but what they seemed to represent was an attempt by Earhart to communicate her location and situation. The situation seems to have been pretty desperate: they were apparently on the ground, but with water rising fast. Noonan (presumably—a man's voice) was heard breaking in from time to time or in the background, not very coherent. Sounds of an argument were recorded, implication of near panic. But what Betty wrote down was mostly fragmentary phrases and numbers: "Where are you?" "Waters knee deep—let me out." "South 391065 Z (or E)," "3E MJ3B," "George," "Get the suitcase in my closet," "Watch that battery."

Gillespie had actually heard of similar transmissions. Back in 1990 Mabel D. of Vermont had written that she had heard an SOS from Earhart, reporting the plane down on an uncharted island, partly in and partly out of the water. She had been living in Amarillo, Texas, when she heard the message in 1937, she said. In 1991 Thelma L. of Ontario, Canada, had reported hearing someone say "Can you read me? Can you read me? This is Amelia Earhart. . . . We have taken in water, my navigator is badly hurt." Thelma had been living in St. Stephen, New Brunswick, at the time. What was different about Betty is that she'd written down what she heard and kept her notebook, which she made available to TIGHAR.

Analysis of the notebook is ongoing, but so far it looks authentic. The right kind of notebook for the period, and all the songs and movies noted in it were popular around the time of Earhart's disappearance. No one on the Earhart Forum has been able to find record of any other broadcast—such as a *War of the Worlds*–type piece of radio fiction—that might have produced such a message. Betty herself, whom Gillespie interviewed in November 2000, seems to be a very credible witness.

But could somebody in Florida—or Amarillo, or New Brunswick—have heard a message from the South Pacific? Radio experts Mike Everette and Bob Brandenburg say it is possible, and Brandenburg has done a detailed analysis of the matter. It appears to be unlikely that Betty could have heard a message during daylight hours on one of Earhart's standard frequencies, but she could have heard it on a harmonic of such a frequency.[8]

The message fragments don't make much obvious sense. This is discouraging in some ways but encouraging in others; one would expect a hoax to include more "leading" information. And it's possible that the message contains what Gillespie calls "occult references"—references to things that nobody could have faked at the time but that in fact mean something. For instance, Betty's notes include repeated references to "N.Y." Betty thinks it's possible (she can't be sure) that this was her shorthand for "New York City." Which could be what *Norwich City* sounded like to Betty. Did the *Norwich City* have her name on her bow, where Earhart could have seen it? We don't know; it's the subject of ongoing research, as are other possible "occult" references, the actual age of the notebook, and the relationships between Betty's message and those reported by others.

But why didn't Betty report her message to the authorities? Why didn't she take action to save Earhart? According to Betty, she did—she says she notified her father, who reported it to the Coast Guard, and was told that the matter was under control.

So What's Next?

Where do we go from here? There are several directions in which we'd like to go, and by the time this book finds its way into the hands of readers we will almost certainly have explored some of them.

We need to search for plane parts on the Nutiran reef ledge, in the sandbar that runs across the lagoon-side end of Tatiman Passage, and on the lagoon floor beyond the sandbar. The ledge search will involve swimming transects over the ledge, examining the bottom, and sweeping it with metal detectors, then excavating hits. The searching shouldn't be hard; the excavation may be something else again, particularly since we'll want to minimize damage to the organisms that make up the reef.

The lagoon bottom next to the sandbar also shouldn't be too hard to survey, though it's a more extensive piece of real estate than the ledge. It's also almost certainly made up of soft silt that will obscure anything lying there, and at times reduce visibility to zero. The sandbar also covers a lot of territory and it's probably dynamic—it probably grows and shrinks, and moves around somewhat. It's also probably full of *Norwich City* debris, as well as other stuff swept in on the strong currents that run through the passage when nor'westers strike. Sorting out little bits of aluminum from great big hunks of iron won't be hard when divers have them in front of their faces, but from a distance, using metal detectors or some other remote sensing technology to figure out where to dig, recognition will be a lot more difficult, if not impossible.

Digging, of course, in this case will mean dredging, and that raises other problems. Niku's natural environment is sensitive, and we'll have to be careful not to damage it. We don't think this is insurmountable, but here again we'll need some serious expertise we don't currently have, in how to control impacts on tropical reefs and lagoons.

Another thing we ought to do is search the village much more thoroughly than we have been able to in the past. Give every house site the kind of attention we gave to the Manybarrels site. This will involve a long, tedious job of coordinated ground clearing and archaeological documentation—mapping, photographing, metal detecting, occasionally excavating.

Meanwhile, we need to go over the bones discovery site, wherever it is, very carefully. Though the survival of bones from sixty years ago seems unlikely in Niku's hyperactive environment, it's not impossible, particularly if they went down a crab hole, thus escaped the notice of the 1940 searchers, and stayed buried thereafter. But if they are buried, how are we going to find them?

One of the things that makes it so tempting to regard the "Seven" Site—the water-catcher site on the southeast corner—as the bones discovery site is that it contains the hole that Gillespie and his 1996 colleagues thought was an aborted well. If this represents where Koata buried and Gallagher dug up the skull, then there might still be teeth in the hole or around it. It would take a lot of digging and sifting sand, but the hole and its surroundings don't represent a huge area; one *can* dig it.

But of course, we're not sure that the Seven Site is where the bones were found, or that the hole is where the skull was buried. We could end up moving a lot of sand and coral rubble to no avail, if we can't nail down the site more accurately. Right now there's enough evidence pointing toward the Seven Site to make it worth a good hard look, but Aukaraime South is still in the running, too. The association of the shoe with the fire there continues to make no evident sense, and there's no particular reason to think that the shoe remained right where it was dropped from whenever it was dropped until 1991. There's a lot of territory that could be searched at Aukaraime South, a lot of fronds to be dragged, coconuts to be tossed. And as Spading keeps reminding Gillespie, King, and anyone else who will listen, there are holes in the ground at Aukaraime South, too, and ridges that just might relate somehow to whatever it was that Bevington and Maude saw there.

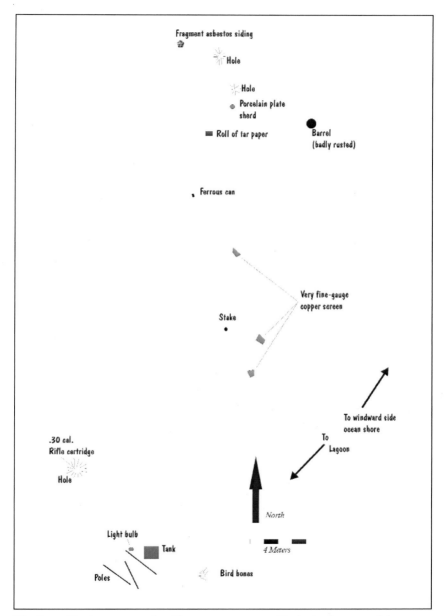

The Seven Site is a scatter of artifacts, structures, and holes in the ground, between the lagoon and the windward shore on Aukaraime North. (After field map by Ric Gillespie)

Gillespie and King protest that the whole area was worked over by coconut planters in the early '40s, but it's certainly not beyond possibility that Spading is on to something. And of course, it's also entirely possible that neither Aukaraime South nor the Seven Site—nor Kanawa Point—is the actual location of the bones discovery. It would be helpful to find something to make us more certain about just where the bones were found: a map drawn by Kilts's informant, for example, or by Gallagher, or those photographs that were itemized in Gallagher's effects.

This brings us to things we need to do in places other than Niku itself:

We need to spend some serious time in Tarawa, capital of Kiribati, to consult with the government about future plans and to conduct interviews and archival research. It's not impossible that the Fiji bones have wound up in Tarawa. It's far more likely that there are pertinent records in the Kiribati National Archives, or that there are people on Tarawa who lived on Niku or heard stories from their elders. Their stories will by definition be only anecdotal, but every little bit of information helps.

Getting back to Funafuti would be time well spent, too. Mrs. Sikuli's brother lives there, and may know more than she does about whatever it was that was found on the reef edge in 1940. Others probably have stories of Nikumaroro, and documents may be available as well. During his enforced sojourn in Funafuti in 1997, looking around for something to do, Spading was directed to the library at the local branch of the University of the South Pacific. After he had scanned a few books the reference librarian asked if she could help. Spading explained his mission, and she suggested that he try the nearby Tuvalu National Archives. Kicking himself for not thinking of it on his own, Spading jumped on his rented moped. In the dusty stacks of the archives, his cursory survey produced a range of manuscripts authored by Harry Maude and others, but he didn't have time to do an in-depth review. He later learned (and Foua Tofinga confirmed) that some of the WPHC files had been sent to Funafuti when the WPHC in Suva closed up shop. Given what we know from the 1998 trip to Hanslope Park, a return trip to the Funafuti Archives could be productive.

It would be good for someone to spend serious time in Nikumaroro Village in the Solomons, consulting with its residents more thoroughly than Dirk Ballendorf was able to during his brief visit. In New Zealand, we need to put some real effort into finding surviving members of the Kiwi survey party, or more records of the expedition, or both.

We need to get back to Hanslope Park and spend more time with the WPHC records. Also in England, we need to review Sir Harry Luke's papers, which he donated to Oxford. We need to look for Gallagher's effects. King is pursuing surviving WPHC veterans and their descendants, with the generous help of Sir Ian Thomson, Sir Harry's aide-de-camp.

We could productively spend more time in Fiji pursuing both the bones and other sources of information. Medical officer Lindsay Isaac[10] died in Fiji after years as a leading figure in the expatriate community; he may have left pertinent papers. So might have Henry Harrison Vaskess or Dr. Jock MacPherson, both of whom also lived out their days there. The National Archives and the records of the Colonial War Memorial Hospital are rich resources that we've barely tapped. And persistent rumors about the bones need to be discretely investigated.

Meanwhile, the possibility still exists that one of Kilts's colleagues will remember something, even have something on paper. Jeff Glickman is continuing his photoanalysis of the "dot and dash" photos and other images. And if the opportunity presents itself, there's a dump to dig on Kanton for Bruce Yoho's engine. Other possibilities arise all the time, and what we can do is limited only by time and money.

In September 2000, serendipity struck again when Gillespie received an e-mail from Gerard Gallagher of Scotland, investigating a story his grandfather had told him about a relative who had died in the Colonial Service in the South Pacific. Gerry Gallagher—Gerald's second cousin, it turns out—was rather overwhelmed by the information that landed on him in response to his innocent query, but recovered quickly and is hard at work on his own program of interviews and documentary research in England, Scotland, Ireland, and Fiji. Gallagher—"Little Karaka," as he sometimes calls himself—is as generous and hardworking as his ancestor, it seems. By the time this book is published he will almost certainly have greatly increased the world's knowledge of the man who, with Koata and their less well-documented colleagues, may have found Amelia Earhart.

Help!

Whatever hypotheses we may spin from the data we have, one thing we have found over the last dozen years is that our research often gets redirected by totally new data, coming in from unexpected sources. Bauro

Tikana's son-in-law sends Gillespie a note, Peter McQuarrie discovers a file, a crab turns over a leaf, "Betty" sends in her notebook. There may be—almost certainly are—important bodies of information out there in the world that we have no knowledge of whatsoever. So, dear reader, if you know anything that might bear on our quest, please, please contact TIGHAR. If this project has taught us nothing else, it's taught us some humility, and about the need to remain open to new possibilities.

Speaking of Possibilities . . .

It would hardly be fair to bring this book to a close without saying something about the alternatives to the Nikumaroro Hypothesis that others have brought forward, and without saying something in response to the critics of TIGHAR's approach.

There are two major bodies of hypothesis other than TIGHAR's about the loss of the World Flight:

Crashed and Sank

Crashed and sank is in many ways the most conservative of the hypotheses, explained in great detail by Elgen and Marie Long in their 1999 *Amelia Earhart: The Mystery Solved*. It is certainly a plausible hypothesis, but the precision with which the Longs locate the crash site requires making a lot of assumptions that can't be verified about things such as fuel evaporation and head winds. And this theory doesn't account for the post-loss radio signals or for any of our discoveries on and about Nikumaroro. Right now, too, crash-and-sank advocates can produce only negative evidence to support their premise. Earhart and Noonan didn't get to Howland and haven't unequivocally been found anyplace else; ergo, they must have crashed and sunk. Until there's evidence acceptable to advocates of this theory that shows that Earhart and Noonan *did* wind up elsewhere, there's no way to prove this premise wrong. What's more important, though, is that there's still no real evidence to indicate that it's right.

Captured by the Japanese

This is probably the most popular hypothesis, advanced by Fred Goerner and others in several permutations—flew to Saipan, crashed in the Marshalls and taken to Saipan, landed in Chuuk. Executed on Saipan, executed in Chuuk, brainwashed and became Tokyo Rose. The major problem with the capture theory is that there's nothing but anecdotal evidence to support it, and it's hard to give much credence to a lot of the anecdotes. Americans started asking Micronesians about Earhart as soon as the islands were taken from the Japanese; today, telling stories about Earhart has become a virtual cottage industry in places like Saipan and Chuuk. To what extent it had achieved this status when Goerner and others started their work in the 1960s is something we just don't know. But we do know that anecdotal evidence is something to be dealt with cautiously. Did people see a short-haired woman imprisoned and killed on Saipan, or in Chuuk? Maybe. Was it Earhart? Maybe, or maybe it was some other woman—a European, American, Australian, New Zealand, German, or French missionary, perhaps. Did people see a two-engined airplane that was different from others they had seen? Maybe, but there were an awful lot of airplanes around the Japanese mandate islands of Micronesia in the 1940s, and a fair number even in the late '30s. We're not going to find out by collecting more anecdotes. By now—as, most likely, by the time Fred Goerner did his research—stories have had plenty of time to grow, elaborate, and evolve.

Another problem with the capture theory is motive. Why would the Japanese have captured and killed Earhart and Noonan? Because the flyers had seen all kinds of fortifications under construction, advocates of this theory propose. But there has been pretty exhaustive historical and archaeological study of the former Japanese mandate islands since World War II, and although it's clear that the Japanese were building things on Saipan at least by 1937 that could be used for military purposes, it's equally clear that from the air they wouldn't have looked particularly suspicious. There weren't fleets of bombers sitting on runways; there were runways, which could as easily be used for commercial purposes as for military, and Japan was engaged in a vigorous program of economic development in the islands. Warships were steaming around and anchored in harbors, but this was permitted by the League of Nations mandate under which Japan administered the islands. If there was nothing truly suspicious for Earhart and Noonan to see and report, what motive did the Japanese have for capturing and killing them? Add to this the fact that any overflight would have happened in the dead of night, and the fact that it would have required more fuel than the Electra was recorded as carrying, or even able to carry, and you have a lot going against the captured hypothesis. What's going for it are some anecdotal accounts that are very hard to evaluate, and a lot of suspicions that its proponents attach to both the Japanese and the U.S. governments.

Of course, we're using a lot of anecdotal evidence, too, but it's not all we have, and we don't rely on it as our sole basis for validating the Niku hypothesis. Indeed, we don't use it at all as a basis for *validating* the hypothesis; it's a means of generating test implications for the hypothesis that we can explore for hard evidence.

Other hypotheses include proposals that Earhart survived and lived for years, is even still alive, in the Philippines, in Kiribati, even in New Jersey, and that she was captured by aliens or zipped off to another dimension. Maybe so, but it seems like there are more efficient ways to account for what we know about the disappearance.

And As for Our Critics . . .

Criticisms of the Nikumaroro Hypothesis also tend to fall into several overlapping categories.

First, there's the "Gillespie's making it up" charge. Some people—including some of the authors, on some days—simply don't like Gillespie. Some of these people—*not* including the authors except on *really* bad days—see our project as Gillespie's personal schtick, and reject it as such. When called upon—as they rarely are—to explain their rejection in other than personal terms, some darkly hint that Gillespie has pulled the wool over the eyes of his faithful followers while salting the island with artifacts, forging documents in files on Tarawa and in England, and coaching informants about what to say. If these charges were true, we would all have to be a good deal dumber than we think we are, even in our most insecure moments, and Gillespie would clearly be in the wrong business.

Then there's the charge that our hypothesis is so preposterous that it can't possibly be true. This charge is usually leveled by crash-and-sank proponents, and is often coupled with platitudes about how we should "get past what happened to Earhart and honor what's really important about her"—her courage, the example she provides to young women, and so on. Needless to say, we don't think that what we're pursuing is preposterous, and as to dishonoring Earhart by continuing to try to figure out what happened to her, we don't think that's true either. We have a world of respect for Earhart, though we don't overlook the possibility that she had some flaws—like an amazingly cavalier attitude toward radio communication. We don't think that trying to find out what happened to her in any way denigrates her memory.

The Nikumaroro Hypothesis, in fact, is based on the assumption that Earhart was a better pilot than she would have to have been to make the crash-and-sank hypothesis work. Barring some catastrophic systems failure, that hypothesis requires us to assume that Earhart mismanaged her fuel to such an extent that she went down well *before* she would have if she followed Kelly Johnson's carefully developed fuel conservation guidelines. It also requires us to think that she and Noonan had little in the way of backup plans if they arrived in Howland's neighborhood and couldn't find the island.[11] If the Nikumaroro Hypothesis is correct, she managed her fuel correctly and responded professionally when she couldn't find Howland, flying efficiently toward the more numerous and visible islands of the Phoenix Group. And the Nikumaroro Hypothesis has her landing competently on an island without landing facilities, from which she would have been rescued if the Navy had put a little more effort into its search.

We *are* keenly aware that our evidence seems to be leading to the conclusion that an icon of U.S. history was eaten by giant crabs—it's easy to imagine what the tabloids may say. But if that's where the evidence leads, we don't see an alternative to following it—other than, of course, just declaring the mystery insoluble or not worth solving, and we're not ready to do that. And as one of the Airhearts said with a shrug: "Everybody gets eaten by *something* after they die."

We're sometimes charged with making overblown claims—with claiming to have "solved the mystery." Well, back in the early '90s, in the wake of the shoe discovery and artifact 2-2-V-1, there were some rash things said. They were unfortunate, though understandable in context. Nowadays we—and Gillespie, most of the time at least—try hard to avoid repeating such mistakes. It's notable, though, that some critics reject as grandstanding even the cautious statement that Burns, Jantz, King, and Gillespie put out in 1998 about the reanalysis of Dr. Hoodless's measurements—that they suggested an individual consistent with Earhart's sex, stature, and racial background.[12]

Some people in Fiji, we have heard, are critical of the questions we've raised about Dr. Hoodless and Dr. Isaac (Verrier), both revered figures in twentieth-century Fijian history. We certainly haven't meant any offense by asking questions, or any disrespect to either of the late doctors. There are curious things about the role of each in the bones saga. Why was it Dr. Hoodless, rather than the seemingly more experienced Dr. MacPherson, who made the analysis? Why did Dr. Isaac become so excited about the bones when they arrived at Tarawa, and then so dismissive? Why did he go so far as to throw a quarantine over the harbor? We don't know whether these questions have anything to do with whether the bones were Earhart's, but it's hard not to ask them. We can only hope that people will understand that we are not asking them in a spirit of disrespect, or in an effort to air dirty linen, but simply in an effort to understand.

TIGHAR is sometimes criticized for being a "one-trick pony," with only the Nikumaroro Hypothesis to investigate. Why don't we investigate crashed and sank, we're sometimes asked, or run an expedition to Saipan? The answers are simple; based on what we know at present, we think the Nikumaroro Hypothesis has an excellent chance of being right, and TIGHAR isn't about to dilute the limited resources it can devote to testing it by extending those resources over a number of other possibilities. And we don't know how we would test the crashed and sank or captured hypothesis. Testing the first would require a monstrously expensive search of the ocean floor over a tremendously wide area; anyone who thinks he can pinpoint where the plane crashed and sank, we think, is fooling himself. As for Saipan—well, it's easy to get to, but "eyewitness" testimony there has been polluted by at least forty years of leading questions about Earhart sightings. Physical evidence, if it ever existed, has almost certainly been obscured, if not destroyed, by the massive landscape transformations caused by the last fifty years of economic development. We think the chances of finding reliable evidence on Saipan is virtually nil—assuming it was ever there in the first place.

Finally, and most generally, our critics continue to emphasize the fact that we haven't found the "smoking gun." Guilty as charged, but we're doing what we can to correct this deficiency. And of course, not every murder investigation produces a smoking gun, but people are still convicted on a preponderance of evidence. Not every archaeological project produces data that unequivocally demonstrate that specific events happened at specific times, but we are still able to reach responsible conclusions about the past based on what such projects *do* produce. We think the preponderance of evidence points toward the Nikumaroro Hypothesis, that the odds in favor of it being correct are at least better than even. As Gillespie put it in an Internet exchange early in 2000:

What are "the chances" that a given island that "happens" to be on the LOP described by Earhart will "happen," three years later, to yield the bones of a castaway which "happen" to appear most similar to those of a woman of Earhart's stature and ethnic background and that a search of the same island will "happen" to produce the remains of a shoe which appears to match Earhart's and aircraft-related artifacts which "happen" to be consistent with the Lockheed Model 10. . . . Is there a way to quantify this heap of coincidence?

There isn't, of course, nor is there any quantitative way to decide whether the existence of all these "coincidences" is enough to justify concluding that the Nikumaroro Hypothesis is correct. All we can do is keep looking.

But about That Shoe . . .

"Wow!" she said. "That's quite a story!"

The plane had crossed the Sierra Nevada and was descending into the Bay Area. King grimaced.

"Well, however, there is one more twist."

"Oh?"

"Yeah, it looks like the Aukaraime shoe isn't hers. Or at least it's probably not the one in the Bandoeng photograph."

"Oh dear."

"Yeah, that's what I said, too. What happened is, a couple of months ago Rollin Reineck, one of TIGHAR's severest critics, put out a note on the Internet saying that as he measured the heel in the Bandoeng picture, vis-à-vis the rivet spacing, it was a good deal shorter than the Aukaraime heel. Our first reaction was to say he was all wet—hadn't considered the fact that the shoe wasn't exactly parallel with the rivet line, and so on. But it had to be checked, so Gillespie dredged up the two thousand bucks for a thorough analysis by Photek."

"And they agreed with—what's his name?"

"Reineck. Yeah, basically. The report's loaded with equations that I don't pretend to understand, but the bottom line is, Photek sees the heel as a shade under two and a half inches long, and the Aukaraime heel is about three inches."

"Couldn't the heel have swollen up in the rain and sun, or something?"

"Not likely; if anything it's probably shrunk."

"What about the whole shoe?"

"It looks shorter, too—about a size six and a half."

"But what about the reports that Earhart had bigger feet?"

"I dunno. Maybe she wore bigger shoes, stuffed with socks, when she was actually flying up in the cold sky. Who knows?"

"But that could mean she had another pair of oxfords!"

"Actually, the photographs show that she did, but we can't tell how big they were."

"Well, so . . ."

"Well, so. It's one piece of what seemed like real hard evidence that's suddenly gotten real soft. But the argument doesn't turn on one piece of evidence. There are the bones, the shoes Gallagher found, the sextant box, the dado, the skin. And there's still the question of how a 1930s woman's shoe, of whatever size, came to be at Aukaraime South."

She looked out the window for a while as the plane banked over Silicon Valley, and waved her hand rather apologetically.

"Look, I don't want to seem critical, but . . ."

"No offense taken. But?"

"It kind of seems like you find stuff that looks good just long enough to get the money to keep going, and then . . ."

"Well, there's some truth in that. Gillespie's accused of it a lot; the rest of us are just accused of being dupes."

"I didn't mean . . ."

"Don't worry about it. I've been called worse things, and so has Ric. But if you'll forgive me, the shoe doesn't fit. The fact is that in any piece of research you wind up being wrong a lot more than you're right, even when you're basically on the right track. You wind up making a lot of missteps, running off down blind alleys."

"Two steps forward and one step back."

"Whatever size shoes you're wearing. And it's worse with something as soft and squishy as historical and archaeological research. But the fact that you're wrong about some stuff doesn't mean you're not right overall. Does that make sense?"

"Well . . ."

"Look, Heinrich Schleimann was wrong about the stratigraphy of Troy—what he thought was the Trojan War level wasn't—but he still found Troy. Hiram Bingham insisted that Macchu Picchu was the Incas' last stand; it wasn't, but he'd actually already found the city that was their last stand, just hadn't recognized it for what it was. It happens all the time."

"I guess we're kind of conditioned to expect neat solutions. But you've got to admit that the timing's suspicious. The grave looks good just long enough to let you find the shoe . . ."

"The grave never looked good."

"Okay, but you get the point. The navigator's bookcase looks good long enough to get the money to go back to the island and find the shoe and the skin, and then it washes up . . ."

"Sure, but here's the rub. The research wouldn't have gotten done to show that the navigator's bookcase probably wasn't from the Electra if Ric hadn't kept himself and the rest of us engaged in the work, and kept contributors interested enough to keep contributing the necessary money. We wouldn't have gone to the island in '97, and gone on to get the wreckage stories and the bones papers, if we—and the people who contribute the money to make it happen—hadn't thought that the shoe was good evidence. And we honestly did think it was good evidence—hell, I'm not convinced that it's not, even now. Something weird was going on on that island to produce the stuff that we've found, and that Gallagher found. And the hypothesis that Earhart and Noonan wound up there is still the most efficient way I can think of to account for it all."

"So when do you go back to look for more?"

"September 2001 is the plan. We've got *Nai'a* reserved, and the money's coming in—it costs about three hundred thousand bucks to put on an expedition—and we're planning to sail from American Samoa in late August."

"What are you going to do this time?"

"We figure to check out the Nutiran reef ledge and the north end of the lagoon, and dig the bejeebers out of the hole at the Seven Site, and—well, there's that other grave on the Nutiran shore."

"You think you'll find her?"

"Well, sure, or we wouldn't be going. Though that's not really true. We think we're going to find *something,* but whether it'll be the smoking gun that proves what happened—well, that's another matter."

"What do you *hope* you find?"

"Oh, well—a whole bunch of teeth at the Seven Site, with good DNA that matches Earhart's. An engine with an ID plate that can be matched with the Electra. A skeleton in the grave on Nutiran—if it's a grave—with a gold watch inscribed 'Best Wishes Fred, from your friends at Pan Am.' But finding any of those kinds of things would be a real, real long shot. And if experience is any guide, what we'll actually find is something we don't expect at all."

"Like the shoe."

"Like the shoe, or the airplane skin, or the navigator's bookcase—or something from a completely different direction, like the Tarawa file or the Funafuti stories. Something that—even if it turns out *not* to be a clue, like the bookcase did and maybe the Aukaraime shoe did, keeps us at it and sends us off to look at new possibilities."

"It's really like a detective story."

"Sure, and some detectives solve the mystery and some don't, and some solve the mystery by finding a smoking gun, and some by pulling together a preponderance of evidence. Ric Gillespie really wants to find that smoking gun—that's why he's so disappointed every time we leave the island without one. I sympathize, but I'm not so sure there's a smoking gun out there to find."

"But without the smoking gun . . ."

"We see what the preponderance of evidence indicates, and right now—well, I think it points in a pretty clear direction."

"Still, it'd be nice to have proof."

"You bet, but on the other hand, not every mystery gets solved, and in a lot of ways it's more fun to *try* to solve it than to actually succeed."

The 757 landed with a bump and the roar of reversed thrust. She had to shout.

"I don't suppose you need an English lit major on the next expedition . . ."

King smiled, wondering why he hadn't had a line like this to use when he was young and single.

"Desperately. But unfortunately there are about twelve hundred people ahead of you in line. I can give you our Web site though...."

To follow TIGHAR's continuing adventures in the search for Earhart, visit www.tighar.org and click on the "Amelia Earhart Search" button.

CHAPTER 27

Epilogue: 2001 and Beyond

Future is mortgaged, but what else are futures for?
—AMELIA EARHART[1]

Dear Cynthia,

Thanks for your note. Of course I remember our conversation on the plane to San Francisco, and I'll be happy to bring you up-to-date on TIGHAR's continuing quest for Amelia. I know the website can be a bit confusing; there's an awful lot on it, and it's constantly evolving.

Where to begin? Well, as I recall, when we left off in our conversation, I was talking about next steps, like planning our 2001 expedition. . . .

The Rust-Colored Patch

Late in 2000, Ric Gillespie was able to work out a three-way deal among TIGHAR, the National Oceanic and Atmospheric Administration (NOAA), and Space Imaging Corporation, operators of the IKONOS imaging satellite, to get high-quality satellite imagery of Nikumaroro. This would prove tremendously helpful in navigating around the island. It would show such objects as trees standing out from the shore and high clumps of buka that could be used as visual reference points on the ground. Moreover, everything on it would be "georeferenced"—that is, precisely located in space. With Global Positioning Satellite (GPS) technology we could then plot courses to wherever we wanted to go, follow our instruments to get there, and make

333

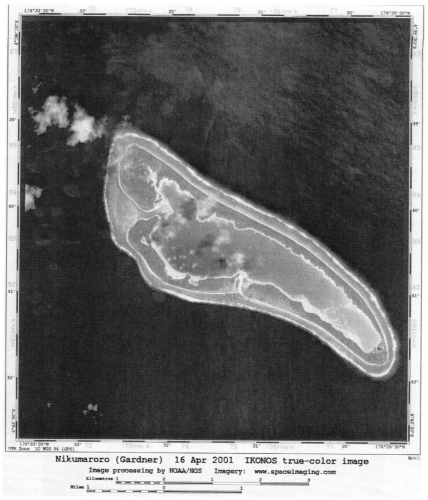

Nikumaroro (Gardner)   16 Apr 2001   IKONOS true-color image
Image processing by NOAA/NOS   Imagery: www.spaceimaging.com

Niku from space, April 2001 (Space Imaging for TIGHAR and NOAA).

accurate maps of where we'd been and what we found. Further, of course, the image might reveal something we couldn't see from the ground.

When NOAA was ready for a showing, Ric and I visited their head-quarters in Silver Spring, Maryland. The picture on the screen was riveting. There was "our" little island, all scaevola green and coral golden in the deep blue sea. A couple of wispy clouds fuzzed western Nutiran, but otherwise the image was crystal clear. There was Kanawa Point, there was the Seven

Site. It was a nostalgic moment, and exciting; there was a lot we could do with this image.

Over the next several months, Ric and others, including Jeff Glickman with his serious image-analysis capability, pored over the image to capture any data they could.[2] The main item of interest that emerged was a cluster of rust-colored pixels on the reef-edge north of the *Norwich City*.

Rust colored? And north of *Norwich City*? The current along this stretch of reef, after flowing around the north end of the island, normally runs down the shore to the southeast, so pieces of the shipwreck should move consistently southeast, not north. But what *was* north of the wreck, of course, was the site where Emily Sikuli had reported the heavy steel plane wreckage.*

Ric tried to be cautious. "I don't need another cruciform," he muttered. But Space Imaging was more bullish, and after all, it was their image. So, before long the media began to trumpet the news—high technology had (perhaps, they acknowledged) found Earhart.

Through the sale of media rights to Mike Kammerer, a New Mexico television executive, TIGHAR raised the money for an expedition that would have four major goals:

- Investigate the rust-colored patch;
- Search the northern lagoon and the shelf on the reef face southeast from Emily's reported wreckage site;
- Investigate the possible grave site found on the Nutiran shore but not excavated in 1999, and
- Give the Seven Site and its mysterious hole a good hard look.[†]

Mission to Tarawa

Before we headed back to the island, however, we needed to get a better handle on the history of the place, especially during and after Gallagher's time. The major unsearched archive we knew of was on Tarawa, capital island of the Republic of Kiribati. So, in March of 2001, Ric Gillespie and Van Hunn made the somewhat complicated air trip to that famous atoll to examine its national archives, consult with government officials about plans

*See chapter 23.
†See chapters 14 and 26.

for work on Niku, and see whether there was further anecdotal evidence to collect.

Ric and Van spent a week on Tarawa. Their discussions with the government were pleasant and productive, and they were able to pay a sentimental visit to the wreck of the *Nimanoa*—the Royal Colony ship that had carried Harry Maude and Eric Bevington to Niku in late 1937 and taken the bones to Fiji in 1941. *Nimanoa* was grounded later that year to prevent her capture during the Japanese invasion,[3] and later turned into a machine gun emplacement that harassed the U.S. 2nd Marine Division as it struggled ashore to retake the atoll in November 1943.

Few people came forward with anecdotal information while Ric and Van were in Tarawa, and there was really not enough time to make a serious effort to contact people. But the National Archives proved to be a rich trove of information.

No, no smoking guns, and not even the files that Ric and Van had most hoped to find—the prewar papers of the administrative officer on Tarawa (Gallagher's contemporary, David Wernham) and the files of the resident commissioner of the Gilbert & Ellice Islands Colony (Jack Barley) on Ocean Island. Not surprisingly, but disappointingly nonetheless, these had apparently not survived the war. But a great many documents did prove worth photocopying. Among these were the following:

- Diaries kept by John T. Arundel, who established coconut plantations on Nikumaroro in 1892. These included a description of the buildings he had put up there—which proved very interesting to us later:

```
1 storehouse—8 sheets iron
1 dwelling—12 sheets iron
1 cookhouse—6 sheets iron
```

- Detailed information about the 1938–1941 settlement process, including the names of the men involved, their wives and children, and what they brought with them—showing among other things that six pigs (notoriously good at scattering bones) were brought ashore in April 1939.

‡See chapters 19 and 26.

- Evidence strongly suggesting that Teng Koata, the island magistrate when the bones were found, had not returned to the island after his trip to the hospital on Tarawa in September 1940.[‡]
- A large-scale (1 inch equals 100 feet) hand-drawn map made by Gallagher and dated March 19, 1941, showing land parcel assignments on Aukaraime South. It appears that the "shoe site"[§] was in a parcel assigned to the Anibuka family. No indication of anything special about it.
- Another hand-drawn map on the reverse of the preceding, showing the entire island with various land divisions. On this map the southeast tip of the island is labeled "Amerika," which dates it to some time after 1943 and probably later. Most interesting is a land parcel shown all by itself embracing the Seven Site. The key ascribes ownership of this parcel to "Komitia," which is the Gilbertese rendering of "Commissioner," a generic term for the local British authority.

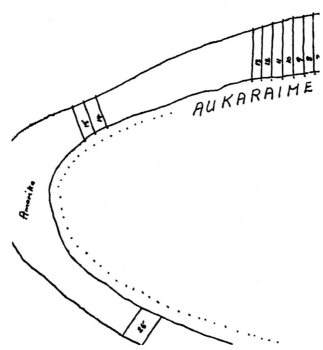

Part of the undated map; Parcel 25 is assigned to "Komitia."

[§]See chapters 12 and 15.

- Yet another map designating island landholdings, drawn by District Officer J. N. Freegard on October 15, 1954, with the same parcel labeled "Karaka" (the Gilbertese rendering of Gallagher). Whatever was intended by this map and the "Komitia" map, they certainly indicate official interest in the Seven Site.

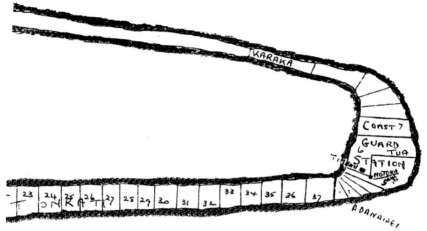

Part of the Freegard map; parcel containing the Seven Site assigned to "Karaka."

- A letter from Gallagher to Acting Magistrate Iokina dated June 2, 1941, giving him detailed instructions about what to do while Gallagher was in Fiji. No mention of clearing operations at any distance from the village or of any work at Aukaraime South, Kanawa Point, or the Seven Site, but—
- A series of telegrams to and from Gallagher *before* his arrival at Nikumaroro in September 1940, which detail the situation there and Gallagher's interactions with Public Works Officer Kimo Jack Petro, who was on the island trying to put the water situation aright. In one of these, sent on June 18, 1940, Gallagher asked:

```
Please telegraph whether there are forty kanawa
trees on Gardner good enough to send to Rongorongo
to be sawn into planks.
```

The next day Petro replied:

```
kanawa trees over hundred on Gardner.
```

Did Gallagher's interest in getting kanawa planks lead to a tree-cutting expedition at the southeast end of the island, in turn resulting in the discovery of the skull? The archives are silent on that point, but the timing is about right, because in September of 1940 Gallagher said that the skull had been found and buried "some months" earlier. In any event, the archives suggest that Petro was on the island during the period when the skull was found, and that could prove to be useful information.

Ric and Van also copied lots of documents describing the postwar progress and eventual decline of the Phoenix settlement. They indicate that Sydney Island (Manra) was abandoned as early as 1956. By the late '50s Hull (Orona) was becoming overcrowded and there was increasing pressure to settle more people on Nikumaroro than the island was ready to accept. A new village on Nutiran was contemplated and begun but apparently never finished. Beginning in about 1960, drought conditions began to impact the settlements on Orona and Nikumaroro. By early 1963 conditions were

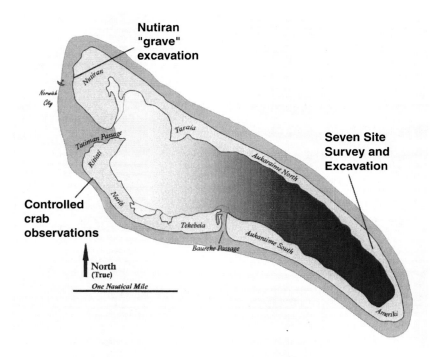

The 2001 expedition focused on the Seven Site and Nutiran.

desperate. Water was being shipped in and people were rationed to one pint per day. There was no alternative to evacuation of both islands, and the residents of Nikumaroro sailed for the Solomons on November 17, 1963.

Moose Antlers on Nikumaroro?

On August 30, 2001, *Nai'a* anchored in the lee of Nikumaroro, and its TIGHARs—old-timers Gillespie, Clauss, Hunn, Gifford, Kennedy, Quigg, Burns, and me, first-timers Walt Holm and Jim Morrissey from California, Andrew McKenna from Colorado, and Bill Carter from Idaho, together with producer/cameraman Mark Smith and cameraman Dan Zaphir—dispersed in three teams to check the reef and lagoon, the "grave site" on the Nutiran shore,** and the Seven Site.

Not to put too fine a point on it, the rusty spot on the reef turned out to be a patch of reddish brown algae. And the reef face and northern lagoon gave no joy to the divers and waders who searched them. An old jeep tire, a coral-encrusted pipe flange with wire wrapped around it, some other miscellaneous detritus from the village, but that was it. Pretty disappointing, particularly in view of the media hype that had built up around the rusty spot.

The reef flat survey was not without interesting results, however. Casual observation in 1999 had suggested that the flat was smooth enough to land on over an area at least 700 feet long. Now Gillespie, Gifford, and Quigg did a detailed topographic survey with transit and rod and found that the smooth area north of the *Norwich City* was more like 3,000 feet long, well in excess of the landing distance required by a Lockheed 10. Only an occasional pothole marred the surface, and Gifford,[4] whose thirty years as an airline pilot and trainer have given him lots of landing experience, declared the reef flat to be entirely acceptable as a place to put down a plane. Inshore from this smooth area, however, the surface becomes very rough. So, landing on the reef is feasible, but bringing the airplane very close to shore is not.

At the putative grave site, Kar Burns and Gary Quigg[5] dug down over two meters through coral rubble and found nothing at all except very interesting natural stratigraphy similar to what they'd observed in excavating the first Nutiran grave in 1999.[6] They finally concluded that the "gravestone" marking the site was an old property boundary marker similar to "coral-henge" on the Nutiran mudflat.††

**See chapter 23.
††See chapter 8.

The excavation of the "grave," coupled with a fortuitous visit by the tuna boat *Jeannine* and her helicopter, gave us an interesting opportunity to test how much the Colorado pilots would have been able to see during their 1937 overflight of the island. Ric Gillespie and Mark Smith were able to fly around the island in the chopper, passing over Nutiran at about 200 feet—less than half the altitude that Lt. Lambrecht and his colleagues had flown. The team members digging at the grave—even Bill Carter in his still-white T-shirt—were virtually invisible.[7]

At the Seven Site, without surprise, we found the place thick with scaevola, well seasoned and nearly impervious to bush knives. Luckily it was not impervious to a chain saw in the capable hands of John Clauss and Jim Morrissey.

John, of course, is the veteran of veterans on Niku; he's been a mainstay of every expedition. Jim Morrissey was new to the project but had his own special credentials. Not only is he Earhart's great-nephew (grandson of AE's sister, Muriel Morrissey), he's also a highly trained expedition medic, with an amazing store of woodlore. Jim—dubbed "Medic Gadget Man" for his stock of peculiar tools and the élan with which he used them—was fascinating to watch. He gave me a real sense of what Earhart must have been like—highly organized, skilled, down-to-earth, and perfectly mad. Jim hated the drudge work of archaeology, the basic hacking and digging and screening, but he

The Seven Site. TIGHAR photo by Tom King.

loved to explore, to disappear into the bush to see what he could find. And, my oh my, he could handle a chain saw.

So, John and Jim cut, and the rest of us dragged the cut 'vola. And dragged, and dragged, and dragged.

The Seven Site lies on a low ridge of coral rubble that makes up the backbone of the island's southeast end. The "Seven" itself—the long natural clearing—is a bit northeast of the ridge crest, which was wooded in buka and maybe kanawa in 1937 but today has just a few *Tournefortia* and *Morinda* trees and lots of scaevola. The hole is down a steep slope southwest of the ridge, with the tank and scatter of bird bones close by. We cut a path in from the lagoon, and another across the Seven to the sea, and as Jim and John cleared the hole vicinity, we dragged the cuttings up and piled them in the Seven.

Temperatures hovered between 100 and 120 degrees, and the air around the hole was dead still. On the ridge, however, the trade winds and tree shade made it pretty comfortable, so it was there that we dropped to rest, sweat, pant, drink water, and nibble the food bars that Bill Carter, in real life an attorney for the Albertsons supermarket chain, had supplied in huge numbers. And it was there that I laid down my backpack one day on a curiously shaped piece of . . .

The moose antler.
TIGHAR photo
by Tom King.

"Ric," I said, "what do you think this is?"

"Looks like a moose antler," he opined, "but I don't suppose that's likely."

It was, in fact, a bony plate from the shell of a sea turtle.

"Remains of fire, turtle, and dead birds . . ." Gallagher had said.[‡‡]

We cleared the area and went down on hands and knees. Andrew McKenna, who had spent his childhood on his father's paleontological expeditions,[8] proved particularly adept at finding the fish, bird, and turtle bones that turned out to litter the ground. We found that there were at least two patches of burned coral rubble with bones, each about two meters across, and when we excavated them we found that they were only about ten centimeters deep. The remains of campfires? Where some castaway had cooked birds, fish, and turtles? We certainly meant to find out.

Over the next two weeks we found five such "burn features" and excavated three of them. We also found two elongated clusters of clam shells—*Tridacna squamosa,* one of the giant clam species, but these were each about the size of two human hands, along with a thick deposit of smaller butterclams (*Anadara* sp. and/or *Gafrarium* sp.) mixed with charcoal.

And a lot of corrugated iron, all reduced pretty much to rust—a rather well-defined patch next to the tank and a large deposit of it, as though sheets of it had been spread over the ground, extending along the ridge out from the vicinity of the clamshell clusters and burn features into the scaevola to the southeast. We didn't have time to trace out how far it went. We were able to ascertain that the corrugated iron had lain on top of the roll of asphalt siding noted in 1996 (which was still there). It was also apparent that siding from the roll had been spread out over the ground, covering the deposit of butterclams, and several pieces of it were found in our excavations, one of them folded into what looked like a container of some kind.

Meanwhile, the Mighty Quigg, fresh in from his fruitless excavation on the Nutiran shore, went after the hole. Gary, Kar, and several screeners dug that hole like few holes have ever been dug. They gridded off both the hole and its adjacent backdirt pile and took them down in controlled levels. Everything was dumped into one-quarter-inch screen and sifted, creating huge piles of coral rubble and very small piles of organic detritus. The latter they then passed through one-eighth-inch screen. With decreasing size,

[‡‡]See chapter 19.

343

the shape of each piece was less and less obvious, so they turned to using ultraviolet light. Bones and teeth fluoresce; coral doesn't. The only problem was excess light. The solution was to leave a small team ashore overnight. Kar and a few volunteers spent two nights sifting through mounds of rubble under the eerie glow of black light.

But all to no avail. Except for some bird and fish bones that fell out of what may have been a crab hole in the excavation's sidewall, nothing turned up.

Speaking of crab holes, another objective of the expedition was to get a handle on what coconut crabs do with bones. Kar very much wanted to put out a pig carcass and observe what happened to it, but she had to make do with a leg of lamb, which she observed and made notes on morning and night. Within a day it was covered with juvenile *Birgus latros*; in a bit over a week it was gone. I did more informal experiments with lamb bones left over from one night's dinner. Within an hour the pile of bones I'd stuffed in an old shirt my wife hated was covered with juvenile crabs, the shirt pulsating as though it were alive. The crabs dragged bones off across the forest floor and reduced them to ragged scraps—eventually either eating them completely or hiding them someplace. Interestingly, though, putting even a few centimeters of dirt and rubble over the bones discouraged the crabs completely.

The crabs also got into our food supplies, our tool caches, and anything else we left around. Camping on the island during the black light scanning was a challenge; the juvenile crabs were delighted with the opportunity to crawl into the clothes of anyone who would hold still, and the bigger ones

Ric Gillespie examines the Seven Site hole during excavation. TIGHAR photo by Tom King.

seemed attracted to human hair. Both would cheerfully begin to nibble if they weren't promptly removed.

"Americans," Bill Carter grumbled, picking a juvenile crab off his leg and lobbing it into the bush; "the other other white meat."

Jim Morrissey dragged up some cargo netting from the beach and rigged hammocks, but the crabs climbed the trees and dropped in from above. Sleeping in the moored boat turned out to be the only escape; it was a grim reminder of what must have happened to the castaway.

Every morning at 0600, Ric would place a call back to TIGHAR Central, on one of the several satellite phones with which we were equipped this time, to report the previous day's progress and get the news from back home. So, on the morning of September 11, he appeared ashen-faced in the cabin where we early birds were drinking coffee, and announced what had happened in New York, Washington, D.C., and Pennsylvania.

The next few days were surreal. Of course there was nothing we could do but worry about our loved ones back home, our country, what the hell was happening, and burn up the batteries on the sat phones trying to get information. Jim strung up an antenna in the scaevola and we listened to Radio New Zealand as we went through the motions of digging and screening. There was a sort of World War II feeling to it, huddled around the shortwave. I kept expecting to hear a gravelly voice saying "We will fight them on the beaches. . . ."

Nai'a's crewmembers were superb, giving us every imaginable kind of support. On our last night at the island they put on the traditional "leaving the island" feast, but with Fijian and American flags and the singing of national anthems. It was strange, disorienting, to be belting out the Star Spangled Banner on Nai'a's gently rolling deck, with the Southern Cross riding above, trying to grasp the enormity of what was going on at home.

In the days remaining to us on the island we did as much work as we could on the Seven Site and then closed it down, spreading tarps over excavations in the hope that depriving the scaevola of sunlight would inhibit its regrowth. But we were just going through the motions; finding Earhart just didn't seem nearly as important as it had on the tenth.

So, we returned to the United States—almost disappointed that nobody tried to seize our plane, because Jim had briefed us on counterhijacking strategies, and we all wanted to do something—and tried to figure out how to relate to the world as it had now become. Kar went almost straight to the

World Trade Center processing area on Staten Island to locate and identify human remains brought in from Ground Zero, and Jim started preparing for possible attacks on Alameda County, California, where he's employed to deal with nuclear, chemical, and biological disasters. The rest of us were left with nothing to do but our regular jobs and follow-up on the expedition. This was, at least, a distraction.[9]

What We Found[10]

We'd ended up excavating three burn features and recording two more. We'd also brought home one of the clusters of *Tridacna* shells—these clusters came to be called "clambushes" when someone speculated that the clams had been ambushed by Coast Guardsmen during some lemming-like migration across the island—and an assortment of artifacts found in our excavation units and through surface scanning and metal detecting. A lot of the artifacts clearly reflected the presence of the Coast Guard from the loran station—lots of .30-caliber shell casings,[11] Coast Guard crockery shards—probably used like skeet—the remains of a large radio vacuum tube that must have made a satisfying pop when used successfully as a target.[12] A lot more—we thought but couldn't be sure—represented something the colonists had been doing at the site, perhaps after the loran station was abandoned—the corrugated iron, the asphalt siding first noted in 1996. Some artifacts and features may have reflected Gallagher's "intensive search."

Mapping the deposit of corrugated iron near the tank showed that it had been the roof of a structure of some kind, which had doubtless drained rainwater into the tank. Its form showed how the structure had torqued as it fell away from the tank when its posts (two of which remained on the ground) gave way. The larger deposit of corrugated iron on the ridge southeast of the burn features remained (and remains) mysterious.

The asphalt siding also was (and still is) a head-scratcher. Gary Quigg has looked into the history of asphalt siding and found that it was introduced in ready-to-roll form in the 1880s, but that techniques for coloring the granules embedded in it weren't perfected until the early twentieth century. The material at the Seven Site has green granules, but we don't yet have a firm date for it. Because it overlay the butterclam feature, it must have been laid down after the clams were, but because the corrugated iron was on top of it, it was deposited before the iron. We have no documentary, photographic, physical, or anecdotal evidence of it at the loran station, but did

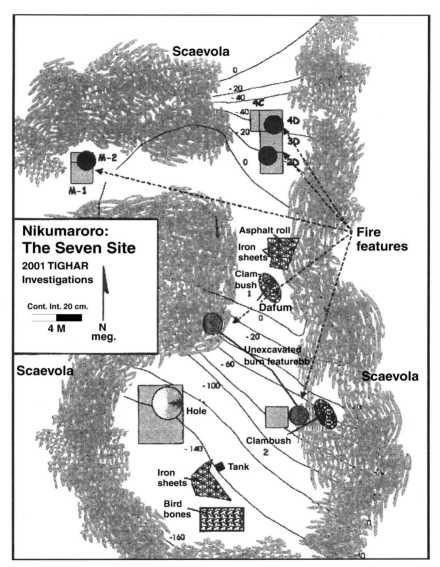

The Seven Site

find a piece nailed to the wall of the radio shack in the village. The folded-over piece from the Seven Site, which was found in the roots of a tree on the edge of one of the burn features, looks a lot like part of a sandal or slipper.

There was a tight cluster of three glass fragments from three different objects—identified by historic glass expert Richard Fike as a wave-washed drinking glass, a piece of sheet glass, and a Japanese fishing float—looking for all the world like things someone had picked up on the beach and brought to the site. When complete, the glass and float might have made good rifle targets, but what we found were just the three fragments, all in a group like they'd been in a bag or pocket. A castaway's collection of cutting tools? Rob Jackson, an archaeologist expert in stone cutting tools, looked them over carefully and couldn't find any evidence of use or modification, but the edges were sharp enough to cut, and cutting soft stuff wouldn't leave a mark.

A round piece of metal that looked like a knob of some kind gave us quite a run for our money; it looked like it might be a knob from an instrument—such as a sextant. Subjected to scanning electron microscopy at the U.S. Naval Academy, it turned out to be made of lead, which seemed pretty weird for an adjustment knob. There were raised numbers on it that couldn't be read by ordinary eyes or even by the microscope, but Jeff Glickman's magic made them translatable. They turned out to make up a patent number—for a gun-oil container, undoubtedly associated with the Coasties' target practice.[13]

Two weird little items remain unidentified—handmade aluminum pieces pierced with wood screws, with scalloped ends. The wood screws are of American manufacture. In October 2003 I gave a talk about the project at the Naval Air Station Patuxent River, Maryland, and my picture of them rang a bell with one of the attendees, Ron Glockner. Ron was sure he'd seen something similar, and after a bit of digging around, he found it—a toothed tab on a pair of garden shears, that engages a toothed washer around the central pivot screw to prevent the screw from twisting loose. Because our toothed items are far too fragile to have worked on such a tool and are mounted on wood screws, Ron's research doesn't tell us what the items are, but it does suggest one possible function, as arresters on some kind of turning mechanism. Our first impression, though, was that they were latches of some sort, and they remain a puzzle.

We had of course collected all the bones from the burn features and a sample of the tremendous number of fish scales we'd found there. These were analyzed by Claudia Milne, a specialist with John Milner Associates, and were found to represent a variety of reef fish, all readily available either in the lagoon or in tide pools on the reef flat; a castaway could have caught them by hand, but then, so could anybody else. Helen James of the Smithsonian Institution examined the bird bones and found almost all of

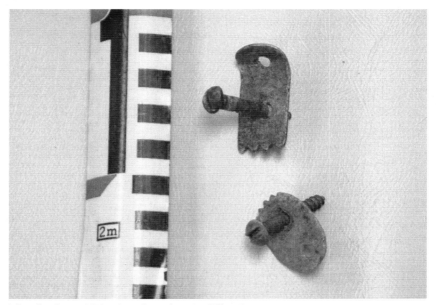

The "latches." TIGHAR photo by Ric Gillespie.

them to be from frigate birds, which nest in the trees around the site. The surface scatter noted by the 1996 survey team near the tank was made up entirely of wing bones, whereas the bones in the burn features were from more edible parts. We think the wing bones may have nothing to do with the bones in the burn features—they probably represent bird hunting by the colonists, cutting off wings before taking the bodies home to the village. Turtle expert George Balazs of the Smithsonian's Honolulu Marine Turtle Research Lab examined the turtle bones and found that they were from a green turtle *(Chelonia mydas)*, most likely only one individual. They were from only the carapace and plastron—in other words, the shell.[14] Green sea turtles nest on the beach near the Seven Site.

All were critters that could have been harvested by a castaway, but also that could have been taken by others. The Coast Guardsmen we interviewed said they hadn't had any cookouts at the site or anyplace else, and we're still trying to get in touch with people who lived on the island in the 1950s—now living at Nikumaroro Village in the Solomons—to find out if they did anything of the kind.

The clambush we'd brought home turned out to be especially intriguing. *Tridacna* clams spend their lives on coral and other submerged surfaces,

349

Each fire feature contained an
assortment of bird, fish, and
sometimes turtle bones.
TIGHAR photo by Tom King.

sitting quietly with their shells open to strain food out of the water. Island
fishermen harvest them by sneaking up almost as quietly as the clams, sticking a knife into the open "mouth," and cutting the tough adductor muscle
that powers the shells. The clam then can't close up and is fairly easily
brought up and deprived of its meat—or deprived of its meat without bringing the shells up at all.[15]

The *Tridacna* in Clambush 1 hadn't been harvested that way.

There were some thirty shells in the clambush, representing seventeen
clams. Of these, several showed evidence of chipping along their edges, as
though they'd been closed when brought to the site and someone had tried
to pry them open. Three of them appeared to have been opened in an even
odder way—or at least that someone had tried to open them—by jamming
a pointed implement of some kind into the hinge side of the shell. The shells
were chipped and broken at this point, and the chipped-out place on one
perfectly matched the tip of a little piece of iron we found about ten meters
away. Another six clams had been opened in a more drastic way—one shell
of each had been bashed to smithereens, probably with a chunk of coral.

It looks like somebody carried the clams up to the site and had a very
frustrating time trying to open them in ways that island people would never
dream of trying.

If not islanders, who *would* try to open a clam in such a way? Well,
according to Eleanor Ely, author of a Rhode Island Sea Grant Fact Sheet
available on the Internet[16]—and referring to quahogs (*Mercenaria mercenaria*), large clams not unlike small *Tridacna*: "To open a clam, hold it in
your left hand (if you are right-handed) and use your right hand to work a
special shucking knife . . . into the space between the shells."

Chipped clam with iron piece. TIGHAR photo by Tom King.

Smashed clam from Clambush 1. TIGHAR photo by Tom King.

Molly Stevens, in the journal *Fine Cooking*,[17] says: "Clams are easier to open than oysters. Their shells allow you to slide a knife between them without having to twist or pry your way in." But if it's not so easy . . . "Oysters, on the other hand, can be quite tenacious. They're best opened by boring the tip of the oyster knife between the shells, near the hinge at the pointed end. Twist and push the knife with a fair amount of force until the shell pops open."

And the late Julia Child says, of oysters: "When the oysters have a slight gap at the closed hinge, you can make quick work of them either with a beer can opener or a stout oyster knife."[18]

Did someone used to opening clams and oysters in the United States or Europe try to apply the same techniques to the *Tridacna* of Nikumaroro? Maybe, and for what it's worth, Muriel Morrissey, in *Amelia, My Courageous Sister,* writes of digging clams with her husband-to-be, Amelia, and Amelia's friend Sam Chapman at Marblehead, Massachusetts.[19]

The Geologist

Howard Alldred is an engineering geologist in New Zealand (though he also runs an olive processing and export company there). An avid diver with much experience in coastal processes and coral reefs, he first learned of TIGHAR from a 1991 television special and was intrigued. Ten years later he noticed an item on the Internet about the 2001 expedition, which had just arrived at the island, and promptly e-mailed TIGHAR offering his assistance. Pat Thrasher at TIGHAR Central passed his comments on to Ric by sat phone, and we knew that Howard was someone we had to have on the team.

Based on his knowledge of atoll geology and the way the ocean interacts with it, Howard was able to offer some knowledgeable opinions about what would have happened to the airplane if it were washed off the edge of the Nutiran reef. Nothing good, of course; it would have been torn apart, though largish pieces might have survived for some time. As we'd thought, the pieces would have moved southeast along the lee side of the island, but Howard's models didn't point to their being sucked or pushed into the lagoon, as we'd thought. Instead, the models suggested deposition along the western shore of Ritiati—the shore adjacent to the village. Handy for collection by the colonists and also an area where there's been a great deal of overwash by storm surges, depositing layers of sand. A good place to find buried fragments, perhaps, and a place where we'd never looked carefully.

This is only one example of the insights that Howard has given us; he's brought a tremendous body of expertise, talent, and energy to the project— to say nothing of greatly improving the group's sartorial image by always wearing a tie and track shoes (except when in the field, where he wears as little as possible). But he could do only so much without actually seeing the island, so we began working on plans to get him there and to take a hard look at the overwash area.

The EPAC and the Forum

The meetings at which Howard shows up in his tie and tennies are those of the Earhart Project Advisory Committee (EPAC), a volunteer group organized in 2002 to better use TIGHAR's increasingly large and diverse collection of talent. As of early 2004 there were 35 people on the EPAC,[20] including veterans such as John Clauss, Kar Burns, Lonnie Schorer, Randy Jacobson, and me, and a wide range of Earhart Syndrome sufferers with pertinent credentials. Some examples:

- Bob Brandenburg, retired U.S. Navy destroyer skipper and antisubmarine operations officer, expert in the use of mathematical models and computer simulations.
- Jeff Glickman, computer scientist and engineer with a specialty in forensic imaging; Certified Forensic Examiner and Fellow of the American College of Forensic Examiners, plenty of other titles; can discern the most amazing things in photo images.

- Roger Kelley, retired Los Angeles police officer now living in Washington State, who knows investigative methods backward and forward.
- Fr. Martin X. ("Marty") Moleski, S.J., Ph.D., professor of Religious Studies at Canesius College in Buffalo, New York; Marty specializes in the study of why people believe what they believe and can shave very close with Occam's razor.
- Jim Thompson, geographic information systems (GIS) coordinator for the city of Northampton, Massachusetts, who is gradually coaxing TIGHAR into organizing its by-now very extensive database using GIS technology.
- Dan Postellon, a pediatric endocrinologist with lots of anthropological experience, who alone among the members can talk shop with Kar Burns.
- Tom Roberts, a structural engineer with Lockheed, who can actually read and understand Electra specifications.

The EPAC tries to meet as a group annually—a three-day session of presentations, hands-on analyses, and brainstorming—and interacts continually by e-mail. The information and ideas that fly back and forth among such an array of experts are—well, *stimulating* puts it too mildly. I don't think I've ever learned as much about so many things as I have from my EPAC colleagues.

Beyond the EPAC, the Earhart Forum continues to operate as a place for general discussion of all manner of things related to our work, and its participants regularly spin off into their own research on post-loss radio messages, navigation, artifact identification, and a wide range of other topics. One mad Australian known as "Th' Wombat"[21] has cast himself away on an uninhabited island. He's found out how many coconuts it takes to keep him alive with no other source of water (about fifty per week), how well he can get along walking barefoot on coral rubble ("First week is the worst," he reports, and it's "hard on the ankles," but tolerable), and how uncomfortable it was to wear one set of clothing for four weeks, washing daily in saltwater. Not too bad, he found, but "I could almost guarantee our castaway did not wear underwear for more than the first couple of days."[22]

Tide and the Reef

Speaking of saltwater, Randy Jacobson, Bob Brandenberg, and Howard Alldred have devoted major effort to figuring out what tidal conditions most likely were at Nikumaroro in the late morning hours of July 2, 1937, and how they were expressed on the Nutiran reef flat. Obviously a critical matter; the reef at Nutiran would have had to be pretty dry—or at least not too wet—for Earhart to have landed there safely. And if the Electra was the source of at least some of the post-loss radio messages, it had to have sat on the reef for several days and nights. Which means that the tides would have had to stay relatively low for several days, before getting high enough to flood the plane or move it into the surf zone at the reef edge, where it would begin to break up.

Everyone who's spent time at the beach knows about tides—low and high, usually two sets per day, in and out. And most of us also know that the height of the tide—both high and low—varies through time with a pretty high degree of predictability. This is why the newspapers can print tide tables—it's possible to forecast how high the tide will be tomorrow or next year based on the long cycles of tidal heights over the years. The same can be done backward in time—that is, we can *hindcast* when the tide should have come in and when it should have gone out, how high it should have gotten and how low it should have gone, on any date in the not-too-distant past.

But tides vary from place to place in complicated ways, so although oceanographers know the gross mechanisms that make them vary, a tide table can't be made up for a particular place—either forecast into the future or hindcast into the past—without a record of what tides have done in that place over a period of time, the longer the better.

Naturally, nobody has been collecting tidal data on Nikumaroro, but they have done so on Kanton, starting in 1949. Randy contacted the Tropical Ocean-Global Atmosphere (TOGA)[23] Sea Level Center at the University of Hawaii for help in analyzing the data. TOGA's Gary Mitchum (now at the University of South Florida) took a year's worth of measurements from 1949 to 1950 and from this database predicted what the tides should have been like in 1986. The results were virtually the same as the actual measurements taken in that year. Then confident that he had a solid base from which to work, Mitchum hindcasted conditions on Kanton for July 1937.

Meanwhile, Bob Brandenburg located a piece of software called AutoTide,[24] designed for use in tidal forecasting and hindcasting worldwide, using a database derived in large part from the records of Her Majesty's

Hydrographic Office in the United Kingdom—including data from Orona (Hull Island), only 145 miles from Nikumaroro. This, of course, made it relatively easy for Bob to hindcast tidal conditions at Orona on the morning of July 2 and thereafter.

The Kanton and Orona hindcastings agree with one another pretty well. On both islands the tide appears to have been low at about six in the morning on July 2 and to have peaked at about noon or shortly after. This was consistent with Randy's original projections,[§§] but the refined hindcasting indicated something else: even at its highest that day, the tide was relatively low, and the high tides stayed that way (as, of course, did the lows) until the afternoon of the fifth, when the high was about eight inches higher than it had been on the second.

So, if the tide at Niku was behaving like the tide on Orona and Kanton apparently did, then depending on how long after their 8:43 A.M. "157-337" radio message Earhart and Noonan arrived at the island (assuming they did), the Nutiran reef flat should have been dry or slightly awash. The high tides would have remained relatively low until the afternoon of July 5, perhaps making it possible for the plane to have remained parked on the reef flat, with its radio available for use by the castaways.

Of course, the question was: are and were the tidal patterns at Nikumaroro about the same as those at Kanton and Orona? We had no way of knowing for sure. Bob had made estimates of maximum tidal heights based on photos showing water marks on the *Norwich City* wreckage, and during the 2001 expedition Ric had tried to collect some timed measurements to help him, but we really needed to take accurate measurements on the Nikumaroro reef over at least a period of a few days, which could be calibrated with the Kanton and Orona tide tables. Another reason to get back to Niku.

The tide also isn't the only important variable, when it comes to figuring out how long an airplane could remain parked on the Nutiran reef flat. The weather is another important factor. Although Jacobson and Brandenberg can argue about it at great length, what they can extrapolate from the logs of the *Itasca* and *Colorado* suggest that the weather during the whole period was pretty benign—probably not much of a threat to a parked airplane until the tide got high enough to let waves begin to jostle

[§§]See chapter 26.

it around. This highlights two other variables: where the plane was parked, and what the elevation of the reef was at that point. We couldn't answer the first question, of course, except to say that the roughness of the near-shore reef flat would keep the plane from being parked very close to the beach, but we could get a handle on the second. We could measure the slope of the reef and get an idea of what the possibilities were for survival at different locations—*if* we could get someone there to take the measurements.

Post-Loss Radio Messages

Bob Brandenburg, Randy Jacobson, and Mike Everette have continued working on the post-loss radio messages—the many radio signals received in the week or so after the disappearance that people at first thought might have been from Earhart but that were later rejected as hoaxes. In 2002 Ric Gillespie turned his own formidable attention to them. Ric adopted a typically straightforward, if daunting, approach. He prepared a minute-by-minute graphic time line of the 408 hours following the disappearance, and on it he plotted every event he could find record of in which a message of some kind was allegedly received—184 at the time of this writing—with data on its duration and character. To this he added hours of daylight and darkness in the central Pacific and the probable state of the tide on the Nutiran reef (assuming that it was similar to that at Kanton and Orona). He then set out to see if any patterns were discernible. The study has gotten so big that he's planning a book on this subject alone, and the results are by no means yet complete, but from what he's been able to report so far:

- Contrary to a lot of accounts, the vast majority of events (69 percent) were reported not by amateur radio operators but by professionals aboard *Itasca* and other search vessels, at Pan American, and at other listening posts.
- There's nothing to suggest that any of the events represent misunderstandings by one station of another station's calls *to* Earhart.
- Events are most common in the first three days after the disappearance,[25] and then drop off dramatically, ending altogether on July 13.
- Most of the events happened at night in the central Pacific; there's a regular pattern of intensive events at night, virtually none during the day.

- Most of the events occurred—that is, the transmissions were received—within 2,000 miles of Howland Island, and nearly half within 1,000 miles; none are reported in a band 2,000 to 3,000 miles from Howland, but quite a number were received in the 3,000- to 4,000-mile zone, mostly by amateur radio operators.
- Some events can be discarded as not credible—on frequencies that Earhart couldn't use, or voice transmissions saying the airplane was floating in the water (from which it would be impossible to transmit). Others are questionable because of what's known of the individuals involved and the circumstances of the alleged reception. This leaves a large number of events that must be seen as credible—that is, possible (though not certain) transmissions from the Electra.
- Radio direction finding (RDF) fixes were taken by Pan American and the Coast Guard on several signals; the bearings taken strongly suggest that the signals originated in the vicinity of Nikumaroro.
- Four people in different parts of North America—Betty Klenck, Nina Paxton, Thelma Lovelace, and Mabel Larremore (later Duncklee)—say they heard distress calls from Earhart on shortwave, though only Ms. Klenck kept detailed notes on what she heard.*** Their accounts are strikingly similar, and Bob Brandenburg's analysis suggests that it is possible they heard messages carried on frequencies that radio people refer to as "harmonics" of Earhart's preferred frequency, 3105 (6210, 9315, etc.).††† Such harmonic signals go out with less power than the main signal, but can travel great distances.[26]

The post-loss messages, of course, were at first taken by the Navy to be genuine; the *Colorado* was dispatched to the Phoenix Islands in large part because of them. Newspaper headlines read "Amelia's Radio Signals Heard" and "Noonan Sends SOS from Earhart Plane." When the search proved fruitless, the official conclusion became that all the events were the results of hoaxes or misunderstandings by one station of another's transmissions. But no one until now has pulled them all together and tried to make sense of them. The sense that Ric and his coworkers are making of them doesn't support the official conclusion.

***See chapter 26.
†††See chapters 26 and 8.

More Bones Stories and a Return to Fiji

Ever since we returned from the 1999 Fiji bones search, we'd gotten stories suggesting that the bones had been seen and talked about in Fiji at various times over the last fifty years. Sort of like the many stories of Earhart's execution on Saipan, in Chuuk, and elsewhere, but it never pays to discount such stories entirely, and in any event there was lots more research to do in Fiji. At the 2002 EPAC meeting Marty Moleski and Roger Kelley volunteered to make a month-long trip there, themselves covering much of the project's cost. The opportunity to put a Jesuit priest and a retired L.A. cop on the trail of the missing bones was far, far too good to pass up, so on May 14, 2003, Marty and Roger headed for Suva.

The Wheel of Fortune Expedition[27]

Roger and Marty weren't the only TIGHARs to launch in the summer of 2003. A small team under Van Hunn's leadership—including Howard Alldred, John Clauss, and Walt Holm—returned to Niku. Their trip was designed to nail down the relationship between Niku and Kanton/Orona tides, to get elevations and record the general topography of the Nutiran reef, to give Howard a good hard look at the island, to do a preliminary reconnaissance of the overwash area on the Ritiati shore, and to give the reef-slope off Tatiman Passage a close going-over for wreck debris. But it also had a less widely advertised purpose—indeed, a purpose that wasn't advertised at all beyond the EPAC until the team was on island. This purpose was to check out another reported discovery—another possible smoking gun.

Nai'a had returned to Niku in 2002 on a biological tour of the Phoenix Islands, sponsored by the New England Aquarium in Boston and the National Geographic Society.[28] While walking along the south shore of Tatiman Passage perusing the sea life, biologist Greg Stone had seen something out in the water, about twenty feet offshore. He waded out and found that it was a wheel of some kind, quite broad in cross section—like an airplane wheel. He tried to move it, but found that it was cemented into the coral. Thinking that the wheel must have given those TIGHAR guys quite a start, he left it alone and didn't mention it until *Nai'a* was Fiji-bound at the end of the trip. Rob Barrel, *Nai'a*'s owner and veteran of the 1997 expedition, refrained from throwing Greg overboard and instead put him in touch with Ric. Ric immediately sent him a series of photos of various airplane wheels, asking him to identify the one or several most like the one he'd seen. You guessed it: without knowing the identity of any of the wheels pictured, he identified the one from an Electra as most similar to what he'd seen. He also marked TIGHAR's satellite image with the approximate location of what we had by now come to call the "Wheel of Fortune."[29]

Anxious to avoid another cruciform or rusty patch incident, Ric kept a lid on the "WOF" story, sharing it only with the EPAC. It obviously had to be checked out, so this became another goal of the 2003 expedition. In some ways the most exciting goal, though it felt a little like the "engine in the woods" stories that TIGHAR had so often pursued through the forests of Maine.[30]

The first plan for this expedition involved sending three or four TIGHARs aboard *Nai'a,* whose owners were planning another biological tour. The tour failed to attract enough paying customers and had to be canceled. But in the meantime Howard Alldred had lined up fellow New Zealander Ken Durey and his family—wife Louise and seven-year-old daughter Mollie—and their boat, also named *Mollie. Mollie,* like her namesake, was much smaller than *Nai'a*—a fifty-six-foot sloop, but she was sufficient to carry four TIGHARs and a Kiribati government representative, and luckily the Dureys' schedule was very flexible. Very luckily.

Getting *Mollie* and her crew to Niku turned out to be a Herculean task that tested even Gillespie's ability to dodge and weave. *Mollie* was to meet the guys in American Samoa, but after she got there, and when they were packing to leave the States, storm damage caused the runway at Pago Pago to be pronounced unfit for landing and closed. A frantic scramble ensued to find another way—via Apia in the "other" British Commonwealth, Samoa. The price was going to be high and the routing complicated, but . . . And then it was reported that the runway might be fixed; and then it wasn't; and then it was. And Aobure Teatata, the Kiribati government representative, had to be gotten to Samoa from Kiritimati Island, via Hawaii, which presented logistic and diplomatic problems complicated by heightened airport security, and then a series of miscommunications left him stranded in Honolulu, with Ric on the phone to the Kiribati foreign minister frantically seeking permission to visit Niku unescorted. Which was very graciously granted, but the whole business created a series of frustrating delays. It was with a great deal of relief that we stay-at-homes learned that Howard, Walt, John, and Van were safely aboard the sloop, beating upwind for Kanton (to clear customs) and Niku.

They got there and back safely, and Roger and Marty made it home from Fiji. From August 15 to 17, the EPAC met in Delaware to welcome them and hear their reports.

What They Found in Fiji[31]

To cut to the chase—Roger and Marty came home with no bones in hand. They did find out with considerable certainty where the bones are *not*, and they gained a good deal of suggestive new information.[32] They interviewed dozens of people who might have first- or secondhand knowledge of the bones and their disposal. Roger thoroughly searched the government's burial and cremation records, housed with the Bureau of Prisons, and found no evidence that unidentified bones from Nikumaroro (under any name he and Marty could think of) had ever been thus disposed of. They learned a great deal about Dr. Lindsay Isaac/Verrier, who intercepted the bones en route from Nikumaroro to Fiji and just might have done so again, but they haven't yet been able to track down his effects. They visited Dr. Gerard D. Murphy, Verrier's best friend, but he had nothing from Verrier (he did have a box left him by one of his patients, containing a clipping about the Earhart monument on Howland and five short manuscripts by Noel Coward;[33] these were entertaining but not enlightening). They read six years' worth of correspondence from the Central Medical Authority and found no mention of the bones. They revisited Dr. Hoodless's house and garage and moved heaven and earth trying to find papers that he might have left, but to no avail. They collected much more data on Henry Harrison Vaskess, the Western Pacific High Commission (WPHC) Secretary who had kept the bones files, and became convinced that if this "prince of bureaucrats"[34] had done anything with the bones, he would have recorded it.

Marty and Roger gave special attention to the collections of Dr. Kenneth J. Gilchrist, principal of the Fiji School of Medicine from 1965 to 1970; some people had said that Dr. Gilchrist, who died in 1993, had at one time had the bones in his possession, and his will provided for dividing his huge collection of shells and "fossils" between the University of the South Pacific and the Smithsonian Institution. We thought that perhaps the word "fossil" had been used with some journalistic license in the news accounts of Dr. G's bequest. Kar Burns had already checked the Smithsonian, which has nothing but shells from the collection. Marty and Roger waded into the university's collections, and there too found only mollusks: 5,300 specimens representing 1,050 species.

Marty flew on to Auckland to reexamine the files of the WPHC, recently relocated there from Hanslope Park in England. He concentrated on the post-1940 period, through the demise of the Commission, looking for indications that the bones might have been packed off somewhere along with the WPHC's possessions or disposed of in some way. Lots of fascinating data, but not about the bones.

Marty and Roger's conclusion was that the bones might well still be in Fiji somewhere, and that there was more work to be done there and elsewhere in their pursuit, but they brought home no hot leads.

As for the stories about the bones being seen in relatively recent years, the jury is still out. Roger and Marty got more stories, but these were always vague and secondhand. Marty concluded that what they were getting was a sort of feedback from our own research, as reported in the Fiji media. People had heard or read about the 1999 search and were recounting their fuzzy memories. Roger isn't so sure; his cop's sense tells him there's more to the stories than meets Marty's eye. Perhaps some day we'll find out, or perhaps not.

What They Found on Niku

As the team went ashore on Niku, it became obvious that the island had been hit once again by a serious storm from the west.[35] Lots of vegetation stripping and beach erosion along the Ritiati shore, a good deal of evidence of overwash, well into the village, lots of broken coral thrown up from the reef face. Baureke Passage had been resculpted and was draining the lagoon much more efficiently than it ever had in our experience; the lagoon was almost crystal clear. Although it looked like there'd been a lot of damage, Howard said the event had done wonders for the atoll's health.

Which made everyone very glad, but unfortunately, it had also apparently taken the Wheel of Fortune. The WOF was nowhere to be found.

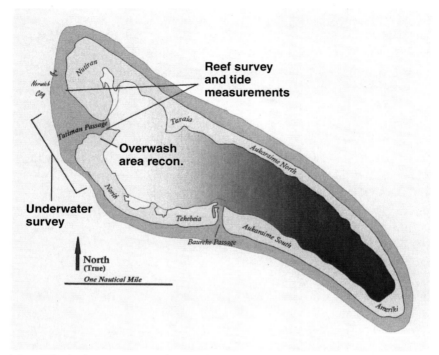

The "Wheel of Fortune" expedition concentrated on the neighborhood of Tatiman Passage.

Assiduous searching, intensive phone consultations with Greg Stone to explore possible errors in his or our understanding of where he'd seen the thing, further searching and re-searching, yielded nothing at all. The WOF appears to be gone for good.

And so are any other parts of the plane that remained on the reef or got washed along it by the currents sweeping around the island, Howard concluded. By now, he opined, such remnants would be somewhere along the Aukaraime shore, but they'd have been ground to powder. So, it wasn't surprising to him that Van and Walt, diving the reef slope off Tatiman Passage, came up empty-handed.

The overwash area along the Ritiati shore didn't yield anything to visual search and metal detecting, but a short distance into the village, near the radio shack, they did find and recover several pieces of aluminum. Well, one was actually alu*minium*, because Howard found it. Two of the pieces were relatively large and rectangular, though one had had pieces cut out of it. The

"Howard's dado." TIGHAR photo by Pat Thrasher.

one that was cut was in pretty good shape, whereas the other, found buried in rotting coconut debris, was only a corroded ghost of its original self. But it still retained its shape and such key features as attachment holes. It was another dado, and so was its cut-up mate.

A dado, you'll recall (or maybe won't), is a finish piece from the interior of an airplane, typically placed where a bulkhead or the inside of the fuselage meets a deck, to make the interior smooth and to cover up things like wires and control cables. They're normally found in civilian passenger planes, not military aircraft, because their function is largely cosmetic.[36]

The first dado, found in 1989, had—we thought—come from "Noonan's Tavern," the now-lost site southwest of the radio shack along the Tatiman shore.[†††] Upon closer examination of notes and videotapes, it turned out that I'd mixed up two artifacts during the cataloguing process. The dado had in fact been found in the area between Noonan's Tavern and the radio shack, and there was another rectangular piece at the tavern. But upon inspection, this one too looks a lot like it had been a dado. It's the right size and shape, but someone—presumably whoever lived at the tavern—cut off the distinctive edges.

Which means that we have at least three and maybe four dados, all from the part of the village adjacent to the shore of Tatiman Passage, and each representing a piece that would be pretty easy to salvage from a wreck—no cutting required. And the 1989 specimen has nonstandard attachment holes on the side that would have met the deck, and pry marks, suggesting that its lower edge was nailed to a wood floor and subsequently pried off. Earhart's Electra had a wood floor (TIGHAR has a sample from a contemporaneous plane). Probably some, if not many, of the planes that

†††See chapters 9 and 10.

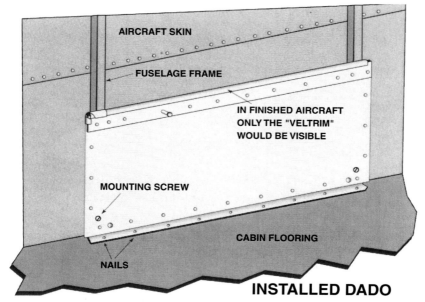

AIRCRAFT SKIN

FUSELAGE FRAME

IN FINISHED AIRCRAFT
ONLY THE "VELTRIM"
WOULD BE VISIBLE

MOUNTING SCREW

CABIN FLOORING

NAILS

INSTALLED DADO

Reconstruction of installed dado.

operated through Kanton during and after World War II had wood decks, too, but few if any military planes had dados (as far as we know). And every part of a military plane was stamped with a part number. None of our dados has a part number.

Van's gang also succeeded in collecting the tidal data they'd gone out for—which suggest that Niku's tides closely match those at Orona—and mapped the reef flat to permit accurate modeling of what waves and tides would do to an airplane parked at different locations. They also visited the Seven Site, and to everyone's unsurprised dismay found the scaevola growing high and healthy in the areas we'd cleared in 2001. All the tarps we'd spread over the excavations were reduced to tatters.

Details on the Dados

The dados went promptly to the Maryland Archaeological Conservation Laboratory—Maryland's state-of-the-art facility for the conservation and analysis of artifacts—whose staff had generously offered to x-ray them and apply conservation treatments as needed. X rays revealed obscured attach-

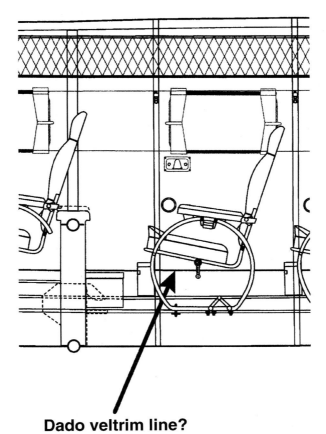

Dado veltrim line?

Electra interior, based on Lockheed drawing.

ment holes and other details, permitting a closer match with aircraft plans and drawings, if these could be found. Ric's earlier research had indicated that Electras had dados, but we didn't know what they had been like. So, Ric, Tom Roberts, and Lonnie Schorer went to the National Air and Space Museum's Garber research facility near Washington, D.C., to pore through archived Lockheed specifications.

The spec's proved incomplete, ambiguous, and hard to interpret, but in drawing number 48551, "Cabin Furnishings," there's a line that's not identified but is precisely where the "veltrim" line (the only part of a dado that's visible in a finished airplane) should be if dados ran along the inside of the passenger cabin.

Needless to say, a dado committee has been set up within the EPAC to delve more deeply into the questions of (1) whether Earhart's airplane had dados, (2) whether any *other* aircraft that operated in the area, for example, through Kanton during and after the war, had dados, and (3) whether anybody's dados much resemble our dados. It's going to be a long and complicated task. Electras still flying today have all been heavily modified, so our research at the moment is focusing on three more or less contemporary Electra crash sites—one in New Zealand, one in Alaska, one in Idaho. Howard Alldred has helicoptered in to the wreck site on New Zealand's Mt. Richmond and found it seriously picked over by collectors, though he did see some interesting fragments. With the cooperation of the U.S. Forest Service, Walt Holm is coordinating trips planned for the late summer of 2004 to find and inspect the sites in Idaho and Alaska.[37]

At the moment all we can say is that someone along the Tatiman Passage shoreline—or several someones—had a bunch of dados to cut up, presumably for use in making handicrafts, combs, and the like. And to judge from the pry marks on the 1989 dado, they were gotten by prying them off aircraft or aircraft wrecks. It's tempting to imagine a piece of wood decking with dados attached floating up on the beach and being seized upon as a source of raw material.

Insights into Artifacts

Having done research years ago on Civil War–era uniform buttons, Lonnie Schorer has taken on the responsibility of researching a button found at the Seven Site during the original 1996 reconnaissance. It's a rather ordinary brown button with some staining on it. It had been examined in 2000 by the FBI Laboratory, which had determined that its surface retained evidence of human DNA. Unfortunately, back in '96 no one had thought to wear latex gloves when picking up such items, so there's not much to be done with that. Lonnie set about finding out what kind of button it was, where it might have come from, and what it might have been attached to. She carried it to button experts in museums, button companies, and button collectors' shows, carefully protected in an old piece of Amelia Earhart brand luggage. Opinions about it were diverse, but the best current judgment is that it's an American thermal injection molded plastic button from the 1930s or 1940s, probably a trouser fly button.

The obvious source of an American button from the first half of the twentieth century on Niku is, of course, the loran station, but did the Coast Guardsmen wear anything with buttons of this kind? Jeff Glickman went to work on a photograph of the station's CO and concluded that the button at the top of his fly was probably metal. Coast Guard loran veteran Tom Brink[38] found one of his old uniforms with buttons—nothing similar to ours. Cindee Herrick, museum curator at the U.S. Coast Guard Academy in New London, Connecticut, compared photos of the Seven Site button with buttons on every type of Coast Guard uniform in the Coast Guard Museum's collection and found no matches. So, while we're still browbeating our Coast Guard veterans to rummage through their seabags and see if they held onto their old tropical shorts, right now it looks like we have a nonmilitary, brown button from the United States at the Seven Site. Tests conducted by Ric Gillespie on similar buttons that Jerry Hamilton got from a cooperative button dealer suggest that the discoloration on the button may have resulted from exposure to fire.

A couple of artifacts that we don't have in hand, but wonder about, are the "small corks on brass chains" that Dr. Steenson mentions in his 1941 WPHC minute on the package of artifacts sent from Nikumaroro by Gallagher. He thought they were probably "from a small cask," but if so, where was the cask? One night in mid-2003 I woke around midnight thinking "water bags"—remembering the self-cooling canvas bag in which I'd carried water on bike trips in my youth. Mine had a screw top on a chain, but would one from the '30s have had a cork? A quick visit to eBay revealed that, yes indeed, there was an "antique desert water bag" for sale, and it had a cork on a chain. A few weeks later I came upon a March 7, 1937, *New York Herald Tribune* article, reproduced in Muriel Morrissey and Carol Osborne's *Amelia, My Courageous Sister,* about what Earhart was taking with her on her first (east to west) World Flight attempt. Water, it said, would be carried in "two desert water bags."[39] Nothing definitive here, but an interesting coincidence.

In September 2003 we received the results of tests run for us by Professor Pat Moran of the U.S. Naval Academy's Department of Mechanical Engineering on samples of corrugated iron from the Seven Site, the loran station, and a collapsed postwar house on Nutiran.[40] All the corrugated metal from both the Seven Site and the loran station turned out to be iron, not steel, but the sample from the Nutiran house was steel. The metal from the roof of the structure built over the tank at the Seven Site was galvanized (as at the loran station and the Nutiran house) but the sheets covering the ground on the ridge were not. Gary Quigg has looked into the history of corrugated metal and found that although galvanized corrugated was available in the United States and United Kingdom by the latter part of the nineteenth century, it was relatively expensive and didn't supplant nongalvanized iron until 1910 or thereafter. So, while the tank structure was probably built during colonial times, and the house on Nutiran certainly was, the sheets on the Seven Site ridge might be earlier. We know that Arundel brought structural sheet iron[41] of some kind to the island in the 1890s; Ric and Van had found that out from his diaries in Tarawa.[42] But Arundel set up his operations on Nutiran, where their ruins were noted by a *Norwich City* survivor in 1929[43] and the Kiwi survey party in 1938; they're not visible today. So, did someone drag old corrugated down from Nutiran to the Seven Site and spread it on the ground? I wonder if Gallagher, expecting to come back and do more searching, was trying to do the same thing we did with our tarps in 2001—inhibit growth in his search area by covering it up. In our case we used tarps, in his case perhaps he used a bunch of old metal sheets from Nutiran that weren't needed in the village. Ric points out that there wasn't any scaevola on the Seven Site when Gallagher did his search, so he wouldn't have needed to cover it up; Ric likes to imagine the castaway(s) hauling the stuff down to catch rainwater. I think that's outlandish, and counter that there's stuff growing on Niku that's not scaevola, and stuff falling from the trees, that would make covering up your search area a good idea if you were going to leave it for a time and come back. And Gallagher must have had some long-term interest in returning to the site, because according to the maps found in Tarawa, he set it aside for "Komitia." More analysis of more samples is needed, but it won't happen in the near future; ours were the last ones processed by the Academy's scanning electron microscope before it and the lab that contained it were destroyed by Hurricane Isabel.

Arthur Rypinski and the Engine on the Reef

In the summer of 2002, economist Arthur Rypinski of Rockville, Maryland, and his family went to visit his father-in-law Jack Porth, a retired helicopter pilot. Arthur's daughter, Tatiana, had just finished reading a biography of Amelia Earhart and had gone with her father to see Earhart's Lockheed Vega at the Smithsonian. The family was chatting over dinner one night, and Tatiana asked: "What happened to Amelia Earhart?"

"Nobody knows," Arthur replied. "Well, she probably ran out of fuel and fell in the ocean, but some people think she may have been on a spy mission and captured by the Japanese."

Whereupon his father-in-law said casually that when he was out in the Pacific, he had found an old engine and had always regretted never checking it out. Arthur assumed he had seen a World War II wreck and didn't think any more about it. Then . . .

> A couple of weeks later, the conversation with Tatiana popped back into my mind. I thought to myself, that if there was anything to the story about Amelia being captured by the Japanese, the relevant papers would surely have been found in some archive by now, and this being the 21st century, there would be some trace of the story on the Internet. So, I fired up Google and went looking for information on Amelia Earhart in the hope that I could give Tatiana a more definitive answer to her question.
>
> Eventually, I found my way to the TIGHAR web site, and began reading the various research papers there, which I found fascinating, even addictive. I read the reports on the Canton engine, which I didn't find particularly interesting.

But Arthur was intrigued by TIGHAR and the Earhart search, so he began looking at old Earhart Forum postings,

> in which some correspondent asked Ric what had happened with the Canton engine. Ric replied, in effect, that what we really needed was to find one of the helicopter pilots who could confirm Bruce Yoho's story. At that instant, all my synapses started firing in unison, and I smacked myself smartly on the forehead, because I suddenly realized that I actually knew a helicopter pilot who had been working on some remote Pacific Island at about that time."

When he got home, Arthur queried his wife, Jacqui:

> "Didn't your father have a job flying on some Pacific island when you were young?"
>
> "Yes."

"What year?"
"I think it was 1970 or 1971 or so."
"What island?"
"The Phoenix Islands."

Thus, another hapless soul fell victim to the Earhart Syndrome. Arthur got in touch with TIGHAR and volunteered to run the "engine on the reef" stories to ground. Ric accepted gratefully and added Arthur to the EPAC. Through his father-in-law, Arthur was able to contact four SAMTEC pilots and crew members, interview them, and pore through their documents and photographs. His conclusions, as presented at the EPAC meeting, were these:

- Jack Porth's engine was almost certainly not on Niku, because Jack was sure he'd never been there and his logbooks showed no record that he had. Jack thinks the engine was on Orona (Hull), but is puzzled that he recalls seeing the engine only once, because he made dozens of trips to Orona. Jack made only four trips to Manra (Sydney), where a SAMTEC mechanic photographed a World War II aircraft engine and we know a C-47 crashed in 1943.§§§
- Bruce Yoho's engine was probably not on Niku either. Niku was visited by scientists early in SAMTEC's program to assess environmental conditions, but this was before Bruce arrived in late 1970. SAMTEC didn't build anything on Niku, and Niku's distance from Kanton makes it an unlikely destination for a casual visit. One of Arthur's informants recalled a single flight to Niku during 1970–1971. No one remembers finding or airlifting an engine from Niku or anywhere else.
- Bruce certainly *did* find an engine; two of Arthur's informants recall seeing it in the shop. Bruce's supervisor remembers it as an R-1830, used on B-24s, PBYs, and many other World War II aircraft. There's also a photograph of Bruce, with two other guys, wielding shovels next to a World War II aircraft prop, sticking out of a beach, with bits of engine attached. No one is quite sure where this photo was taken, and Bruce doesn't remember it at all.
- No one other than Bruce recalls slinging an engine under a helicopter and bringing it to Kanton from another island, but someone did sling an old cannon in from Enderbury Island.[44] Perhaps two incidents have gotten

§§§ See chapter 17.

compressed in Bruce's memory—bringing in an engine from someplace else on Kanton, and bringing in the cannon from Enderbury.

- The best candidate for the source of Bruce's engine is a B-24 crash site on the reef off the east end of the Kanton runway. The helos routinely passed over it at a low enough altitude to see something the size of an engine, and B-24s had radial engines. The wreck was probably scavenged by local residents, too, and some of the parts could have wound up on Niku—accounting for the identifiable B-24 pieces we've found there.

I have to say (as, I think, would Arthur) that the jury is still rather out on this one, though I'm tremendously impressed with the volume and quality of Arthur's research. Niku is a long way from Kanton, and there wasn't much reason to go there, but in addition to the pilot who remembers a single flight to the island, a former contractor recalls a visit to Niku because "the guys just decided to fly over there." It seems like there was at least some unscheduled, undocumented flying[45] being done by the doubtless bored helicopter crews. If someone could sling in a cannon from Enderbury, it's not beyond belief that someone could have slung in an engine from Niku. But I agree with Arthur, and Ric, and the EPAC, that the evidence doesn't justify our giving the search for the Kanton engine very high priority for scarce research dollars.

What We've Not Done

There are some things we've intended to get done**** that we haven't yet been able to pursue. For one thing, we haven't made any progress on figuring out what sizes of shoe Earhart actually wore on the flight. The same newspaper article that says she was carrying desert water bags also says that she was taking along a pair of hiking boots, "just in case," but we don't know what "hiking boots" means in this particular context. There's a good picture in the Earhart Birthplace Museum in Atchison, Kansas, that shows her foot next to a line of rivets; we'd like to get a copy of it to compare with the one we already have, but haven't been able to make that happen yet.

We haven't been able to get anyone to Funafuti to check the archives there and to hunt up people who, like Emily Sikuli and Tapania Taiki, lived on Niku in the past. And we haven't been able to get anyone back to

****See chapter 26, "So What's Next?"

Nikumaroro Village in the Solomons. The money just hasn't been there for everything we'd like to do, and in the case of the Solomons the political situation has been pretty unstable. However, we have been fortunate enough to be put in contact with Gideon Tiroba, an official in the Solomon Islands government who's the son of Nikumaroro Village residents and has e-mail. Mr. Tiroba has promised to interview people from the village when they come to the capital, Honiara, or when he visits his birthplace; he has a set of important questions to ask about use of aluminum, what was done at the Seven Site in the 1950s, and other topics. And late in 2003 another descendant of Nikumaroro colonists, Baoro Koraua, contacted us from New Guinea, eager to help. Astoundingly, Mr. Koraua is the son of Paul Laxton, whose article on the colony guided us in exploring the village back in 1989. And his sister Hilary Laxton Kerrod, in New Zealand, has also been in touch and is in possession of many papers that their father left. Moreover, Mr. Koraua has enlisted the help of another Nikumaroro expatriate, Dr. Eritara Tekieru, who practices medicine in Australia. Suddenly, we have a whole new group of colleagues, with access to unique data that may help us sort out what happened on the island in the 1940s and 1950s.

Finally, I should mention that we keep getting urged to conduct deepwater robotic searches for aircraft wreckage—notably the engines—on the face of the Nutiran reef. This would be a good thing to do, but frightfully expensive—far beyond the limits of anything we can expect our fundraising to accomplish. And the likelihood of success is uncertain. Once one goes over the lip of the shelf that runs along the reef face—which our divers searched pretty carefully in 2001 with no results—the reef and its underlying mountainside plunge sharply to a depth of over three miles. There's a lot of territory down there in which an engine could hide.

The Other Hypotheses

As we've moved along testing the Nikumaroro Hypothesis, proponents of other hypotheses haven't been letting the grass grow under their feet, either. In 2002 Nauticos Corporation, a Maryland-based deep water search and salvage company, undertook an ocean-bottom survey of some 900 square miles in the area where Elgen and Marie Long projected the Electra to have gone down.[46] They haven't released results yet, but we're pretty sure they would have if they'd found the plane. And my friend and colleague Jennings

Bunn, the Navy's archaeologist on Guam, is investigating the account of a World War II Marine who says he was shown Earhart's and Noonan's graves on Tinian.[47] I've told him that if he nails down the site and gets authorization from the Northern Marianas authorities, I'll be happy to help him dig; Gary Quigg and Kar Burns say they'll go too. Every hypothesis deserves testing, and the project has great musical potential.

As this is written, our old friend Col. Rollin Reineck has published a book resurrecting the hypothesis that Earhart survived and assumed the identity of Irene Bolam, a New Jersey resident who died a few years ago. If you're interested in this notion, take a look at Ric's review of the book on the TIGHAR website.[48] In a nutshell, Reineck's argument is based on several pieces of "evidence" that don't hold up when exposed to careful scrutiny.

Where We Are Now

So, to sum it up, we continue to think that the Nikumaroro Hypothesis looks pretty good as the explanation for what happened to Earhart, and better than any of the others. We still don't have a smoking gun, but the data continue to pile up. The study of post-loss signals suggests that some of them may well have been genuine, which would mean that the plane had to be on land. The dados suggest that a chunk of a civilian passenger plane was available to the Niku colonists at some point in time, in the area where our hypothesis predicts wreckage would have washed ashore. The Tarawa maps indicate an interest in the Seven Site by Gallagher that reinforces our premise that it's where the bones were found, and our work there in 2001 shows that someone was doing something there that involved cooking birds, fish, and turtles and opening clams. And someone tried to open *Tridacna* the way clams and oysters are opened in the United States and bashed others open with a rock. But the Seven Site is complicated, with its dispersed burn features, its enigmatic hole, and its strangely stratified clams, asphalt siding, and corrugated iron. It's evidently been used on at least two or three different occasions by different people—colonists, Coast Guardsmen, maybe the castaway(s)—and it's hard to sort out who was responsible for each of its many features. It's a complex, stratified archaeological site, with all its strata compressed into a few centimeters.

There are lots of leads to be pursued, lots of lines of evidence to be run out, lots of analyses to be completed, but we think we know enough now to plan a major expedition to the island in late 2005, concentrating on the village shore along Tatiman Passage and on the Seven Site.

Of course, the big problem is how to fund such an expedition—and our other research and basic operating expenses—in these times of fiscal constraint and world peril, when frankly, most people have more pressing things to do with their money than to invest it in looking for long-lost aviators. In 2000 I was interviewed about the project by *U.S. News & World Report*, and I said I didn't think that it had "any redeeming social significance" but was "an intellectually engaging form of recreation." That's true, but what the *U.S. News* writer went on to say is also true—that it's "a mystery that can't be put down."[49] We may very well be close to solving the mystery, and none of us is prepared to stop now, even when there are lots of other demands on our own discretionary money and the contributions of donors. Like Earhart as she prepared for the flight, TIGHAR has mortgaged its future on testing the Nikumaroro Hypothesis; here's hoping we can find a way to pay the bill.

Thanks again, Cynthia, for giving me the opportunity to write about my favorite gig. Please feel free to contact me again, and of course keep checking the website—www.tighar.org—for breaking news.

Tom King

Ric Gillespie (in Sir Harry Luke Memorial Headgear) and Tom King at the Seven Site, 2001. TIGHAR photo by Andrew McKenna.

Acknowledgments

LTHOUGH NO ONE BUT THE AUTHORS ARE RESPONSIBLE for this book and its contents, it would never have come to be without the assistance of many, many people, governments, organizations, and enterprises. We are grateful to everyone who has helped us, and although we do not ourselves speak for TIGHAR, we are equally grateful to those who have supported the organization over the years.

First, we thank TIGHAR itself, and Ric Gillespie and Pat Thrasher, without whom there would be no search of Nikumaroro for Amelia Earhart, and who have assisted us in innumerable ways — to say nothing of putting up with us with (most of the time) a great deal of courtesy and understanding. We also appreciate the institutional support of TIGHAR's board of directors: Chairman John Sawyer and members Peter Paul Luce, Richard Cobb, Skeet Gifford, Dick Reynolds, Bill Thursby, and Don Widdoes. (Author Tom King also serves on TIGHAR's board.)

TIGHAR's work on Nikumaroro would be impossible, of course, without the approval and support of our host nation. We owe a great debt of thanks to the people and government of Kiribati, in particular:

His Excellency Teburoro Tito, president; His Excellency Ieremia T. Tabai, former president; Dr. Tetaua Taitai, secretary of State; Natanaera Kirataa, member of Parliament from Onotoa; Meita Beiabure, permanent secretary to Cabinet; Kautuna Kaitara, director of Customs; Manikaa Teuatabo, deputy director of Customs; Tonganibeia Tamoa, Customs agent.

Much of our work is also done in Fiji, and Fiji is usually the port of origin for expeditions to Nikumaroro. We have received tremendous support and help from the people and government of Fiji, and express particular gratitude to:

His Excellency the Right Honorable Ratu Sir Kamisese Kapaiwei Tuimacilai Mara; Dr. Apenisa Kuruisaqila, Speaker of Parliament; Joseph Browne, personal secretary to the president; Mrs. Stanley Brown; Ratu Epeli Nailatikau, permanent secretary, Ministry of Foreign Affairs; Paula Kunabuli, chief protocol officer, Ministry of Foreign Affairs; Luke Rokovada, permanent secretary, Ministry of Health; Dr. Asinate Boladuadua, acting permanent secretary, Ministry of Health; Nemani Buresova, permanent secretary, Ministry of Women and Culture; and Filimoni Kau, principal information officer, Ministry of Information.

We also express our gratitude to the many individual Fiji citizens and organizations acknowledged below.

Special thanks are due to the Fiji Museum, TIGHAR's partner in the search for the bones sent to Suva in 1940 from Nikumaroro. We are especially grateful to:

Kate Vusoniwailala, director; Tarisi Vunadilo, head, archaeology department; Sela Raya; Kalpana Nand; Francis Fitzpatrick; and Sagale Buadromo.

We would of course have no book at all were it not for our colleagues on the various expeditions to Nikumaroro, McKean, and Kanton islands and in our research in Fiji. Without their brains, hearts, machete-arms, and contributions of time and treasure the Nikumaroro Hypothesis would remain untested: Much gratitude and *kung butae* to:

John Clauss; Bill Decker; Mary DeWitt; Veryl Fenlason; Tom Gannon; Skeet Gifford; Ric Gillespie; Joe Hudson; Van Hunn; Johnny Johnson; Jerry Ann Jurenka; Chris Kennedy; Dutch Kluge; LeRoy Knoll; Jessica Krakow; Lee Kruczkowski; Joe Latvis; Tommy Love; Russ Matthews; Barb Norris; Alan Olson; Gary Quigg; Dick

Reynolds; Ron Rich; Lonnie Schorer; Kris Tague; Pat Thrasher; Aysa Usvitsky; Bart Whitehouse; Diane Whitehouse; Don Widdoes; Tom Willi; Julie Williams; and Bruce Yoho.

Many government officials, professional colleagues, archivists, librarians, and specialists in a wide variety of fields have helped us and TIGHAR, and many people in all walks of life have provided the organization with financial support, in-kind services, and the loan of equipment. Regretfully, we do not have the names of every such person, but we are grateful to them all just the same. We know, and greatly appreciate, the fact that the following individuals, organizations, agencies, and enterprises have assisted us each in our research, or have taken part in or supported TIGHAR in its work:

ABC News; Rev. Aberaam Abera; the crew of the research vessel *Acania;* Air Pacific; U.S. Air Force Museum, Wright-Patterson Air Force Base; The Airhearts: Michael Baillargeon, Michael Bertha, Katie Chandler, Ethan Goldblum, Adam Goto, Katie Henderson, Jessica Sabato, Jackie Sharpe, Kate Sokolowsky, Robin Tan, Matt Thigpen, Alex Tremblay, and Tony Yacenda; Alcoa Aluminum; Faiz Ali; American Merchant Marine Museum; Dr. Atholl Anderson; Dr. Susan C. Anton; Louis V. Aronson; Wing Commander Desmond Ashton, Royal New Zealand Air Force; Atlantic Aviation; Australian National War Museum; Autometric Inc.

Dr. Avinanash Buharadwaj; Sydney Bailey; Dr. Dirk Ballendorf; David Baker; N. D. Bambard; Dr. Warne Baravilala; Robert Barrel; Barr Smith Library, University of Adelaide; Dr. Stan Benkowski; Robert Benzinger; Bruce Bevin; Eric Bevington; Bilt-Rite Shoe Company; Bernice P. Bishop Museum; Roy A. Blay; Lee ("Chuck") Boyle; Velina Bowen; Shiu Bradab; LCDR Bob Brandenberg, USN (Ret.); Ronald Bright; William Brisk; Janice Brown; Joseph Brown; Steven Brown; Capt. Stanley Brown; Douglas Brutlag; Turtle Bunburry; David Bush; Gilbert Butler.

Alan Caldwell; California Highway Patrol; Sandy J. Campbell; Dr Roel B. Cayari; members of TIGHAR's "Celestial Choir"; David Charlwood; Alexander A. Chasan; Dr. W. T. Chase; Charles Chiarchiaro; Dierdre Clancy; Dr. Roger Clapp; Dr. Paul Chattey; U.S. Coast Guard Museum; Howard Cohen; Colonial War Memorial

Hospital, Fiji; Commonwealth of the Northern Mariana Islands Historic Preservation Office; William Conover; Alika Cooper; Special Agent James E. Corby; Dr. Ron Crocombe; Dr. Thomas Crouch; Sr. Aileen Crowe; Larry Crutsinger; Cultural Resource Analysts Inc.

Gene Dangello; David Taylor Research and Development Center, U.S. Navy; Capt. Eugene L. Davis; Ron Dawson; U.S. Defense Mapping Agency; Nicholas Del Cioppo; Satya Deo; Ross Devitt; Herman DeWulf; Dr. John Diebold; Hon. Larry Dinger; John Dipipo; Discovery Channel; Wesley and Susan Dixon; Bill Doty; Sidney Dowdeswell; Peter Downey; Prudence Draper; Dr. William Dudley; Dr. Fred Duennebier; Amanda Dunham; Mabel Dunklee; Christian Duretete.

Alexxis Edwards; Elixir Apartments, Suva; Peter Elliott; Joe Elms; Simon Elwood; U.S. Embassy, Fiji; Joe Epperson; Kunei Etekiera; Dr. Richard K. Evans; John Evaskovich; Mike Everette.

Nancy Farrell; U.S. Federal Bureau of Investigation; Federal Express Co.; Dr. James Ferris; *Fiji Times*; Fiji School of Medicine; Risasi Finikaso; Mike Firczuk; U.S. Fish and Wildlife Service; Foreign and Commonwealth Records Center, Hanslope; William F. Foshage Jr.; the late Dr. Raymond Fosberg; Frank Fournier; Freer Gallery, Smithsonian Institution; Fresno County Sheriffs Department; Sue Fukuda; R. E. Fullenwider; Craig Fuller; Moira Fulmer; Francis O. Furman.

G&N Services Inc.; Leo T. Gallant; Frances Gale; Gerard Gallagher; members of TIGHAR's Gallagher Project; Tom Gannon; Geonics Inc.; David Gee; Rob Gerth; Jeff Geiger; Heather Gillespie; Rodney Glatt; Jeff Glickman; the late Fred Goerner; Dr. Ward H. Goodenough; Dr. Roger Green; Rick Grigg; Grocery Hall of Fame; Dr. Joel Grossman; Dr. Gordan Groves; Tarab Ata Groves; University of Guam; Joseph Guerrero; James Guest; Margaret Guthrie.

Hagley Museum and Library; Florence N. Hall; Jeff Hamilton; Jerry Hamilton; Toni L. Han; John Hathaway; Agnes Henson-Derby; Dr. Jerry Harasewych; Dr. Leslie Hartzell; Paul Harubin; Fr. Francis Hezel; Hiller Museum; Bill Hillier; Louis O. Hilton; The History Channel; Matthew Hockey; Jul Hoehl; Walt Holm; Cat Holloway; Dr. Rob Hommon; Joe Hudson; Hudson Homes Inc.; Tony Hughes; Bernadette Hussein.

Peter Ifland; Dr. Richard Jantz; Capt. Victor Jhonnie; Tim Johnson; Richard Johnson; Don Jordan; Paul Jordan-Smith; Dorothy K. Josselyn.

John Kaitu; Mitchell Kalloch; Felipe Kamakorewa; Ann Kambara; People of Kanton Island; Hon. Nancy Kassenbaum; Robert Keith-Reid; Roger Kelley; David Kelly; James Kelly; Greg Kennedy; Kay Kepler; Radio station KGMB, Honolulu; Dr. Alick Kibblewhite; George Kidd; Rachel King; Dr. Patrick Kirch; Erenite Kiron; Robert Klaus; Vern Klein; Kenny Kosar; Walter Kozak; Bob Krebs; Robert Kujawa; Dr. Apenisa Kuruisaqila; Mike Kutzleb.

Warren Lambing; Lamont-Doherty Earth Observatory, Columbia University; Dan Lann; Bruce Lawson; Hugh Leggatt; *Life* magazine; Terry Ann Linley; Dr. Mark Leone; Dr. William Lipe; Mary Liscombe; Dr. Litadamu; Cathy Lloyd; Lockheed Corp.; Frank Lombardo; Elgen and Marie Long; Elmo Long; Donald Lopez; Thelma Lovelace; Michael D. Luke.

Buddy Macon; Dr. Ann Macintosh; "Bo" McKneeley; Robert Marsh; Howie Masters; owners and crew of *RV Matagi Princess II*; Richard Mater; James Mathews; Dr. James Maragos; University of Maryland, Department of Anthropology; Masonic Lodge of Suva; Harry and Honor Maude; Aleric Maude; Steve McCollum; Dennis McGee; Andrew McKenna; Joan McPherson; Peter McQuarrie; John E. Meekings; Dr. Teinamati Mereki; Dr. Etika Mesulama; Mike Meunich; Midway Phoenix Inc.; Dr. Pete Miller; Dr. Ann Millbrook; Dr. John Mims; William Moffet; Herb Moffitt; Metuisela Mua; Tony Mucciardi; Melissa Murray; George J. Myers Jr.

N&Z Ltd.; staff of *Nai'a* Cruises, and the crew of *Nai'a*; U.S. National Air and Space Museum; National Archives of New Zealand; National Archives of Fiji; National Archives of Kiribati; National Archives of Tuvalu; U.S. National Archives and Records Administration; U.S. National Museum of Naval Aviation; U.S. National Museum of Natural History, Smithsonian Institution; U.S. National Oceanic and Atmospheric Administration; U.S. National Transportation Safety Board; U.S. Naval Historical Center; U.S. Naval Oceanographic Office; Hiroshi Nakajima; Tarawa Nataua; NBC Productions; Kathleen Neary; Peter Newell; New England Air Museum; New Zealand Embassy to the United States; Dr. Peter Ng;

Tyjuana Nickens; people of Nikumaroro Village, Wahgena Island, Solomon Islands; Nimitz Museum; Charles Niquette; Patrick Nolan; Richard Noonan; members of TIGHAR's Noonan Project; Jeffrey Norris.

Otira O'Brien; David Obura; Oceaneering International Inc.; Cathleen O'Connor; Rachel O'Flynn; Robert L. Ogintz; Carol Osborne; David Osgood; Owl's Head Transportation Museum.

Owners and crew of *Pacific Nomad*; Pacific Society; Sam Painter; Brent Parker; Rose Passadori; William Paupe; Dr. Mark Peattie; Bob Perry; Phillips Screw Company; Photek Corp.; Richard Pingrey; Louis C. Pentages Jr.; Karen Pery-Johnston; Rachel Pery-Johnston; Dick Phillips; Placer Dome Inc.; Harry Poole; Janet Powell; John Powrzanis; Brijesh Prasad; Prentice Thomas & Associates; Public Record Office, Kew; Purdue University Special Collections; Terapa P. Pyatt; Pyrene Corp.

Robert Opie Museum of Packaging and Advertising; Dr. Constance Ramirez; William Rankin; Capt. R.L. Rasmussen, USN; Michael Real; Col. Rollin Reineck, USAF (Ret.); Dr. Elizabeth Reitz; William Renz; The Richards Corp.; Robbins Engineering Instruments; Tom Robinson; Leonard Rochwarger; Rohm & Haas Ltd.; Gary Rogan; Denise Rowntree; Royal Air Force Museum; Royal New Zealand Air Force Archives; Jimmie Rush; Joe Russell; Scott Russell.

Saint Andrew's Presbyterian Church, Suva; Dr. Jimione Samisone; San Diego Aerospace Museum; Dr. Salesi Savau; Capt. W. E. Scarborough, USN (Ret); Schonstedt Instruments Inc.; Lou Schoonbrood; Laura Carter Schuster; Pam Sedgman; Jack Seiderman; Dr. Jona Senilagakali; Susan Shaner; Robert Sherman; William Sherman; Dr. Mary Shramm; Dr. Richard A. Schreiber; Helen Shroyer; Rick Siciliano; Emily Sikuli; Maria Simpson; Aloha Smith; Arthur Smith; Page W. Smith; Tim Smith; Pulekai Songivalu; Charles Sopko; Stanley Sorenson; University of the South Pacific; Michael P. Speciale; U.S. State Department; the late Virgil Stennett; Sterling Last Co.; Dr. Joe Stewart; Stihl Chain Saw Company; Margot Still; Pam Stone; Dr. Charles Streck; Richard G. Strippel; Michael Swean; University of Sydney.

Tapania Taiki; Setareki Tale; Robert Tallman; Jordan Tannenbaum; Takaua Tataua; Thermos Corp.; Allen Thomas; Thomas & Betts Co.; John Thompson; Mark Thompson; Sir Ian Thomson; the late Bauro Tikana; Foua and Selepa Tofiga; Trimble Instruments; Vasemaca Tuisawa; Mark Turner; Phil Turner; Diane Tyler.

United Airlines; United Technologies Corp; Dr. Douglas Ubelaker; Sir Leonard Usher; Uwchlan Hills Elementary School.

Apaitia Vakacegu; Elaitia Vakarau; Vandenberg Air Force Base; Angie Vandereedt; J. Gordon Vaeth; Eduard Van der Nordaa; Thomas Van Hare; Gerson Van Messel; Vasiti; U.S. Department of Veterans Affairs; Vokker Aerospace.

Colin Wagner; Ray Wagner; Daniel Ltd.; Wagner and Associates; Joanna Wallington; Warner-Lambert Co.; Cam Warren; Farley Watanabe; Jon Watson; Larry Webster; White's Electronics; Dr. Peter White; Ted Whitmore; Barbara Wiley; Tom Wili; Dr. Roy Wilkens; Willis and Geiger Outfitters; Larry Wilson; Winterthur Museum; Susan Woodburn.

Paul Yat Lum, Bruce Yoho; Larry Zerbe; Janet Zisk; Keith Zorger; William H. Zorn.

Special thanks are due to Dr. James Carucci and to Amy and Adam Kleppner for their critical and helpful reviews of this book in draft. In no way, however, should their contributions be taken to imply any endorsement of the views presented here.

In preparing the second edition, we're grateful to Art Carty, Dan Postellon, John Pratt, Tom Roberts, and Lonnie Schorer for special editorial assistance. Others who've helped in the research since 2001 are noted in the text or endnotes; we're grateful to them all.

Marty and Roger express particular thanks to all those in Fiji and New Zealand who helped them—especially Risasi and Tau Finikaso, Joeli Lau, Taniela Masirewa, Etie Batirerega, Tokai Toribau, Apaitia Vakacegu, Anthony Cooper, Fr. Kevin Barr, Michael Benefield, Fr. Michael Bransfield, Mrs. Stan Brown, Bruce T. Burne, Fergus Clunie, Anthony Cooper, Eni Etuati, Ron Gatty, Stephen Innes, Linda Crowl, Elise Huffer, Ragini Mudaliar, Molly Murphy, Denise Murphy, Susan, William, and Sufi Parkinson, Margaret Shanta Patel, Joan Teiawa, Foua and Eseta Tofiga, Taraiasi Vakamoci, Imeri Waibuca, and Matt and Emilita Wilson.

Finally, we are grateful to Mitch Allen of AltaMira Press for his unwavering support, his critical editorial reviews, his willingness to work with us in bringing this book to fruition, and particularly his patience, and to Dorothy Smith of Rowman & Littlefield for her careful and understanding editorial work.

Notes

Chapter 1: Where in the World Is Amelia Earhart?

1. While based on a real incident, this conversation and its continuation in the last chapter and epilogue are fictional.
2. Admittedly, a proposal advanced only in tabloid newspapers from time to time, and in variant form in an episode of the television show *Star Trek: Voyager.*

Chapter 2: The Lady in Question

1. Backus 1982, 126.
2. See Long and Long 1999 for a good summary, Morrissey and Osborne 1987 for details, Backus 1982 for "her own words."
3. Backus 1982.

Chapter 3: The Navigator and the Airplane

1. TIGHAR Tunes is a running collection of mostly very bad lyrics produced on various TIGHAR expeditions.
2. A project of the Earhart Forum, an Internet discussion group sponsored and moderated by TIGHAR. Jerry Hamilton, Don Jordan, and Ron Dawson are among the major contributors to Noonan research.
3. New Orleans *Times-Picayune,* July 6, 1937.
4. Goerner 1966, 33.
5. See for instance Brock 1978.
6. Noonan 1937.

7. Grooch 1939, 212–214. Like much else we now know about Noonan, Grooch's information was rediscovered by TIGHAR's Noonan Project, headed by Jerry Hamilton.
8. See for instance Long and Long 1999, 182.
9. See for instance Long and Long 1999, 179.
10. Gillespie, personal e-mail communication to King, 2000, describing telephone conversation with Furman.
11. Marshall 1937.
12. Further analysis of the film by several Earhart Forum participants has revealed some gaps and breaks in the imagery, suggesting that it represents several short clips patched together. Some analysts see some of the shadow patterns in some of the images to be inconsistent with the time of day the Electra took off on its fatal flight. If true, this might indicate that some of the images were shot the previous day, when Earhart and Noonan took the plane for a test flight. If this were the case, Noonan's chipper condition would not necessarily reflect how he felt on July 2. This leaves us a little less certain than we otherwise might be about the significance of the Lae imagery to the question of Noonan's drinking, but in the end, it doesn't prove that Noonan either was or was not impaired during the flight from Lae.
13. Lovell 1989, 229.

Chapter 4: Disappearance

1. Earhart 1937.
2. GCT. Also called Greenwich Mean Time or GMT.
3. On the original log, "circling" has been typed in over another word that had been erased. Some have suggested that the original word was "drifting." Gillespie has suggested that "listening" makes better sense.
4. The material in the square brackets, a direct quote from the log, is interpreted to mean that they were flying north and south along the 157-337 line; the numbers are the operator's notations on frequency, mode of transmission, and signal strength.
5. U.S. Navy 1937c, Enclosure D.
6. U.S. Navy 1937c, cover report, first section, p. 6; U.S. Navy 1937d.
7. The United States sought the permission of the British government for this enterprise only rather belatedly, which caused some alarm in the Crown Colony of the Gilbert and Ellice Islands. British authorities cooperated in the search, however.

8. U.S. Army Intelligence 1949a; NCDC n.d.; Maritime Safety Agency 1951.
9. Western Pacific High Commission 1937a; U.S. Department of State 1937; U.S. Navy 1937e; Spading 1997.
10. Parker 1938. See also Thompson 1937 and U.S. Navy 1937c: see page 4 of Annex D to Attachment K (*Lexington* report).
11. At this writing, Jacobson and King are preparing a lengthy paper on this aspect of the search.
12. Putnam 1937.
13. Western Pacific High Commission 1937b; TIGHAR 1999a, Section 3:B.
14. The Western Pacific High Commission, or WPHC, administered British colonies and interests in the area, including the Gilbert and Ellice Islands Colony. The WPHC will figure prominently in later chapters.
15. Western Pacific High Commission 1937b; TIGHAR 1999a, Section 3:B.
16. Ibid.
17. Luke 1945, 112.

Chapter 5: After the Search

1. Cooper 1937, 10.
2. *Smith's Weekly* 1937.
3. See for instance Peattie 1988.
4. U.S. Navy 1937a, 1937b, 1937c; Peattie 1988, 249.
5. Goerner 1966, 79.
6. See for instance Brink 1994, 161 (Earhart as Tokyo Rose), U.S. Navy 1939c.
7. Backus 1982, 239.
8. U.S. Army Intelligence 1949a, 1949b; Mutsu 1949.
9. Patton 1960.
10. Goerner 1966, 318–319. Some time later Goerner changed his mind about the Mili Connection; in a letter to TIGHAR member Rob Gerth dated April 13, 1989, he said that, based on interviews carried out in the Marshalls, he was convinced that Mili had not been Earhart's landing place. He continued to believe that she and Noonan had been picked up by the Japanese, however, and taken to Saipan.
11. Examples include Loomis with Ethell 1985, Devine with Daley 1987, Brennan 1988, and Donohue 1987.
12. Vansina 1985, 107.
13. Many critiques of Goerner's work simply write him off as paranoiac about U.S. government secrecy, or gloss over his allegations without

actually rebutting them. To the best of our knowledge there has never been a thorough, documented, point-by-point rebuttal of Goerner's interpretations—though Goerner himself, in personal correspondence upon being confronted with strong contrary evidence, responsibly backed away from some of his arguments.

14. Strippel 1972.
15. Long and Long 1999.
16. Klaas 1970.
17. McKenchnie 1975, 897.
18. Bahn 1989, 60.
19. Even finding them elsewhere might not be enough for real Japanese capture aficionados. As one reviewer of this book in draft asked: "What if the Japanese captured them, interrogated them, and then abandoned them on a desert island to die of starvation?"
20. That is, the artifact that "any idiot" would accept as legitimate.

Chapter 6: Getting Hooked on Earhart

1. Inaccuracies in Noonan's dead reckoning could result in his LOP actually being somewhat beyond or somewhat short of Howland Island, which would have added to his difficulties. On the other hand, the LOP couldn't be thought of as a narrow line but as a band whose width represented the swath of ocean visible from the air. The Toms felt that Noonan's navigational skills were such that this band should have included Howland.
2. U.S. Navy 1937c.
3. Lambrecht 1937, 4.
4. Goerner to T. F. King February 29, 1992: "After your last communication I went back to the letters and the transcripts of our phone conversations. With respect to John Lambrecht I gave you a bad read in my first letter. John said he saw what appeared to be stone walls or construction of some kind on McKean Island. On Gardner he saw what appeared to be markers of some kind."
5. Maude 1968.
6. Laxton 1951.
7. Scarr 1960.
8. Thanks to John Marks of the Earhart Forum for succinct articulation of the "Razor."
9. For information on "Project Midnight Ghost," see www.tighar.org (September 1, 2000).

10. See for instance King and Parker 1984, including "The Guns of Tonnachaw" by King and James Carucci.
11. Luke 1945.

Chapter 7: McKean, Gardner, and the PISS

1. Maude 1968, 332.
2. A nautical mile is about 1.15 statute miles.
3. TIGHAR, in progress, VII.F.1.b.1.
4. Coconut crabs are reported in various encyclopedia articles and other popular sources to rip up fallen coconuts to get at the meat, to break fresh ones on the ground, and to climb trees to twist nuts off their stems. These stories are generally unsubstantiated in the technical literature we have been able to review, however (see for instance Brown and Fielder 1991). Coconut crabs are apparently omnivorous; they eat rotting fallen coconuts, but they eat all kinds of other organic material as well, including meat. We have observed them eating rats, but don't know whether they found them dead or caught them alive.
5. Maude 1968, 328.
6. The Solomon Islands Protectorate, the British part of the Anglo-French "condominium" of the New Hebrides, the Line Islands, the Colony of Pitcairn Island (of *Bounty* fame), and the protection provided by the British to the Kingdom of Tonga.
7. Maude 1968, 328.
8. Arundel's plantation workers were on the island for several years, leaving at least a couple of buildings and several groves of coconuts. The latter survived into the late 1930s, and their locations would become important to TIGHAR's research. The buildings were observed by castaways from *Norwich City,* which was wrecked on the island in 1929. These buildings might account for Lambrecht's "signs of recent habitation."
9. Maude 1940, 13.
10. In the language of Kiribati, Teng or Ten is an honorific male referent similar to Mister in English.
11. Luke 1945, 221.
12. Maude 1968, 341; Laxton 1951, 141.
13. Luke 1945, 222.
14. Much later, we found notes from Gallagher in WPHC files that he had signed as "Irish," apparently a nickname.

15. In the language of Kiribati, Nei is an honorific term for a woman, like Mrs. in English.
16. Laxton 1951, 142.
17. Western Samoa 1929; *London Times* 1929.
18. Three bodies washed ashore and were buried on the beach by the survivors; the remaining bodies were not found. This fact would become important to us later.
19. Ward H. Goodenough personal communication to T. F. King, 1998 (Goodenough did ethnographic research with Teng Koata and Nei Aana in Kiribati in the 1950s—see Goodenough 1963).
20. Laxton 1951, 150.
21. Gibson 1939 and Lee 1939 describe the expedition.
22. More candidates for the "signs of recent habitation" seen by Lambrecht.
23. Royal Navy 1937, 1938; U.S. Navy 1937a, 1937b, 1939a, 1939b, 1941.
24. Goerner 1989.
25. Maude 1968, 328; TIGHAR 1996c: Tab 4:27 (excerpt).

Chapter 8: First Time on Niku

1. The Fijian term for kava, a mildly narcotic drink consumed both in ceremony and recreationally.

Chapter 9: Can't Find That Train

1. Laxton 1951, 159.

Chapter 10: Hope Springs Eternal

1. TIGHAR 1991b, 4–5 ("The Darwin Photo").
2. Corby 1990, TIGHAR 1991a, 5 ("Summary of Evidence").
3. TIGHAR 1996b, 13–14 ("Found Objects").
4. TIGHAR 1996b, 14 ("Found Objects").
5. Maude 1997.
6. Maude 1937a. See also Maude 1937b, 1938a.
7. Maude 1940.
8. Gallagher 1940a, 1940b, 1940c, 1941a, 1941b; Maude 1938b, 1939a, 1939b.

10. Gallagher 1941a.
11. Gallagher 1941b.
12. Tikana 1991.
13. TIGHAR 1990, 3–5 ("Nor Any Drop to Drink").
14. Laxton 1951, 150–151.

Chapter 11: The Grave, the Skin, and the Shoes

1. By this time it had become necessary to elaborate on the numbering system. The first "2" means the Earhart Project, the second means the second expedition, "V" means "village," and "1" means it's the first artifact collected in the village.

Chapter 12: "We Did It!" or Not

1. TIGHAR 1992a, 1.
2. Schelling 1992, 74.
3. Weber n.d.
4. Fenn 1992.
5. Sledge 1988; Robinson 1992.
6. If Earhart's foot was considerably smaller than the size of her shoe—something we can't be at all sure of—it's not unreasonable to imagine that she wore larger shoes when flying to accommodate thick socks; an airborne aluminum airplane could undoubtedly get cold.
7. Cuca 1992.
8. In one of her press releases Earhart mentioned being nauseated by gas fumes in the cockpit during the South Atlantic crossing because the tanks had been overfilled. Later she reported that while in Java she and Noonan partook of a very rich traditional banquet that left them both feeling like they had eaten too much—as they probably had. We can find no other documentation of stomach trouble.
9. Artifact 2-2-G-5 was identified by Tim Johnson, science teacher, Kasson, Minnesota.
10. Gilbert Islands 1978.
11. Since then TIGHAR members have examined half a dozen other Electras, with similar results.
12. Bureau of Air Commerce 1937.

13. TIGHAR 1996b, 16–18 ("Found Objects").
14. TIGHAR 1992a, 1–7 ("We Did It").
15. Gillespie 1992, 74.
16. See for instance Schelling 1992, 74; TIGHAR 1992b, 4–7 ("Through the Flak").
17. Sagan 1996.
18. Bevington 1990.
19. Bevington 1937.
20. Maude 1996.
21. TIGHAR 1996b, 12–13 ("Part Number 40552") and 20–21 ("Found Objects").
22. Ernest Zehms, who served at the Nikumaroro Loran station, commenting on Gillespie's *Life* article in the San Francisco *Chronicle*, Thursday, March 19, 1992, page A6, said that he and his colleagues sometimes brought pieces of aircraft aluminum to the station from Canton Island.
23. Knudson 1964.
24. Ballendorf and Hoehl 1996.
25. This is generally consistent with the recollections of the Coast Guardsmen, and with the records of the station, which indicate only short visits to the village by liberty parties of unspecified size about every other weekend.
26. Videotape of the interview raises questions about whether Erenite Keron actually saw the ghost or heard about it from someone else.

Chapter 13: The Skeptic and the Kiwis

1. Jacobson 1994.
2. A Monte Carlo simulation plots the possible end results of a scenario in which there are many variables, each with a probability distribution. In this case Jacobson plotted the Electra's flight path given the probability distributions of all the known variables—both those Earhart was aware of (for example, amount of fuel, known weather forecasts) and those she did not know (for example, actual weather conditions). This resulted in two paths—the one Earhart should have thought she was on given what she knew, and the one she might actually have been on given what we know. The latter ended about 117 nautical miles southwest of Howland at the time of her "cannot see you" last transmission. Jacobson cautions that there is much room

for error in this kind of analysis, and many variables that we can't control.

3. Gibson 1939.
4. Lee 1939.
5. Unfortunately, Henderson is the only surviving member of the party we have thus far been able to locate.

Chapter 14: Back to the Windward Side

1. Airphotos found to date are:
   - 1937: Lambrecht photo, first noted in Donohue's book *The British Connection* in 1989. Also found in 1990, reproduced in a 1942 intelligence monograph about the "Islands North and West of Samoa at the U.S. National Archives." Actual print acquired from the New Zealand National Archives in 1992.
   - 1938: Two aerial views of the island taken from plane launched from HMS *Leander* December 1, 1938. New Zealand National Archives 1992.
   - 1939: Aerial mosaic taken by plane from USS *Pelican* on April 30, 1939. Found in U.S. National Archives 1989.
   - 1941: Seven aerial views of the island taken by USN PBY on June 20, 1941. Four found in U.S. National Archives in 1989. All found in New Zealand National Archives 1992.
   - 1942: Two aerial views taken by a USAF plane November 26, 1942. Found at USAF Historical Center, Maxwell AFB, Alabama, in 1995.
   - 1944: Two aerial views taken by Charles Sopko, commanding officer of Loran Unit 92, provided by Sopko to TIGHAR in 1996.
   - 1953: Eight aerial views from mapping photos taken May 1, 1953 (photographer unknown). Found in New Zealand National Archives 1992.
   - 1975: Ten aerial views taken by Smithsonian survey from a USAF helicopter. Provided by Smithsonian Institution ornithologist Roger Clapp in 1989.
   - 1978: Aerial view taken as part of Geomarex mineral survey. Provided by former Geomarex employee in 1990.
   - 1988: Five aerial views taken by Royal New Zealand Air Force patrol flights. Via RNZAF Air attaché through RNZAF 12 Squadron, Wellington, in 1991.
2. TIGHAR 1996a, 12–13 ("Part Number 40552").
3. TIGHAR 1996b, 20–21 ("Found Objects").

4. The resettlement plan, though still on the books, had not been carried out as of 2004.

Chapter 15: The Shattered Shores of Niku

1. Gallagher 1941a, 1.
2. TIGHAR 1993a, 8 ("The Beast of Bombay Hook").
3. Simple holes, plotted on a map, dug by shovel and quickly screened, to get an idea of the distribution of artifacts and other phenomena.

Chapter 16: Harassed by Hina, Favored in Funafuti

1. Who now plays rugby—loose head prop, to be precise—for the San Mateo (California) Rugby Club.
2. Laxton 1949, Appendix.
3. King is a Patrick O'Brian fan.
4. TIGHAR 1997, 9–12 ("I Saw Pieces of an Airplane").

Chapter 17: After the Storm

1. *TIGHAR Tracks* 1997, 12.
2. Photek 1997, TIGHAR 1997, 12–13 ("Corroboration").
3. Gilbert Islands 1978.
4. TIGHAR 1996b, 11–12 ("Found Objects").
5. TIGHAR 1998b, 15–18 ("The Crash at Sydney").

Chapter 18: Kanton in the Rain

1. Yoho 1998, 5–6.
2. The Sherman tank and other military vehicles (including landing craft) had engines that could easily be confused with an R1340; we don't know of any such vehicles that went missing in the Phoenix Islands, but there would probably be less chance of such a loss being recorded than there would of an aircraft loss.
3. See for instance U.S. Air Force 1974a.
4. U.S. Air Force 1974b; TIGHAR 1998a, 3 ("The Kanton Mission").
5. U.S. Air Force 1975; TIGHAR 1998a, 3 ("The Kanton Mission").
6. This time including Gillespie and his daughter Heather, King, Clauss, Spading, Matthews, Love, and expedition sponsors Dick Reynolds, Joe Hudson, Lee Kruczkowski, and Johnny Johnson.

7. Gasoline for airplanes. Nobody smokes on TIGHAR expeditions anyway.

8. When they got back to the United States Clauss prepared a report that King got routed through government channels to the U.S. Air Force's Center for Environmental Excellence, which handles such matters, describing the problem and urging that it be looked into. There was no response.

Chapter 19: Bones for Real

1. See for instance McQuarrie 2000.

2. Western Pacific High Commission 1940–1941a; TIGHAR 1997, 18–31 ("The Tarawa File").

3. A British size 10 would be about a size 12 according to the system then used for shoe sizing in the United States, considerably longer than the Aukaraime South shoe. We really don't know what to do with Gallagher's "size 10" and Kilts's "size 9" anecdotes. The only shoe we can be sure about is the one that we've actually measured and compared with the photo of Earhart's shoe—the one from Aukaraime South.

4. It's possible that Gallagher meant a higher stand, since there is no evidence that he had a chart on which the mean high water mark would be indicated, and since in his quarterly report for October–December 1940 he comments on the damage done by "high spring tides."

5. In Great Britain this term is sometimes applied to a debate that has been cut off for some reason, so Isaac's reference here may be simply to the fact that higher authority had intervened and directed him to send the bones on.

6. Simpson 1998; Spading 1998.

7. Guthrie 1979.

8. See for instance Guthrie 1979; University of the South Pacific 1971.

Chapter 20: Flesh on the Bones

1. Western Pacific High Commission 1940–1941b.

2. Western Pacific High Commission 1938–1939; Spading 1998.

3. Decarbonizing doesn't seem to have been such a complicated process that it should have required a month in port, but *Nimanoa* may have needed further patching up as well; she went into the yard for a significant overhaul when she reached Suva.

4. We do not know why Dr. MacPherson didn't examine the bones. As the forensics expert, he was probably more knowledgeable about bones

than Dr. Hoodless. He may have been off the island at the time, but we haven't yet researched his movements during the period.

5. Luke 1945, 129.
6. Noonan 1935; TIGHAR 1998a, 11 ("The Noonan Project").
7. Cluth 1968; TIGHAR 1998a, 11 ("The Noonan Project").

Chapter 21: Whose Bones, and Where?

1. There are several kinds of anthropologists—cultural, physical, linguistic, archaeological, and medical, among others. A physical anthropologist who does forensic work with bones is a forensic osteologist.
2. See Burns 1999.
3. Moore-Jansen, Ousley, and Jantz 1994.
4. "Race is so complicated that it is tempting to try to ignore it altogether . . . (but) race is still important to the process of identification. . . . The analyst needs to find ways to cope with the difficulties of racial identification rather than avoiding them. This can be accomplished through thorough description and explanation" (Burns 1999, 153).
5. For example, a single family group may be characterized by brown eyes, red hair, type A blood, and diabetes. But brown eyes occur most frequently, and diabetes occurs least frequently. The red hair is more consistently present than is type A blood. DFA includes all the relevant characteristics, but gives the most weight to eye color, then hair color, then type A blood, and finally, diabetes. The numerical weight of each characteristic is statistically determined.
6. For example, Key and Jantz 1990; Jantz 1997; Ousley and Jantz 1998.
7. TIGHAR 1998b, 9.
8. Burns et al. 1998.
9. MacPherson had suggested the same thing in a note dated October 23, 1940.
10. There's nothing in the files to suggest that he did send them on, and investigations into the files of the anthropology and anatomy departments at the University of Sydney, and into Professor A. P. Elkin's papers, which are housed at the university, have revealed no evidence that the bones were ever received.
11. Laxton 1949, 1; emphasis added.
12. Laxton 1951, 150.
13. Maude 1937a, 7; emphasis added.
14. Maude 1939b, 16; emphasis added.

15. Laxton 1951, 151.
16. Bevington 1937, 18; TIGHAR 1996c, Tab 2:4.
17. Clauss didn't know he had found it at the time. He climbed it to shoot pictures, which wound up including some leaves. Gillespie's later comparison of the photos with illustrations provided by the Smithsonian Institution revealed that Clauss had climbed a kanawa.

Chapter 22: Meanwhile . . .

1. At this writing, the Web site gets about 1,400 hits per day.
2. Noonan 1937.
3. It turned out that Gallagher had died of sprue, a radical thinning of the intestinal wall. The files included a long report by MacPherson, criticizing the government for its failure to provide people like Gallagher with the nutritional food and rest needed to avoid such illnesses.
4. Western Pacific High Commission 1936–1937; TIGHAR 1999a: Tab 2:A–D.
5. Western Samoa 1929; TIGHAR 1996c: Tab 3:8.
6. Hamer n.d.
7. Carrington 1977.
8. Royal Navy 1946–1947.
9. TIGHAR 1997, 15 ("Is This Earhart's Electra?").

Chapter 23: Where the Plane Came Down

1. Gallagher had counted only eleven, but Dr. Hoodless had counted thirteen. The two not mentioned by Gallagher (a rib and a foot bone) were presumably found during the "detailed search" ordered by Vaskess.
2. The original Airhearts have now moved on, and parts of Norris's curriculum are now being used in other schools around the country. This may be the best legacy the project leaves, and it's doubtless one that Earhart would approve of.
3. TIGHAR 1999b, 14–15 ("Fiji Bones Search") and 19–20 ("Mrs. O'Brian").

Chapter 24: Trying to Make Sense of It All

1. TIGHAR 1999b, 25–34 ("The Carpenter's Daughter").
2. Earhart Forum discussion group; report in progress.
3. Evening, Nauru time. Evening of July 2 on Niku.

4. Brandenburg in The Earhart Book: See TIGHAR, in progress.
5. Best known for *Island of the Blue Dolphins* (1960), O'Dell ran a writing school in the 1960s.
6. U.S. Coast Guard 1943–1949.
7. TIGHAR 1993b; TIGHAR, in progress.
8. Laxton 1951, 150–151.

Chapter 25: What Happened on the Night of July 2?

1. Knox-Mawer 1995.
2. Collopy 1937, 1.
3. Kelly Johnson 1937.
4. Lovell 1989, 343.
5. Chater 1937.
6. Long and Long 1999, 232.
7. Williams 1937.
8. Chater 1937, 8.
9. Chater 1937, 8.
10. Purdue University Special Collections.
11. Further complicating the matter, Jacobson found that the calculated positions reported were not actual celestial fixes; rather, they were extrapolated from observations taken hours earlier, based on time in flight assuming still air.
12. U.S. Department of State 1937.
13. Dowdeswell 1992.
14. Irving Johnson 1940, 1.
15. TIGHAR, in progress.
16. FAA/CAA 1937.
17. Long and Long 1999, 113.
18. Hooven 1982.
19. See for example Warren 2000.
20. Chater 1937, 3.
21. Marshall 1937.
22. Fullenwider 1994.
23. Thompson 1937, 47.

Chapter 26: And Then? And Now?

1. *Itasca* started making smoke just after dawn to mark her position. Based on what we know of pre-World War II ship propulsion systems,

however, it appears that the ship could make substantial amounts of black smoke for only a short time without damaging her boilers.

2. U.S. Navy 1939b.
3. Obura 2000.
4. Bob Brandenburg has examined this proposition—which he calls the "Resurrection Hypothesis"—in some detail, modeling the forces likely to act on the shelf and Tatiman Passage given the predictable strength of storm surges against the reef face. He regards it as very likely both that pieces of debris would be tossed up from the shelf onto the reef flat from time to time, and that more debris would have worked its way through the passage to the north floor of the lagoon.
5. Knudson 1964, 48.
6. See for instance Brown and Fielder 1991, 5–6; Fletcher, Brown, Fielder, and Obed 1991, 39. Both the technical literature and consultation with specialists indicate that coconut crabs are omnivorous, and specialists have opined that they would be able to carry bones around.
7. Guerrero 1999.
8. What's a harmonic? For nonspecialists in radio, here is Bob Brandenburg's description.

A harmonic is just a multiple of some frequency. Take 200 Hertz, for example. The second harmonic is 400 Hertz, the third harmonic is 600 Hertz, and so on. If you look at a vibrating string, you'll note that it vibrates in a wavelike fashion producing what is called a sine wave, which looks like a tall thin letter "S" turned on its side.

It's possible to add sine waves of different frequencies together. For example, you can combine vibrations at 200, 400, 600, 800, etc., Hertz. But when you do, a strange thing happens—the shape of the combined wave is no longer a sine wave. As you add more harmonics, the sides of the wave become steeper and its top becomes flatter until, when you have added a very large number of harmonics together, the resultant wave looks square, and is actually called a square wave.

A modern radio transmitter generates and radiates, through an antenna, an electromagnetic field which oscillates at some desired fundamental frequency, such as the frequency of your favorite radio station. The transmitter's output power is generated by switching on and off, at the desired frequency, the current flowing through a power amplifier. This on-off current switching, which is the most efficient way to generate output signal power, produces square wave pulses that are applied to an electronic circuit (called a tank circuit) which responds to the pulses in much the same way that a tuning fork responds to being struck. Except, instead of physically vibrating, the tank circuit produces an oscillating voltage which is applied to the antenna to generate the radiated electromagnetic field. But since each pulse is a square wave containing harmonics of the fundamental frequency, the tank circuit's output voltage oscillates at the harmonics as well as at the fundamental. A special filter circuit is interposed between the tank circuit and the antenna to prevent radiation of the harmonics.

However, the design of Earhart's transmitter did not include a filter between the tank circuit and the antenna. Consequently, any harmonic oscillations present in the tank circuit were passed directly to the antenna and were radiated along with the fundamental frequency. Although the power radiated at harmonic frequencies is less than the power radiated at the fundamental, it still is high enough to allow the harmonics to be received at long distances from the transmitter under appropriate propagation conditions. (e-mail to T. F. King, March 2001).

9. Isaac changed his name to Verrier during the war, and became a well-known figure in Fijian politics and society.
10. Gene Vidal reported, after the fact, that Earhart's "Plan B" had been to backtrack into the Gilbert Islands; this is possible, but not very plausible. It's a long way back, and a chancy piece of navigation if you don't know where you are when you set out.
11. Burns et al. 1998.

Chapter 27: Epilogue: 2001 and Beyond

1. Telegram dated May 17, 1937, to Purdue University president Edward Elliott: "Our second attempt is assured. We are solvent. Future is mortgaged, but what else are futures for?" Quoted in Muriel Morrissey and Carol Osborne, *Amelia, My Courageous Sister*, 208.
2. For details, see http://www.tighar.org/Projects/Earhart/Bulletins/07_12_01%20Bulletin/Nikusatphoto.html (November 2003).
3. The invasion trapped the island's WPHC staff, including Dr. Lindsay Isaac, who had played such an interesting role in the voyage of the

bones. Most of them, including Isaac, later escaped in an epic small-boat voyage to be rescued in the Ellice Islands. This story is detailed in Peter McQuarrie's *Conflict in Kiribati.*

4. Skeet has made thousands of landings in a wide variety of airliners as an Air Force pilot, a United Airlines captain, a United training instructor, and a consultant for Lockheed Martin and NASA. He coauthored the *Big Boeing FMC User's Guide,* a pilot's technical manual for operation of flight management computers on Boeing wide-body aircraft.

5. With the help of Bill Carter and others, but Gary won the shoveling prize hands down.

6. Which showed at least two old surfaces covered by coarse debris, deposited by storm events.

7. The resulting videotape, *An Aerial Tour of Nikumaroro,* is available from TIGHAR.

8. The noted paleontologist Malcolm C. McKenna, retired from the American Museum of Natural History and now affiliated with the Department of Geology and Geophysics at the University of Wyoming.

9. For Ric Gillespie's summary of the fieldwork, see "Niku III: A Summary from a Jet-Lagged Perspective," at http://www.tighar.org/Projects/Earhart/NikuIIIsumm.html (November 2003).

10. For details, see "Mysteries of the Seven Site" at http://www.tighar.org/Projects/Earhart/Bulletins/11_20_01%20Bulletin/mysteriesbull.html, and "Artifact Analysis, Step Two," at http://www.tighar.org/Projects/Earhart/Bulletins/02_22_02Bulletin/artifacts.html.

11. Along with a few .22-caliber casings. The .30-caliber rounds are undoubtedly from Coast Guard M-1s, but there's no evidence that .22s were issued to Coast Guardsmen. A list of Gallagher's effects made after his death indicates that he had a .22, however.

12. One loran station veteran reported having participated in a target shoot that put a hole in the tank, prompting complaints by the colonists and an order from the CO to patch it up. We found that the tank had two .30-caliber-sized holes in it that had been patched with American bolts, nuts, and washers. Skeet Gifford was able to plot where the shooter must have stood to make the two holes, and upon searching the location found a spent .30-caliber casing.

13. See "The Knob That Wasn't" at http://www.tighar.org/Projects/Earhart/Bulletins/knob_id_Bulletin/knob_idbulletin.html (November 2003).

14. Turtle "shells" aren't like the true shells that shellfish have; they're systems of bony plates covered with scales made of keratin (the same substance

that forms nails, claws, hooves, and horns). We found both the bony plates and pieces of keratin.

15. Dr. Frank Thomas, archaeologist with the Republic of the Marshall Islands Historic Preservation Office, who has studied the ethnoarchaeology of shellfish gathering in Kiribati, advises that this sort of "field processing" is the most commonly used approach.

16. Rhode Island Sea Grant Fact Sheet http://seagrant.gso.uri.edu/factsheets/fsquahog.html (October 6, 2003).

17. Stevens, "Shucking Clams and Oysters," *Fine Cooking* 22 (1997): 68.

18. Julia Child, *The Way to Cook* (New York: Knopf, 1999), 118.

19. Morrissey and Osborne 1987, 76.

20. Members of the EPAC include the following:

- Howard Alldred, engineering geologist, Geodata Consulting Ltd., Waiheke Island, New Zealand
- Robert Brandenburg, retired naval officer with an M.S. in Operations Research, a field that uses mathematical models and computer simulations to study systems of people, machines, and procedures
- Doug Brutlag, American Airlines international captain (Boeing 757/767), student of celestial navigation
- Karen Ramey Burns, forensic anthropologist, college professor, human rights consultant, and National Disaster Medical System employee
- Alan L. Caldwell, retired Air Force instructor pilot and currently a practicing Texas attorney
- Arthur Carty, retired computer industry executive in Bonita Springs, Florida
- John Clauss, high-tech sailboat manufacturer in Lake Tahoe, California
- William Carter, senior litigation counsel for Albertsons, Inc., and scuba diver
- Veryl Fenlason, a semiretired farmer and co-owner of a golf club and event center in central Minnesota; pilot, member of the Experimental Aircraft Association, airplane restorer, and veteran of fourteen TIGHAR expeditions
- Skeet Gifford, retired United Airlines pilot and consultant to NASA, member of TIGHAR's board of directors

- Jeff Glickman, forensic examiner specializing in the examination of photographic imagery for law enforcement, government, and the legal and scientific communities; Board Certified Forensic Examiner, and a diplomate and fellow of the American College of Forensic Examiners
- Jerry Hamilton, marketing and advertising executive in the San Francisco Bay area; extensive historical research experience; head of TIGHAR's Noonan Project
- Walt Holm, electrical engineer specializing in instrumentation design, pilot, scuba diver with dive master certification, Menlo Park, California
- Van Hunn, retired Air Force colonel, pilot, and scuba diver
- Randy Jacobson, geophysicist with extensive experience in oceanographic sensors and measurements
- Roger Kelley, retired sergeant, Los Angeles Sheriff's Department, with thirty years of investigative service
- Thomas F. King, archaeologist, would-be writer, and specialist in cultural resource management
- Tommy Love, hyperbaric and diving physician, scuba diver, retired Air Force colonel with extensive experience in aircraft accident investigation and air-sea rescue
- Russ Matthews, independent film producer in Hermosa Beach, California, in charge of video documentation on several TIGHAR expeditions
- Andrew McKenna, specialist in commercial and industrial energy management, with extensive paleontological experience with the American Museum of Natural History in the Western United States, Greenland, and Egypt; also a scuba diver and pilot, actively involved in search and rescue missions
- Martin Moleski, SJ, Ph.D., Jesuit priest, professor of religious studies at Canisius College in Buffalo, New York
- Barbara Norris, TIGHAR's development director for education; currently teaching elementary gifted education and writing curriculum based on TIGHAR's research in Downingtown, Pennsylvania
- Ryan Parr, Ph.D., forensic DNA specialist with Genesis Genomics in Thunder Bay, Ontario, Canada
- Robert Perry, Ph.D., chemist and research and development executive with extensive experience in the chemical and electronics industries; participated with his group in the postmortem analysis for

NASA on recorded data tapes recovered from the ocean six months after the loss of the *Challenger* space shuttle

- Daniel C. Postellon, M.D., pediatric endocrinologist at Spectrum Health in Grand Rapids, Michigan
- John Pratt, a physicist at Los Alamos National Laboratory
- Gary Quigg, associate director for historical resources at Indiana's Conner Prairie Museum, with archaeological field experience in the Midwestern United States; independent producer of historical/environmental documentary videos, and private pilot
- Dick Reynolds, retired engineer/businessman and member of TIGHAR's board of directors
- Tom Roberts, a structural engineer with Lockheed Martin Aeronautics Company, specializing in special-purpose modifications of transport aircraft
- Arthur Rypinski, an economist with the U.S. Department of Energy
- Lonnie Schorer, architect/designer and private pilot, formerly head of design for the *World*, a 43,000-ton new concept shipboard community at sea, now working on programs to facilitate travel and residence by private citizens in outer space
- Kristin Tague, specialist in archival, museum, and library systems and management of documents and artifacts; veteran of eight TIGHAR expeditions
- James Thompson, Geographic Information Systems coordinator for the city of Northampton, Massachusetts; uses specialized software to collect, analyze, manage, and disseminate information about spatial environments
- Jon Watson, detective sergeant, Police Department, Golden, Colorado
- Don Widdoes, owner and CEO of Marine Computer Technology in Chadds Ford, Pennsylvania

21. Also known as Ross Devitt.
22. E-mail report to Earhart Forum by "Th' Wombat," November 16, 2003.
23. The Tropical Ocean-Global Atmosphere observing system, supported by the National Oceanic and Atmospheric Administration.
24. Produced by Linden Software; thanks to Linden's Steve Taylor for his assistance and support.
25. The drop-off after three days—that is, on July 5—coincides with the time when the tide rose about eight inches higher than it had since

before the second, assuming the Orona/Kanton data apply to Nikumaroro. Combined with wave action, this may have been sufficient to break up the airplane and/or transport it off the reef, eliminating the possibility for further transmissions. However, July 5th is also when the Navy took over the search from *Itasca,* and *Itasca,* which had recorded most of the events, stopped monitoring the radio.

26. For details, see Robert Brandenburg, "Could Betty Have Heard Amelia Earhart on a Harmonic?" at http://www.tighar.org/Projects/Earhart/Bulletins/03_15_01Bulletin/03_15_01bulletin.html (November 2003).

27. Also known as the Niku Vp Expedition. For details, see http://www.tighar.org/Projects/Earhart/nikuvp/dailies.html (November 2003).

28. See Gregory S. Stone, "Phoenix Islands: A Coral Reef Wilderness Revealed," *National Geographic,* February 2004, 48–65. The centerfold coconut crab on pages 48 and 49 is guarding the south shore of Tatiman Passage.

29. For details, see "Wheel of Fortune," at http://www.tighar.org/Projects/Earhart/Bulletins/04_15_03Bulletin/04_15_03Bulletin.html (November 2003).

30. In search of *l'Oiseau Blanc,* in which Charles Nungesser and Francois Coli perhaps crossed the Atlantic before Lindbergh; see "Off to the Phoenix Islands" in chapter 6 and http://www.tighar.org/Projects/PMG.html (November 2003).

31. For Fr. Moleski's full report, see http://www.tighar.org/Projects/Earhart/Bulletins/07_15_03Bulletin.html (November 2003).

32. We've learned that the bulk of the Fiji School of Medicine files that could have shed light on the fate of the bones were thrown away during a cleanup in 1954. Toni Hawley, wife of former principal Guy Hawley, advised Kris Tague that "a completely wrong headed Acting Principal . . . destroyed all the FSM records before 1954 because they 'took up too much room'!"

33. Who once lived in Fiji. With the rest of the box's contents, these were left with Dr. Murphy's family.

34. As he was described to us by Sir Leonard Usher in 1999. Sadly, Sir Leonard passed away in 2003.

35. Possibly Tropical Cyclone Zoe, which formed in the general vicinity but at a considerable distance in December 2002; but there are other candidates. The source and effect of whatever it was are the subject of hot debate among EPAC members versed in meteorology and ocean science.

36. For details, see "The Dado, Part One," http://www.tighar.org/Projects/ Earhart/Bulletins/09_15_03Bulletin/09_15_03.html, and "Dados Galore," http://www.tighar.org/Projects/Earhart/Bulletins/10_08_03 Bulletin/10_08_03.html (November 2003).

37. In July and August 2004, with the cooperation of the U.S. Forest Service, TIGHAR teams reached the two wrecks. The Idaho wreck proved to have lost its entire fuselage, probably to scrap salvagers during World War II. The Alaska wreck proved to be much more complete, and contained some intriguing features, which are under analysis as this book goes to print. Reports on both wrecks and the analysis are forthcoming on the TIGHAR website (www.tighar.org).

38. Mr. Brink served on Atafu Island, south of the Phoenix Islands.

39. In Morrissey and Osborne, 192, crediting Enid Williams and Schlesinger Library, Radcliff College.

40. Bob Perry of the EPAC analyzed the results of the U.S. Naval Academy (USNA) tests.

41. His diary doesn't say whether it was corrugated, but Irvine C. Gardiner, writing of Arundel's roughly contemporaneous guano operations on Kanton and Enderbury Islands, reported in 1938 that "the huts used by the guano collectors are entirely flattened, only the corrugated roofing remaining." See Gardiner, "Crusoes of Canton Island," *National Geographic* 73, no. 6 (1943): 766, and thanks to the ever-alert Arthur Rypinski for finding this source.

42. Arundel's diary also lists "tin paint" among the materials he shipped to Nikumaroro. The stuff on the Seven Site ridge, while clearly iron, has traces of aluminum that may represent paint. Aluminum paint was in use as early as the 1890s in heat-shielding and reflecting applications. Was it referred to as "tin paint"? We don't know.

43. *Norwich City* survivor J. Thomas actually reported, "Near the palms (on Nutiran) we found two disused *galvanized* roof huts and a large water tank, all of which were in a state of collapse" (emphasis added). Of course, we do not know whether Thomas knew the difference between galvanized and nongalvanized iron, and Arundel is the only person we know of who was on the island early enough to have imported nongalvanized iron.

44. The photograph Arthur obtained shows what looks like an eighteenth-century ship's cannon; he was told that it was a "nine pounder carronade" and that it was subsequently thrown into the Kanton lagoon.

45. Arthur says maybe so, but he doubts if it included trips to Niku, which is just too far away for people to hop over to it on a lark.
46. For details, see http://www.nauticos.com (October 7, 2003). Marie Long passed away on June 20, 2003.
47. For a précis, see "Earhart Search Continues," *Explorers Journal*, Winter 2003–2004, 7.
48. Rollin Reineck, *Amelia Earhart Survived* (Orange, Calif.: Paragon Agency Publishers, 2003). See also the review by Ric Gillespie at http://www.tighar.org/Projects/Earhart/BookReviews/reviewlist.html, and the Gillespie–Reineck exchange at http://www.tighar.org/Projects/Earhart/BookReviews/reineck/discussion.html (both April 6, 2004).
49. Holly J. Morris: "Mysteries of History: Elusive Truths," *U.S. News & World Report*, July 24, 2000, 30–82.

Bibliography

Backus, Jean L. 1982. *Letters from Amelia: An Intimate Portrait of Amelia Earhart.* Boston: Beacon Press.

Bahn, Paul. 1989. *Bluff Your Way in Archaeology.* West Sussex, England: Ravette Books.

Ballendorf, Dirk A., and Jul Hoehl. 1996. The Waghena Island Connection. Report of a Trip to Nikumaroro Village on Waghena Island in the Solomons. TIGHAR 1996c: Tab 7:4 (excerpt).

Bevington, Eric. 1937. Phoenix Islands Expedition. Personal diary, typescript, TIGHAR 1996c: Tab 2:4, or view at www.tighar.org (September 1, 2000).

——. 1990. *The Things We Do for England, If Only England Knew.* Salisbury, Wilts, England: Acorn Bookwork, Laverham Press.

Brandenburg, Robert. 2003. "Could Betty Have Heard Amelia Earhart on a Harmonic?" TIGHAR. View at www.tighar.org/Projects/Earhart/Bulletins/30_BettyHarmonic/30_Bettyharmonic.html (April 2004).

Brennan, T. C. ("Buddy"). 1988. *Witness to the Execution—The Odyssey of Amelia Earhart.* Frederick, Colo.: Renaissance House.

Brink, Randall. 1994. *Lost Star: The Search for Amelia Earhart.* New York: W. W. Norton.

Brock, Horace. 1978. *Flying the Oceans: A Pilot's Story of Pan Am 1935–1955.* New York: J. Aronson.

Brown, I. W., and D. R. Fielder, eds. 1991. *The Coconut Crab: Aspects of the Biology and Ecology of Birgus Latro in the Republic of Vanuatu.* Canberra: Australian Centre for International Agricultural Research.

Bulfer, Bill, and Skeet Gifford. 1991. *Big Boeing FMC User's Guide: Advanced Guide to the Flight Management Computer.* Kingwood, Texas: Leading Edge Libraries.

Bureau of Air Commerce, U.S. Department of Commerce. 1937. Lockheed Engineering Orders and telegram approving them, Lockheed Electra 10E, Serial Number 1055, May 19. Oklahoma City: Federal Aviation Administration (FAA) microfiche; TIGHAR Files.

Burns, Karen Ramey. 1999. *Forensic Anthropology Training Manual.* New York: Prentice-Hall.

Burns, K. R., R. L. Jantz, R. Gillespie, and T. F. King. 1998. "Amelia Earhart's Bones and Shoes?" Paper distributed at the annual meeting of the American Anthropological Association, Philadelphia. *TIGHAR Tracks* 14:2 (December 4). View at www.tighar.org (September 1, 2000).

Carrington, George. 1977. *Amelia Earhart, a Report* (1987, 1993). Vancouver, B.C.: Britnav Services.

Chater, Eric H. 1939. Letter dated July 25 to M. E. Griffin, Placer Management Ltd., San Francisco. Copy given to TIGHAR by Placer Dome Ltd., Vancouver, B.C. View at www.tighar.org (September 1, 2000).

Child, Julia. 1999. *The Way to Cook*. New York: Knopf, 118.

Cluth, W. A. 1968. Letter dated June 6 to "Whom It May Concern," National Museum of Naval Aviation Accession Files, Pensacola, Fla.

Collopy, James A. 1937. Letter dated August 28 to Secretary, Civil Aviation Board. U.S. National Archives, Washington, D.C. View at www.tighar.org (September 1, 2000).

Cooper, Daniel A. 1937. Expedition to the American Equatorial Island in Connection with the Amelia Earhart Flight. Report to Commanding General, Hawaiian Department, July 27. U.S. National Archives Record Group 94/407, Office of Adjutant General, Central Files 1926–1939, 580.81, Trans-Pacific and Round the World Flights of Miss Amelia Earhart. Washington, D.C.; see TIGHAR 1993c: Document No. 11 for a copy.

Corby, James E. 1990. Report to TIGHAR on analysis of navigator's bookcase, FBI Laboratories, Washington, D.C., December 31.

Cuca, Claudia B. 1992. Memorandum to Richard Gillespie, TIGHAR, dated January 15, tracing the history of the use of the "Omnis Orbis" globe trademark. Includes photocopies from the "Modern Drug Encyclopedia" and an obituary of Gerard B. Lambert.

Devine, Thomas E., with Richard M. Daley. 1987. *Eyewitness: The Amelia Earhart Incident*. Frederick, Colo.: Renaissance House.

Donahue, J. A. 1987. *The Earhart Disappearance: The British Connection*. Terre Haute, Ind.: Sunshine House.

Dowdeswell, Sidney. 1992. Letter dated December 24 to Randall Jacobson. TIGHAR Files.

Earhart, Amelia. 1937. *Last Flight*. New York: Harcourt, Brace & Co.

Explorers Club. 2004. "Earhart Search Continues," *Explorers Journal* (Winter 2003–2004), 7.

FAA/CAA. 1937. Federal Aviation Administration/Civil Aeronautics Administration Central Files, 835, Amelia Earhart. U.S. National Archives, Record Group 237.

Fenn, Al. 1992. Personal communication to Richard Gillespie, TIGHAR. Long Island City, N.Y.: Sterling Last Corp.

Fletcher, W. J., I. W. Brown, D. R. Fielder, and A. Obed. 1991. "Moulting and Growth Characteristics." In *The Coconut Crab: Aspects of the Biology and Ecology of Birgus Latro in the Republic of Vanuatu*, edited by I. W. Brown and D. R. Fielder. Canberra: Australian Centre for International Agricultural Research.

Fullenwider, Robert. 1994. Personal communication to Richard Gillespie.

Gallagher, Gerald B. 1940a. Phoenix Islands Settlement Scheme. Quarterly Progress Report, January–March 1940. Public Record Office, British National Archives, Reference CO/225/328/86059/3; TIGHAR 1996c: Tab 4:19.

———. 1940b. Phoenix Islands Settlement Scheme. Quarterly Progress Report, April–June 1940. Public Record Office, British National Archives, Reference CO/225/328/86059/3; TIGHAR 1996c: Tab 4:20.

———. 1940c. Phoenix Islands Settlement Scheme. Quarterly Progress Report July–September 1940. Public Record Office, British National Archives, Reference CO/225/328/86059/3; TIGHAR 1996c: Tab 4:21. View at www.tighar.org (September 1, 2000).

——. 1941a. Phoenix Islands Settlement Scheme. Quarterly Progress Report October–December 1940. Public Record Office, British National Archives, Reference CO/225/328/86059/3; TIGHAR 1996c: Tab 4:22. View at www.tighar.org (September 1, 2000).

——. 1941b. Phoenix Islands Settlement Scheme. Quarterly Progress Report January–March 1941. Public Record Office, British National Archives, Reference CO/225/328/86059/3; TIGHAR 1996c: Tab 4:23.

Gardiner, Irvine C. 1943. "Crusoes of Canton Island," *National Geographic* 73:6, 766.

Gibson, E. A. 1939. New Zealand Pacific Aviation Survey Expedition. General Report on Activities and Results, February 28. Public Record Office, British National Archives, Reference FO/371/22792; also in TIGHAR files.

Gilbert Islands, Government of. 1978. *Report of the Expedition to Nikumaroro 1978.* Bairiki, Tarawa: Government Printing Division.

Gillespie, Richard. 1992. "The Mystery of Amelia Earhart." *Life* 15:2 (April), 69–74.

Goerner, Fred. 1966. *The Search for Amelia Earhart.* New York: Doubleday & Co.

——. 1989. Letter of April 13. TIGHAR Files, courtesy Rob Gerth.

Goodenough, W. H. 1963. "Ecological and Social Change in the Gilbert Islands." *Proceedings of the Ninth Pacific Science Congress,* vol. 3:167–169.

Grooch, William. 1939. *From Crate to Clipper with Captain Musick, Pioneer Pilot.* New York: Longmans Green & Co.

Guerrero, Joseph P. Deleon. 1999. Memorandum Serial 16131, File 1.3, March 30. Historic Preservation Officer to Commissioner, Department of Public Safety, Commonwealth of the Northern Mariana Islands, Sapian. Subject: Recovery of Human Remains from Crime Scene in As Matuis (#99-003055).

Guthrie, Margaret W. 1979. *Misi Utu: Dr. D. W. Hoodless and the Development of Medical Education in the South Pacific.* Suva, Fiji: Institute of Pacific Studies, University of the South Pacific, in association with the South Pacific Social Sciences Association.

Hamer, Daniel. (n.d.). "Stranding and Subsequent Rescue of the Survivors of the *Norwich City.*" Manuscript, TIGHAR Files, from Janet Powell.

Hooven, Frederick J. 1992. "Amelia Earhart's Last Flight." Unpublished paper on file at the National Air and Space Museum Library, Washington, D.C.

Jacobson, Randall S. 1994. "Where in the World Are Winslow Reef and Amelia Earhart?" *EOS* 75:24 (June 14): 265–268. Transactions of the American Geophysical Union, Washington, D.C.

Jantz, Richard L. 1997. "Cranial, Postcranial and Discrete Trait Variation." In *Bioarchaeology of the North Central United States,* edited by D. W. Owsley and J. C. Rose. Fayetteville, Ark.: Arkansas Archeological Survey Research Series, vol. 49.

Johnson, Clarence L. 1937. Three telegrams dated March 11 to A. H. Marshall, Pratt & Whitney Aircraft Co., Hartford, Conn., Fred Goerner Files, Nimitz Museum, Fredricksburg, Texas. View at www.tighar.org (September 1, 2000).

Johnson, Irving. 1940. Letter dated June 4 to Bessie M. Young, microfilm. Washington, D.C.: National Air and Space Museum Library.

Key, P., and R. L. Jantz. 1990. "The Statistical Assessment of Population Variability: A Methodological Approach." *American Journal of Physical Anthropology* 82:53-59.

King, T. F., and P. L. Parker. 1984. *Piseken noomw noon Tonnachaw: Archeology in the Tonaachaw Historic District, Moen Island.* Micronesian Archeological Survey Report no. 18. Carbondale, Ill.: Southern Illinois University at Carbondale Center for Archaeological Investigations Occasional Paper no. 3.

Klaas, Joe. 1970. *Amelia Earhart Lives.* New York: McGraw-Hill.

Knox-Mawer, June. 1995. *The Shadow of Wings.* London: Orion Publishing Group.

Knudson, Kenneth E. 1964. Titiana: A Gilbertese Community in the Solomon Islands. Report of a field study for the Project for the Comparative Study of Cultural Change and Stability in Displaced Communities in the Pacific, Department of Anthropology, University of Oregon, Eugene.

Lambrecht, John O. 1937. "Aircraft Search of Earhart Plane." Weekly newsletter, Bureau of Aeronautics from Senior Aviator, USS *Colorado,* July 16. U.S. National Archives Record Group 72, General Correspondence (1925–1942), file A7-1/BB45.

Laxton, P. B. 1949. Gardner Island or Nikumaroro. Memorandum of April 6 presumably to WPHC. TIGHAR Files from Barr Smith Library, University of Adelaide, Australia.

———. 1951. "Nikumaroro." *Journal of the Polynesian Society* 60(2/3):134–160.

Lee, E. W. 1939. "Pacific Islands Survey Expedition, Gardner Island." March 28. Typescript, New Zealand National Archives; TIGHAR 1996c: Tab 2:6.

London *Times.* 1929. Articles on wreck of *Norwich City,* December 2, 3, and 5. Public Record Office, British National Archives.

Long, Elgen M., and Marie K. Long. 1999. *Amelia Earhart: The Mystery Solved.* New York: Simon and Schuster.

Loomis, Vincent, with Jeffrey Ethell. 1985. *Amelia Earhart: The Final Story.* New York: Random House.

Lovell, Mary S. 1989. *The Sound of Wings: The Life of Amelia Earhart.* New York: St. Martin's Press.

Luke, Sir Harry. 1945. *From a South Seas Diary, 1938–1942.* London: Nicholson & Watson.

Maritime Safety Agency, Japan. 1951. *Hydrographic Bulletin,* 981(8).

Marshall, Sid. 1937. Film footage of Amelia Earhart's takeoff from Lae, New Guinea. Guinea Airways. Copy in TIGHAR Files. View at www.tighar.org (September 1, 2000).

Maude, H. E. 1937a. *Colonization of the Phoenix Islands by the Surplus Population of the Gilbert and Ellice Islands.* Confidential Report, Gilbert and Ellice Islands Colony. Suva: Government Press. Public Record Office, British National Archives, Reference CO/225/309/86059/3; TIGHAR 1996c: Tab 4:6.

———. 1937b. Memorandum of December 3 to Acting Secretary to Government, Gilbert and Ellice Islands Colony, regarding reconnaissance of Phoenix Islands. TIGHAR Files from Barr Smith Library, University of Adelaide.

———. 1938a. Memorandum of January 6 to Acting Secretary to Government, Gilbert and Ellice Islands Colony, providing details of implementing Phoenix Island Settlement Scheme. TIGHAR Files from Barr Smith Library, University of Adelaide.

———. 1938b. Phoenix Islands Settlement Scheme. Preliminary Progress Report. Memorandum of December 14 to Acting Secretary to Government, Gilbert and Ellice Islands Colony. Public Record Office, British National Archives, Reference CO/225/317/86059/3; TIGHAR 1996c: Tab 4:10.

———. 1939a. Phoenix Islands Settlement Scheme. First Progress Report. Memorandum of March (no date specified) to the Secretary to Government, Gilbert and Ellice Islands Colony. Public Record Office, British National Archives, Reference CO/225/317/86059/3; TIGHAR 1996c: Tab 4:11.

———. 1939b. Phoenix Islands Settlement Scheme. Second Progress Report. Memorandum of November 29 to Secretary to Government, Gilbert and Ellice Islands Colony. TIGHAR 1996c: Tab 4:15, from Barr Smith Library, University of Adelaide.

———. 1940. Report on the Phoenix and Line Islands with Special Reference to the Question of British Sovereignty. Secret Report to the WPHC, F. W. Smith, Suva. TIGHAR Files from Barr Smith Library, University of Adelaide.

———. 1968. "The Colonization of the Phoenix Islands." In *Of Islands and Men: Studies in Pacific History,* edited by H. E. Maude, 315–342. Melbourne: Oxford University Press.

———. 1996. Personal communication to T. F. King, November 6.

———. 1997. Personal communication to T. F. King, June 26.

McKenchnie, Jean L., ed. 1975. *Webster's New Twentieth Century Dictionary of the English Language.* New York: Collins World.

McQuarrie, Peter. 2000. *Conflict in Kiribati: A History of the Second World War.* Christchurch: Macmillan Brown Centre for Pacific Studies, University of Canterbury.

Moleski, Fr. Martin. 2003. "Fiji Bones Search: Final Report." TIGHAR. View at www.tighar.org/Projects/Earhart/Bulletins/42_FijiBoneSearch.html (April 2004).

Moore-Jansen, P. H., S. D. Ousley, and R. L. Jantz. 1994. *Data Collection Procedures for Forensic Skeletal Material,* 3rd ed. Report of Investigations no. 48. Knoxville: Department of Anthropology, University of Tennessee.

Morris, Holly J. 2000. "Mysteries of History: Elusive Truths," *U.S. News & World Report* (July 24): 30–82.

Morrissey, Muriel Earhart, and Carol L. Osborne. 1987. *Amelia, My Courageous Sister.* Santa Clara, Calif.: Osborne Publisher.

Mutsu, Ian. 1949. "The Earhart Mystery: UP Tracing of Story Famed Aviatrix Was Nabbed by Japanese Still Proving Futile." United Press release published August 29, *Nippon Times.* TIGHAR Files.

Nauticos. 2004. "Amelia Earhart Website Launched." View at www.nauticos.com (May 2004).

New Orleans *Times-Picayune.* 1937. Article published July 6.

NCDC. (n.d.) Bridge logs of *Kamoi.* Jacobson files from U.S. National Oceanic and Atmospheric Administration, National Climate Data Center, Asheville, S.C.

Noonan, Fred. 1935. Letter to Commander P. V. H. Weems, Weems School of Navigation. TIGHAR Files.

———. 1937. Letter from Dakar, Senegal, to Eugene Pallette. TIGHAR Files, courtesy Earhart Forum member Don Jordan.

Obura, David, CORDIO East Africa. 2000. Personal communication to Richard Gillespie and Earhart Forum.

O'Dell, Scott. 1960. *Island of the Blue Dolphins.* Boston: Houghton Mifflin.

Ousley, S. D., and R. L. Jantz. 1998. "The Forensic Data Bank: Documenting Skeletal Trends in the United States." In *Forensic Osteology: Advances in the Identification of Human Remains,* edited by K. J. Reichs. Springfield, Ill.: C. C. Thomas.

Parker, Stanley V. 1939. Memorandum to Pan American Airways, March 22. U.S. Navy Historical Center, U.S. National Archives Microfilm, Records Group 26, Washington, D.C.

Patton, Joseph M. 1960. Memorandum to IO-COMNAVMARIANAS dated December 23. Subject: Earhart, Amelia; Information re. location of grave of. In *Eyewitness: The Amelia Earhart Incident,* ed. Thomas E. Devine and Richard M. Daley (Appendix). Frederick, Colo.: Renaissance House.

Peattie, Mark. 1988. *Nan'yo: The Rise and Fall of the Japanese in Micronesia, 1885–1945.* Honolulu: University of Hawaii Press.

Photek Inc. 1997. TIGHAR/Earhart, 1953 Aerial Recon Photos and Niku 1988 Aerial Photos, processed by Jeff Glickman, Photek Inc., Hood River, Oregon, June 2. Report to TIGHAR.

Putnam, George P. 1937. Telegram to the U.S. Chief of Naval Operations, July 17. U.S. Navy Historical Center, Earhart Files, File: Leahy, OP38, CNO Radio Traffic, Washington, D.C.

Reineck, Rollin. 2003. *Amelia Earhart Survived*. Orange, Calif.: Paragon Agency Publishers.

Rhode Island Sea Grant. 2003. Rhode Island Sea Grant Fact Sheet. View at http://seagrant.gso.uri.edu/factsheets/fsquahog.html (October 2003).

Robinson, Nancy. 1992. "Ex-Customs Agent Remembers Earhart's Big Feet." *Abilene Reporter-News* (October 31).

Royal Navy. 1937. Notes on the Various Islands of the Phoenix Group (Visit of HMS *Leith*). Typescript, May 28. From Barr Smith Library, Adelaide, Australia; TIGHAR 1996c: Tab 2:2.

———. 1938. Report of Proceedings of HMS *Leander* covering the period October 1 to December 31. Public Record Office, British National Archives, Reference CO/225/317/86059; TIGHAR 1996c: Tab 2:6.

———. 1946–1947. Deck Logs of HMS *Adamant*. Public Record Office, British National Archives, Reference ADM 53.

Sagan, Carl. 1996. *The Demon-Haunted World: Science As a Candle in the Dark*. New York: Random House.

Scarr, Lew. 1960. "San Diegan Bares Clue to Earhart Fate." *San Diego Tribune* (July 21): 1. Retyped transcript at www.tighar.org (September 1, 2000).

Schelling, Frank. 1992. "An Opposing View." *Life* magazine 15:2 (April): 74.

Simpson, Maria. 1998. Letter to Kenton Spading dated February 2. Subject: The Search for Amelia Earhart, Foreign and Commonwealth Office, Library and Records Department, Retrieval Services, Hanslope, England, FCO Reference LRE 335/001/98. Extract in Spading 1998.

Sledge, Peggy. 1988. *The Littlest Smuggler and Other True Stories: U.S. Customs on the Rio Grande*. Privately published. Abilene, Texas: AAA Printers.

Smith's Weekly (Australia). 1937. "USA Does Australia a Secret Service." (October 16; XIX:33:1).

Spading, Kenton. 1997. Letter to Richard Gillespie, Executive Director, TIGHAR, July 31, transferring Western Pacific High Commission documents received from the Foreign and Commonwealth Office, Library and Records Department, Hanslope, England (FCO Reference LRE 334/001/97). See Western Pacific High Commission (1937a).

———. 1998. Letter to Richard Gillespie, Executive Director, TIGHAR, dated February 20, transferring Western Pacific High Commission documents received from the Foreign and Commonwealth Office, Library and Records Department, Hanslope, England (FCO Reference LRE 335/001/98). See Simpson (1998) and Western Pacific High Commission (1938–1939).

Stevens, Molly. 1997. "Shucking Clams and Oysters." *Fine Cooking* 22 (August/September): 68.

Stone, Gregory S. 2004. "Phoenix Islands: A Coral Reef Wilderness Revealed." *National Geographic* (February): 48–65.

Strippel, Richard. 1972. *Amelia Earhart: The Myth and the Reality*. Jericho, N.J.: Exposition Press.

Thompson, Warner K. 1937. Memorandum to Commander, U.S. Coast Guard, San Francisco Division, July 19. U.S. National Archives, Record Group 26, General Correspondence, 1910–1941, 601, Entry 283B, Box 469. Washington, D.C.

TIGHAR (The International Group for Historic Aircraft Recovery). 1990. *TIGHAR Tracks* 6:4 (September 29).

———. 1991a. *TIGHAR Tracks* 7:2 (April 8): 5.

———. 1991b. *TIGHAR Tracks* 7:3 (June 20): 4–5.

———. 1992a. *TIGHAR Tracks* 8:1–2 (March 12): 1–7.

———. 1992b. *TIGHAR Tracks* 8:3 (April 30).

———. 1993a. *TIGHAR Tracks* 9:1 (January 15).

———. 1993b. *The Earhart Project: An Historical Investigation,* 7th ed. Wilmington, Del.: TIGHAR.

———. 1993c. *The Earhart Project: Companion,* 3rd ed. Wilmington, Del.: TIGHAR.

———. 1996a. *TIGHAR Tracks* 12:1 (March 31).

———. 1996b. *TIGHAR Tracks* 12:2–3 (September 30).

———. 1996c. "The Niku Source Book." Updated July 1997. Wilmington, Del.: TIGHAR.

———. 1997. *TIGHAR Tracks* 13:1–2 (September 30).

———. 1998a. *TIGHAR Tracks* 14:1 (May 15).

———. 1998b. *TIGHAR Tracks* 14:2 (December 4).

———. 1999a. "The Niku Source Book, Volume 2: Records of the Western Pacific High Commission." TIGHAR Files.

———. 1999b. *TIGHAR Tracks* 15.

———. "Analysis of the Satellite Photo." View at www.tighar.org/Projects/Earhart/Bulletins/32_SatPhoto/32_Nikusatphoto.html (May 2004).

———. "Artifact Analysis, Step Two." View at www.tighar.org/Projects/Earhart/Bulletins/36_ArtifactAnalysis2/artifacts.html (April 2004).

———. "Dados Galore." View at www.tighar.org/Projects/Earhart/Bulletins/44_DadosGalore/44_DadosGalore.html (April 2004).

———. "Expedition Updates." View at www.tighar.org/Projects/Earhart/nikuvp/dailies.html (April 2004).

———. Gillespie and Reineck exchange of views. View at www.tighar.org/Projects/Earhart/BookReviews/reineck/discussion.html (May 2004).

———. "Is This Amelia Earhart? Review of Reineck's Amelia Earhart Survived." View at www.tighar.org/Projects/Earhart/BookReviews/earhartsurvive.html (May 2004).

———. "Mysteries of the Seven Site." View at www.tighar.org/Projects/Earhart/Bulletins/33_SevenMysteries/33_SevenMysteries.html (April 2004).

———. "Niku IIII: A Summary from a Jet-Lagged Perspective." View at www.tighar.org/Projects/Earhart/NikuIIIIsumm.html (April 2004).

———. "Project Midnight Ghost." View at www.tighar.org/Projects/PMG.html (April 2004).

———. "The Dado, Part One." View at www.tighar.org/Projects/Earhart/Bulletins/43_DadoPart1/43_Dado1.html (April 2004).

———. "The Knob That Wasn't." View at www.tighar.org/Projects/Earhart/Bulletins/39_KnobThatWasnt/knob_idbulletin.html (April 2004).

———. "Wheel of Fortune." View at www.tighar.org/Projects/Earhart/Bulletins/41_WheelofFortune/41_Wheel.html (May 2004).

——. In progress. *The Earhart Project Book,* 8th ed. View finished portions at www.tighar.org (January 1, 2001).

Tikana, Bauro. 1991. Personal communication by fax to Richard Gillespie, August 13. TIGHAR, 1996c: Tab 7:3.

University of the South Pacific. 1971. Medical Education in the South Pacific: A Report by an International Mission 1971. Typescript. Fiji: Fiji Museum Library.

U.S. Air Force. 1974a. Environmental Survey of the Phoenix Islands, Central Pacific Ocean. August; EHL(K) 74-18. U.S. Environmental Health Laboratory, Kelly AFB, Texas. Vandenberg Air Force Base, Calif.: Office of the 30th Space Wing Historian.

——. 1974b. Environmental Conditions of Canton Island, P.I. Memorandum to SAMTEC/SUD compiling documents dating between September 23 and November 21. Vandenberg Air Force Base, Calif.: Office of the 30th Space Wing Historian.

——. 1975. Environmental Protection (Canton Island). Memorandum: Global Associates to Lt. Col. Philip J. Stack, USAF, Commander SAMTEC/OL, January 15. Vandenberg Air Force Base, Calif.: Office of the 30th Space Wing Historian.

U.S. Army Intelligence. 1949a. G-2, GHQ Inter-Office Memorandum, August 4; "Compilations" to Deputy Chief, CJ Div, through Col. Smith, citing "Mr. Perry." "Information Concerning Amelia Earhart." CI Div/Opns Contl/LGS:Comp/ME/as. TIGHAR Files.

——. 1949b. G-2, GHQ Inter-Office Memorandum, August 8; "Compilations" to Deputy Chief, CJ Div, through Col. Smith, citing "Mr. Yamada." "Report on Amelia Earhart Dated 3 August 1949." CI Div/Opns Contl/LGS:Comp/ME/as. TIGHAR Files.

U.S. Coast Guard. 1943–1949. Records of Coast Guard Loran Unit 92, Gardner Island. Phoenix Chain General File. Washington, D.C.: U.S. National Archives.

U.S. Department of State. 1937. Telegrams and correspondence. Record Group 59, State Department 1930–1939, 800.79611—Putnam, Amelia Earhart. Washington, D.C.: U.S. National Archives.

U.S. Navy. 1937a. Deck log of USS *Colorado.* Record Group 24. Washington, D.C.: U.S. National Archives.

——. 1937b. Deck log of USS *Swan.* U.S. National Archives, Record Group 24, Washington, D.C.: U.S. National Archives.

——. 1937c. Earhart Search Report. Commandant, 14th Naval District, Compiled by Admiral Orrin Murfin. Date stamped July 31. Records Group 181, Entry 49, File A4-3. Washington, D.C.: U.S. National Archives.

——. 1937d. Map, Earhart Search, 14th Naval District, undated but probably July 5 or 6. Hand-drawn lines crossing in the vicinity of the Phoenix Islands illustrate bearings taken on radio signals. Records Group 181, Entry 49, File A4-3. Washington, D.C.: U.S. National Archives.

——. 1937e. Radio messages, including Japanese. Record Group 80, Secretary of Navy, General Correspondence, 1926–1940, Box 146 Earhart publicity—A4-5(5) (361030).

——. 1939a. Deck log of USS *Bushnell.* Record Group 24, Washington, D.C.: U.S. National Archives.

——. 1939b. Deck log of USS *Pelican.* Record Group 24, Washington, D.C.: U.S. National Archives.

——. 1939c. Report on bottle found on beach alleging Earhart a captive at Jaluit Atoll. Record Group 38, Office of the Chief of Naval Operations, Division of Naval Intelligence, File A4-3/Earhart A., January 7. Washington, D.C.: U.S. National Archives.

———. 1941. Reconnaissance of Phoenix Islands—Report on. Memorandum from Commander Patrol Wing Two to Commander in Chief, U.S. Pacific Fleet, covering memorandum of June 28. Commander Patrol Squadron 22 to Commander Patrol Wing 2. TIGHAR 1996c: Tab 2:11.

Vansina, Jan. 1985 *Oral Tradition As History.* Madison: University of Wisconsin Press.

Warren, Cam. 2000. E-mail Response to Richard Gillespie dated September 25. TIGHAR Earhart Forum Highlights, September 24–30. View at www.tighar.org (January 15, 2001).

Weber, Helen Hutson. (n.d.) Note in box with shoes loaned to TIGHAR.

Western Pacific High Commission. 1936–1937. Gallagher, G. B., Cadet Officer, G&EIC; Personal File. WPHC List No. 4, IV, Vol. for 1936–1937, M.P. No. 3597/1936. Hanslope, England: Foreign and Commonwealth Office, Library and Records Department.

———. 1937a. Jack C. Barley, Resident Commissioner, Gilbert and Ellice Islands, Report for August 1937. Hanslope, England: Foreign and Commonwealth Office, Library and Records Department. Extract in Spading.

———. 1937b. File: Subject: "Flights of Amelia Earhart–1937," WPHC List No. 4, IV, Vol. for 1937–1937, M.P. No. 957/1937 (M.G.) (Formerly M.P. No. 138(s)/1937). Hanslope, England: Foreign and Commonwealth Office, Library and Records Department.

———. 1938–1939. "Fiji: Annual Medical and Health Report for the Year 1938–1939." WPHC List No. 4, Vol. 2, IV, M.P. No. 923/1940. Hanslope, England: Foreign and Commonwealth Office, Library and Records Department. Extract in Spading, 1998.

———. 1940–1941a. "Discovery of Human Remains on Gardner Island." Kiribati National Archives List: KNA 11/1, File F13/9/1. Republic of Kiribati, Bairiki, Tarawa: Ministry of Education, Training and Technology, National Library and Archives Division. (Also see TIGHAR 1996c: Tab 4:29.) View at www.tighar.org (September 1, 2000).

———. 1940–1941b. "Skeleton, Human—Finding of on Gardner Island." WPHC List No. 4, IV, Vol. for 1940–1941, M.P. No. 4439/1940 (G&E). Hanslope, England: Foreign and Commonwealth Office, Library and Records Department. (Also see TIGHAR 1999a: Tab 3:A.) View at www.tighar.org (September 1, 2000).

Western Samoa, Administration of. 1929. Memorandum from Claude Arthur Johnson, British Merchant, Apia and Lloyd's Agent (and three other signatories) to the Assistant Secretary, Board of Trade, London, England, dated December 9, transmitting evidence from a Naval Court of Inquiry referring to the wreck of the *Norwich City* on Gardner Island. Reference MT/9/1967/M4294/30. London: Public Record Office, British National Archives.

Williams, Clarence. 1937. "Flight Planning Charts Prepared for Earhart Prior to the 1st World Flight Attempt." West Lafayette, Ind.: Purdue University Library.

Yoho, Bruce. 1998. "The Pilots Thought I Was Nuts." *TIGHAR Tracks* 14:1 (May 15): 5–6. View at www.tighar.org (September 1, 2000).

Index

About the Authors

Dr. Thomas F. King serves as project archaeologist for the Amelia Earhart Project, sponsored by The International Group for Historic Aircraft Recovery (TIGHAR). He holds a Ph.D. in anthropology from the University of California, Riverside, and has extensive archaeological field experience in California and Micronesia. His professional work emphasizes the preservation of historic places and cultural traditions. In the United States he is recognized as a national expert on cultural and historic preservation laws and practice, about which he teaches dozens of courses annually and has authored five books. He is a former program director at the Advisory Council on Historic Preservation, and was the primary author of many historic preservation regulations and guidelines. He also served as an archaeologist and historic preservation specialist in the former U.S. Trust Territory of the Pacific Islands, as archaeologist for the National Park Service, and as head of archaeological surveys at three universities. He helped create the Micronesian Archaeological Survey, based in Saipan. King can be contacted at tfking106@aol.com.

Dr. Randall S. Jacobson is a geophysicist with the U.S. Navy, currently working on airborne mine hunting and mine countermeasure systems. Jacobson has a Ph.D. in oceanography/earth sciences from Scripps Institute of Oceanography, taught geophysics at Oregon State University, and was a program officer in geophysics at the Office of Naval Research, responsible for evaluating and funding proposals. He has written extensively on underwater seismic propagation, evolution of oceanic crust, and was the state seismologist for Oregon in the 1980s. His work has involved going to sea, using sonar, magnetometers, ocean bottom seismometers, and other geophysical systems. He is an avid historian, and enjoys restoring classic cars.

Dr. Karen Ramey Burns is a forensic anthropologist, an expert on human identification from bones, with a specialty on understanding victims of violence. She has taught this subject to college students and police officers for more than a decade. Burns has been asked by various human rights groups and government agencies to find, examine, report, and testify on victims of political violence in Haiti, Iraq, and Guatemala. She has also worked crime scenes and natural disaster sites in Georgia, helped identify the remains of victims of the September 11, 2001, attack on the World Trade Center, and studied the cemeteries of ancient Carthage. Burns is a fellow in the American Academy of Forensic Sciences, a certified trainer at the Georgia Police Academy, and author of a major college textbook on forensic anthropology. She has been responsible for the analysis of bones and forensic reports of the Amelia Earhart Project.

Kenton Spading has served as the technology and remote sensing coordinator for the Amelia Earhart Project as well as other projects sponsored by The International Group for Historic Aircraft Recovery. He has conducted archival research for the Earhart Project in England, Kiribati, Tuvalu, New Zealand, and the United States. He has a bachelor of science degree in civil engineering from the University of Minnesota Institute of Technology and is a registered professional engineer with the state of Minnesota. He is a hydrologist with the U.S. Army Corps of Engineers, St. Paul District, and currently works in the water control section that oversees thirteen locks and dams on the Upper Mississippi River as well as numerous flood control reservoirs in the upper Midwest.